Eyewitness to War

Volume II

The US Army in Operation AL FAJR: An Oral History

Kendall D. Gott
General Editor

Interviews by
John McCool
Matt M. Matthews

Transcribed by
Colette Kiszka
Jennifer Vedder

Edited by
Jennifer Lindsey

Additional Interviews by
Dr. Christopher K. Ives

Combat Studies Institute Press
Fort Leavenworth, Kansas 66048

Library of Congress Cataloging-in-Publication Data

Eyewitness to war : a US Army oral history of Operation al-Fajr / Kendall D. Gott general
editor ; interviews by John McCool ... [et al.].
    p. cm.
  1. Fallujah, Battle of, Fallujah, Iraq, 2004. 2. Unified operations (Military science) 3.
United States. Army--History--21st century. 4. Iraq War, 2003---Personal narratives,
American. I. Gott, Kendall D. II. McCool, John. III. Series.
DS79.766.F3E93 2006
956.7044'342--dc22

2006035657

Cover photo by SSG Kimberly Snow, National Guard Combat Camerawoman.

CSI Press publications cover a variety of military history topics. The views expressed in this
CSI Press publication are those of the author and not necessarily those of the Department
of the Army, or the Department of Defense.

A full list of CSI Press publications, many of them available for downloading, can be found
at http://www.cgsc.army.mil/carl/resources/csi/csi.asp.
—   —

For sale by the Superintendent of Documents, U.S. Government Printing Office
Internet: bookstore.gpo.gov Phone: toll free (866) 512-1800; DC area (202) 512-1800
Fax: (202) 512-2250 Mail: Stop IDCC, Washington, DC 20402-0001

ISBN 0-16-077465-9

Foreword

Eyewitness to War The US Army in Operation AL FAJR: An Oral History is a unique publication for the Combat Studies Institute. It is our first publication to make exclusive use of oral history. This study is a derivative of the CSI Operational Leadership Experience (OLE) project, a program that collects and archives first-person experiences from the Global War on Terror. It can also be considered a companion to the recently published CSI Occasional Paper #20: Operation AL FAJR: A Study in Army and Marine Corps Joint Operations. Interviews collected for the OLE project formed the basis for that occasional paper and were so compelling, we felt a need to publish those interviews in a book series.

In November 2004, the second battle for Fallujah was a brutal and bloody fight so characteristic of urban terrain. Under the overall command of the 1st Marine Division, four Marine infantry and two US Army battalions (Task Forces 2-2 Infantry and 2-7 Cavalry) were committed to the streets of Fallujah. At this same time, the Army's 2d Brigade, 1st Cavalry Division formed a cordon to hold and isolate the insurgents in the city. Using the firepower and mobility of the Army's heavy armor and mechanized units to full effect, the Marine Regimental Combat Teams were successful in destroying the enemy and securing Fallujah in ten days.

Eyewitness to War interviews span a wide spectrum of participants, from commanders and senior non-commissioned officers at all levels to the first-hand accounts of combat and combat service support personnel on the battlefield. We make no claim that this history is a comprehensive work, as these 37 people are but a fraction of the thousands who took part in the operation. This is primarily an Army oral history, though one of the Marine Regimental Commanders agreed to provide his story. The USMC bore the brunt of fighting in Fallujah and this study does not attempt to overlook their tremendous accomplishments.

The individuals featured in this work volunteered to work with our staff over many months. Their stories are a tremendous testimony to the skill, flexibility, and bravery of the US Army today.

This collection of personal experiences is the raw material history is made of. It is a riveting and useful way to study the past. And it is our hope that the insights derived from their roles in the second battle for Fallujah will better prepare the US Army for tomorrow's endeavors. *CSI – The Past is Prologue!*

Timothy R. Reese
Colonel, Armor
Director, Combat Studies Institute

Introduction

The Combat Studies Institute (CSI) was established at Fort Leavenworth, Kansas in 1979 with the mission to conduct original, interpretive research on historical topics pertinent to current doctrinal and operational concerns of the US Army. CSI's further mission is to publish these results in a variety of useful formats and to conduct battlefield staff rides for the US Army. Today, CSI also assists the US Army's Combined Arms Center in the development and implementation of an integrated progressive program of military history instruction. CSI's mission further includes writing contemporary Army history, overseeing the Frontier Army Museum, and serving as the Command History Office for the Combined Arms Center.

In 2005, the US Army Training and Doctrine Command (TRADOC) gave CSI the mission to conduct oral and videotaped interviews with officers who recently participated in operations in the Global War on Terrorism, including Operation Iraqi Freedom (OIF) and Operation Enduring Freedom (OEF). The Operational Leadership Experiences (OLE) section accomplishes this by arranging these interviews and providing transcription, archival support services, and website implementation. Digital copies of all interviews are posted on the Combined Arms Research Library (CARL) and CSI websites: http://www-cgsc.army.mil/carl/contentdm/home.htm and http://usacac.army.mil/CAC/csi/.

Since its inception in the summer of 2005, the OLE section has conducted over 350 interviews of returning veterans. Many officers interviewed were conveniently located at Fort Leavenworth as students of the Command and General Staff College, the School for Advanced Military Studies, or for one of the Pre-Command Courses. However, numerous other officers, soldiers, and civilians interviewed volunteered from units or posts located all around the world. The wide range of experiences and perceptions preserved for posterity is remarkable and continues to grow.

Eyewitness to War The US Army in Operation AL FAJR: An Oral History is the first series of published interviews by the OLE section. The accounts in this book and successive volumes are the experiences of actual participants told in their own words. It is history in raw form, recorded for future generations by key leaders on the ground and the men and women there to see and hear the events unfold. The CSI staff only lightly edited the contents for clarity, to remove the occasional use of excessive profanity and the rare injurious personal attack. However, the content and tone describing the operation remain untouched. No classified information was used or included in this book and the opinions expressed by the participants are their own.

The bulk of this book consists of Army interviews, which are presented in order of rank. Two Marines, one airman, and a journalist are also included and provide interesting insight to the cooperation achieved between the services. A glossary and index are also included. Volume I provides an overview chapter of the second battle of Fallujah, named Operation AL FAJR (Dawn) by the Iraqis. This is a modified version of a chapter featured in *Breaking the Mold: Tanks in the Cities*, published by CSI Press in 2006. Matt Matthews authored an additional work of great interest in the CSI Occasional Paper #20 *Operation AL FAJR: A Study in Army and Marine Corps Joint Operations*.

My thanks go foremost to the men and women who took the time and effort to be interviewed, provide statements, and review the final transcripts. Additionally, the fine work of the OLE team, namely John McCool, Dr. Chris Ives, Colette Kiszka, and Jennifer Vedder who made this work possible by their untiring efforts to locate key personnel and to persevere under tight deadlines. High recognition and praise also go to Mr. Matt Matthews for identifying, tracking down, and interviewing a significant number of the featured participants. Thanks and appreciation also goes to our editor, Jennifer Lindsey and also to Mike Brooks for his fine work in designing the cover. Lastly, this project could not have seen fruition without the support and sage advice of Colonel Timothy R. Reese and Dr. William G. Robertson.

Kendall D. Gott
Senior Historian
Research and Publication Team

Contents

Abstracts

Captain James Cobb, Fire Support Officer for Task Force 2-2: Captain Cobb was attached to Marine Regimental Combat Team 7 for purposes of this combined-joint urban assault, he speaks about the artillery-related planning and coordination conducted with the Marines, his observer plan and his work in terms of the preparation and execution of the initial breach into the city. He also speaks to the overall fire support plan throughout the decisive fight. For Cobb, a variety of communications issues posed significant challenges and caused no small amount of frustration, particularly the order to change COMSEC in the middle of the battle. In addition, he discusses embedded reporters, gives his explanation for the successful outcome of the battle, and also comments at length on the experience of high-intensity combat.

Captain Jeff Emery, 1st Platoon, Alpha Company, Task Force 2-2: As Senior Platoon Leader, Captain Emery was in charge of four Bradleys, two tanks and two dismounted squads during Operation AL FAJR. In this interview, he discusses the role his unit played in its successful prosecution. His duties changed upon the company losing both its commander and executive officer; tragic and difficult events, which he discusses in great detail.

Captain Michael S. Erwin, Assistant S2, Task Force 2-7: As the assistant intelligence officer for 2d Battalion, 7th Cavalry Regiment, Captain Erwin's principal duties during the assault to retake Fallujah were in the intelligence, surveillance and reconnaissance realm. Working with Task Force 2-7's Raven unmanned aerial vehicle and coordinating with the Marine UAV effort, Erwin focused mainly on Fallujah's Jolan District and provided real-time information on enemy locations and movements to the maneuver forces. In addition, Erwin discusses the unique situation in which his Active Duty battalion was attached to a National Guard brigade: the 39th Enhanced Separate Brigade out of Arkansas.

Captain Natalie Friel, Assistant S2, Task Force 2-2: Deployed with 2d Battalion, 2d Infantry Regiment from February 2004 through February 2005, Captain Friel served as the battalion assistant intelligence officer. While officially the AS2 during a time of transition for the unit prior to the battle, Friel acted as the primary S2 and oversaw Task Force 2-2's intelligence preparation of the battlefield. Once the operation commenced, she was stationed in the tactical operations center, but would go forward to brief commanders in the field on the latest intelligence assessments. In this interview, she shares her far-reaching visibility over the entire intelligence picture, focusing on enemy tactics and capabilities; information gleaned from human, signals and imagery intelligence sources. She also discusses experiences with US Marine Corps intel officers and USMC assets, particularly unmanned aerial vehicles; and her overall insights into why the operation was a success.

Captain Peter Glass, Commander of Charlie Company, 3d Battalion, 8th Cavalry Regiment: Captain Glass and his company were attached to Marine Regimental Combat Team 1 during the battle to retake Fallujah. In this interview, he discusses his company's role, which included securing the Martyrs Cemetery, clearing areas of the Jolan District and doing what he calls "mini thunder runs." The taking of company casualties, dealing with mosque fires, and having his own tank disabled by an anti-tank mine are but some of the experiences Glass relates. He also describes his unit's working relationship with the Marines and some of the difficulties they encountered.

Captain Jeff Jager, Liaison Officer to the Marine Regimental Combat Team 7: In March 2004, Captain Jager joined 2d Battalion, 2d Infantry Regiment at Forward Operating Base Normandy in Iraq and, in early November, was sent over to Marine Regimental Combat Team 7 as the officer in charge of a liaison team. He speaks at length about the responsibilities to understand the command and control structure of RCT-7, determine their operational plan and targeting process, and to find and reconnoiter Task Force 2-2's attack position. In this interview, Jager also discusses communications difficulties he experienced in dealing with Army and Marine systems and the challenges with respect to good situational awareness. Providing unique insights into the execution of the operation from the battalion and regimental levels and shedding light on a myriad of personnel and task organization issues, Jager also talks about embedded reporters and how their remarkable access had both positive and negative consequences.

Captain Christopher Lacour, Assistant Fire Support Officer for Task Force 2-2: A recent addition to 2d Battalion, 2d Infantry Regiment as the onset of the operation, Captain Lacour served as the assistant fire support officer during the fight to retake Fallujah. A key participant in the pre-mission planning and coordination, Lacour discusses the fire support plan and his liaison role in great detail. In addition, he talks about the rules of engagement, relates a number of communications-related difficulties between the Army and Marines. Lacour comments at length on the firing of two missions using white phosphorous rounds, and describes the challenges of coordinating indirect fires in a city that was a "gigantic, pre-planned, waiting-for-the-invasion maze." From his vantage point, Lacour had solid visibility on many of the key leaders and their decision-making processes from both 2-2 and RCT-7, which he shares in this interview. He also touches on the lack of availability of Marine air assets and, additionally, for the benefit of young field artillery lieutenants, discusses and evaluates some of the fire support equipment he used during this operation.

Captain Gregory McCrum, Physician Assistant, Task Force 2-2: A former medic with the 82d Airborne Division and a Special Forces-qualified medical sergeant, Captain McCrum was assigned to 2d Battalion, 2d Infantry as the battalion PA. He discusses his simultaneous provider and command and control responsibilities, as well as all aspects of the medical support given to the soldiers of his unit. Among the many topics covered are the measures he took to ensure the task force was as self-sustaining as possible in terms of medical supplies; the layout, capabilities and movements of the forward aid station as well as the non-doctrinal innovations employed and the emergency care administered.

Captain Edward Twaddell III, Commander of Alpha Company, Task Force 2-7: CPT Twadell was the commander of Alpha Company, 2d Battalion, 7th Cavalry Regiment, which was attached to Marine RCT-1 for the operation. His interview focuses on the role his two platoons of Bradleys and one platoon of tanks played in the overall operation, Twaddell discusses pre-mission planning, the initial breach into the city, the seizing of company objectives and the unit's engagement and destruction of enemy forces. In this detailed, day-by-day account, he also talks at length about his company's cooperative relationship with Marine Corps units and how the taking of casualties affected him and his soldiers. Twaddell relates the story of his own command Bradley being penetrated by a rocket-propelled grenade, leading to the death of his Iraqi interpreter and the wounding of three others.

Captain Coley D. Tyler, Fire Support Officer for Task Force 2-7: Captain Tyler served as the fire support officer for 2d Battalion, 7th Cavalry Regiment which, during this decisive urban fight, was attached to Marine Regimental Combat Team 1. In this interview, Tyler talks at length about his unit's relationship with the Marines, his own perceptions and, indeed, his original misconceptions of them. Tyler discusses the operation itself in great detail, including the initial reconnaissance in force, his role in observing and calling for fires, the rules of engagement, and his work with unmanned aerial vehicles.

Captain Neil Prakash, Platoon leader, Alpha Company, 2-63 Armor: Captain Prakash was in charge of two tanks, two Bradleys and two infantry squads worth of infantry while his unit was attached to the Brigade Reconnaissance Troop, operating with Task Force 2-2 Infantry. Tasked initially with a screen line mission that involved "softening the targets, staying static, observing, keeping a low profile and hitting anything that was moving," Prakash's platoon soon escalated to directly engaging enemy sniper positions that were menacing US forces. Prakash recounts the time he was pinned down by a sniper in the middle of a minefield after his own tank hit and disabled by a mine, as well as a near-fatal friendly fire incident. In addition, he discusses the outstanding logistical support his platoon received, his experiences fighting in a combined-joint environment, the benefits of ad hoc task organization, and speaks at length on what he considers the necessity of maintaining a vigorous "armor footprint" in any fight.

Command Sergeant Major Darrin Bohn, Operations Sergeant Major for Task Force 2-2: As the operations sergeant major for 2d Battalion, 2d Infantry Regiment CSM Bohn quickly found himself thrust into the role of command sergeant major when the battalion's original CSM was killed early in operation. In this interview, Bohn discusses this leadership challenge in great depth and shares his unique perspectives into the overall role his heavy mechanized battalion played in this decisive battle. He details the emotional lows and highs of the soldiers and the unit. In addition, Bohn covers a variety of training and equipment issues, the joint aspects of working with Marines and Air Force, and comments at length on the enemy forces they faced.

Command Sergeant Major Timothy L. Mace, Command Sergeant Major for Task Force 2-7: CSM Mace joined 2d Battalion, 7th Cavalry Regiment only five weeks before the battle for Fallujah. Occupying a key position in the Bradley of Lieutenant Colonel James Rainey, the 2-7 commander, Mace followed the lead assault elements into the city. In this interview, he provides a wealth of insight about this decisive operation. Speaking at length on the joint aspect, Mace insists that all services worked well together as an integrated team. In addition, he discusses the impact of taking casualties, his impressions of principal leaders, embedded reporters, as well as the Iraqi soldiers who fought with 2-7 and the enemies who fought against them.

Sergeant Major Peter Smith, First Sergeant for Alpha Company, Task Force 2-2: At the time of Operation AL FAJR, Sergeant Major Smith was serving as the first sergeant for Alpha Company, 2d Battalion, 2d Infantry Regiment and, in this interview, relates his and his unit's role in this fight. The recipient of the Silver Star for his actions in this battle, Smith conducted the evacuation of his company executive officer from the center of an ambush, returned to prepare for another fight. In an extraordinary move by the battalion commander Smith was placed in command of the company for over 18 hours when the commander and XO were killed in action. In this interview, he also discusses working with the Marines and the problems associated with communications.

Sergeant First Class John Urrutia, Platoon Sergeant for 2d Platoon, Alpha Company, Task Force 2-7: The platoon sergeant for 2d Platoon, Alpha Company, 2d Battalion, 7th Cavalry Regiment, Sergeant First Class Urrutia discusses his unit's role in the assault to retake Fallujah. He relates the clearing of Jolan Park, which was a key insurgent location. In addition, in this day-by-day account of the fight from his perspective, Urrutia describes the enemy and coalition tactics, the taking of casualties, his working relationship with Marine Corps units, the experience of having two Marine engineers attached to his platoon, the extensive captured enemy ordnance missions he participated in, and the vehicle-borne improvised explosive device factory his platoon secured.

Staff Sergeant Jimmy Amyett, 2d Platoon, 3d Brigade Reconnaissance Troop: During Operation AL FAJR, Staff Sergeant Amyett was the second highest-ranking noncommissioned officer in 2d Platoon, 3d Brigade Reconnaissance Troop – a 20-man, four-Humvee unit attached to Task Force 2-2 Infantry. He discusses the intense training regimen his platoon went through in preparation for its role in this operation and the actions that followed. A significant event is the decisive leaders' reconnaissance that demonstrated the supreme value of the Long Range Advanced Scout Surveillance System (LRAS) in identifying and then calling in artillery and air strikes against enemy locations and individuals. For the first few days, Amyett was one of the principal set of eyes behind the task force's only LRAS device. Later in the battle, Amyett's platoon was tasked with a variety of dangerous dismounted house-to-house clearing duties, during which they encountered weapons caches, the enemy's extensive underground tunnel network, as well as insurgents lying in wait. Amyett also speaks to a number of weapons issues.

Staff Sergeant David Bellavia, Squad Leader of 2d Squad, 3d Platoon, Alpha Company, Task Force 2-2: Staff Sergeant Bellavia was recommended for the Medal of Honor, nominated for the Distinguished Service Cross and received the Silver Star for his actions on 10 November 2004 in which he "single handedly saved three squads of his platoon that night, risking his own life by allowing them to break contact and reorganize. He then entered and cleared an insurgent strong point, killing four insurgents and mortally wounding another." This interview details Bellavia's experiences in the intense room-to-room, at times hand-to-hand, combat that characterized that one night in particular. He offers the ultimate on-the-ground insider's story of this seminal urban operation. As perceptive and introspective as it is raw and action-packed, Bellavia's account touches on everything from doctrinal, training and technology recommendations to his warm recollections of his 2-2 comrades.

Staff Sergeant Matthew Horgan, USAF, Tactical Air Control Party specialist assigned to 3d Brigade, 1st Infantry Division: As a US Air Force joint tactical air controller (JTAC), Staff Sergeant Horgan was the noncommissioned officer in charge of the JTAC teams that served with Task Force 2-2 Infantry in this decisive urban fight. Placed with the Brigade Reconnaissance Troop for the duration of the battle, Horgan called in close air support as well as strafing missions from a variety of platforms, including F-18s, F-16s, F-15s, AC-130s, and Marine Super Cobra helicopters. Although he estimated having made requests for 500-pound bombs probably once every two hours for a period of 10 days, Horgan only ended up getting a total of eight – which he says was a point of frustration. In addition, Horgan describes significant communication problems between Army and Marine Corps units.

Sergeant Wes Smith, Medical Platoon, Task Force 2-2: Primarily assigned to Alpha Company, 2-2 Infantry, Sergeant Wes "Doc" Smith served in the evacuation section of the medical platoon as an evacuation NCO during his February 2004 to February 2005 deployment in support of Operation Iraqi Freedom. Smith discusses his experiences going in and out of Fallujah time and again to retrieve and provide early treatment of battalion casualties. In particular, he talks at length about the under-fire evacuation of the Alpha Company executive officer, First Lieutenant Edward Iwan, actions for which he himself received the Bronze Star with "V" Device. Another tremendous loss for Alpha Company was the death of its commander, Captain Sean Sims, which Smith also discusses, as well the concomitant psychological impact it had on the company as a whole.

Jane Arraf, CNN Senior Baghdad Correspondent, embedded with Task Force 2-2: As CNN's senior Baghdad correspondent, Jane Arraf was embedded with the US Army's 2d Battalion, 2d Infantry Regiment during that unit's participation in Operation AL FAJR. Arraf benefited from remarkable access to and cooperation from the battalion commander and operations officer, and shares her unique visibility and frontline, often harrowing experiences during this decisive urban fight. In addition, she discusses media-military relations at length, the differences between working with Army and Marine Corps units, and the relationship between news coverage and public support for Operation IRAQI FREEDOM. She outlines what she considers the best and worst parts of being an embedded reporter in a time of war, the latter being "that horrible soul-destroying aspect of seeing so much destruction."

Captain James Cobb
2 June 2006

MM: My name is Matt Mathews (MM), an historian with the Combat Studies Institute. Today is 2 June 2006 and I'm interviewing Captain James T. Cobb (JC) who, during Operation Phantom Fury, was the fire support officer (FSO) for 2d Battalion, 2d Infantry Regiment, or Task Force 2-2. If you could, sir, please give me some background on yourself: where you went to school, how you got commissioned, where you were born, that sort of thing.

JC: I was born in western Tennessee, north of Memphis, and my family moved to just outside of New Orleans when I was in middle school. That's where I finished growing up. I went to high school right outside of New Orleans and went to the University of New Orleans, which is where I graduated from. When I was a senior in high school, I enlisted in the Louisiana National Guard in December 1989 as a 13B, which is a cannon crew member in the artillery. I stayed in the Guard unit until after I graduated college and was commissioned in 1998. I was commissioned field artillery, went to the Officer Basic Course (OBC) at Fort Sill, then I did a 12-month assignment at the Artillery Training Center as a battery executive officer (XO). Then I went to III Corps Artillery, in 1-14 Field Artillery where I was a battery XO in a multiple launch rocket system (MLRS) unit. Later, I was a battalion fire direction officer (FDO) in the same unit and a fire control officer for the brigade, the 214th Fires Brigade now.

MM: Could you talk me through your first introduction to Task Force 2-2 and your assignments in that unit up until Operation Phantom Fury? What was going on?

JC: I graduated from the Captains Career Course and had an assignment to the 1st Infantry Division (ID) in Germany. I showed up in Germany in December of '02. I was assigned to 1-6 Artillery out of Bamberg and they further assigned me to be the FSO for 2-2 in Vilseck, Germany – it's about a 90 kilometer difference. When I got to Vilseck, 2-2 had already deployed to Kosovo for KFOR 4B. In January of '03, I went to Kosovo and joined up with them. We stayed there until late July of '03. While I was there as the FSO, there really wasn't a lot of fire support action going on in Kosovo so I was the information operations (IO) officer. I was also the S5, which is the civil-military operations (CMO) officer. That was a pretty good learning experience for me. It was a complete stability and support operations (SASO) type mission, non-lethal targeting. We did some artillery training missions but we really didn't focus on it until we got back in Germany and started training up for our Iraq rotation. I pretty much had the same job the whole time I was in Germany assigned to 2-2. I was the task force FSO, the IO and the CMO.

MM: Could you talk me through what you remember when you first arrived in Kuwait and everything that happened between then and the start of Operation Phantom Fury? Maybe a short history of what you participated in.

JC: Sure. We got to Kuwait and that was just a 30-day suck-ex. It just sucked. You're living in a tent in the desert and you're just waiting on equipment to come in before you head north. I went forward on the torch party – me and two other guys from the intelligence (S2) shop. We went up there and met up with the unit we were replacing, and then about a week and a half later the main body showed up. We did a right seat/left seat ride and then in April the insurgent offensive kicked off all across Iraq. We were fighting in the Diyala Province pretty thick and Moqtada al-Sadr kicked off down in Najaf. They told us to form a task force and we sent a battalion-minus down to Najaf. We stayed there for about 25 days just trying to secure the area until more forces came in.

MM: Do you remember if you guys worked at all with the Marines while you were there during that time period?

JC: I do not remember working with the Marines. I remember working with the Hondurans and another Central American contingent that was down there. I didn't work with any Marines, but of course at that time I didn't get out a whole lot. I pretty much stayed on Forward Operating Base (FOB) Duke except for the few recons we ran into Najaf.

MM: Could you talk me through when you first heard that Task Force 2-2 might have to participate with the Marines, with Regimental Combat Team 7 (RCT-7), in the assault on Fallujah? Could you also talk me through the planning process and the role you played in all of that?

JC: Sure. I had just gotten back off of my R&R leave; and any time you leave Iraq for any amount of time, everything has changed so I was trying to catch up on what was going on in my sector. We got the warning order (WARNO) that we might have to go to Fallujah and help the Marines out. Okay, right on. So we started working through the imagery and the Marines had a great intel packet that they put together – great imagery and targeting. They knew what was going on in that town and where the insurgent hangouts and caches were. We were able to start wargaming that and, as task force FSO, I'm helping Major John Reynolds, the operations officer (S3), work through the targeting, how we're going to support the maneuver, how we're going to do the breach if we need to. We wargamed that for about a week. In the meantime, myself, Major Reynolds and the S2 flew to Camp Fallujah a couple times to talk to our Marine contingent that we were going to be supporting, and I thought that was a good idea. We were not going to be the main effort. We were going to be the supporting effort; and any time you're the supporting effort and you want to do good things and still support the overall plan, you have to be self-sufficient. You're supporting them for a reason – because they're focusing somewhere else. That being said, every time we asked for information about our area, we got it. They had a lot of this stuff already produced so it was pretty much off the shelf for them.

MM: When you found out you were going to be the supporting effort, was it you or somebody else in your command that recommended you take the Paladins with you?

JC: As soon as I found out we were going down there and I asked what the task organization was – because I knew we were going to be a supporting effort. I also know if you're a supporting effort, you're so low on the priority of fire list that you might as well not even be on it, especially if you're going to do a serious urban fight that we were looking at. So we asked to take some of our Paladins and I initially asked for a three-gun platoon, which got cut down to a two-gun platoon with a fire direction center (FDC). That really wasn't what I wanted. I wanted more, but a two-gun Paladin platoon with its own FDC is a pretty formidable fighting force for a battalion; and since they were organic to us, we didn't have to worry about any priority of fire issues or cross-boundary coordination.

MM: Did you know the men who would be handling those guns? Had you met them before?

JC: I didn't know the gun crews but I knew the platoon leader, the FDO and a couple of the non-commissioned officers (NCOs) that were working in the FDC.

MM: You were pretty satisfied then that once you got into the fight these guys would be able to put steel on target where you wanted it?

JC: I would have much rather had an opportunity to do some training with them because, like it or not, most of what you do in the military is personality driven. What does panic sound like in my voice on the radio? When I say I need fire now, I don't want some PFC on the other line thinking Captain Cobb's just freaking out again and ignore me. That being said, I was fairly comfortable dealing with the platoon we had. I would have much rather had more practice with them, though.

MM: As Task Force 2-2 goes out to set up in their attack positions on November 7th, could you talk me through what's happening and what you're doing? What vehicle are you in? Who are you with as they're getting ready to conduct this breach at 1900 on November 8th?

JC: Okay. Can I also talk about what my observer plan was?

MM: Of course.

JC: When I got the mission to go down to Fallujah, I already had a short section. I had 20 personnel and I was allowed 33 by the modified table of organization and equipment (MTOE). So I'm shorthanded to begin with and then I had to split my forces again because I still had the counterfire mission back at FOB Normandy. So I took a handful of soldiers – about 12 – and only one lieutenant: Lieutenant Chris Lacour, who by the way is a stud; one of the smartest young officers I've ever worked with. Anyway, I left him back on Camp Fallujah in the tactical operations center (TOC) to do my cross-boundary coordination for me and coordinate with higher. I left one soldier with him – PFC Romero – who was another stellar soldier. He had actually been injured a few days prior to that in a car wreck and had 30 stitches in his arm, but he still came down and did a great job. Those two guys lived at the radio for 96 hours straight.

MM: Were you the one that assigned Lieutenant Lacour as the liaison officer (LNO) before this to stay with the Marines?

JC: When it came up during the planning and I knew I was taking him and had a good idea what I was going to do with him, I recommended he go as the LNO early to start building those relationships with the people he was going to be talking with later. I think that's always a good idea. I've been a liaison before and you're pretty much the redheaded stepchild trying to beg, borrow and steal information and resources, so the sooner you can build those relationships, the better off you are. So I recommended him. He probably hates me for it because it sucked, but he supported the unit and I think that was a key call there.

MM: Is there anything that happened as you guys went out to set up in the staging area in your tactical command post (TAC) site before doing the breach?

JC: Sure. I had one FST team-minus with Alpha Company (Mech), which was Captain Sean Sims' company, and basically that was an E-6 working as the company FSO and he had a radio telephone operator (RTO). I had platoon forward observer (FOs) out there with these guys. I had Alpha Tank who showed up with an FSO as a lieutenant, but he didn't have any RTO or any NCOs with him – and he ended up getting wounded on the second or third day and was out of action. Then I sent Sergeant Raymond Sapp – one of my FOs – with the Brigade Reconnaissance Team (BRT) and I templated an observer location for him, an observation point (OP) on the north-south highway north of the cloverleaf where it intersected with the rail line. I told him before we left to get out there and start observing, doing your drills, get with the BRT guys and use their Long Range Advanced Scout Surveillance System (LRAS) and start lasing some targets. We had the Ground Laser Designator System (GLDS) with us but we didn't have a vehicle to support Sergeant Sapp, so he was pretty much piggybacking with somebody else. From up there, he was able to confirm or deny the intel we had, the templated positions, and tell us whether or not targets were still good. He actually started engaging the enemy observers and rocket-propelled grenade (RPG) teams early with artillery.

MM: This is well before even going to the breach?

JC: Yes, sir. This was early to mid afternoon and it was still daylight, which was great because he was able to find these positions in the daylight, lasing them in and getting good target data to them. So if we had to shoot them later at night –

MM: He's using the BRT's LRAS to do this?

JC: He had a Viper and Mk-7s with him, which are laser range finders that give you direction. They're handheld devices and are pretty good, but they're very sensitive to any type of movement. The LRAS is vehicle-mounted, it has all types of great optics on it, and he can observe and lase as well with that thing as probably anything else we had in the inventory.

MM: Will that give you a 10 digit grid coordinate?

JC: Yes, sir.

MM: So far, the people I've talked to have said that that was just an amazing piece of equipment.

JC: It is and, to tell you the truth, we'd never worked with it before. Fortunately for Sergeant Sapp, he was in a vehicle with a trained crew from the BRT and they kind of schooled him up on it. They all took turns lasing targets. As an FO, he just needed somebody to lase and get the data for him; he can work the rest of it. Once you get the initial data, you can make adjustments, or if you get a first round on target you can just call fire for effect after that. It worked out pretty well.

MM: Was he involved in the mission that came later on when they actually had to fire across the 1-3 Marines' boundary line over into 1-8 Marines' area?

JC: He was not. When we had to do that – and you're talking about the annex or the mosque, I think.

MM: Right. It was one of them.

JC: I don't know where we got that intel. I think it was an unmanned aerial vehicle (UAV) from the Marines that saw a bunch of insurgents running in and out of this building, using it as a headquarters or a weapons cache. We tried to call close air support (CAS) on it but they had trouble identifying the target. It took a long time and I don't know what the problems were; but while we were waiting I went ahead and called the mission to the artillery, to our platoon, and had them working on the data just in case. When CAS finally could do it – and the target had been dwelling a long time; and when you do that, you start losing effects. The people you want to kill in that target are going to filter out, so you have to hit it pretty quickly. Lieutenant Colonel Peter Newell looked at me and told me to fire the artillery. We had a grid from the UAV but we didn't have an observer on it, so I called BRT and asked them to send somebody down there. I think it was Lieutenant Neil Prakash from the BRT – great kid. He went on to win the Silver Star in Ba'qubah later on. He got his tank with his wingman and drove across boundary – way behind enemy lines – so he could lase the target, verify the grid and then observe for me about 800 meters away. After I was satisfied that we had a good accurate location – because we're firing next to a mosque and I wanted to limit the collateral damage as much as we could. And by the way, CNN had a camera stuck about 12 inches away from my head watching me do all this. So, no pressure, right? I sent a platoon, a 20 rounds fire-for-effect mission – which if you had two guns shooting and you ask for 20 rounds, that's 40 rounds of high explosive (HE) coming down. I asked for a converging sheaf. Usually when you fire artillery you want to get a large dispersion area and the computer will plot the aim points so you can cover more area with your impact and your blast. I asked for a converging sheaf which had one aim point for both tubes, so it would be more accurate and I would have less dispersion of the rounds. The lieutenant called back and told me we had multiple target hits, building's been hit multiple times, there's dust and it's smoking. But there were still some people moving so he asked to repeat the mission, we shot it again, and after that we had no more problems out of that building. I think that was around November 9th. We weren't sleeping a whole lot. The first three days sort of all blended together there.

MM: Can you talk me through your actions as the breaching operation was preparing to kick off?

JC: Sergeant Sapp was on that great OP earlier and he was able to confirm or deny some target houses. We also adjusted our smoke; and the way you do that is by shooting HE in first and then you can record the last data. Then we shoot the smoke on the last target information we had and the smoke is right where you want it. So it saves us time when we were actually going to do the breach. We had always planned on shooting smoke on the breach because, for a doctrinal breach, we use the abbreviation SOSRA: suppress, obscure, secure, reduce and assault. So the first two – suppress and secure – are pretty much the artillery and the maneuver forces suppressing any enemy positions; then artillery obscures the breach so the bad guys don't know what we're doing. So we had always planned on shooting smoke into the breach and I had three targets planned for that. We adjusted the first one in, which was outside of town but between the railroad and the first houses. From there, from the observer, we were just going to add to the target, add to the range, so we could move that smoke out and leapfrog it back until we had it where we wanted it. Since Sergeant Sapp had observed these targets early and had confirmed the intelligence, we also planned on shooting some of those known enemy locations with our 120 millimeter mortars so we could suppress those or destroy them so they couldn't fire on our tanks and Bradleys as they were going through the breach.

MM: These 120s that you mentioned, were they co-located back with your Paladins?

JC: No. Actually, the 120 mortars don't have the range that a Paladin does so they stayed on the east side of the berm most of the time, but they were right up there with us. I think initially they were co-located with Captain Fred Dente's element out there in the attack position and then we jumped them a little further south so we could cover more of the city. We jumped them a few times. They did great work.

MM: What vehicle were you in and who were you with as the battle is progressing and the breach goes through? Can you give me some sense of how you got your communications system set up and who you were talking to and that sort of thing?

JC: I was operating out of an M1114 Humvee. The driver and the gunner were two of my observers who were part of my crew from back at Normandy. We had all been together since Kosovo, and that's an extremely long time for a group of soldiers to be together. Private James Peterson and Private First Class Nick Brzeski – great heroes. The other person in the truck was the S2, Captain Ray Pemberton, who was a recent addition to the team. I also had an Air Force joint tactical air controller (JTAC). As far as comms devices, I had two single channel ground to air radio systems (SINCGARS); one had a power amp so I could talk long range, and I also had a Blue Force Tracker. The JTAC had his whole comms suite, but since he didn't have his own vehicle he was pretty much man-packing all that stuff. When we would stop somewhere, he would run up the hill, set up his long whip and try to talk to aircraft, and that probably wasn't the best way of doing business, but there you go.

MM: Did you have any problems communicating with the Marines? Apparently they were using some sort of chat system during this fight. Were you able to talk to them and were they able to get you on the line? How did that work?

JC: If you're talking about mIRC Chat, which was like a chat room on the computer, Lieutenant Lacour had that whole system wired tight back at the TOC on Camp Fallujah. He could mIRC Chat with those guys both laterally across to our adjacent units and up to higher and could send that information to me over the radio. I think they had good commo over that system and would push any info to us over Blue Force Tracker or the radio. If they had problems with that system, they must have ensured that we didn't see them where we were. That was sign of good staff work.

MM: He would just send that to you over the standard FM?

JC: Yes. And I had my own fire support net, so the only thing that was on that was fire missions or anything fire support related. I was also monitoring the battalion command net, but I was co-located with the S3 so I really didn't need to monitor the command net. I could bounce back and forth to other nets on that other radio – that was my short range radio, though.

MM: So there wasn't any problem for you guys. I have heard other people telling me how difficult it was to talk to the Marines because of the mIRC Chat system. That doesn't appear to be a problem for your light TAC out there.

JC: Well, it wasn't for me because my commo always works. One of the things an FSO prides himself on is that he's always able to talk. When a fire supporter can't talk to anybody that means he's not doing anything. Sergeant First Class William "Billy" Hight, my platoon sergeant at the time, he started beating into the soldiers from day one to take care of their comms equipment, because it will take care of them. So we were parked right next to the S3's truck and we could talk back to the TOC and hear him clean, and the S3 couldn't. He would have problems. So we'd go over there and school the young soldiers on how to maintain that commo equipment and that's basically all it was. The S3 had a pickup team as far as who his crew was. They rotated the battle captain in and out. His driver wasn't his historical driver. He was working out of a different truck. For me, I had one crew and we had always worked together, so that was easy for me.

MM: Do remember having any difficulty with communications security (COMSEC) and fills and getting new load sets? Do you remember having any difficulty prior to the complex ambush that took place where Lieutenant Edward Iwan was killed, having to go back or the S3 having to go back and get a new load set?

JC: I remember thinking it was the craziest and most idiotic thing I had ever heard of – changing COMSEC in the middle of the fight – unless of course COMSEC has been compromised; and I never heard of a report that said COMSEC was compromised. To me, it seemed like it was one of those standard, "We change COMSEC every Wednesday no matter what, so let's change COMSEC." "Well you know what guys? I'm kind of busy right now." I wasn't going to change COMSEC until everybody had the COMSEC available because if I do, I can't talk to anybody who still has the old fill. There are ways to work around it; you just have to think through it.

MM: Can you talk me through as the task force goes through the breach, what you recall up until this complex ambush that takes place a few days later?

JC: The funniest thing I remember was that my driver and I were bouncing all over the place driving under blackout with night observation devices (NODs) on.

I had to tell him that he was probably the worst night driver I had ever seen – and he said, "Hey, sir, this is the first time I've ever driven with NODs on, give me a break." That was something I really didn't need to hear right then. We executed the suppression of the enemy positions with our 120s. We were shooting the white phosphorous (WP) in and the fire support plan was on track, just like I planned it. Quite frankly, I was surprised because I know a plan never survives first contact, but so far mine had. We were adjusting the smoke and doing what we wanted to. The mortars actually stopped firing the known targets and we were just waiting for targets of opportunity. Again, Sergeant Sapp down at the cloverleaf was spotting these bad guys popping up and moving around and he was able to bring some mortar fire on them. I remember the mine-clearing line charge (MCLC) going in and that was just an awesome sight. When it detonated, you could see the improvised explosive devices (IEDs) kicking off into the sky and exploding. It looked like fireworks from where we were. Then things settled down and the actual heavy lifting of the breach went in. I remember Alpha Tank and Alpha Mech getting in in good order, but the Iraqi Army had a difficult time getting their trucks over the rail lines. The heavy tracked vehicles had eroded all the dirt that was supporting it, so when the Iraqi trucks went over they were just bottoming out on the rails. We ended up blowing those rails, and somewhere in there is when Sergeant Major Steve Faulkenburg was killed while guiding the Iraqi Army to their positions, because it was night and they couldn't see without NODs. When I heard about it, it was such a shock; but at least for my guys and me it steeled our determination to get on with the fight and make them pay. We moved the TAC a couple times and ended up on top of the highway, looking down into the city about 500 meters away from the cloverleaf where the BRT was set up. We're north of the cloverleaf and Alpha Tank and Alpha Mech are working through town hitting their objectives, clearing buildings. Actually, we didn't fire a lot of artillery into town at that time just because we couldn't see the targets. We were fighting in a city and we couldn't see that far away. Every time one of my observers would go to a roof to try and establish an OP, the units they were supporting would tell them to get down and get back because they had to move on, so it was just a fast paced event and they didn't have time to establish OPs. The few times they did try to establish one, they'd get shot at, so it was probably not the best place to conduct an indirect firefight. So we let the guns and my observers rest. Now, Sergeant Sapp was shooting because from where he was, he could see all the way down from east to west on Phase Line Fran. He was able to see insurgents moving back and forth across the road, and if they stopped he could call a fire mission on them. I think he put a priority target down there at one point, but I don't remember. I think around 0400, visibility dropped down to pretty low and we were hitting a lull in the fight. Major Reynolds wanted me to focus more of my fire down Phase Line Fran to try to interdict any of those guys running across. Sergeant Sapp was down there and said he didn't have any targets. So since we knew there were IEDs on the other road and they were in the obstacles, why don't you target a couple of the obstacles down there on Phase Line Fran. When the Iraqi Army had left the area, they had left all their HESCO bastions full of dirt there at the checkpoint and the insurgents took them over. They ended up putting IEDs in them, so if you were to drive through the checkpoint and you have to slow down anyway, they could detonate the IEDs. So Sergeant Sapp fired a couple of them and it detonated the IEDs, and that worked out pretty good. We started shooting linear targets up and down Phase Line Fran in our sector to try and clear out some of the IEDs, so when our guys eventually got down there they wouldn't have to deal with them as much. It worked pretty well.

MM: The sun comes up on the morning of 9 November and basically Task Force 2-2 is at Fran. Did you think you would have been able to get down there that quick? Was there any sort of consternation? It was my understanding that the Marines in 1-3 are still up at their own line of departure (LD). Do you recall anything about that?

JC: I don't know the details of why they were still that far up north, but quite frankly I knew we would get to Phase Line Fran by sunrise. We were supposed to be in a less heavily defended area so there weren't supposed to be as many fighters. Also, we had mechanized units; we move faster. I thought it was a fairly safe bet that we'd get there by sunrise. Intuitively, I knew we'd be ahead of the Marines. I knew their plan was to do a detailed clearing of what I thought was each house that was an enemy fighting position. What I didn't know until later was that they were doing a detailed clearing of each building. That takes a long time and uses a lot of manpower. As far as 1-3 not being able to get their breach in, I didn't know about that. I just knew they had requested to use our breach lane and send some forces through there. I don't know why. It didn't matter to us at that time because we were done with the breach lane. We were sending forces back across the berm to our logistics point so they could get ammo and fuel and stuff like that, so I didn't care.

MM: So you're all at Phase Line Fran. Can you talk me through the rest of the operation as you go south through the rest of the city?

JC: Okay. As far as the artillerymen, we had a target package for the stuff south of Phase Line Fran, but it wasn't very robust. I think most of the effort had been on the first couple phases – breach and get into the northern sector. So me and Lacour over the radio finalized that fire plan so when we did actually go south we could support with artillery fire, and I think we did a pretty good job. But it was difficult to observe down in that area because the tall industrial buildings limited your observation. I had Sergeant Sapp confirming and denying some targets down there and he could see the exposed buildings, but once you get past the screen of them, he couldn't tell much. The UAV helped out. We sent the Raven over there a couple

18

times targeting some stuff. Then we fought through the industrial area, came back up to Fran and then, the next day, we turned around and went back through it. When the Marines finally caught up, we pushed back down south and were fighting through that residential area to the south – and that was pretty hard fighting. They had prepared some positions and kill zones and ambush sites. I don't know all the details of Iwan getting killed, but I know he got killed down there as well as Sean Sims. I carry some guilt about Sean because I had been pressuring his observer team – Sergeant Sean O'Brien – to get up on high ground on some of those buildings and occupy an OP and start lasing some targets for us. I think they were jumping his command post (CP) to a new building and were using the same building to establish an OP. So when he got killed, two of my soldiers were following right behind him into the door; and I think the JTAC that was with him got wounded in that engagement too.

MM: So all three of these guys just went into this building, turned left, and the bad guys were in there and got them?

JC: I never did get all the gory details because I really didn't want them. All I know is that Sergeant O'Brien was the third or fourth guy walking into the building behind Captain Sims and he said all hell broke loose. He actually got separated from everybody else for about 30 to 40 minutes. He was pinned down somewhere. So I was freaking out. One of my best friends had been killed, my JTAC was wounded, and I can't find two of my guys. Holy smokes! What is going on up there? That rocked me a little bit. I had lost Iwan the day prior – who was a great guy and one of my friends – and then I lose Sean the next day and two of my guys are missing. That was a bad couple days for me.

MM: Had you known Captain Sims on prior assignments?

JC: Just from being in 2-2. I think we met in Kosovo when he came down. He was working as a plans officer in the S3 shop and he just had a great personality. As soon as you met him and he gave you his grin, you liked him. I don't know anybody who had a bad thing to say about Sean, ever. He was a great guy and a hard worker.

MM: Let's jump forward to 13 November and Task Force 2-2 had gone back up to do a hot rearm and refuel and then they were going to come back down and do a passage of lines with 1-8 Marines over in the west. Do you recall any special coordination that had to be done artillery-wise with the Marines to accomplish this?

JC: I think that was the mission we planned when we were at the potato factory – and that was the first time I had had any real sleep since two days prior to kicking it off, so it's all kind of fuzzy.

MM: I was just wondering if there was anything special you needed to do in that instance. It just seems to me that that was a pretty complicated maneuver to do a passage of lines with the 1-8 and I didn't know if it required any special activities from the FSO or not.

JC: It probably did, but I can't remember right now. I think that's also when Sergeant First Class Hight finally got back from Germany. He'd been detained by the MPs in Germany because they wanted him to testify in a court martial and we're screaming at him to get back to Iraq. Finally, someone called General John Batiste and asked what he wanted to do with this guy. "Get his butt to the fight."

MM: That's what I've heard from interviewing Major Erik Krivda and some of the others. All these days just blend into each other. Are there any other big events you can remember or are there any solid lessons learned that you'd like younger officers to know?

JC: From the whole fight and the entire rotation, I was just amazed and astounded and in awe of the amount of random violence that happens in combat. You watch the movies and you think there's a lot of violence and a lot of bad things happening; but until you're actually standing there, smoking and joking and talking to your guys and then the world starts to explode around you for no reason, that's difficult to prepare for. The second thing is that combat is a come-as-you-are event. You're either trained or you're not; but when you get there, it's too late to figure it out. One of the things Sergeant First Class Hight and I did when we were back at Normandy – under Lieutenant Colonel Newel's direction – was to keep training on fire support tasks and keep working on our fire missions. This did a couple things. It kept the guns we had at Normandy in practice and us in practice in case we had to do something. I think at least every other week we'd go out for four or five hours and shoot indirect artillery into our impact area. We had an impact area there so it was a good training environment. We worked danger close missions up there and any range control manual or safety regulation in the world would have de-certified me in a heartbeat for some of the stuff we did up there. It was safe training and no one got hurt, but it was realistic and it worked out pretty well. I had observers who were confident enough to adjust rounds into about 150 meters of their position which, if you think about that in a city environment – that's about two streets. They have rounds impacting a block or two blocks away and they're walking them in and feeling pretty confident about it. They had the tactics, techniques and procedures (TTPs). We used Blue Force Tracker with the imagery program so we could actually see which building our guys were in and which building they were targeting, so if something had happened to them – if they were getting shot at and they couldn't observe the rounds – we could help them out with the imagery we had available. It was right there in my laptop.

MM: So you give a big thumbs up to the Blue Force Tracker?

JC: Yes and no. The sending of messages was good. Captain Natalie Friel, who was the S2 back at the TOC, could type of a quick intel summary and fire it out to everybody, and it worked well. I think we tried to send a couple overlays through Blue Force Tracker and it failed miserably – too much bandwidth, I think. But as a planning tool, Major Reynolds and I could sit there and look at the imagery and move it around and plot locations, just like using a paper map but I could do more stuff to it. It was actually more current than the photo imagery we had in our hands. Blue Force Tracker was a good planning tool.

MM: During the course of this operation, did you ever have to use any of the Marine towed 155s or call for any Marine indirect fire to help you out?

JC: I think we did a couple times. When our guns had to go down for maintenance or something, Lacour coordinated to get some coverage from the Marine guns. When that big underground bunker complex was found deep down south and they wanted us to try to pound it with artillery to break its back, I think we used some Marine artillery for that. We used about 150 rounds for that and, in my opinion, it was a waste of time, but higher headquarters wanted it done so we shot it. Unless it was planned, it was extremely difficult for us to get the responsiveness from the Marines; and I understand that because they had their own priority of fires they had to contend with, which is why we brought our own Paladins.

MM: What about Marine air and CAS? Were they very responsive to your needs?

JC: The Keyhole CAS airspace deconfliction concept worked pretty well. I think it would have worked better if we had had time to rehearse it in a training environment instead of actually on the objective. The way the concept was supposed to work is that the CAS is stacked up somewhere else and it comes in through a small piece of air that we don't fire any artillery or mortars into. They come in and do their run and then they pull back out. The way it's supposed to work is you don't turn off the artillery or the mortars except in the airspace that the bird is flying. Well, in actuality, we had to shut down all the artillery for a portion of time, at least in the beginning stages, because people weren't confident that the artillery wouldn't fire through that airspace. Where I'm from and the training we did, that was standard – you don't shoot through an airspace coordination area (ACA), but we didn't do it. A couple times we had to shut down all the artillery to let CAS come in, but it actually worked out pretty good for the guns because they needed a break. We were just smoking them.

MM: Speaking of which, didn't you at one point almost go black on your 120 millimeter rounds?

JC: We almost went black on 120, 155. We were down to about 20 rounds of 155 at one point and about 50 or 60 of 120 millimeter mortars.

MM: Did you guys actually shoot more 155 with those two Paladins than the Marines shot with a whole battery?

JC: I have no idea. I just know we shot close to 1,000 rounds of 155 – but that included HE and the WP and all that stuff. We shot a lot and, actually, I won 100 bucks off of that too, because the battery FDO bet me that we wouldn't shoot over 100 rounds. Yeah, I won.

MM: Is there anything else you want to leave us with?

JC: I think we were successful and I don't think anybody can argue that. We were successful for a couple reasons. One was that we had a team that had been together for almost two years straight – since Kosovo. We had done a lot of training together and we had lived together. We were in our eighth or ninth month of the deployment at this point and we knew how to conduct a combat operation. That being said, I think the capstone training event we did in Germany before we left – the mission readiness exercise (MRX) at the Combat Maneuver Training Center (CMTC) – did not prepare us for this fight. I think that prepared us more for SASO and small unit patrolling and stuff like that. The training events that prepared us for this fight were each individual leader's training experiences throughout their entire careers. I was doing stuff there that I did at the National Training Center (NTC) as a lieutenant. Sergeant First Class Hight was doing the same stuff there that he had done as a young E-6 at Fort Polk. Lieutenant Colonel Newell, who had been in the Ranger Regiment and had done all these great training events, he knew how he wanted to do the fight. Major Reynolds had deployed as a lieutenant to Somalia with 10th Mountain Division. He had done stuff like this before. All the senior guys had done things like this before, so we were able to fall back on that. It wasn't the recent training we had done; it was that we are all products of our experiences, and I think we all had the experience and the training level we needed to go be successful in this.

MM: What were your perceptions of working with the Marines?

JC: I liked working with them and I'm going to give you the reason why. It sounds extremely simplistic, but it's the way I feel. Since we were their supporting effort and we weren't a Marine unit, they pretty much gave us our area, validated our plan when we briefed it, and said, "Okay, good luck. Go out there and fight your fight." Colonel Craig Tucker, the RCT-7 commander, would come down and check us out every couple days during the fight and he had nothing but good things to say. I don't think he ever came down there and told us we were doing something wrong or that he wanted us to do something different. We had our left and right boundaries; we stayed within them. I liked it, but I like autonomous missions. I like it when they just give me a mission and some resources and then go forth and execute.

MM: I could be wrong on this, but it seems like you guys do in fact start out as the supporting attack of the supporting attack. However, I would safely say that by the morning of November 9th, you're clearly no longer the supporting attack. It seems to me that you guys were actually leading the show for RCT-7. Do you have any views on that?

JC: I would agree with that, but the objectives we were given weren't the high profile objectives like the main effort got. The main effort was in the middle of town, they had a very difficult sector to go through, and they needed to be the main effort. I don't even want to speculate, if they had put 2-2 Infantry in the main sector, how we would have done. It would have been a completely different fight. Yeah, we were ahead, but I don't think anybody in 2-2 ever said they needed to make us the main effort now. I think we were all completely satisfied with our own little piece of battlespace and just go through there and kick ass, take names and do our job.

MM: What were your observations on the enemy in general? What were your views on the foreign fighters and the insurgents?

JC: The foreign fighters were pretty good. I think later on when they established those kill zones down south, it was obvious they had some level of training. The guys further up north on the first night, we pretty much killed them early with overwhelming firepower. I was behind the tanks and the Bradleys and the artillery going in, and I was awestruck. No way on Earth would I have wanted to be on the receiving end of all that. You can't imagine what it's like to be a dismounted insurgent with an AK-47 or a RPG and a couple mags of ammunition looking at a tank. Hell, I'd quit, but they kept coming at it. They were more brave than smart sometimes, and I'm okay with that as long as we kill them. We killed a lot of bad guys and I'm okay with that, because I know they would have just as easily killed me if they had had the opportunity.

MM: 2-2 had an overabundance of media with them for some reason. What were your observations of all the media types being with Task Force 2-2?

JC: Initially I was pretty hesitant about them because that was how I was brought up: don't trust the media types because they're going to cast you in a bad light if given the opportunity. After I got to know them, though, they made an honest, concentrated effort to get to know us and become friendly; and I think part of their motivation was that the friendlier they are to us, the more we'll open up and give them the good intel, and that's okay. I think generally they stayed out of our way as much as they could and still get their job done. I liked most of them. Scott

Rutter from Fox News was a great guy. Jane Arraf and her crew from CNN were good as well. She almost got killed a couple times.

MM: Have you read her interview that we have online?

JC: No, not yet.

MM: When you get a chance you should. I think you'll really like that.

JC: I liked all those guys, except for the guy who took pictures of Sean Sims' body and then sold them on the Internet. I never met him, but that guy's really lucky he got pulled out after that because he probably would have met with an unfortunate accident in the combat zone. Alpha Company loved their commander – and to disgrace him like that? I'm not going to say somebody would have capped him, but he would not have had a good time. There are a lot of emotions in a fight like that and, once again, everything is personality driven.

MM: I think that just about covers everything. Thank you for your time.

Captain Jeff Emery
17 July 2006

MM: My name is Matt Matthews (MM) and I'm an historian at the Combat Studies Institute at Fort Leavenworth, Kansas. Today is 17 July 2006 and I'm interviewing Captain Jeff Emery (JE) who, at the time of the Battle of Fallujah – Operation Phantom Fury – was a platoon leader and executive officer (XO) for Alpha Company, 2-2 Infantry. Let me start out by saying that this is an unclassified interview, so if we get into anything that's classified, just tell me you can't talk about it and we'll move on. I want to start off with some background on you, where you were born, where you grew up, and how you received your commission.

JE: Sure. I grew up and went to high school in northern New Jersey, then went to the University of Delaware for college where I did ROTC for four years and got commissioned on 1 June 2004. From there, I went into the infantry down at Fort Benning, Georgia, and spent a year there going through all the schools – Basic Course, Mechanized Leader, Airborne, Ranger – and then went to Germany. My first duty assignment was the Big Red One, Hohenfels, Germany, with 2-2 Infantry. I started out as a platoon leader in Alpha Company, 2-2.

MM: Can you talk me through what you did prior to going to Iraq, what your unit was involved in?

JE: When I got there they were just returning from Kosovo, so we were kind of going through refit operations where we were trying to plus-up manning, receive any type of new weapons and equipment, get familiarized with that. Pretty much immediately, we went into small arms and Bradley gunnery, all the way up through Table 12 – we did a whole gunnery rotation. Aside from the Brads, we put a lot of concentration on small arms marksmanship, close quarters fighting, and military operations on urban terrain (MOUT) training, urban warfare fighting. We also worked with explosives for room entry techniques and to blow breaches. The biggest training event we did was a field problem rotation, 30 days at Hohenfels – a bunch of platoon and company exercises, kind of like mission readiness exercise (MRE) training – to prepare us for all the types of missions we'd face in Iraq: react to improvised explosive devices (IEDs), squad/platoon attacks, enter building/ clear room, that kind of stuff.

MM: You were the 1st Platoon leader, correct?

JE: Yes, 1st Platoon, Alpha Company.

MM: Could you also give me some background, before you get to Iraq, on who the company commander was, the executive officer (XO), and if there were any changes in leadership?

JE: When I got there, Captain Doug Walter was the company commander, Peter Smith was the company first sergeant and First Lieutenant Jeff Jager was the XO. By the time we deployed to Iraq, First Lieutenant Cole Namken became the XO and Jeff Jager went up to the battalion and was the assistant operations officer (AS3) there. And then right as we deployed – and I'm talking like three days before we flew – they replaced Captain Walter with Captain Sean Sims, because Captain Walter – when he came back from Kosovo – was pretty sick and the colonel made the decision that he wasn't going to deploy with the task force, although he did deploy several months later.

MM: So Lieutenant Edward Iwan wasn't the XO at this point?

JE: No, Iwan deployed as the mortar platoon leader.

MM: He eventually becomes the XO after the unit's already been in Iraq.

JE: Yes.

MM: Okay, so tell me about your arrival in Iraq and any incidents that occurred up until Phantom Fury, what went on and any changes in Alpha Company.

JE: We first deployed to Kuwait, did a three-week train up there and headed to Iraq in the first week of March – did a replacement with guys from 4th Infantry Division and started doing patrols in our area, which was Muqdadiyah, about 45 kilometers northeast of Baghdad. As far as highlights, 8 and 9 April 2004 was our first major contact when there was a large push of insurgents in the city of Muqdadiyah, so we engaged in back-to-back fighting, street fighting for two days. They were probably six hours of continuous fighting per day. At that point in time, An Najaf was flaring up and we – after fighting those two days back to back – got the call that they were taking our task force down to An Najaf. We were stationed there, based out of Forward Operating Base (FOB) Duke, which was just in the desert. I think we were there for close to three weeks. We didn't do a whole lot; we were just basically the show of force. I think only one of our units actually went into the city of Najaf, more or less to just take Colonel Dana Pittard and set up security for him. Most of our time down there was spent doing security patrols outside the city, getting a sense for what the local population was feeling towards us, and making sure no one else was getting in. After we returned from that, there weren't too many other highlights. We got back in May. Just in terms of what was going on in Alpha Company, we got back from An Najaf in mid May and I was hit with an IED on one of my patrols. I was actually evacuated back to Germany, spent six weeks out of Iraq, and then came right back and ended up retaking 1st Platoon. They didn't replace me. The big change in the company, however, came while I was hurt. Cole Namken, our XO, on one of his patrols a Humvee flipped on his leg and he was evacuated back to Germany too. When that happened, that's when Ed Iwan moved from the mortar platoon to became the Alpha Company XO, First

Lieutenant Chris Walls – the 3d Platoon leader – moved to take the mortar platoon, and First Lieutenant Joaquin Meno took 3d Platoon.

MM: As you discuss the platoon leaders, could we go over the task organization for Alpha Company? Were those three pure Bradley platoons at this time?

JE: No. The way it was organized, you had a headquarters element, which was the commanding officer (CO), the XO and the first sergeant in two Bradleys and a '113. You had three line platoons. 1st and 3d Platoons were Bradley-pure and 2d Platoon was a slice from the 82d Engineers, so we actually had an engineer platoon task organized to our unit for the entire year's deployment in Iraq. When we deployed, we had four platoons, which is pretty uncommon; but we sliced out two in infantry platoons to different units and we received one back, being the engineers.

MM: What did those engineers have in terms of equipment?

JE: They showed up with pretty much the regular modified table of organization and equipment (MTOE). I think they were a 20-something man platoon, maybe 24, 26. They had either four or six '113s, two ACEs, a M548 and a C-truck, and then they had a lot of demolition equipment for breaches, obstacle reductions and so forth.

MM: They didn't have a mine-clearing line charge (MCLC) with them, did they?

JE: I don't think we were given MCLCs at Fallujah.

MM: Tell me about when you first found out or had an inkling that you might be sent to support Operation Phantom Fury.

JE: I believe there was talk in October and, at first, people were saying it wasn't going to happen – then it was on and off. Finally, we were going but then it was just a matter of when. Once we were definitely going, our task force pulled all the maneuver units that were going to Fallujah and they stopped patrolling, just kind of training up and getting plused-up on all our supplies – ammo, food, any type of equipment we needed, swapping out vehicles to ensure we had the best stuff to go fight. I'd say there were at least four days where we were definitely going, and then the next morning when we woke up we found we were not going after all. It was right after the US presidential election, right after George W. Bush won – I think it was the next day or two days later that we got the call that we were going to Fallujah. Basically we just assembled at FOB Normandy, loaded up on the heavy equipment transporters (HETs), drove down to Warhorse, refueled there, got a quick refit, and then continued the road march down to Fallujah.

MM: Once you get down to Camp Fallujah, did you encounter any problems working with the Marines, any interaction with them?

JE: We didn't have too much interaction with Marines. We got there first and they had an area already sectioned off for us. There were some Marine units in our area but not too many.

MM: Let's start when you guys rolled up Route Michigan and go into your staging area prior to the attack. Were there any incidents you recall or anything you want to talk about?

JE: I don't recall too much. The Brigade Reconnaissance Troop (BRT) had gone in the night before and they were calling a lot of indirect fires and we rolled in and set up. I think we might have changed our position one time but once we were set in our assembly area we didn't move until we were actually attacking into the city. I think we were there for quite some time and the leaders had gone up to the berm right on the highway just looking to see where they were going to be headed at night; and while that was going on, BRT was calling indirect fire and we were watching what they were doing and witnessing some of the effects.

MM: Did you go on this visual daylight reconnaissance?

JE: I did. We tried to send all the leaders up there – the colonel, the platoon leaders, company commanders – and maybe if you were lucky a few squad leaders, just to see the route we were going to take up to the berm and go over the highway. For the engineer guys, it was mainly to try and pinpoint the breach during the day.

MM: Can you talk me through what you recall happened on the night of your movement from the attack positions into the line of departure (LD) and going through the breach?

JE: Sure. The attack positions – we just moved into an assembly area first and then we moved into an attack position right before we crossed the berm. My platoon was nearside security of the breach so we jumped out in front of Alpha Company, led them in, set up nearside security and started firing into the town at targets of opportunity. The commander came up once we had our nearside security set, put some eyes on the area and called up the engineer platoon. They came up, set the breach and blew the MCLC, marked the lane, swept for mines and did everything pretty much textbook. They opened a great breach lane and once that was completed, 3d Platoon went right through the breach. I think when they were going through they hit some mines, but the reason was that the Bradleys that got hit went outside of the breach lane and they felt some effects from some kind of an explosive.

MM: Did it take out their Bradleys?

JE: No, there was no damage whatsoever.

MM: When you say 3d Platoon, we're still talking about the Bradleys, right?

JE: Yeah. 2d Platoon was the only engineer platoon. Everybody else was pretty much Bradleys.

MM: What platoon was the attached armor platoon that was with you guys?

JE: We had a platoon from Bravo Company, 1-63 Armor.

MM: Did you guys call them 3d Platoon?

JE: We called them 4th Platoon. And they were actually split: the commander gave two tanks to me in 1st Platoon and two tanks to First Lieutenant Meno in 3d Platoon, and we used them as point men to lead us through since they had the heavier armor and more firepower. They could go through and clear any types of obstacles rather than having the engineers reduce them.

MM: So to clear this up in my mind, you have 1st Platoon Bradleys, 3d Platoon Bradleys, 4th Platoon is your tanks and really the engineers had no platoon designation?

JE: No, they were 2d Platoon and they were riding in '113s. Once we got to Fallujah , we split 4th Platoon. I got a section of tanks and 3d Platoon got a section of tanks so, in essence, I was in charge of four Bradleys, two tanks and then I had my two dismounted squads, and 3d Platoon looked identical to me.

MM: Your actual 2d Platoon, Alpha Company, 2-2, was sent over to Alpha Company, 2-63, is that correct?

JE: No. Our 2d Platoon, Alpha Company, 2-2, was sent to the 82d Engineers. Our 4th Platoon, Alpha Company, 2-2, was sent to the BRT. The way we deployed was that our 2d Platoon deployed with the 82d Engineers and 4th Platoon deployed with the BRT to support their brigade. When we went to Fallujah, the BRT received a section of Bradleys from 4th Platoon and the other section of Bradleys went to Alpha Company, 2-63. First Lieutenant Gregory and his wingman went with Captain Paul Fowler in 2-63 and Sergeant First Class Lanpher and his wingman went with Captain Kirk Mayfield who was the BRT commander. I believe the BRT also received a section of tanks from 2-63. I believe First Lieutenant Neil Prakash was with BRT the whole time in Fallujah and he was under Mayfield.

MM: The MCLC fires at about 1915. Could you talk me through what happened from there?

JE: The lane was cleared and 3d Platoon rolled right through. They immediately started clearing houses and everyone else was still on the far side of the breach. So they immediately gained a foothold into the city, and once they were set they held their position. There was one house they were supposed to go into and they decided against it because they thought the house was rigged to blow up, so they jumped to the next one and called back to the company commander. I don't remember if he went first or if I did, but I just remember that I pushed my platoon through and we continued going down to our first objective. We ended up overshooting it and just cleared back to it, so we probably cleared back about three or four houses. The most resistance we received was sporadic gunfire. We were using our thermal sights to spot the enemy and placing effective fires for them. Once we were set, they pushed 3d Platoon through us and they jumped to their objective; and then once they were set, we jumped up to Objective Wolf and this was when daylight was starting to break. Up until then, we were looking at very minimal resistance. We reduced some obstacles on the way to our second objective, Wolf, which was a school. We were going to set up a hasty defense there and conduct a tactical pause to refit but it didn't quite work out, because once daylight hit and we were trying to get set up we started taking pretty heavy fire. The sun had come up, the enemy knew where we were and was focusing in on all of us.

MM: Is this when you were approaching Phase Line Fran, also known as Highway 10?

JE: Right, but we were still not quite there yet. We were 200 to 400 meters shy

MM: It looks like it may have been Phase Line Linda maybe.

JE: Yeah, that may have been it. So we were held there for awhile and encountered a lot of small arms fire. I don't remember a lot of rocket-propelled grenades (RPGs) being shot. I remember a lot of small arms sniper fire, machine gun fire and sporadic gunfire, and we were pretty much shooting from the windows at where we saw or heard gunfire coming from.

MM: Were most of your guys still in the Brads?

JE: No, we were all dismounted at this time because we had dismounted to clear Objective Wolf, the school. Once we did that, we set up shop there because that was going to be our first refit; and then as that was happening, that was when we started taking a lot of fire. We went up to the rooftop and, while we weren't pinned down, we took heavy fire up there as well. So anyway, we popped smoke, got off the rooftop, went back inside the building and just kind of fired from the windows. We used the Bradleys to surround our position and suppress the enemy.

MM: Were you calling in a lot of indirect fire at this time?

JE: I wasn't calling in any and I don't know if the Alpha Company commander, Captain Sean Sims, was. I'm sure he must have been talking to the colonel to find out what his plans were. There was a lot of on-the-ground fighting, but mostly shooting from the windows at targets. That went on for a couple hours and we finally got the call that 2-63 was already down on Phase Line Fran. The original thought was that we were going to go house to house all the way down to Phase Line Fran – and this is probably where the story will start to conflict because, up until then, everybody was on the same page and now this is when what you wanted to have happen didn't. What I was told by my commander was that we were behind schedule and the colonel wanted us down at Phase Line Fran ASAP.

MM: You're of the opinion that they were in a hurry to get down to Phase Line Fran?

JE: Well, that's what happened. It's not my opinion; it's a fact. We were in Objective Wolf – and I know this from my platoon and it had to be the same for Alpha Company. The commander said that this had gone on long enough and we've been there too long, so we mounted up and did a bounding overwatch all the way down to Phase Line Fran. It was basically a mounted movement from Objective Wolf to Phase Line Fran. The original plan was to clear house to house to Fran, but that is not what happened.

MM: So you kind of had a separate mission because, when you guys crossed the LD, it was get to Fran as fast as possible but also clear all the houses?

JE: Right. Our mission was get to Fran, control and clear it, and open it up for logistical purposes. Initially the plan was to have a mounted movement to Objective Wolf and then a house-to-house clearance from Linda to Fran. And then really, we went into the city not knowing if we were going further than Phase Line Fran because we knew that next was the industrial area and then the Queens District: that was 2-2's lane. We had the eastern side of the city and that was what we had. So we knew it was LD, mounted movement up to Phase Line Linda, hit our objectives, refit, and then house-to-house clearance from Phase Line Linda to Phase Line Fran. Once we got to Fran, we were to reconsolidate, refit, and then wait for guidance because we didn't even know if we were going past Phase Line Fran. I don't know if Captain Sims made the call or if the colonel just said to get to Phase Line Fran now. All I know is what Captain Sims told us, which was that we were doing a mounted movement from Phase Line Fran because we need to get up there because everybody else was waiting on us, so that's what we did. We conducted a bounding overwatch movement to Phase Line Fran. When we hit Phase Line Fran, it was chaotic and disorganized for at least 20 minutes. We were on the highway and now we were exposed to everything.

MM: Were you taking fire from across the south side of the highway?

JE: Yes, and that was the problem. That's when I remember the RPGs flying left and right. I remember counting RPGs impacting buildings where we had troops. We got up there, took some fire, dropped off dismounts in the buildings and cleared so they could get a foothold and get in the fight too. And once that happened, RPGs were just being launched from the south side of Highway 10 and they were fairly accurate. They were actually impacting the buildings where we had dismounted troops and were impacting pretty close to the vehicles. That's where it was kind of chaotic until we finally got a plan together to get some more dispersion and get everyone up there on line and shooting in sync as opposed to just a couple vehicles up there just doing their own thing. Once everyone was up there and we got some dispersion and everyone was moving around, it got better. We were drawing a lot of fire from that south side because no one had crossed over there yet.

MM: When you're sitting on Highway 10, you were up a ways, so did the enemy in the buildings have a good angle on you?

JE: Yes, they had good standoff distance. They could still feel effects from our weapons but they certainly had enough distance and cover to where they could take pretty well aimed shots at our vehicles that were just sitting up on the highway. Once we got up there, it was kind of confusing because 2-63 was too far to the east so everyone was shifted over and we started doing some relief in place; and once we got everyone back in their original assigned lanes, that's when we captured that diversion and got guys set up in better observation points (OPs) and better fighting positions. We just kind of hunkered ourselves in and fortified our positions and that's when we started to really use our indirect fire assets. Once that started happening, the enemy attacks started calming down. Once we hit Fran, even the colonel wanted us to come up and do something with CNN just to show our progress, and initially they had to call that off because it wasn't secure enough to do that. I'm not sure when the decision came to go further south, because after we secured Fran we stared doing clean up or search-and-attack missions back up into the northern part of Fallujah. We started having the engineer platoon clear the major roads and they started clearing Fran of all IEDs from phase line to phase line. And then whatever that route was that went to the easternmost part of the city – I don't remember the name – but they started clearing that.

MM: Was it Phase Line Dan?

JE: Yeah, maybe. Their main job was to become the bomb squad, to clear from phase line to phase line all the IEDs on the route; and once they finished that, they leapfrogged back and did Fran. For 1st and 3d Platoons, our major mission became going back and doing search-and-attack missions from the south all the way back up to the LD. We got down there so fast and had that part where we didn't do house to house, we went mounted, so we had to backtrack and clear all that up. 1st Platoon didn't encounter a lot of heavy resistance: the caches we found were minimal, small contacts, sporadic gunfire, a lot of empty houses. 3d Platoon had the most resistance doing that. I don't know if it was that day or the next night, but that was when Staff Sergeant David Bellavia and 3d Platoon encountered heavy resistance in a house they entered. This is the action that Bellavia was nominated for the Medal of Honor.

MM: Where did this happen?

JE: On the north side of Phase Line Fran.

MM: Were you told anything about the Marines running behind schedule or anything like that?

JE: I initially assumed the Marines were ahead of schedule, but I think once we got to Phase Line Fran was when we realized that it was just our units that were up there. The Marines hadn't made it yet. We starting hearing that the Marines were moving kind of slow, they're dismounting the whole way, and that's when we were doing those search-and-attack missions and waiting for the Marines. We spent two nights on Fran, and both of those days and nights were spent doing search-and-attack missions all the way back.

MM: Do you recall whose call signs were Tango 5, Tango 6 or Tango 36?

JE: It sounds like those were Terminators, because we were the only Ts out there. You had 2-63 who were the Avengers, the BRT were all Phantoms –

MM: Alpha Company was all Terminators, correct?

JE: Right. I was Terminator 16 and then there was Terminator 26 and so on. So if they were saying Tango, they were probably talking about us.

MM: Was Sims Terminator 6?

JE: Yes. Then we had the 2-2 scouts in there but they were Stalker and the mortarmen were Thunder, so it's possible that you could have some mortars in there.

MM: Terminator 5 was the XO?

JE: Yes. That was Ed Iwan, and then Terminator 7 was First Sergeant Smith. If you see any other Ts that don't sound like a Bradley platoon and they're doing a lot of call for fire, that's probably the mortarmen. They were Thunder 6.

MM: You said you were at Fran for about 48 hours to rest and refit?

JE: Yes, but we were also doing search-and-attack missions back up into the city. One of those nights was when Bellavia and 3d Platoon had that heavy resistance, and I think it was also the night where we ended up calling a joint direct attack munitions (JDAM) on a building we had already pushed through. We had been fighting around this other building but we couldn't really get into it because they had barricaded everything – and this is when the scouts took some casualties. No one died but they had about three 2-2 scouts get shot based on just trying to enter this one house. We tried to help them out and I guess Captain Sims was trying to push more guys into this house. We tried to draw them out with psychological warfare and we had psychological operations (PSYOP) up there playing the theme song from the movie *Team America: World Police* and all types of heavy metal stuff, just trying to piss them off and get them to make a mistake so we could get in there. We tried to shoot them with our main guns and they were still in there so we ended up backing everybody up, pulling everybody up to Phase Line Fran, calling in the JDAMs, and we eventually destroyed the building like that. I think the next morning was when we started to push south and that's when we set up in the industrial area.

MM: Talk me through the fight south of Fran.

JE: The industrial area – I believe we were told it was going to be more of a mounted fight. We ended up going back in the industrial area a lot of times after the fight in the north was done. We rolled into the industrial area and did a lot of mounted land navigation, a lot of mounted movement, minimal dismounting through the industrial area. I would say we didn't dismount at all while we were there; if we did at all it was very minimal. It was a pretty quick movement from Phase Line Fran through the industrial area to the border of the Queens District.

MM: The night you guys crossed the LD and did the breach, what was the weather like?

JE: I don't remember too much. I don't think it rained, and I don't think it rained once while we were in Fallujah. It was pretty decent because it got almost chilly the nights we were in Fallujah. We actually had pretty decent weather all the way through. I remember it being pretty cool at night.

MM: Can you take me through the fight south of Fran up until the complex ambush that killed Lieutenant Iwan?

JE: There was talk of firing another MCLC. I think there was talk of that once we got through the industrial part. There was a large linear danger area with very open terrain, very uneven, and to go through it at night with the Bradleys would have been chaos to try, with the night vision, to see all those holes in the ground. We probably would have gotten some vehicles stuck. The plan wound up being a large show of force just north of the Queens District and we weren't even allowed to fire for quite some time. We were feeling the effects of the enemy weapons and we couldn't return fire; and then we almost had an on line end of exercise (ENDEX) of ammunition once the colonel felt like he wanted to return fire. The plan was to show force in hopes of drawing the enemy into our range; and once he was ready and was satisfied that he'd drawn them out of hiding, that's when he gave the command to open fire and we started using the TOW missiles and the indirect. We did all that and it was almost like one element at a time. Because we all took the same route, a single-file line, and we finally went out and around this whole danger area, skirted it, and then came back into position. So basically we had to go out and around, come back in and get lined up again in our lanes.

MM: The date now is 12 November and you guys have been fighting all night. At 0600 that morning you find yourself in this position. Are you personally involved in this complex ambush that takes place where Lieutenant Iwan is killed?

JE: Yes. In this complex ambush, at this time we were down by Phase Line Jenna and were close to Phase Line Isabelle. I think we actually attacked too far and then we came back; and I think the initial thought was we were going to be done fighting in the morning, but then we get the call saying we're going to keep pushing. So we push further south and I'm not sure exactly where Ed was killed, but what happened was the whole company was fighting different battles at the time Ed was killed. Each element was of our company was being engaged by a different enemy. What made things even more difficult was that Captain Sean Sims was dismounted, which made it hard for the platoons to communicate with him and vice visa. He's in some pretty heavy contact, taking a lot of fire and is fighting the fight personally now. This led to the company fighting as separate elements instead of as a unified company. At this time, 3d Platoon was taking some heavy RPG fire and Lieutenant Iwan's Bradley was right in the middle of things. I didn't actually witness him being shot, but the next thing I know an RPG hit him. I think it came from the southwest and struck him right in the plate. It hit part of the Bradley right up top where the commander is – a piece of metal right in front of where the commander's head would stick out. It dented that, blew through him and damaged his commander's hatch.

MM: Was his vehicle Alpha 55?

JE: Yes. It was a tan Bradley, one of the old ones.

MM: Is there anything else you can tell me about this incident? I guess First Sergeant Smith went up there and got Lieutenant Iwan off the Bradley?

JE: I can tell you what I know. His gunner reports that he was hurt pretty bad and Terminator 6 is back up on the net trying to get someone from Terminator 5, not knowing he'd been hit because he kept saying, "Terminator 5, Terminator 5!" And his gunner said something to the effect of, "He's hurt" or "He's been hit" or something like that, and added that it was really bad. I know the colonel was up there out of his Bradley with Ed and I know Sergeant Dove jumped out of his vehicle and was yelling, "XO! XO!" First Sergeant Smith was in the vehicle with Sergeant Dove, but I don't know what his actions were. I don't know who actually dragged Ed out of the commander's hatch; I don't know who actually put him in the vehicle; but I do know he was evacuated in the first sergeant's '113. The first sergeant went back but I'm not sure who he went with – and they were taking RPG fire on that evac. I did hear that one RPG hit their .50 cal and damaged it. At this point, we were kind of all down in this big open area, the far side was all buildings, and we were getting shot at from all directions. Ed had already been evacuated and we were still fighting; and at some point we were told to pull back. There was a tank there that had thrown tracks so we had to first bring a mechanic forward to fix them as we were getting shot at. Once that's done, that's when everyone finally consolidated back up to Phase Line Isabelle.

MM: So you get back up there, consolidate on Isabelle and, at this time, Alpha 2-2 – you guys are on the far eastern part of the city when you reconsolidate. Talk me through what happened after you reconsolidated.

JE: We reconsolidated and switched lanes. The colonel's new plan was that since we encountered so much resistance, he wanted to do a whole other wait-until-it-gets-dark, do a whole other attack at night and go as far as he could into the Queens District and hold there.

MM: It does look like the two companies switch.

JE: Yeah. Alpha 2-63 flips over to where we just attacked and then we go to where they were. We had that eastern flank and then you had the scouts way out in the boonies over on the far side. We went down – and that's when they decided we were going to use another MCLC, another deliberate attack with the breach, to fire a MCLC as a shock effect. This was around the time when we got advice that told us to shoot everyone twice. Like, if you see someone on the ground and they're not dead yet, then shoot them again because we had reports that they were faking death. We were told that if they weren't dead, we needed to kill them. Don't assume they're dead. Unless they were surrendering – if they were on the ground and moving around, there were reports that they were faking it and they may have grenades under them or they'd shoot you. So the engineers fired the MCLC and we started our second organized attack into the Queens District. The platoons attacked simultaneously just giving reports back to the commander and we didn't wind up clearing too far because we kept finding cache after cache after cache of weapons, so we couldn't really wait for the engineers to come and blow them up. That's what we were doing at first but, then, it was taking so long that we ended up blowing up a lot of it ourselves. The intent was for us to get a lot farther into the city that night, but we probably didn't even wind up going 1,000 meters past where we LD'd from Phase Line Isabelle. In every house we searched, we just kept coming up with mortar rounds or automatic weapons, and that's where we got a bunch of enemy kills. We went in, they were still in there, and we were actually shooting them in the building. We were finding weapons, body armor, explosives, and we were just finding paperwork and all that kind of stuff. We had to secure it to some degree – whether it was consolidating it in one room, mark it, write everything down, record it, and then just move on and deal with it later. That's what was going on. After the initial attack, we didn't encounter that much resistance at all.

MM: So you guys do the consolidation and there's an attack planned for 13 November. Can you talk me through the death of Captain Sims?

JE: Night comes and they were getting pretty drained. And so by midnight, wherever they were at, they finished what they were doing, hunkered down, set up security, and they all went to sleep because the next day he knew he was planning on going from wherever we stopped that night all the way through house to house to the limit of advance (LOA). That was his plan. We stopped and the next morning came and we got the call to come back to Phase Line Isabelle, refuel and refit. We had all the dismounts basically retracing their steps last night going over all those caches and making sure we disposed of all of them and brought them all up. The next morning we found a bunch more because it was daylight, we could see a lot better, and we were in a search mode. At this time my platoon was tasked to take CNN around, show them the cache sites and do some interviews, and I can only imagine 3d Platoon was doing a similar search-type mission. While this is going on, Captain Sims moves up until he was on line with the lead element of the company. I had two Bradleys up there but no dismounts, 3d Platoon was up there, and that's when he decides to get on the ground himself because he wants to get to a rooftop. He wants to get a better vantage, see the rest of the city and pick out his attack lanes. At this time, my platoon, the dismounts, are still going through all our cache sites. About 1030 he told us to wrap it up with CNN and get them out of there, so we dropped them off. Then I take one squad of dismounts in my section of Brads, drop them off, and tell them go into a building, clear it again, set up and then wait for another squad. I go back up and pick up the second squad and, when I get there, I noticed that my squad hadn't cleared the building. I told them I needed them to clear the building and they said there were a bunch of headquarters guys on the ground that had a bunch of casualties and they didn't know where the CO was. So Sergeant First Class Kimball says, "Give me the casualties right now and I'll evac them." So the first thing we do is drag the headquarters casualties onto two of my Bradleys. Sergeant First Class Kimball and Sergeant Galvez (ph) put the casualties in the Bradleys and they take off back to the forward aid station (FAS).

MM: Was First Sergeant Smith with them while this was going on?

JE: I don't know where he is during this. I can, however, tell you where he was *not* – and that was anywhere near me for that fight. While that was going on, Sergeant Richie (ph) and Sergeant Alvey (ph) get on the ground and I told them to clear from here to the east to look for the CO because we didn't know where he was. They had to go clear the buildings in this manner because the headquarters dismounts did not know which building he was in. I told them that, as soon as I reported our situation, I would get on the ground and join them. Sergeant Richie (ph) was one of the senior squad leaders and probably one of the best and smartest guys in the battalion, and I knew he could handle the task of moving a squad-plus through a couple buildings. So I send him out and report up saying there were two casualties from the headquarters element. I told them where I was located, that the CO was missing, and that we were clearing west to east looking for him. I get a call from my squad leader saying they were getting shot at and that they were taking some heavy resistance – getting shot at and having grenades thrown at them out of windows. To my south, the BRT was clearing from east to west with the 2-2 scouts – they were coming across. To my left, I had another section of BRT or Alpha 2-63 with tanks, and we were all packed in there and it was way too tight. There were way too many people in that one small area. So I pulled up all the way to Captain Mayfield and Lieutenant Namken and said, "We don't know where our CO is." I told them that whatever they were doing, do it, and that I wasn't going to get in their way and wasn't going any further south of where I was right then. But I told them I needed to find the rest of the company. I had guys hurt, guys shot, and the commander was missing so I was trying to let those other units know why I was there because I knew they were looking at me wondering why I was in their way.

MM: Were you the XO for Alpha Company by this point?

JE: Not really. When Ed died, Sergeant First Class Ryan – who was part of the S3 shop – commanded that Bradley, so he became essentially the CO's wingman. As far as the XO duties, I really hadn't started taking over. He had not been dead that long and I think the commander, Captain Sims, just wanted to leave me commanding my platoon, that he and the first sergeant could just pick up the XO's duties because Ed was just doing a lot of reporting and gathering reports and keeping track of supplies. I think the commander and the first sergeant figured they could just tag team that and then when they needed extra help they would have thrown stuff to me. As Captain Doug Walter came, I started picking up XO duties then, but it didn't happen before because we were just busy fighting. So anyway, we stay and fight and I get a report saying they found the CO, they secured the building and they told me he was dead. So I got on the ground and told them I wasn't going to call it up until I see him because I didn't want any confusion. I run into the building, see that he's dead, made sure we got everyone and that the building was secure. I said to go to the Bradleys and get a stretcher – and we only ended up having white body bags. I said there was no way we were putting the commander in a fucking white clear body bag so I told them to get a stretcher and a blanket, cover him up and put him in the back of my Bradley. I said, "I don't know where the f------ first sergeant is and we have to get him out of here and reconsolidate." I told my squad leaders to account for everyone in Alpha Company, to let me know when they had a positive headcount and get everyone on the ground. I went back to my track, reported the KIA and gave our current SITREP. I told them I had the commander but he was KIA, and said we're putting him in my Bradley and bringing the rest of Alpha Company back to Phase Line Isabelle once we had 100 percent accountability. It was unfortunate because we already had six guys in my Bradley already. We had reporters and camera guys and were really crammed in there, and we had to put the commander in the Bradley and everyone had to pile in and try not to step on him as they got in there. We just threw as many people as we could from headquarters into my Bradley too so we could get them back to reconsolidate. So we get back to Phase Line Isabelle and everyone gets out of the Bradley. This is when the first sergeant is up on the rooftop trying to call for fire in the direction where the CO was killed. The colonel asks me for the grid where the CO was killed because he wants to drop a JDAM on that building, so I give it to him and they drop a bomb. After that, the colonel wanted to attack right now south to the LOA from Phase Line Isabelle and he wanted to know when I could have the company ready. I told him I could have the company ready in about 30 or 45 minutes, and we pulled the leaders into this little courtyard. We were debating on what our plan was going to be. At this time the first sergeant joined us and stated that we were not going to dismount and that he was going to ride in the commander's Bradley. I was pretty sure Lieutenant Colonel Newell wanted us to dismount and clear house to house, but the senior NCO was dead set on not dismounting. I decided to go along with his plan rather than argue with the senior enlisted guy in the company minutes after the CO was killed. (Looking back on my decision, however, I should not have accepted that plan and instead insisted that we dismount). I told them I was going to go between 1st Platoon and 2d Platoon and we're going to go down the western flank, and 3d Platoon and the headquarters element will go down the eastern flank and that's how we're going to attack through to the LOA. First Sergeant Smith jumped in the commander's Bradley – so it was his Bradley, 3d Platoon and the XO's Bradley – and then my side was my whole platoon and then 2d Platoon behind me. We ended up calling this attack "Rolling Thunder" and we were basically doing bounding overwatch on two flanks and shooting anything in the middle while we were calling fire just ahead of us. We were calling a lot of indirect fire and close air support (CAS) right on top of us and were just walking it down.

MM: Let's go back to when Captain Sims was killed. Did Lieutenant Colonel Newel put out any word that said First Sergeant Smith was the new company commander?

JE: No. If anything, I was in charge then because when I got out of that Bradley, Sergeant First Class Ryan said the colonel wanted to speak to me. He asked for me and told me the plan. No one came down there. It wasn't like he came down and gave me a face to face. No one came down and asked what I needed or anything like that. It was just a radio transmission, very simple and to the point, and we were going to continue to attack to the LOA. He wanted to know how long it would take for me to get the company ready. I said 30 to 45 minutes – "Let me just talk to the leaders and I'll get back to you."

MM: I was just going off the unit after-action review (AAR) where it says, "Following the evacuation of wounded, First Sergeant Smith and First Lieutenant Emery meet with task force commander at the tactical command post (TAC) to discuss Alpha Company's ability to meet an LD time."

JE: No, it was a radio call that was given to me. The first sergeant was up on the roof calling fire where he thought the commander was killed, but he didn't know because he wasn't there. He was still generally calling it in the right spot but he wasn't there. I talked to the colonel, told him 30 to 45 minutes, and then once we got everyone there, the first sergeant came down and we decided on no dismounting. Once we pushed through to the LOA, we took a left turn, drove back up to where the colonel had his TAC set up and met there. That's the first time we got out and saw the colonel. He asked how it went and we said it went pretty smooth; we were talking, everything was in sync, and there was no problem. Then we got the call to help out the Marines, go in their sector and do the same thing, and the first sergeant's big thing was he wanted to do it before it got dark. So we were rushing to get everything set and get over there, and we meet the Marines and they give us some bullshit about how we can't go through their defenses because they're set up, they have their colonel down there, and they aren't letting anyone through. We were trying to tell them we were coming to help them and they still wouldn't let anyone through. We ended up taking this roundabout way that took us an extra 35 to 45 minutes to get into position. So we line up the same way – 3d Platoon, headquarters, me and then 2d Platoon – and we're trying to get this off before dark. We finally get together and I had Sergeant Larid calling for fire, but what I told him to do he didn't understand. I wasn't on the ground with him because I stayed in the Bradley to be able to talk to battalion, company and the platoons. I was trying to give him adjustments and he didn't understand where I wanted it. So he stops calling for fire and First Sergeant Smith ended up taking over calling for fire. He's trying to call for fire and it takes us forever to adjust fires on – and if you want to hear this story you should talk to Lieutenant Chris Walls. He can tell you what happened because he was listening to the fire commands coming across the net by First Sergeant Smith and could enlighten you on how "good" they were. We finally get the fires where we want them and start pushing through. We were so far ahead of the Marines and we ended up taking a lot of contact from our western side because there's no one up there but the enemy, because the Marines are so far behind. Then it gets dark and visibility is pretty limited. The road had lot of obstacles in the way and a lot of debris, then we end up getting a tank stuck in a ditch. We didn't even get to finish that mission or anything because we got halfway down to the LOA and the colonel said that's it, recover the tank and bring everyone back. He said we weren't going to continue. At this point, we ended up coming back, the first sergeant was leading everyone out, and then he and his vehicle just took off. His two-man element was gone. The first sergeant was our guide and he probably didn't realize we were so far behind him, because we were pulling a tank and you can only go 10 miles an hour. He just took off so we actually had to call ahead, he had to stop and wait for us, and it was very slow moving all the way back. We went to see the colonel, he gave us a 24-hour breather, and that next whole day was a wash. I don't think we sent out any missions or anything. We had Major General John Batiste come down and we figured out what we needed. The first sergeant realized that the best thing for the company was to ask for Captain

Doug Walter to retake the company. I know the colonel asked General Batiste to get him back and have him lead the company. I wasn't really involved with that decision at all. I think the first sergeant talked to the colonel and I don't know what the hell he said to him; but the next thing you know, Lieutenant Colonel Newell is talking to the general.

MM: They actually managed to get Captain Walter back in 24 hours or so?

JE: Captain Walter was working for brigade with the Iraqi Army and they basically just picked him up. I wasn't there when he got there. We ended up running two missions. We ran one mission with 3d Platoon, some kind of reconnaissance mission in the city, because I knew the next day we were definitely attacking through the city. 3d Platoon went up there and then, later on that night, my platoon went down there and spent the night in the city. We were the only element from Alpha Company that was in the city. We knew what lane we were going to be in and were basically the key for the company. We went in the night before, cleared the buildings, set up a hasty defense and secured a foothold, and then that's where we spent that night. Sometime that night, Captain Walter showed up. The next morning, we were going to go at 0630 or 0700 and we were waiting for the indirect fires to hit in the southern part of the city. Captain Walter called us and asked where we were. He told us what he wanted to do and we got everyone set up. He came in, put the platoons in order, and he fought the company as if he never left. He had my platoon in the middle, 3d Platoon to the left and then 2d Platoon to the right; and as we fought down, this is when I started doing some extra duties. I was in the middle and I was up front, so he was having me report the status of 2d and 3d Platoons – because I was the senior platoon leader and he also had no XO. I would tell him how many buildings we've cleared, where we were sitting and that I was secure. I would let him know the status of 2d and 3d Platoons and where they were located. He gave the order for 3d Platoon to hold and for 2d Platoon to bound up to 3d Platoon and then that's how we were doing it. It was basically him and I doing it. He was doing it but he was using my eyes to move the company. When Captain Walter got there, that was the house-to-house fight. We went through every single house down to the LOA, and when we hit the LOA we established a command center. We found a good house with good fields of fire, good security, and he basically came up to me and said we were going to use the house I found as the company tactical operations center (TOC). After that, we did some more search-and-attack missions. We got to the LOA and attacked backwards, but it wasn't so much attack as it was search and attack, looking for caches.

MM: On 19 or 20 November you guys did a battle handoff and headed home, correct?

JE: Yes. We got to go back to the base and had to rotate some platoons back to the base, but we did a handover with the Iraqi Army first and then we bounded back to Phase Line Fran and spend a day or two going through the industrial area. We probably spent three days going through every part of the industrial area, breaking open every lock, opening every shop up and tearing stuff apart. We found a lot of IED factories and a lot of anti-aircraft weapons, machine guns, missiles and mortars – you name it, we found it. We basically were blowing up ordnance because, by now, the fighting was done; and at some point in time, Lieutenant Colonel Newell wanted to turn his lane over to the Marines completely done. So he figured that since we'd cleared it, searched it and gotten rid of everything in it that shouldn't be there, he could hand it over to the Marines and we could go home, and that's what he did. The Marines came in, we showed them the area, and then we pulled out, went to Camp Fallujah and that was it.

MM: Could you give me a brief assessment of some of the following individuals? What did you think of Lieutenant Iwan?

JE: Probably the best XO in terms of really understanding what an XO's job is and doing just an XO's job – not trying to be a platoon leader and not trying to assume more of an authority role than he had. He used to be a mechanic when he was enlisted so he understood vehicle maintenance very well; he understood what it took to keep vehicles running and how to keep the company in the fight from a logistical standpoint. He was very smart when it came to that. He was very organized and knew how to keep his reports straight. He always was asking you for reports and always at the right time. He wouldn't interrupt you during a fight and ask if you needed water. He knew when the time was right, he knew what you would be low on and he was very good at getting you stuff you needed. Whenever you had a question and you weren't going to the CO, you went to Ed and he knew the answer.

MM: How long was he enlisted for and on Active Duty?

JE: I don't know if it was Reserves or Active Duty but he was enlisted as a mechanic for a while. Like I said, he was the best XO in terms of knowing his job and doing it. He was great. You didn't have to worry about him. You knew he was going to get it done.

MM: What about Captain Sims?

JE: He was probably one of the smartest men I've met in the Army – officer and enlisted. He was very intelligent and, from an officer standpoint, he understood doctrine to a T and probably knew it better than anyone. He knew what he was supposed to do and what the books said. He was just a good person, had heart. He wasn't the type who was going to bend the rules or cut corners. He believed in his mission and took care of soldiers to the best of his ability. Any mission he got, he believed in it and wasn't going to pawn it off on anyone else. He would say it was our mission and we would do it the best we could. He was probably the calmest man in any situation you could ever meet in your life. He never raised his voice – and he never had to. He was able to remain calm no matter who was looking over his shoulder. He was in the spotlight a lot with the colonel; and even when stuff wasn't going right, he was always calm and wanted to figure out what the problem was and find a logical solution – and that's what he did.

MM: What about Captain Walter? Were there any similarities between him and Captain Sims?

JE: Yes. Captain Sims was a gadget guy. He loved them. Any new gadget he had to have. That was his thing. But he always was thinking out of the box, too. If we were doing a recon and we didn't have the equipment, he'd have us take his digital camera, do a drive by, put it on a 90-second video, film the whole strip, and then go examine it later. He could always find a way to get stuff done and that was great. He was putting his own personal camera for use in a tactical aspect: taking footage of targets we're going to do. They were both 101st Airborne Division guys so they had similar light fighter backgrounds. As far as Captain Walter – if you're going to combat, there really is no other person you'd want to go with than this guy, because he really is a soldier's leader and a soldier's warrior. He's a warrior himself and he wasn't going to back down from anyone. He's going to use common sense and he's going to put the best guys in the job. He doesn't care about seniority; that stuff doesn't matter to him. He's going to pick the best guy for the job. He has no problem making a corporal a squad leader if that corporal is better than a staff sergeant. He was a no-quit guy; there was absolutely no quitting. He was not going to fail and he was not going to quit. He couldn't originally deploy to Iraq because he was sick. He was on a diet of vegetables because he couldn't eat anything else; it made him sick. There are plenty of guys in the Army who did everything they could *not* to deploy and here this guy did everything in his power to get healthy and then begged to come down, took a job that absolutely sucked in Iraq just to be there with the unit, and then retook his old company from his best friend. He took them through Fallujah with no casualties and then took the rest of the company home. If you're going to measure an officer, that's the guy you measure him against. You should ask yourself, "How do I measure up to Captain Walter?" That's the type of guy he is.

MM: What about the battalion commander, Lieutenant Colonel Pete Newell?

JE: He's not the most charismatic guy in the world, he doesn't have the greatest personality and he's probably not going to really inspire you with these great Lou Holtz-type pep talks. But he understands his job, he understands how to fight a battalion, and he understands what it takes and how much force he needed to let his battalion use. He pretty much took the gloves off when we went to Fallujah. He knew we were trying to establish a rapport with the people in Muqdadiyah and get on their good side, so he understood when he had to hold us back. But in Fallujah he knew it was a real fight and he knew what that meant. For him to take the gloves off, tell us it was our fight, that we were going to win it, just to give us the freedom to do what we had to do on the battlefield – the fact that he understood that and allowed us to do that was great. That was the type of leader he was. The only real negative hit on him was that he's a little vain and doesn't like to be told he's wrong. In the AAR of the Battle of Fallujah, he stated that he didn't fail to do anything. For example, he insisted that a task force rehearsal of the breach site was conducted, when in fact it was not. He was definitely in the spotlight; he put himself on CNN and was with those reporters all the time.

MM: What about your battalion S3, Major John Reynolds?

JE: He's a real intelligent guy and has a lot of degrees. He's a guy who seems like he spent a lot of time in staff positions. He was very philosophical and he's got these theories and plans, but when it comes down to using common sense and just executing, that's a different story. When you're on the ground, in combat, the main thing is: can you get it done? He's a smart guy and he understands doctrine; he could recite it, he could write it, but when it was time to execute....

MM: I greatly appreciate this. Is there anything else you'd like to leave us with that we didn't cover?

JE: Yes, I would like to address a few things. First is, the leaders of this fight who had to make on-the-spot decisions every day that eventually led to the final outcome of the battle. The Battle of Fallujah was a squad leader and platoon leader fight, company commander at the most. The plan was very simple: start in the north and attack south until you run out of city. If it were not for the company commanders talking to each other on a regular basis, there would have been a lot more fratricide. They did an outstanding job of knowing where their counterparts were and directing their fires in the appropriate lanes. Next is, the guys who were really fighting and making decisions the most were the platoon leaders on the ground and their squad leaders. And last is, the soldiers who did everything they were told: kicked in every door, searched every little dark corner. The platoon and squad leaders really had to make those decisions about what was going to get a guy hurt, what was going to get someone killed, and what will keep them safe and still get the mission done. The guys on the ground almost did it flawless. In a battle like Fallujah or any time it's a house-to-house dismounted street fight, you really have to give the credit to the guys on the ground the whole fight, because they're the ones who are really taking the brunt of it. This brings me to my next point: the awards given out for Fallujah. The Silver Star is one of the highest awards given out to soldiers in combat; but in the case of the Battle of Fallujah, it seemed as if it was given out to senior leadership for simply doing their jobs. The only officer who deserved the Silver Star in the Battle of Fallujah was Captain Sean Sims on the basis that he gave his life for his country and put himself in harm's way for the safety of his men. My intention here is not to bad mouth anybody, just to point out how quick we are to reward leadership to further enhance their careers, while we forget about the ones who are the *real heroes:* the *soldiers*.

MM: Once again, I want to thank you very much for your time.

Captain Michael S. Erwin
19 April 2006

MM: My name is Matt Matthews [MM] and I'm an historian for the Combat Studies Institute. Today is 19 April 2006 and I'm interviewing Captain Michael S. Erwin [ME] who was the assistant intelligence officer (AS2) for 2d Battalion, 7th Cavalry Regiment (2-7 CAV) during Operation Phantom Fury. Could you please give me some information on your background – where you were born, where you went to school, how you got commissioned and the assignments you had in the Army prior to Phantom Fury?

ME: I was born in Syracuse, New York, in 1979. I went to Christian Brothers Academy High School and from there I received an appointment to go to West Point. I graduated West Point in 2002 and was one of around 30 cadets who picked military intelligence (MI) for their branch. A big reason for that was because three weeks before we had to pick our branches was when September 11th happened, and I knew MI was something that was going to be important to our nation's security for many years to come. I came out to Fort Huachuca, learned how to be an intelligence officer, and really the only assignment I ever had was AS2 and then S2 for 2-7 CAV, which later became 1-12 CAV upon redeployment from Operation IRAQI FREEDOM II (OIF).

MM: Can you talk me through when you first arrived in 2-7 CAV and the deployment of the unit to Iraq?

ME: I got there as a young second lieutenant and I had about 16 months experience as an AS2 back at Fort Hood before I actually deployed. Our big train-up was at the Joint Readiness Training Center (JRTC) at Fort Polk, Louisiana. We went there for a training mission in November and December of 2003, just about three months before we deployed, and they did a really good job of simulating what the scenario would be like over in Iraq. That was our first real taste of how we were going to have to run convoys and prepare to predict where you think the enemy might attack. That really was just the ramp-up to deploy. We sent all of our equipment over to Kuwait on the ships.

MM: Where did you go after you left Kuwait and what was 2-7's assignment prior to Phantom Fury?

ME: We made the convoy up north and our location was at Camp Taji, which was one of the old main bases for Saddam Hussein's Republican Guard. He actually had two divisions of his Republican Guard there, the Medina Division being one of them at Camp Taji. Our area of operations was going to be a rural area north of Baghdad. We were the first Active Duty battalion to ever be directly attached to a National Guard brigade. Although organically we were part of 3d Brigade, 1st

Cavalry Division, we were attached the 39th Enhanced Separate Brigade out of Arkansas, so that was unique in itself. We'd always trained with units back at Fort Hood, but now we were going to be working with a brigade of National Guard that we did not really interact and train with until four to five months before the deployment.

MM: Did you have a pretty good working relationship with those guys?

ME: As with all relationships when it was new, there were some things we had to work out, but I think they really appreciated the fact that we brought a lot of Active Duty experience. More importantly, we had guys who were well trained in operating the M1 Abrams tank and the M2 Bradley Fighting Vehicle, two of the most dominant maneuver vehicles on the battlefield today, so that was really helpful to the overall brigade mission. April 2004 was a very hectic time in Iraq. Fallujah was heating up for the Marines, and Sadr City and Najaf and Karbala with the radical Shi'a. So right when we got there – and no one thinks it was coincidence that this was during the main exchange between OIF I troops and OIF II troops. They kind of timed it and planned a time to make their uprising.

MM: Did you have to go to Najaf when they had the uprising?

ME: The uprising that I spoke of, that was the first one. After that, what they thought was put down in May, it turned out that it started back up in late July. The second time that Najaf became a hot spot was in August 2004. What happened there, when things got heated up, was that 1st Battalion, 5th Cavalry Regiment (1-5 CAV) – which was the division ready reaction force – got sent there and it was realized that we were going to need more combat power to handle that mission. At that point, III Corps, who was controlling the theater, decided that 2-7 would go. This was a result of the fact that we did not have an area in Baghdad. We were north of Baghdad, and I say that because Baghdad was the focus of so much of the media and government. If they were going to pull a unit out of Baghdad, that would have a bigger effect in terms of how the Iraqi people were to perceive the whole situation. So they moved us because we were north in a rural area, and they had a unit come in and take our place temporarily. We went down there and it was really a big preamble to Operation Phantom Fury, because that was where our unit demonstrated its confidence and its ability to work with the Marines – and also its ability to destroy the enemy in support of the Marines' mission. It gave our guys on the ground the experience and the confidence so that when Phantom Fury came around, it wasn't our first time going into a city where the enemy held a lot of the buildings and knew the terrain.

MM: When you got there in August, had you personally had any experience working with the Marines? Did you work with them pretty closely in August?

ME: No one in our unit, at least that I know of, had worked with them in the past. I was on the advanced party with Major Tim Karcher – the battalion operations officer (S3) – and a couple of the assistant guys in the plans shop. We got there at 0300 and started going to work right away trying to figure out what they wanted us to do. Right off the bat, we had a pretty close relationship working with them, especially Major Karcher. He came down there as the voice for Lieutenant Colonel James Rainey, our battalion commander, saying we would do whatever they needed us to do, and I think that really played a big role in it. There was no us showing up and expecting a certain mission or a certain role. We just showed up there and knew we were there to help them. We knew they had a tough fight going on, so we were there to support them however we could. This helped with the Marines' perception of us as fighters; and once they gave us one of the tougher missions down there, it gave us the experience and we could prove we could continue to work for them and continue to support their mission.

MM: When did you first hear that you might have to go to Fallujah and might be assigned to help the Marines once again?

ME: After we got back from Najaf in September, we had heard some word – and even just in open sources there was a lot of speculating that since things had gone so well down in Najaf, it was time for coalition forces to go in and take Fallujah back, to enable those people to have the opportunity to vote in the upcoming elections. We did not get the official word until the day I came back from leave in mid-October. We were told to start preparing to fight in Fallujah. Lieutenant Colonel Rainey actually had gone all the way over to Camp Fallujah to meet up with the Marines, to get an idea of what the mission was going to be and what they were going to ask Task Force 2-7 to do. The difference between this and the battle for Najaf was that, in Najaf, we showed up and the fight was already going on. There was no plan to take the city back. We were only fighting because Moqtada al-Sadr's militia forced us to. This was very different because the planning process was several months long. Coalition forces had not been allowed in there since April, so the Marines had been flying their unmanned aerial vehicles (UAVs) over the city for months, gaining intelligence on where the enemy liked to be. It was a much bigger mission in terms of the number of forces we were going to use, and also in terms of the planning process that went into it. Unlike Najaf, this was a well planned, well thought out and orchestrated mission.

MM: Did you make several trips with Major Karcher to go link up with the Marine intelligence people? How did that work?

ME: I actually did not make the trips. My boss, the primary intelligence officer, Captain David Gray, he went out there a couple days early before the rest of the main body, but no one else did. What did happen was Lieutenant Colonel Rainey and Captain Gray had linked up with their intelligence section and basically put us in touch with them. Remember, we still had operations going on in the Camp Taji area, so we had to make sure our guys were accomplishing the mission there. So it wasn't like we could just totally shut down operations there and focus on Fallujah. I was the night shift guy, so I really had a lot of time to do a lot of the preparation for the fight, because that was when things tended to be a lot quieter. I had all the emails and telephone numbers of all the intelligence officers back at Camp Fallujah, and I worked pretty closely with them to get an idea of the type of fight they expected, where the enemy suspected locations were, where the suspected cache sites were and improvised explosive devices (IED) making locations and things of that nature. So I started working closely with them, helping to paint the picture for our task force before we even left Camp Taji for Camp Fallujah.

MM: Did you find that there were some big challenges in urban intelligence collection that maybe you had not been involved with before – other than in Najaf?

ME: One of the big differences between Fallujah and Najaf was the quality of the fighters they had. But in terms of the situation, they were both very similar terrain. There were very dense urban areas with not very many high buildings. But another big difference this time was that no coalition forces had been in there for over six months, so the enemy had a lot longer time to build up – and more than that, they were more experienced fighters. They had a lot of foreign fighters who really knew how to set up sniper locations and call for indirect fire and things like that.

MM: Talk me through from the beginning of the fight on November 8th. Where were you? What was your location? As the fight progressed, what was going on with the intelligence section?

ME: We rolled out of Camp Fallujah to a location about two clicks north of the city where the Marines, 2-7 and 2d Battalion, 2d Infantry Regiment (2-2) had decided the general area of operations would be – and that was because the direction of the attack was going to be from the north to the south into the city. We set up our tactical operations center (TOC), got all of our communications up, and got all of our tracking – our radios and such. The big thing we did was, as soon as we could, we got out task force UAV up in the air. It was called the task force's Raven. It was still relatively new in theater when we were there and it was something that paid dividends for us in this fight. When we were back at Taji, we had had a lot of issues with it because it was a line of sight UAV. However, before our unit had even crossed the line of departure to push into the city, we had the support of the Marine UAVs flying over, letting us know where some enemies were being spotted. But more than that, we also had our own task force Raven and that was really my role.

I was the intelligence, surveillance and reconnaissance (ISR) leader. We basically compared where we thought the enemy were with the routes that our companies were going to take. Once we crossed the train tracks into the city, the tank company would take what we thought was the most fortified enemy route, because the tanks are the most resilient and have the most firepower. So as soon as we flew that Raven, we were able to see the grid and were able to call our 120 millimeter mortar section that was standing by less than 500 meters away. We relayed those positions into those guys and, within a minute, we had rounds on target. Now, if that didn't kill some of the enemy at that time, it certainly moved them and let them know that somehow we knew where they were. This was a pretty key piece of real-time intelligence. We were able to help save soldiers lives by determining where the enemy was before we got there, instead of spotting them with our eyes.

MM: Did you have any problems deconflicting these Ravens with the Marines? The folks in 2-2 said the Marines were on their frequency and caused a couple of these things to crash.

ME: That's a good point. We did have some issues with that; however, we worked a lot of those issues out in the days leading up to the fight. There was a few times where we had gotten on a particular frequency thinking the Marines wouldn't be there, but sometimes the frequencies would cross over and that would cause us to either lose track of it for a while or actually have it lost. An interesting thing about the Raven was that the enemy knew we were flying these over their heads, and one of our Ravens actually came back with bullet holes in it. Believe it or not, it actually made it – and for a small plane that was pretty impressive. I just say that because it was an indicator of how many enemies were down there and how aware they were of what was going on above them.

MM: Did the Marines have you concentrating over the Jolan District with your Ravens?

ME: Our ISR plan was essentially where we knew we were going to go. Lieutenant Colonel Rainey, Major Karcher and Major Scott Jackson – the leadership in our task force – had pretty much outlined to the officers and the senior noncommissioned officers (NCOs) in the TOC what the plan was. Essentially, their guidance to us was that they wanted as much reconnaissance one to two kilometers ahead of where our unit was. So once our unit hit the train tracks, he wanted us looking one to two kilometers past that and to start to paint the picture for the units who were advancing south. We did that through the Ravens, and we also did that through one of the Marine UAVs – the Scan Eagle. We had a terminal for that in our TOC. So we'd have one of our soldiers in the intelligence shop monitoring that system. We really had two different UAV platforms going at the same time. That being said, that was a Marine above-regimental asset. We were definitely not the priority for that. Once we breached the city and led the way in, we no longer became the priority for that, so Lieutenant Colonel Rainey wanted us focusing as much as we could on the Jolan District. If you look on a map, you can see how the Jolan District was set up as a potential enemy strong point or a location where the enemy could fall back to with prepositioned weapons caches. That was also something that intelligence reports had indicated to the Marines. The Marines had passed down to us a lot of intelligence reports; and one of the things they had told us was that, according to their intel, the Jolan District was going to be one of the places where a lot of the foreign fighters were going to make their last stand. That began to concern us greatly once we found out that we could potentially run into upwards of 300 to 400 fighters in one condensed area, if that intelligence was going to be accurate.

MM: Did the difference in tactics, techniques and procedures (TTPs) and systems cause any delays in intel sharing between you and the Marines?

ME: Not really, because the big thing was that we had a good working relationship before we even got there. Also, once we got to Camp Fallujah on November 1st, we had about six or seven days there to be synching our systems with the Marines – and that was one of the things I attribute to great leadership at our task force level. They ensured we got as much face time and communications with the Marines before we even left Camp Fallujah. We did have differences in UAV platforms and that was something we worked out, but really our systems were synched pretty well. We'd use the regular FM radio to put out intelligence reports, letting everyone know what we'd seen in the last couple hours – and that would go up to Regimental Combat Team 1 (RCT-1), since that's who we were attached to. We were also the lead unit for them, so we wanted to make sure they knew where we encountered resistance and where we didn't, because that would really help them as their Marines were basically going to follow Task Force 2-7 several hours after we pushed through. We called these battle update briefs (BUBs), where we would pass that information on. We would also get intelligence from our soldiers out there in the tanks and Bradleys: they would pass it back to us and we would pass it up to higher.

MM: Were you and Captain Gray pretty much co-located during the entire fight?

ME: Yes. Our intelligence shop was located right there at the TOC. I would usually be up the hill, about 100 meters away, working with the Raven.

MM: Who was in the TOC during the most of the fight besides the intel section?

ME: We had our task force logistics officer (S4) who was in charge of coordinating for any ammo, food and water. That was Captain Sheldon Morris. We also had our signals officer (S6), Captain John Ontko, and he was the guy in charge of making sure our TOC could talk to all of our units on the front line. That was a bigger issue as we pushed further and further south and got further away from our jump TOC location. We had Major Jackson, who was our task force executive officer (XO). He was the guy who coordinated everything and put all of the pieces of the puzzle together, coordinating between our S2 section and the fire support guys. Another key player was Captain Coley Tyler and his shop of fire support guys. He and Major Jackson worked closely with our S2 shop and the mortar section to call for mortar fire. We also had attached to us an Air Force liaison officer who was the direct link to the fast movers up in the sky, to call for fire, and also the AC-130 gunship, which attacked hostiles and vehicle-borne improvised explosive devices (VBIEDs) ahead of our other units, so we used those guys quite frequently. It was really a team effort there to make everything go.

MM: Did you have any problem with communications since the Army was on FM and the Marines were using tactical satellite (TACSAT) and mIRC Chat?

ME: That was definitely one of the things that proved that sometimes we just do things differently than the Marines, and one of the ways was in attack aviation. They have the Cobra and we have the Apache. Army soldiers are very comfortable calling in the Apaches and the Marines are not, and vice versa. The Marines rely heavily on TACSAT radio and mIRC Chat – we did not have the ability to establish much of a secret Internet protocol router network (SIPRNET) out there due to our location and how quickly we had to set up. So there were definitely issues talking on the radios between the Marines and us, just due to the fact that we really, almost unfailingly, use FM – and the first time I experienced TACSAT was down in Najaf. Although it was a bit of a challenge, it was nothing we were not able to work through.

MM: Can you talk me through some of the lessons learned that you'd want to get out there and let some of the younger soldiers know about?

ME: One of the big things we learned was that there is a very big difference between an urban fight and the rural fight we had out there at Taji. A very different kind of intelligence preparation of the battlefield (IPB) needs to be done, and Lieutenant Colonel Rainey had a great idea about how to deal with it. He came up with a system, for example, so he knew how wide or narrow the roads were – because that right there impacts whether tanks should go down this road or whether it's better for Humvees. So one of the key lessons learned is that armored forces do perform very well in combat in the cities. Well, before Najaf, we were under the impression that the best way to fight the urban fight was with dismounted soldiers and going building to building. But the big lesson we learned was that armor does a better job at it because they have more firepower and better vision capabilities on their vehicles. You also need to understand the difference between the urban fight and whatever else you may do. I think we learned about teamwork working with the Marines. I think a lot of people were under the impression that it was going to be hard for an Army unit to work with the Marines, with their different radio communications, different attack aviation assets, and different sizes in companies – lots of little things. But the thing we learned was the importance of establishing a good working relationship and a good rapport. Going back to the battle of Najaf where we went in saying we were there to help: taking that kind of approach and attitude made a really big difference in our ability to help them out. Also, we learned the importance of the UAVs from the intelligence side of the house.

MM: So you give a big thumbs up to the Ravens and the Marine UAV assets as well?

ME: Absolutely. We did have problems with the Raven in Taji and other places, but in Fallujah and Najaf, they performed very well. It was definitely a learning point. Really, it was the first time that I got to see the future of MI actually taking place at the present time. That is, if you're able to work those UAVs and prepare them and have a good route for them, you can really see how they can save lives by sending real-time pictures of the battlefield to your soldiers and your commander. We were able to keep people informed about what was going on one or two kilometers ahead of them, and I think that made a difference in terms of our soldiers being prepared. It wasn't just, "Hey, I think the enemy might be here." We were able to say, "We know where the enemy is." We were able to pick up the Jolan District and calm our worries a little bit that it was going to be a place for 300 terrorists to fall back to. We were able to see that there was some movement there, but not a whole lot.

MM: By the end of the fight, did the enemy forces pretty much match what you guys had templated them to look like? Also, did you feel there were in fact a lot of foreign fighters there?

ME: Absolutely. When we got there, it was actually one of their snipers that caused one of our soldiers to be killed in action and several others to be wounded and taken out of the fight. We knew there were foreign fighters from numerous countries who were in Fallujah, and they fought just the way we thought they would. They had numerous chances to leave the city and they continued to turn those chances down; they stayed there and they fought. One of the key things about this fight was that we'd templated that the enemy was going to put up a lot of resistance in the northern part of the city. That first day of fighting, we thought, was going to be the most intense. It turned out that after all the air strikes and traumatizing close air support (CAS) that led the way, a lot of these guys said, "Hey, we don't want to be a part of this initial fight," especially once they saw all these tanks and Bradleys. Some of them were under the impression that it was going to be a lot of Marine dismounts that were going to come walking from the north down to the south. Well, once they saw a lot of Bradleys and tanks and all the fire power that comes with them, a lot of them pushed south and basically retreated. I'm not sure if it was out of shock or if it was out of hope that we really weren't going to push all the way through to the south. I don't know what their reasons were, but they left and pushed south. That's why the initial 24 to 36 hours of the fight, while intense, were not the most intense hours of the fight. It wasn't really until we pushed to the southern part of the city where we started to see that a lot of these guys had come there to take up their last-stand positions. These guys could have turned themselves in numerous times, but they stayed and fought until the end. They were as bold as firing at Marines as the Marines were coming in to clear a building, when they basically knew they were dead. These guys were definitely hardened fighters.

MM: Did you have any contact with the media at all? Were there embedded reporters with you guys?

ME: Yes. Some of the bigger media went with the Marines, and that was just natural because it was their area of operation, their fight, and we were just supporting them. So we were content letting the majority of the media go with the Marines. We did, however, have some smaller time reporters. We had a guy from the Chicago Tribune and a couple other smaller publications. They spent a lot of time in the TOC just following the battle, asking questions of the S4, the fire support officer, and our section – trying to get a feel for what was going on.

MM: Is there anything else you'd like to tell me?

ME: It's interesting to see that there haven't been any fights like Najaf or Fallujah since we've been there. The battle of Fallujah was the last time we had to go in and take a city down, so it was really interesting to be a part of, especially with the whole situation in Iraq and trying to get those guys some stability and get them back on their feet. I think taking back Fallujah was a big step. Of course, the enemy just went north to Mosul and other locations throughout Iraq, but we did go in there and were very successful in what we had to do. It just goes to show that, yes, there were insurgents there and they did have some success in day-to-day operations. But when it came to the real fight, it just demonstrated the unbelievable, overwhelming capability that our armed forces have when we combine Air Force, Marines and Army, when we're on the same page, and when we're working together. It goes to show that we are still that dominant when we have to go head to head with someone.

MM: It could very well be one of the most successful joint operations of all time.

ME: Absolutely. I would think it's got to be up there, just because it was so well orchestrated between the three branches of service and because it was a known enemy stronghold. They had months and months to fortify; and for us to go in there and do the mission we did, I think that speaks volumes for how well we are able to pull off joint operations.

MM: Did you see the interview I did with Colonel Michael Shupp, the commander of RCT-1? He thinks you guys walk on water.

ME: It was a mutual feeling. Being able to go ahead of them in our armored vehicles and set the battlefield up for his Marines. That was something no one can take away from us, when you've got commanders in other units saying they could not have completed their mission if it wasn't for 2-7 CAV. That's something you look back on and you'll never forget.

Captain Natalie Friel
28 July 2006

JM: My name is John McCool (JM) and I'm with the Operational Leadership Experiences Project at the Combat Studies Institute, Fort Leavenworth, Kansas. I'm interviewing Captain Natalie Friel (NF) on her experiences during Operation Iraqi Freedom (OIF) and specifically we'll be focusing on her role in Operation Phantom Fury. Today's date 28 July 2006 and this is an unclassified telephone interview. Before we begin, Natalie, if you feel at any time we're entering classified territory, please couch your response in terms that avoid revealing any classified information. And if classification requirements prevent you from responding, simply say you're not able to answer. Could we start by you giving me some background on your military career and maybe also where you grew up, how you got commissioned, things like that?

NF: Okay. I grew up in Pittsburgh, Pennsylvania, and went to the United States Military Academy at West Point for my commissioning source. My first assignment was in Germany with 3d Brigade, 1st Infantry Division, and one year into that assignment I deployed to Kosovo for about nine months. Five months after we returned from Kosovo, we all deployed together to Iraq and initially I started off in Ba'qubah with 3d Brigade headquarters. About three months into my deployment – around June 2004 – I was assigned to Task Force 2-2 Infantry which was in Muqdadiyah, Iraq, and that was our area of operations (AO). Task Force 2-2 was a mechanized infantry task force and was utilized on several occasions throughout our one-year deployment in Iraq to assist in other areas that seemed to have a surging insurgency population. Task Force 2-2 deployed to Najaf initially in April; we, of course, assisted in Fallujah in November; and then part our unit assisted in Mosul in January 2005. We were jumping around several times during our tour there.

JM: For the record, what was the period of time for your deployment?

NF: We were deployed from February 2004 to February 2005.

JM: What was the specific duty position you held in November 2004?

NF: I was the battalion assistant intelligence officer (AS2). When we got our order to go to Fallujah, there was no primary battalion S2 so I was filling that role at the time. About two days before our actual movement to Fallujah, we received another intelligence officer – a more senior captain than me who came in to be the primary battalion intelligence officer – but for the entire intelligence preparation of the battlefield (IPB) portion of it and previous to that battle, I had been acting as the primary S2.

JM: What happened to the original S2?

NF: It was a time of transition for the unit and he was taking command in Ba'qubah for one of the direct support intelligence companies. He was in transition going to do that and, at the time, he was also on R&R leave.

JM: So you become the acting S2 and, all of a sudden, this warning order comes down for this major operation. What's going through your mind? What are your concerns?

NF: It was kind of a big intelligence gap in my mind because I had been very focused on our sector and didn't know exactly how to get the information about this other sector. First of all, it wasn't even an Army unit, it wasn't in my division, and it wasn't something I could reach out and touch very easily. Immediately upon getting our mission order, we did get to go do a reconnaissance of Fallujah and met with their intelligence section and with the commander we would be falling under for Marine Regimental Combat Team 7 (RCT-7).

JM: How did that recon go? And could you also talk a little bit about how 2-2 was integrated with the Marines and your relationship with them?

NF: That recon went very well and I was received very well by the Marine Corps intelligence staff. They really gave me a whirlwind tour of the big picture of what was going on in Fallujah, brought me up to a map and showed me all the key insurgent strongholds and who all the key players were that we would be looking for. They couldn't really give me an in depth discussion of what our sector would be because, at the time, that was still in flux. The Marine Corps was still trying to decide how they wanted to use this mechanized infantry task force in the fight. He also gave me a number of CDs that had an enormous amount of information. I think it was about 10 CDs worth of imagery, intelligence reports, graphics and assessments of all of Fallujah – so they really had a good package to give us and they had a great terrain team. At that time, the terrain team provided us with some imagery of the area as well.

JM: Who were you principally interacting with, who was your counterpart?

NF: I don't remember his name but it was the RCT-7 S2. He was a major.

JM: Colonel Craig Tucker was the regimental commander, correct?

NF: Yes.

JM: Was he around? Did you have any interaction with him?

NF: He was around and gave our entire staff a briefing but I didn't really interact with him personally.

JM: So you were generally pleased with the intelligence the Marine Corps had already devised?

NF: Yes, I was very impressed. They were very sharp and seemed to have a good picture of things. They were really showing me the bottom line of everything I wanted to see.

JM: What immediately struck you as you were beginning to process these 10 CDs worth of stuff? What were the major things you took back with you to 2-2?

NF: We took those CDs back with us to our unit as well, but just seeing the fact that they had vehicle-borne improvised explosive device (VBIED) factories, they had IED factories and pictures of these kinds of locations – that really struck me. There were also suspected hostage locations, places where US and other nationalities had been taken hostage. All those things we see on the news with people being taken hostage, it was happening in Fallujah. So that struck me as the importance of this operation. Hearing names like Abu Musab al-Zarqawi and Omar Hadid being thrown around – those were major players in the insurgency in Iraq and a lot of their hangouts and places where they met were within Fallujah. It was also interesting to see that many of the mosques were identified as hostile and as meeting locations. That to me was an escalation of what we were used to in our own sector. What was interesting to see was all the unmanned aerial vehicle (UAV) coverage they were able to provide us with, because we weren't used to having that level of support in our own sector in Muqdadiyah. They just had some great UAV feeds showing daisy-chained IEDs that the insurgents were setting up and showing all their defensive positions they had created. Looking at all the pictures, you could see that this was just not a city where people were living normally. It was definitely a fortified zone with huge speed bumps everywhere and concrete barriers along the roads. They had been preparing a long time for us to attack.

JM: With reference to the UAVs and the Marine Corps, were they using those Shadows?

NF: No, we had a Shadow at our brigade level in Ba'qubah. Our battalion didn't have a Shadow. The Marines had two different UAVs: I think they had a Pioneer and a Scan Eagle. Because they had all this corps and division support all focused on Fallujah, they also had Predator and IGNAT, which can provide some really good coverage. We just weren't used to seeing that level of detail.

JM: In terms of this whole IPB process, was there anything you thought could have gone better? Any resources or assets you wished you'd had?

NF: I wish that the specific mission for 2-2 had been better defined sooner because, for awhile, the Marines were only going to use 2-2 as an outside force just sitting on the edges of the city on the southeast corner.

JM: Basically doing a cordon?

NF: Yeah, and just trying to catch insurgents who would be flooding out of the city. They wanted the Marines to be going from north to south and pushing people and then we would be catching them coming southeast. Then our mission changed to be going from north to south starting in the Askari District, which is the northeastern most corner of Fallujah, and that stands for the "military district." I think overall the Marines underestimated how quickly we would be able to do that, because a mechanized task force can move a lot faster than dismounts. We're not going to be distracted by things blowing up at us because we have a little more armor to protect us. I think there was also a difference in opinion in terms of how in depth they wanted us to be clearing things during the initial sweeps. We got the message that they wanted us to get down to Highway 10 – Phase Line Fran – as quickly as possible, but I think their forces were actually clearing every single house as they were going. I think our forces, on the other hand, were only clearing the houses we received contact from and then we continued on. That might have been why the Marines were a lot slower than us as well. We had this follow-on mission that no one really talked about, which was to continue moving south past Highway 10, so I had focused my intelligence effort on the Askari District and the industrial districts which were just south of Highway 10. I didn't really focus on the Shuhada District, which was even further south, and I hadn't done this because I didn't realize we would be going that far, so that had been unclear. I wish I'd known more about and had prepared better for that Shuhada District because we got there so quickly that there wasn't a lot of time to collect information about it.

JM: How long would you say you planned for this limited mission until you got word that it was going to be much more involved?

NF: I think before we got to Fallujah we had about two weeks to do IPB and just give an in depth enemy course of action. We focused that on the industrial district and the Askari District. We looked at the information about Shuhada but there was less information available about that and I didn't push for more because I didn't realize we would be going that far south.

JM: Do you feel the mission that 2-2 eventually did get was the best use of the task force and the best way of complementing the Marine forces?

NF: I think it was. We were given a difficult enough mission and we were definitely well used. I think it was an adequate mission for us, but that's not really my call.

JM: What kind of intelligence did you have on the enemy before the fight and what was your assessment of them? Were they going to be formidable? What were their capabilities?

NF: We did present the enemy as very different and very unlike the enemy we were used to facing in Muqdadiyah. The message we sent was that there were

60

foreign fighters and insurgents who had been preparing for this fight since probably April, so they had many months to prepare their defensive positions. We had been given the impression from the intelligence that the majority of the civilian population had left the city and particularly so in the sector we were going to be in, which was the military and industrial district – and the industrial district was warehouses and things, so we didn't expect to find any residents there anyway. Just based on the pictures and the intelligence reporting we had, it really just looked like a warehouse for bombs and terrorist activity. So the message was that this enemy was more intense and better trained than any of the enemy that we were used to facing.

JM: You mentioned the UAV coverage, but was there also any human intelligence (HUMINT) you all were relying on that you thought was good, bad or otherwise?

NF: There wasn't a lot of HUMINT. Part of the problem was that because the city had been occupied by insurgents and there wasn't a US presence in the city – like in most of our other cities in Iraq – it's hard to get HUMINT sources in there to get information. We did have a few reports but it wasn't as well developed of a HUMINT area as some of our other cities in Iraq.

JM: I guess I was wondering how you were able to distinguish between foreign fighters and guys who were actual Iraqis.

NF: We could get that from some HUMINT sources, so we had a picture of that from HUMINT as well as signals intelligence (SIGINT).

JM: In some of our previous correspondence, you mentioned this issue of the insurgent training ground. Could you expand on this?

NF: When I got the picture that our forces were going to go down into the Shuhada District as kind of a second wave mission, an on-order mission to move south, and that that would be our sector, I started to look back through information the Marines had initially provided me with and there really wasn't as much information about Shuhada as there had been about Askari and the industrial district. So I tried to figure out where I could get some more information about that and asked the Marines at their headquarters where I could get some more information about Shuhada. They gave me a point of contact in another Army unit that had been on the outskirts of the southeast of Fallujah before we had started Operation Phantom Fury. They had pulled out of that area because they would have been in the line of fire once the operation started, but they had been doing some feints into the southeast corner of Fallujah; and their role was to make the insurgents think we were coming from the southeast instead of from the north. They had never actually gone into Shuhada but they had been engaging them and probing at them from the southeast, so they were able to give me some information and some intelligence that they'd gathered from their time there. They showed me all the points they had received fire from, gave me some imagery they had and some intelligence they were able to collect. One thing they told me – and I believe it was from HUMINT – was that there was kind of a gap in between the end of the industrial district in the south and the start of Shuhada further south, and there was this vacant area that didn't have any houses in it. They said they believed it had been used as an insurgent training ground. They also said the insurgents were creating foxholes on the outskirts of the city, which we started to call spider holes that they were using to pop out of, but we didn't realize the extent of this spider hole and tunnel network they had created down south until our forces were actually on the ground. Obviously with them moving a lot underground, the UAVs had not been picking up really anything down there. While our forces were still up north in Askari and the industrial district, we were watching the Predator one day and it picked up a truck driving around down there. We believe it had weapons in the back and was stopping at houses, dropping weapons off and then going to another house, dropping more weapons off.

JM: Like a delivery truck.

NF: Yeah, it was a delivery truck; and since in the tactical operations center (TOC) we were part of the deep fight, we actually targeted that truck with our own artillery. None of our forces were down there to be observers, so the observer was the Predator that was following this truck. Our first tries were pretty far off, but eventually we were able to get that truck with our artillery and that was really the only thing we saw as a sign of life down there.

JM: Talk me through the kickoff of the battle when they blow the breach and cross the berm. Where are you located at this time and what are you seeing?

NF: I was in the TOC which was on Camp Fallujah, and we could hear the battle from there but we couldn't really see anything at that point. We were just monitoring radio traffic and I believe they had to change their plan in terms of the breach and just use one breach point. I think they had planned to use two and they went to one – but I could be wrong about that.

JM: Didn't the Marines have some trouble with their breach?

NF: Yes, that's what it was. The Marines had trouble with theirs so they had to come use ours. It went very quickly. We had been concerned because a couple days before the actual battle we had received some more updated UAV feeds that showed all these tires they had laid out on the roads and more defensive positions up on the northeast corner. We believe they were going to set those tires on fire and try to create a huge smoke obstacle, but I don't think they ever did that and there wasn't really anything to slow down this huge task force that was coming through the breach. They passed that quite quickly. There were certain areas we thought

62

were going to slow our own forces down but it didn't end up slowing them down at all.

JM: Where was the S2 at this time?

NF: He was with the tactical command post (TAC), and the TAC consisted of the operations officer (S3), the battalion commander and the sergeant major and their Bradleys. The S2 didn't have his own vehicle so he was in the fire support officer's (FSO's) vehicle. That situation should have been improved because he didn't have access to a radio and I guess he thought at the time he would be sharing with the FSO. But the FSO was extremely engaged at the time in calling for fire, working with the mortars and the TOC and the artillery, so that radio was absolutely occupied. He didn't really have any good access to anything other than listening to the FSO's radio. In terms of intelligence information, I was receiving the SIGINT and HUMINT and UAV traffic from the Marines in the TOC, so I found that it was hard to try and interrupt on the radio to provide any kind of updates because we were really only using one net – the command net. That's what we were monitoring in order to monitor the fight. There was no operations & intelligence (O&I) net and there should have been, so that could have been improved as well. I started using the Blue Force Tracker to send out messages and intelligence updates; and I could only send out a couple sentences so it had to be a quick update. If there was anything time sensitive I had to report, I would cut into the command net, tell the battalion commander and let him do with that what he wanted.

JM: Could you take me through the battle itself and tell me from your perspective what the major events and turning points were?

NF: It was pretty quick to get from the breach down to Highway 10. The real hardship for us was the fact that, during the breach, we lost our command sergeant major – Steve Faulkenburg – so that was obviously a tough thing to have happen. Sergeant Major Darrin Bohn took over as the command sergeant major and we got to Highway 10 within 48 hours. There were a couple mosques and suspected insurgent houses that our forces were supposed to check out along the way and they did that and didn't find anything there. There was a hospital we had suspected the insurgents were using as a meeting place or maybe as their own hospital, but there was no one there. They did receive a lot of enemy contact and cleared those buildings but I didn't get the impression that that was really the most difficult part of the fight for us. We continued down through the industrial district. I can't remember what the timeline was in terms of what day it was in the fight that this happened, but I don't think they received hardly any enemy contact when they went through the industrial district, which was a surprise because we thought there would be at least some insurgents down there. Then the Marines wanted us to go back up and re-clear every single house in the Askari District, so I think one of our tank companies was attached to one of the Marine companies and they went back and cleared house by house. We were then given our on-order mission to continue down through the Shuhada District; and at that point, I was scrambling trying to pull together a good picture of that sector. I went out to meet with all the commanders and the staff and brought them new imagery showing the southern sector, because we didn't even have any imagery of that sector to start with. I gave them the best intelligence update I could at that time, and that was the first time they had heard an enemy course of action on that district or had even seen what it looked like on imagery. I know we started off our movement down to that area with another white phosphorous (WP) blast just as we had started off up north with the breach.

JM: What was the purpose of the WP?

NF: It was to give us some cover and concealment. We felt like the top northeast corners of both Askari and the Shuhada Districts were going to be hot spots because of the intelligence we had. We knew those were fortified positions and UAVs had seen activity there, as well as anti-aircraft weapons. Going down into Shuhada, we had to cross that open field so we didn't really have a lot of concealment there. We wanted to clear out that area as we were crossing the insurgent training ground area.

JM: At this point, was there anything surprising you about the enemy, their capabilities or their effectiveness as a fighting force?

NF: Yeah. I felt like this was the big turning point in the battle for the Marines as well as the Army. We didn't know about this extensive tunnel network they had down there or all these spider holes they had created, so they were able to repopulate or go back into a house after we'd cleared it. They could reappear in that house because they had a spider hole or a tunnel from another house back into it, so that was really smart on their part. There was no way we could clear all these houses without getting rid of that tunnel network and I know that, whenever our guys would find one of these holes, they would drop a grenade down there – but they were still able to sneak around us using that system. Our guys were able to find several dead fighters whom either they killed or had been killed by the artillery or the bombing that had occurred before they went down there. They found several foreign passports and that confirmed to us that these were foreign fighters. People from Jordan and Syria – definitely a confirmation that we weren't just dealing with Iraqi local fighters.

JM: Were they more skilled, more fanatical? What did you perceive as the major differences between foreign fighters and Iraqi fighters?

NF: Just that they were probably more prepared to die – more of the suicide mentality – which was not common for the Iraqi fighters who were not suicidal for the most part. Most of the people who were blowing themselves up in Iraq were from somewhere else – at least that's my perception. They were from Egypt, from Jordan, etc., and they were bringing the radical, fundamentalist Islam into Iraq. I knew they were probably able to inspire some of the more hardcore Iraqi insurgents to go along with them but, for the most part, Iraq did not have a fundamentalist mentality to it.

JM: You mentioned briefing commanders on the ground.

NF: Yeah. There were a few times I went out with Major Erik Krivda, who was the S3 in the TOC, to talk to the commanders and just provide an update to them or give them a course of action, either enemy or friendly. They were so tired that they didn't have time to do that out there and they didn't have access to what we had access to in the TOC.

JM: Now, is this a normal AS2 job or is this something the S2 would normally do?

NF: It should be what the S2 is doing and usually the assistant is out in the TAC tracking the battle.

JM: So basically the roles were reversed.

NF: Yes, and that was probably because I had been part of the two reconnaissance missions out with the Marines and just part of the whole IPB. Captain Ray Pemberton came in at the last minute and didn't have a lot of time to get his feet wet.

JM: Were you pretty comfortable in this role of going out and briefing?

NF: I was, but I did feel as though there was a gap I was receiving in terms of battle tracking because the TAC was able to track enemy KIA and exact events that were occurring, and sometimes we missed those because we could only listen to the command net. A lot of that they were getting from company nets and tracking things that way. In terms of the whole battle tracking process, I think I only got about 50 percent of what was going on. So really, all I could feed them was my general assessment of what was going to happen in the future based on this intelligence I was receiving that they weren't getting.

JM: How well do you feel the information you received tracked with what was occurring?

NF: I feel that the S2's job is more to be looking into the future and not reflecting into the past, so I felt like I was doing a good job of giving them something to work with in terms of what I thought was going to happen in the future. But in terms of being able to capture in the TOC what had happened in the past, we weren't able to clean that up until after the fight. We got together with the battle trackers in the TOC and got all the information they'd captured and started plotting it for ourselves. We really only needed that to say how many total enemy were killed and where they all were.

JM: While the battle was going on, did you have any communication with the Marines?

NF: Yes. There were several times I went over to their area and we were both located on Camp Fallujah so that made it easy. I went over there to get new imagery and new information from them. Most of the time I was chatting with them on Microsoft chat, which was their big thing.

JM: Was this the mIRC Chat?

NF: No, the mIRC Chat we used to talk to the Air Force really, for the close air support (CAS) and the Predator and IGNAT feed because they controlled that.

JM: How would you assess the Marines' intelligence info during the battle?

NF: I think they were getting better information because they all had these Microsoft chat things down to a lower level, and so their TAC on the ground was able to be Microsoft chatting spot reports back to their TOC. I felt like they were getting a more up to date feed as far as spot reports. I could see everything that was going on on the Microsoft chat and that was a good way for me to get the big picture.

JM: How would you characterize the whole joint-ness of this operation?

NF: I felt very welcomed, part of the fight and really one team with the Marines – and the Air Force was never a problem. We had some Air Force soldiers on the ground with our commanders who were assisting to call in the CAS. The Marines provided us with several intelligence teams to try and help integrate us into their systems. One was a counterintelligence team that did some interrogations whenever we did have prisoners and they were doing document exploitation whenever we found documents. We also had a small SIGINT team that was providing that kind of support. The only area where I felt where we weren't treated as equals was with the Marine UAV support, and it was probably because their forces were able to Microsoft chat into the Marine TOC and let them know what contact they were receiving, that they needed the UAV to come and look around in a specific area. For us, it was just me trying to Microsoft chat to them and asking if we could see in front of us or behind us. I could only get the Marines to bring their UAV over to our sector whenever we were in some serious contact. I felt like we were only getting about 10 percent of the time with UAV coverage so that wasn't adequate in my mind, especially when they had UAVs up 24 hours a day.

JM: Were you able to get any worthwhile information from the interrogations of these enemy prisoners? Were they able to filter anything back to you?

NF: No, not really. I think they were able to pass it on to the S2 on the ground, but I wasn't getting it. I don't know of anything actionable they got out of it.

JM: What would you say was your overall assessment of this fight and the quality of the intel you saw?

NF: Overall in terms the imagery and the SIGINT, it was a lot more support than we were ever used to receiving. The HUMINT was a little sparse and that was just a factor of they hadn't been able to develop sources very well. It takes awhile to develop that kind of HUMINT relationship. Just the imagery and the UAV coverage were incredible and, for this type of fight, that was really the most important ones we could have had. Just to be able to see all the defensive positions they set up, the location of weapons on tops of roofs, seeing people set up daisy-chained IEDs or vehicles that were rigged to explode – we could see all of that through UAV feeds.

JM: What were some of the unique intelligence challenges of this being an urban operation?

NF: It was just a lot closer together of an area. It really was a small area we were dealing with and we were used to dealing with miles and miles. It's a big city but it was really just a compact fight, so there were so many details in each little road. It was hard that we could never say that a particular area was cleared or safe because they were always being repopulated. Even though initially when we went from north to south in the city – you could say everything is open game and the enemy could be anywhere – but you still didn't feel like things were cleared even when we had passed through that area, so I think it kind of got hazier as we went along. There was a new technique the insurgents started to use down south that I never anticipated them using – and really this is something they could only do in an urban environment and was something of a suicidal technique. They were setting up defensive positions right inside the house, so whoever came through the front door would be just be blasted from multiple directions by machine gun fire or rocket-propelled grenades (RPGs). That was how one of our company commanders was killed and I know that's how a number of the Marines were killed.

JM: Are you talking about Captain Sean Sims?

NF: Yes. I know Staff Sergeant Jason Laser, one of our scouts, was shot in the neck that way as well. Our guys are used to being able to go into a little stack, the first person busts into the room and they start shooting; but it was that initial person going through the door who wasn't going to make it with this technique the enemy was using. So our forces started to respond to that by shooting a tank round or a Bradley round through the door of a house before they would go in. I don't think the Marines did that and, from monitoring their Microsoft chat, I kept seeing more and more Marine casualties occurring from this same technique.

JM: I understand that a lot of times 2-2 would just drop the building all together with artillery?

NF: Yeah, if we knew for sure that it was infested; but if we didn't know they were still shooting a round through the house.

JM: Could you share any impressions you may have of some of the key players you worked with like, Lieutenant Colonel Pete Newell or some of his battalion staff?

NF: About 72 hours into the fight, I think everybody who was out there in the battle – Lieutenant Colonel Newell, Major John Reynolds, Captain Sims and the other company commanders – hadn't slept that whole time and they were just smoked. I had been going down for about two or three hours every night and the same for Major Krivda, so we at least had some semblance of being able to think still. So whenever we got our second and third on-order missions – going down to the industrial district and continue into Shuhada – he and I were doing what a full staff should be doing, which was coming up with the op order, coming up with a plan, IPB and imagery, and then going out to the TOC and delivering that. Those guys were definitely heroes in my mind for what they did: 72 hours of constant fighting and being in a battle that whole time. Captain Sims and Captain Doug Walter really stick out in my mind as does First Sergeant Peter Smith, first sergeant for Alpha Company. When Captain Sims and Lieutenant Ed Iwan, his executive officer (XO), were both killed, Smith really had to be the XO, the commander and the first sergeant for about 24 hours while still in a fight, which was a lot to ask of someone. Captain Walter was pulled from brigade staff. He used to be the Alpha Company commander before Captain Sims and he was pulled down from Ba'qubah and went right into the fight. I think that was one of the best decisions Lieutenant Colonel Newell could have made because they really needed someone like him – someone they were comfortable with after what that company had gone through.

JM: We've actually interviewed Doug Walter and Peter Smith as well, and one of the things we're interested in is this whole issue of when they lost both the XO and Alpha Company commander and when Smith effectively becomes the commander for awhile. Is that your understanding?

NF: He was. I remember there being some confusion about lines of fire at this point of the fight down in the Shuhada District, and there was some danger of fratricide, but that was the point when Lieutenant Colonel Newell made a good decision to pull them back. I think he dropped some CAS at that point to clear it out a little better and also got Captain Walter down there to be the company commander.

JM: Did you ever have any interaction with Major (Dr.) Lisa DeWitt?

68

NF: Not during the battle. She was in a different area where the casualties, the medics, the maintenance and the Headquarters Company were all located. That was where my husband Jamey was as well.

JM: He was the battalion maintenance officer (BMO), right?

NF: Right, and he ended up being kind of the casualty evacuation officer as well because no one was really playing that role. He had to go back and forth a lot to pick up parts and keep things going with the maintenance, but he ended up bringing back several of the KIAs too.

JM: In summary, how would you account for the successful prosecution of this fight? What were some of the major factors that went into it?

NF: I think one of the biggest factors was Lieutenant Colonel Newell's clarification of what the rules of engagement (ROE) were and the fact that he allowed our commanders – based on the intelligence we had received – that if they saw a vehicle just sitting on the side of the street with no one in it, assume it's a VBIED and shoot it so it doesn't blow us up when we get closer. He also allowed commanders to shoot a round through houses before they went in later on in the battle. Those decisions were really important and things I don't think the Marines were doing the same. I think those kinds of decisions on his part really saved our lives. I would say the speed of movement we were able to use was a major factor in our success as well. Definitely the armor helped, and that was something the Marines could have used. The great amount of imagery and intelligence we received before going into the fight was huge. Knowing where there were going to be obstacles and where the tanks and Bradleys were going to have to go around or take a different route – that was critical information.

JM: Are there any other individuals we haven't mentioned whom you think deserve some special recognition for their actions in this operation?

NF: I wasn't close enough to the fight to be privy to particular key players. I know who the key players were in the leadership but there were definitely some real heroes who were squad leaders and platoon sergeants like Staff Sergeant David Bellavia. He was a real hero in the fight.

JM: Were there any challenges you faced being a female officer in an infantry battalion?

NF: No, not really. I thought maybe the decision to not send me out into the TAC had been made because I was a female, but Lieutenant Colonel Newell wasn't that way and I think I was better off being where I was in the fight, having access to the secure internet protocol router network (SIPRNET), the non-secure internet protocol router network (NIPRNET), the imagery and all the intelligence feeds. I was getting hundreds emails all the time with reports to sift through, so I think that's where I needed to be. The Marines were surprised that we had a female in that role but it didn't bother them in any way to work with me. Lieutenant Colonel Newell is a very out-of-the-box-thinking guy and if he feels like someone is going to be an asset to his unit, he doesn't care whether they're a female or not. I think the same thing applied to Major DeWitt being the surgeon for our unit. He knew she was an expert with trauma with all her experience in emergency rooms and probably the best and most experienced surgeon the brigade had, so that what's drove his decision making.

JM: Are there any other issues from the intelligence perspective about this fight that you'd like to highlight or other points you'd like to make?

NF: No, I don't think so.

JM: Well, thank you very much for your time today and for your service as well. It's greatly appreciated.

Captain Peter Glass
29 March 2006

MM: My name is Matt Matthews [MM] and I work for the Combat Studies Institute at Fort Leavenworth, Kansas. I'm interviewing Captain Peter Glass [PG] who was the commander for Charlie Company, 3-8 [3d Battalion, 8th Cavalry Regiment (Armor)] during Operation Phantom Fury. This is an unclassified interview. Why don't you start out by giving me your full name and a little background on where you grew up, where you went to school, how you got commissioned and your assignments prior to Operation Phantom Fury.

PG: My name is Captain Peter Glass. I grew up with a military background. My father was in the military for 29 and a half years. I lived all over. I was born in Schaumburg, Illinois. I went to college at the Citadel and that's where I got my commission through ROTC. My first duty assignment was at Fort Stewart, Georgia, where I was an infantry rifle platoon leader, a battalion adjutant and an infantry rifle executive officer. After that, I went to the Advanced Course, CAS3 [Combined Arms Service and Support School]. Then I went to Fort Bragg, North Carolina, where I was part of the XVIII Airborne Corps, and deployed to Afghanistan. I came back from Afghanistan and went to Fort Hood, Texas, and took over an armor company. Between coming home from Afghanistan and going to Fort Hood, I did a branch transfer to the armor branch and was selected for company command after being at Fort Hood for about three months. I took command of Charlie Company, 3-8.

MM: Can you give me some background starting when you took over Charlie Company, 3-8 and when you were sent to Iraq? Did you go to Iraq with the company?

PG: Yes, sir. I took over command about two months before we went to Fort Polk to participate in JRTC [Joint Readiness Training Center] as the MRE/MRX [Mission Rehearsal Exercise] that they were doing at Fort Polk. I took command of the company on November 7, 2003, and deployed the company to Fort Polk. Came back from Fort Polk after conducting the MRE/MRX and then went to Iraq. I think we left for Iraq around March 17, 2004. I was cross-attached to 2-7 CAV [2d Battalion, 7th Cavalry Regiment] for the duration of the deployment. We actually went to JRTC with 2-7 CAV, conducted our training together, and we were with them the entire time through Iraq. We were stationed at Taji, Iraq, and then we were called upon to go to Najaf and then Fallujah. I got wounded on February 6, 2005 –

MM: In the Najaf operation?

PG: No, I got wounded while conducting a patrol in the Taji area. Then after that, I came home on February 17th and the company remained there until about March 12th when they pulled out.

MM: When you were in Najaf, were you actually working pretty closely with the Marines during that fight?

PG: Actually, not really. I didn't see the Marines until the final push when they started going in the inner circle. We worked kind of as a task force. It was just 2-7 CAV that operated in the south and then I believe it was 1-5 CAV that operated in the north. The Marines came in with the 36th Commandos to actually go in within 300 meters of the Imam Ali Mosque to start securing the northwestern corner and the buildings in there.

MM: The Marines thought you guys did a bang up job, from what I understand. You definitely got the Marines' attention. Can you talk me through when you first found out that you might be attached to Regimental Combat Team 1 and would have to participate in Operation Phantom Fury?

PG: We found out probably about a week before the operation was to commence, so it was probably around November 1st. Of course, we'd heard about it in the press and weren't anticipating the Marines were going to specifically say, "Hey, we want the guys that were with us in Najaf." We were elated to find out that they thought so highly of us, that we had performed so well in Najaf that they had basically requested 2-7 CAV. That was what we were told. We weren't told that they said, "Hey, Army, we need a mechanized infantry battalion with armor assets to come help us." They basically asked for us by name. We received word around the 29th of October and left around the 1st of November to go out towards Fallujah and start intermingling with the Marines, getting under their planning process.

MM: Did you drive your track vehicles?

PG: Yes, sir. We drove them from Taji, Iraq, which is about 30 miles north of Baghdad, down through Baghdad. We skirted the northern portion of Baghdad and then we drove all the way out to Fallujah.

MM: So we're talking about 200 kilometers?

PG: Yes, sir. It wasn't just my company that we had with us. We had additional HHC [Headquarters and Headquarters Company] assets and we had about 25 Strykers from another unit that came with us at the last minute. They fell in on our serial; and since I was the company commander, they gave me the mission of being the serial commander with my XO and my first sergeant. We all convoyed down there. It was about 14 tanks – you're looking at about 35 to 40 vehicles in that serial.

MM: Can you describe what the situation was when you rolled into Camp Fallujah and how you linked up with the Marines? Did you do any prior planning before this?

PG: Yes, sir. We rolled in and they already had tents set up for us. We parked our tanks right next to these tents. The motor pool was right there so we could go do services and get our equipment ready to go into Fallujah. At this time, the battalion staff was incorporated with the Marine Corps. So we had Major [Tim] Karcher, the S3, and Major [Scott] Jackson working with those guys while we were getting our company set and into the tents. Later on in the planning process, when they were getting ready to do their combined arms rehearsal, is actually when we sat down with the Marines and saw the big picture of what was going on in Fallujah. We'd been working in conjunction. The battalion staff was doing their own planning process and we kind of had a read of what was going to be expected of us. When we went to the combined arms rehearsal, we didn't really have a speaking part because it was with Colonel [Michael] Shupp and Lieutenant Colonel [James] Rainey was doing the speaking. We were just sitting in the back going over in our mind what we were supposed to do, what RCT-7 was going to do, and what the whole 1st Marine Division was doing in the theater of operations, as well as the other 1st CAV assets that were there and anybody else that had been attached to the Marines for this operation. So that was the first time we had actually sat down and did a combined arms rehearsal – and that was kind of just on the map. Later on that day and into the early next day, we did a combined arms rehearsal in our vehicles of the breach lane. We went up early on, did a recon and identified the train tracks to the north of Fallujah. Those train tracks presented a serious obstacle for vehicles that have suspension – mainly my tanks. If we had gone up against those, we would have broken several road wheels making the mission inoperable. So the Marines went in and conducted a breach of the tracks, bulldozed them and opened a lane.

MM: That was right over the top of that railroad station and the railroad tracks?

PG: Yes, sir: the train station to the north. All those train tracks, we breached it to the west side of the train station. If you're looking at your map right now, you can see where they all come together. That's where they breached them, and I think it was about eight railroad tracks. That whole area south of the railroad tracks and north of the town was a suspected anti-tank, anti-personnel minefield. So we conducted a deliberate breach of that with our tanks. My first platoon was in the lead under Lieutenant Thompson. They went in first with the tank plow to push any mines that might be left behind and then proofed the lane with the roller.

MM: Was your company task organized? Did you have to give up a tank platoon and get a Bradley platoon or were you pure armor?

PG: No, sir. We had an infantry platoon. Lieutenant Benjamin Polanco was our infantry platoon leader.

MM: Where did he come from?

PG: Alpha Company, 2-7.

MM: You gave up an armor platoon that went to Alpha 2-7?

PG: Yes, sir. I gave up Lieutenant Matthew Wojcik, 3d Platoon, Charlie Company, 3-8 that went to Alpha 2-7.

MM: What happens after you get through the breach and into the next 48 hours?

PG: Before we entered the breach, there was a large air campaign that took out strategic targets, obviously oblivious to the company. We didn't receive any fire going through the breach. We actually thought we would. We turned up Phase Line April and headed due east up April. Came into Phase Line Henry, which runs north/south, and that was the boundary between RCT-1 and RCT-7. We were the furthest flanking.

MM: Any key events during the first 48 hours after the breach? Were you under a lot of indirect and direct fire?

PG: We were held up at Phase Line Donna while we were waiting for Alpha Company and the rest of the Marines to move through. Alpha Company, 2-7 CAV was to secure the Jolan Park area and then the Marines were going to come through and clear that out. They cleared that sector in the first 24 to 48 hours. We were taking sporadic small arms and RPGs [Rocket-Propelled Grenades]. We didn't receive any mortars. We did see a lot of IEDs [Improvised Explosive Devices] and stuff like that, but they were not detonated against us. We just saw them on the road. We engaged those IEDs with our .50 cal and coax just to neutralize them, because in that operation we couldn't afford the time to wait for EOD [Explosive Ordnance Disposal] to come out there. So once Alpha Company got in and secured Jolan, we kind of moved in unison with Alpha Company, securing their flank, and we moved all the way up to Phase Line Fran. We were held there while the Marines were dealing with securing the Jolan area and rooting out all the insurgents. That's when they started doing that deliberate clearance, going house to house and room to room, and making sure they cleared. I would say within 36 hours, I had to go to the Martyrs Cemetery and secure that as my objective. That was supposed to be the endpoint and that was supposed to be the end of Operation Phantom Fury. We were going to secure that and they were going to continue to clear out the Jolan District. We got in there and received some small arms fire. Basically everything

74

was south of Phase Line Fran. If you look at what we refer to as the "pizza slice," Phase Line Fran is where –

MM: Isn't Phase Line Fran, Highway 10?

PG: Yes, I believe it is. It seemed like the larger concentration of enemy forces were down in that area south of Fran. South of Fran and into our battlespace, we received sporadic sniper fire, mortar rounds and RPGs. It didn't look like they had a defined defense. It looked like their defense got more elaborate as we pushed south. When I secured that, I put a platoon in the west, a platoon in the east and the infantry platoon had the inner cordon. They cleared all those schoolhouses in that area.

MM: By the 10th of November, you have gotten onto Highway 10 and headed west towards the bridges. Could you talk me through that?

PG: We went down under cover of darkness. From our experience in Najaf, we knew that the enemy didn't fight at night. They tended to hunker down and gather themselves and rest. So we used the cover of darkness to get behind their lines, and we got in there and we drove to the west. We didn't get all the way to the bridge. We hunkered down and held that area. Now, Alpha Company had a follow-on mission. After they secured the Jolan Park and the Marines had cleared all the buildings and done their actions on the objective, they actually went down and secured a foothold on the east side of the bridge across from the hospital. They secured that area and then the Marines went across and secured that. The company commander for that was Captain [Edward] Twaddell. The report I got was that that bridge was just covered with multiple IEDs. They were prepared to blow that in the event that that was our direction of attack. We had intel that the enemy believed we would not come from the north through the Jolan District, and that we were going to come from the south and head up to the north. That's what they thought. We found this evidence later on when we pushed all the way to the southern portion of Fallujah. Some of their fighting positions were oriented south.

MM: Up to this point, have you taken any casualties?

PG: We had several guys that received wounds from RPGs. The early morning of the 12th, they had actually hit the glass on the tank, shattered the glass around the cupola, and wounded the tank commander, Staff Sergeant Anibal Reyes. The gunner, Sergeant Jonathan B. Shields, was also wounded and he caught a flash burn from the RPG. It had actually shot through the glass and embedded behind the tank commander, so it missed him by inches.

MM: When you're talking small arms fire, you're also including RPG-7s?

PG: Yes. RPG-7s and RPG-14s. I don't know exactly what they were. I'm sure you've read reports. I'm sure most of them are classified as far as the penetration we received.

MM: Captain Twaddell was saying that after his Bradley was hit, one of the tanks behind him blew up, which were his words. That must have been from your tank platoon and, still to this day, nobody seems to know what did that.

PG: Yes.

MM: Was there anybody wounded in that tank behind Twaddell.

PG: Yes. I believe it was a mortar round that may have hit the tops of the tanks. They also had some top-down RPG shots onto the tanks, and the RPG actually penetrated from the loader's hatch and into the small part of the penetrator – not the RPG itself, but the penetrator went into the loader's station and injured Specialist Brian Svendsen. He actually received two Purple Hearts during Fallujah.

MM: So when that tank caught on fire, were you able to salvage that at all?

PG: Yes, sir. That tank rolled right back out. The reason it caught on fire, besides the RPG and the small arms, they actually hit one of the thermite grenades and melted the grenade launcher on the tank.

MM: After Alpha Company took the bridges and you received a change of mission to go south of Highway 10, can you talk me through what happens next?

PG: Yes. We were given the mission to continue to clear the Jolan District. At that point, it was my understanding that the task force's mission was to secure the main highway between RCT-7 and RCT-1, which was Phase Line Henry. As you can see, Iraqi towns are square boxes and they're made up with north, south, east and west running streets. When we received the follow-on mission, if you follow on the map – Phase Line Fran and Phase Line Grace. We split up and I had a tank platoon cover four lanes in the west, a tank platoon cover four north/south roads in the east, and my infantry platoon in the center. So we were platoons on line heading from Phase Line Fran to Phase Line Grace, and we went in and tried to identify insurgent positions and caches. We didn't do any room-to-room clearing but we could identify them through our optics and stuff like that. Any vehicles we saw – intelligence suggested that those vehicles were suspected VBIEDs [Vehicle Born Improvised Explosive Device], because that's where the majority of the VBIEDs in the Baghdad area of operations were coming from – from Fallujah. So any fixed fighting positions we could identify – places with sand bags around windows and on buildings, any fortifications, and any cache we could identify we engaged. We continued to push down to Phase Line Grace and all the way down south to Phase Line Isabella and Phase Line Jenna in that same fashion.

MM: As you're coming down Route Henry, one of my maps shows your company veering off with three big arrows to the west from Henry. Are these individual platoons that you're sending out?

PG: At this time, this was my company on line moving from Phase Line Fran to Grace. We hit Grace and continue to bound south to Phase Line Heather. Everybody bounded in unison, on line, by platoon, by company to Phase Line Heather and we continued on. Obviously, it took a little bit of time to maneuver through the narrow streets; and sometimes we couldn't find how to get through because the road wasn't clear enough, so we would have to back up and find another way through. Then the follow-on portion – the Marines would come through and clear every house between Phase Line Fran and Phase Line Grace with their dismounted forces to ensure we got out all the insurgents and fighting positions. They seemed to take fewer casualties when we went ahead of them with our tanks, so they wanted to continue this momentum. If you look on the map, there is a big empty field in the vicinity of Phase Line Jenna right along Phase Line Henry. There's a building there that we established our command post at, and that mosque was a definite enemy mosque. There were several caches in there. When we started coming down that way, we took multiple RPG rounds, small arms, IEDs; and it's difficult when you're buttoned up in a tank to differentiate between an IED explosion and a RPG, unless you get out after the fact and check the battle damage. But our tanks had taken so much battle damage: an RPG that blows up next to a road wheel looks the same as an IED, so we weren't able to tell. But we knew we took a heavy volume of fire from that mosque, and they were clearly firing from the mosque minaret at us with RPGs. So we backed up, engaged the mosque minaret; and once that was secure, we halted. It took us 24 to 48 hours to get there. We moved in there and held that piece of terrain through the rest of the fight. There was a house there and that was kind of our command post for the company. The tanks were holding key intersections. So I had from that intersection across from the mosque all the way up to Phase Line Fran, and we held each of those intersections with a tank section.

MM: Were there times while you were doing that that the Marines called and asked for help from a tank?

PG: Yes. After we held that area for a while, we were doing a lot of night runs. Before we actually moved towards that mosque, I had spoken to Lieutenant Colonel Rainey and said, "Sir, these guys aren't fighting at night. I'd like to do some mini thunder runs." We called them "mini" because obviously we can't replace the 3d ID and the great work they did. We did that in the night and we didn't get any enemy contact. It was like there was nobody out there. They were all hiding. I asked if we could do it during the day. Well, we did it during one day and my lead tank platoon fired so many main gun rounds that I had to rotate them back to get more ammunition from our forward support company. I put the Bradleys that were trailing behind them on Phase Line Henry to continue to the fight, because we were taking such a large volume of fire from that area near the mosque.

MM: When you went back to resupply your tanks, did you have to go back north up Henry out to the north side of the city to do that?

PG: Yes. If you're looking at a Fallujah map, there is this "S" curve that we had to drive around and that was where the battalion TOC [Tactical Operations Center] was. They would push the ammo and fuel down past this embankment there so we could get back into the fight as soon as possible. But yes, we had to drive all the way back through the breach, get our resupply, and then go back down south.

MM: Who was firing indirect fire for you? Was it an Army outfit?

PG: Yes. I had a company fire support officer who was assigned to our company and he was calling in the 120 millimeter mortars. I only fired one mission with the mortars on a known sniper position. It was a building and that pretty much rendered the sniper ineffective. So that was the only fire mission I had. They were always prepared to fire for us, we just didn't use them. I used a lot of the air assets we had. We worked with Lieutenant Colonel Ron Lewis. He's out at Fort Irwin at NTC [National Training Center] right now, but we worked with him in Najaf and in Taji. They had our frequencies because they were a 1st CAV element, so we worked with them. Since they knew us from Taji, they dropped down to our company push and we would actually talk to Army Apaches. They would come in and do gun runs and fire Hellfires into buildings that we weren't having effects on with our 120s.

MM: Can you talk me through to 20 November when you withdrew and maybe any other incidents that happened between there and the 20th?

PG: Yes. I'd like to talk about the casualties we suffered. Remember I was talking about Staff Sergeant Reyes, the tank commander that got hit by a RPG, the gunner that got a flash burn and the loader who took some shrapnel as well. Because of our battalion aid station and because we were on the move, I put our company command post/aid station with Alpha Company's CP, because they were in a holding pattern waiting for us to continue moving south. That tank crew made the smart choice to try and go to the battalion aid station. As they were going through the breach, the tank flipped and rolled. By this time, my company first sergeant had actually linked up with Staff Sergeant Reyes at the site of the breach point. That was our alternate plan. They transferred the casualties. Staff Sergeant Reyes had gotten off and Specialist Edwin Modeste had gotten off and they were cross-loaded. Sergeant Jonathan Shields had actually taken over as tank commander. He was the gunner, and even though he was wounded, he realized that the tank had to get back because it wasn't functioning properly. It took shrapnel to the main gun and they were worried about penetration on the sleeve of the main gun. As they were taking it back, they fell into a deep hole on the side of the road that no one knew about. The tank actually rolled and flipped and instantly killed Sergeant Shields. It rolled on top of him and crushed him. Specialist Troy Caicedo was the driver of the tank at the time. He survived, but Sergeant Shields didn't make it. We didn't take any other casualties from my company other than him. We continued the mission. We stayed in that area and operated out of our CP. Using those grid squares, we'd go in and clear the streets and avenues of approach, engaging fixed and fortified positions with our main guns, as well as houses that were obviously fortified. And we had great effects. The Marines were going into buildings and finding lots of stuff. I got one report that they found six enemy KIA [Killed in Action]. They had weapons and a cache in there, but they were all embedded with concrete in their bodies from the 120s. So we called these "mini" gun runs. Similar to what the helicopters would do – kind of circling around a target, engaging fixed positions. Then the Marines would come through. My tank got taken out by an anti-tank mine, probably around November 17th or 18th.

MM: When you say it was taken out, did it just blow the track?

PG: It blew the track off, blew the road wheels off. It actually penetrated behind the loader and the ammo well of the tank. We didn't receive any secondary explosions, but there was a hole in there.

MM: Were you wounded again on this?

PG: No, sir. It lifted the tank up, knocked out the communications. My XO had to come up there, hook up to our tank. Specialist Alvin Holloway got out, hooked up the tank, and we drove off. Evac'd that tank and I jumped on another tank with the rest of my crew. I gave my 1st Platoon some down time because they had taken that casualty. We continued to push and went past the city all the way out to the farm country where we identified a two-story house that had sand bags in it that was oriented south. We engaged that with main guns and destroyed that building. Then we pulled up to that building and waited. That was our final set. The Marines would call and ask to clear certain grids. They would give me a box to go clear and I would assign a platoon. We would clear those grids and then the Marines would come through and clear each of those buildings.

MM: When I interviewed Colonel Shupp on Saturday, he just thinks you guys walked on water. Can you tell me what it was like working with the Marines? Did you have any problems? I know Captain Twaddell told me that there were a few incidents when Marines had stumbled in and he didn't know they were out there.

PG: The problem with working with the Marines is that there's no common operating picture. What I mean by that is we have FBCB2 [Force XXI Battle Command, Brigade and Below]; we're able to see ourselves and see where our forces are arrayed on the battlefield. They don't have that. I think they use something else, but it's not compatible.

MM: What about Blue Force Tracker?

PG: I didn't notice any Blue Force Trackers on any of their vehicles. I know that our Humvees all had them, so we were able to know our location. But I'd have to call up to the battalion TOC every night to find out what units were on my left and right, because I was on the border of both RCT-1 and RCT-7. I wanted to make sure there weren't any Marines on my left and right. There were a couple incidents where my guys were securing a corner and they saw some Marines run across the street falling back from small arms fire. They wanted to go over there and help them, but I told them that they can't just run over there and do that. It's a totally different brigade-sized element. To cross somebody's battlespace, we had to get permission and coordinate that kind of stuff. Luckily they didn't, because they saw the tanks pull up and then they fired at the buildings that the Marines were taking some heavy small arms fire from. I don't know what their capabilities were. I know that the Army has FBCB2 and Blue Force Tracker and that's the way we track the battlefield. I had to call the battalion TOC to find out where they were placed on the battlefield, other than using the eyes that we had and the scopes that we had. I really didn't like doing that, because then you had a weapon pointed at them if you were using your scope and it kind of made me nervous.

MM: Colonel Shupp said he was amazed at what the tanks could do and what the 120 millimeter mortars could do, and he said that the medic tracks saved countless lives of his Marines.

PG: Yes. We actually had two Marine engineers with us. They got injured and we got them out of there. Being a tank company and with an infantry platoon attached to me, all my seats were taken. We had the loader seats available on the tank, and I wanted to get them into the fight. I thought they brought another asset to us we didn't have, other capabilities we could bear down on the enemy. They were actually both wounded within the first five to six days.

MM: Were they in the tank when this happened?

PG: Yes. We didn't have any infantry casualties when they were dismounted. It seemed like the majority of the casualties came from RPGs and small arms fire, more so the RPGs fired at us when we maneuvered.

MM: When these two Marine engineers were injured, was everybody buttoned up and it was just something hitting the tank?

PG: There were times when they were maneuvering back to get fuel and stuff like that. We have a heavy fuel load and have to go back every four hours and get fuel. So we had a section going back and, basically, once they passed coalition force lines, they would roll open hatched – and they were actually open hatched and they caught shrapnel. Not a direct bullet or anything like that. I know you probably want some other names and such.

MM: I'd like to identify the S1, the S2, the S3, the S4 and the battalion maintenance officer. I haven't been able to identify those individuals and get their emails.

PG: The S1 is out of the Army. The S2, I can get you all that stuff. Have you talked to Lieutenant Colonel Rainey?

MM: I have not been able to track him down. And, quite frankly, I have just now gotten into the 2-7, because I started out with 2-2. Now I'm trying to put together the full picture of 2-7 and get that organized. I am missing the staff guys. I've got all the key commanders and I interviewed Tim Karcher. He gave me some good stuff and he's apparently heading back to Iraq at some point soon. Is there anything else you'd like to throw out there on how you think this mission went?

PG: There were a couple times when it got hairy and there were a couple close calls with blue on blue, or fratricide, just because the common operating picture between the Army and the Marines is not there. I think if the coalition forces are going to continue to do operations like this, we need to have a broad spectrum where everybody shares the same stuff, has the same picture and has the same FBCB2, Blue Force Tracker, so we can continue to do operations and function like this. I think that's really it.

MM: Thank you very much.

Captain Jeff Jager
17 May 2006

MM: My name is Matt Matthews and I work for the Combat Studies Institute at Fort Leavenworth, Kansas. Today is 17 May 2006 and I'm interviewing Captain Jeff Jager (JJ) who served as a lieutenant in 2d Battalion, 2d Infantry Regiment, or Task Force 2-2, during Operation Phantom Fury, and he was also a liaison officer (LNO) to Regimental Combat Team 7 (RCT-7) during this time. Could you please give me some background on yourself, where you were born, how you got commissioned and the assignments you had prior to Operation Phantom Fury?

JJ: Sure. My name is Captain Jeff Jager. I'm from a small town in western Michigan. I was commissioned out of West Point in the class of 2000 and, from there, I went to Fort Benning for the Infantry Officer Basic Course (IOBC). After that, I went to Ranger School and a couple other schools and then I went off to 2-2 Infantry in Vilseck, Germany, where I spent just under four years. With 2-2, I served as a rifle platoon leader in Alpha Company. I was a battalion mortar platoon leader. I was the executive officer (XO) for Alpha 2-2 and then I moved to the battalion operations shop (S3) where I served in a myriad of different duty positions in the 15 months or so I was there.

MM: Could you give me some background on what you were doing when you first arrived in Iraq and the events leading up to Operation Phantom Fury?

JJ: I arrived in Iraq about three weeks after the rest of the battalion. I joined them in Kuwait about two weeks after they deployed. I attended the Special Forces Assessment and Selection (SFAS) in January 2004 and then I came back to 2-2 as I withdrew from training, from SFAS, and was ready to permanent change of station (PCS) to Fort Benning to attend the Infantry Captains Career Course. I had a [inaudible] slot and everything lined up. There was no stop move/stop loss on my part because I was still in the SFAS program, but my unit deployed me to Iraq and I went. In Kuwait, I spent about three weeks pushing forward the battalion's equipment that was left behind and didn't go forward on the ground assault convoy. There were transportation issues and we needed to push our tracks and other vehicles forward, so I was an infantry officer in charge (OIC) for that event. Then I joined 2-2 in early March of '04 at Forward Operating Base (FOB) Normandy, Iraq. When I arrived there, I spent about six weeks without a real job. I was the special projects officer and the "Hey you" guy for the S3 shop. There was a bunch of captains in the S3 shop and there was not a lot that I did for about the first four weeks. The battalion received a [inaudible] mission to go down to Najaf in April and I became a battle captain. When I returned, I continued those duties as the senior battle captain and then I began change of command inventories for Charlie 2-2.

MM: When you went down to Najaf, did you work with the Marines at all?

JJ: I read in some of the other interviews you did that we may have interacted with the Marine Corps in Najaf but, to my knowledge, no. It was entirely an Army experience. 3d Brigade, 1st Infantry Division (ID) was the brigade headquarters, 2-2 had a battalion-minus, and then there were two other battalions – one Stryker battalion and one light infantry battalion out of Hawaii. These battalions were under 3d Brigade's control for the initial part of that operation. I don't remember any Marine interaction.

MM: When did you first get an indication that something might be happening in Fallujah and Task Force 2-2 might get that mission?

JJ: I think it was at the beginning of October 2004 when I, as a battle captain, first started hearing the concept that we might deploy to Fallujah under the Marine Corps. It wasn't anything official; it was all word of mouth and email traffic. There were no official orders or anything. We didn't receive official orders until quite late into the process. We conducted a lunch meeting that really served as our first reconnaissance or briefing from RCT-7 at the beginning of October. That was the first time we went down; and that was when the battalion commander and staff, along with some brigade planners and logistics officers, went to RCT-7 headquarters in western Iraq and received a briefing from Colonel Craig Tucker and his S3 on what they were looking at for Fallujah.

MM: It's my understanding that, at some point, you traveled down to Camp Fallujah with the brigade commander and Major John Reynolds, the Task Force 2-2 S3, for some sort of link up with RCT-7. Is this true?

JJ: We first went to RCT-7 headquarters for the initial meeting in early October and it was probably two or three weeks after that when things were pretty fluid and we didn't really know what was going on. We kind of had the feeling that we were going to end up going and, as soon as we got the initial warning order – and I'm really not even sure if it was official or if the task organization had even become effective. But we started receiving email traffic from RCT-7 that we were going to be fighting with them, so the battalion began the parallel planning process.

MM: You were actually left there as an LNO, correct?

JJ: Yes. I'd been given the warning order in early October that I would probably be the LNO that deployed. Colonel Tucker actually requested that we send a planner to assist with the integration of our capabilities, which we held off on for a while because we didn't know when we were going to go. As soon as the battalion commander and the S3 felt we were really going to do it, that was when they left me behind at Camp Baharia to serve as LNO. That was the end of October. Around the 27th or 28th of October, the task force conducted another recon and, this time, they went to Camp Fallujah. Camp Baharia sits just north of Camp Fallujah; it's pretty much connected and that's where the RCT-7 headquarters was. That was the meeting where Colonel Dana Pittard, Lieutenant Colonel Peter Newell, Major Ken Adgie – the battalion staff – conducted a meeting with the RCT-7 staff. Colonel Tucker chaired that meeting. After that is when I remained behind with three other individuals to serve as a liaison team.

MM: Were you the only LNO left there?

JJ: No. I was the OIC of the liaison team. For 2-2, we deployed myself, Lieutenant Chris Lacour – who was the fire support officer (FSO) under Captain James Cobb, who was the OIC of the fire support element. But he mostly served in a civil affairs (S5) capacity through Iraq until we went to places like Najaf and Fallujah where he took over as the FSO. So Chris was the OIC of the lethal fires cell. We also had an intel specialist and Captain Jeff Beauchamp, who was one of the senior battle captains at brigade. He deployed as the brigade LNO to RCT-7 and really helped out a lot with transmitting information to brigade to keep them situationally aware.

MM: What were your impressions initially when you were there performing these liaison missions with the Marines? Did you get an understanding of the operational plan at that time?

JJ: Before I deployed, Major Reynolds had given me some very specific tasks to accomplish as an LNO. The first one was to understand the command and control structure of RCT-7: how they talk, how they reported, what they did. The second one was to figure out their operational plan. The third one was to figure out how they used their targeting process to prosecute targets. The fourth was to find and recon the task force attack position. The fifth and final one was to find and recon the battalion living area and where the tactical operations center (TOC) was going to be located. So I had an idea of what I needed to do as an LNO. When I first arrived, we almost immediately began plugging into the RCT-7 command and control structure, trying to understand what they did. The way we were able to do that was through three techniques. The first was that RCT-7 conducted two-a-day battle update briefs chaired by Colonel Tucker, where the last 12 hours of operations were briefed in pretty excruciating detail, and then the next 24 and 48 hours were briefed as well. Those two-a-day meetings really read me into the current operations that RCT-7 executed – and they executed quite a bit of preparatory fires weeks out from when we actually conducted the attack, to mitigate the number of enemy in Fallujah. The second technique that helped a lot was that RCT-7 executed a once-daily targeting meeting. During the meeting, RCT-7 intel and fire support sections briefed Colonel Tucker with what battle damage they caused over the last 24 hours through close air support (CAS) and indirect fires, and then recommended targets for the next 24 hours. Through this process, we were able to see what they were doing as far as targeting the enemy in the RCT-7 sector prior to the attack.

MM: Were these targeting missions also targeting Task Force 2-2's area as well?

JJ: Let me talk about the other two mediums that helped me understand the operational plan as well, and then I'll address that question. The other two mediums were interaction with the RCT-7 S3 and future plans officer, two lieutenant colonels. When we established our LNO section, they put us in the operations tent, which is where the S3 and the future operations officer worked out of, so we were able to personally interact with them to explain what were the capabilities of 2-2 and understand what they needed us to do and what their expectations of an Army mechanized infantry battalion were. Those mediums were the ones that allowed us to get a situational awareness of not only the operations that RCT-7 conducted prior to the attack on Fallujah, but what their plan was for the attack. To address your question of whether they were targeting 2-2's sector initially – no, they weren't. In my mind, the RCT-7 plan initially was for 2-2 to establish blocking positions in the southeast section of the city. But that mission eventually went to another Army element, which gave RCT-7 the ability to use 2-2 in the attack rather than in a blocking position. RCT-7 had initially planned to bypass the eastern part of their sector. Initial intel sort of said that the eastern portion was less heavily populated with enemy and can probably be bypassed, allowing the Marine Corps' two organic battalions to focus on the more densely populated enemy areas and then come back and clean up the eastern part of the city. So in those first few targeting meetings we realized, between Lieutenant Lacour and the intel specialist, that they weren't targeting anything in our sector. From that meeting, we sat down afterwards and said we knew there were enemy there. Lieutenant Lacour and the intel specialist developed a fire support matrix requesting the servicing of targets in 2-2's sector, which RCT-7 began to fire. I don't have the data on what targets they actually fired or what the battle damage was.

MM: Did they start firing missions for you?

JJ: Yes, they did. We weren't the main effort for the RCT, but because they were focused on the more densely populated areas of their sector, they had not considered firing in our area. But as soon as we developed that fire support plan and integrated that into the RCT-7 plan, they began servicing targets in 2-2's sector. I think that really reduced the enemy's presence.

MM: Were you reporting back every day to Major Reynolds?

JJ: At the end of every day, we would either call or send an email, or both send an email and call. Usually send the email and then call to verify receipt. Captain Tom Mitchell was the battle captain and he and I shared battle captain duties – 12 on and 12 off – and then I deployed, so he and Captain Cameron Dow took over my position back at FOB Normandy when I left. It took us a couple days to establish any kind of email connectivity with battalion, so the first couple days I was there were all telephone conversations where I listed the lessons learned, the operational intelligence, and fire support routes for Major Reynolds to disseminate amongst the staff and commanders. There was frustration initially in how the Army and Marine systems didn't talk easily together. We had four secure internet protocol router (SIPR) computers between members of the LNO team, and all of us had our own, but RCT-7 was operating pretty austerely. They weren't at their home base camp; they just had their organic commo equipment so they were very limited in the number of drops they could give us. They gave us one SIPR drop and it took a couple days to get our computers configured so we could talk on their SIPR line back to 2-2 or any Army element. It wasn't like we could just take our computer, unplug it from our SIPR drop, plug it into the Marine Corps SIPR drop and have it work. The RCT-7 commo guys – the signal officer himself was the guy who finally got us connectivity on our computer. We also had the same sort of problems with telephones. Initially, we couldn't dial an Army number from the Marine Corps phone at all. It took a couple days but, eventually, the RCT-7 signal guys were able to figure out how to let us call back to FOB Normandy, but they could only give us one line that they could configure that way. They had to use all the others to talk to their chain of command. So the number we got, we established as the 2-2 TOC. But to call anybody else, like brigade or any other Army phone number, we had to go back through Germany, to a switchboard in Germany, to have them patch us into the Army network, which limited our ability but at least we were still able to communicate.

MM: I get the impression that, during this time, you guys are sending a lot of information back to the S3. Do you know what he was doing with all this information? Was he forwarding it to the task force commander, Lieutenant Colonel Newell, who, it's my understanding, was on leave during this time?

JJ: I'm not sure what overall impact his being on leave had on us. I can only talk from personal experience. I wasn't real read up on LNO integration but I looked at FM 5-01.12, which is Joint Task Force LNO Integration. Had I read that document prior to deploying, I would have known what I needed to do as an LNO; and part of that is knowing my battalion commander's intent and specific tasks for me as the LNO. I didn't have that because the battalion commander was on leave, so the XO and S3 were pulling double duty there. I had some good guidance from the S3 on what to execute, but that was the S3's guidance and not the battalion commander's.

The entire time I was in Fallujah, I was operating off the S3's guidance, which wasn't the same as what the battalion commander's guidance would be given how things changed after the battalion commander got in the loop when he arrived back on the ground. I'm not sure what happened to the information I sent back via SIPR email to the S3. I know most of it didn't go to the people it should have gone to. Tom Mitchell sent me a note when I told him I was writing a monograph about my LNO experience. He was a battle captain back at FOB Normandy. He would know I had called and verified that Major Reynolds got the notes I was sending. Tom commented that there wasn't good dissemination of what information I was sending back. The stuff I was sending back was mostly in regard to the current Fallujah set – what RCT-7 was doing to set the conditions, what the intel picture said about what the enemy was doing inside, how RCT-7 was targeting our sector, what we experienced when we were there, and what lessons we learned.

MM: You said in your previous email to me that you actually stood up on 5 November and were going to brief the 1st Marine Division (MARDIV) commander, General Richard Natonski, on what you believed was the course of action. Did that somehow change?

JJ: Going back to the military decision-making process (MDMP), the first part is receipt of the mission; and when I left FOB Normandy at the end of October, we conducted a modified MDMP at the battalion level. I say modified because without the battalion commander's input, it's kind of hard to do an MDMP properly, so it was modified. I knew the plan for what the S3 had put together because I was a battle captain and in the area when he was developing it. I knew what he wanted to do, and part of my job as the LNO is to go to these rock drills and rehearsals and brief 2-2's part of the RCT-7 plan. Around the 3d or 4th of November, when Lieutenant Colonel Newell got back, there was a final division-level rehearsal for the operation and the Task Force 2-2 staff. The commander and the company commanders were required for the rehearsal and getting them from FOB Normandy to Camp Fallujah was hard, so they didn't arrive in time to start the division rehearsal. I was prepared to brief the plan, as I knew it from the S3, in the division rehearsal. I had actually been briefing for about five minutes when the task force arrived to the rehearsal. Major Reynolds allowed me to continue until he realized that I hadn't been briefed on the new plan and then he stopped me and started the brief over. I wasn't back at FOB Normandy so I don't know what exactly happened. I know this was the first time the company commanders had seen the battalion commander's course of action. Major Reynolds briefed it to the division commander during the rehearsal and then, afterwards, Lieutenant Colonel Newel and the company commanders took a knee around the digital imagery blow up of Task Force 2-2's sector. Lieutenant Colonel Newell gave them their task and purpose and what the concept of the operation was, what the course of action was. It differed pretty significantly from what I had been briefing. I wasn't at FOB Normandy so I'm not sure at what point the S3 was able to establish SIPR connectivity and send his plan back to the battalion commander. Apparently, Lieutenant Colonel Newell was able to review the S3's plan while back in Germany, but he wasn't able to influence it until he came back to Iraq, to FOB Normandy. It's my understanding that once Lieutenant Colonel Newell returned to FOB Normandy, the staff stayed up all night conducting an MDMP, based on the colonel's directed course of action, and produced a new course of action, which is what Major Reynolds briefed in the division rehearsal the following day. Then Lieutenant Colonel Newell briefed the company commanders after the rehearsal.

MM: One of your jobs as the LNO was also to go and find potential attack positions for Task Force 2-2. Can you tell me a little bit more about that?

JJ: One of the directed tasks Major Reynolds gave me before I left was to find where our attack position was, recon it, and make sure it's what we need. Doing a map recon was fairly easy. Route Mobile, which runs north to south past Fallujah on the eastern side of the town, sits on a large earthen berm which provides cover and concealment from direct fire from the city of Fallujah. The Marines were planning on establishing their attack positions to the far side of that berm. The future operations officer for RCT-7 said we had two or three choices. We could go north, south or east and establish our attack positions there. The map recon was easy, but actually conducting the reconnaissance proved a little more difficult based on the fact that I had no transportation assets myself and RCT-7 was pretty busy executing their preparations for combat. It was pretty hard to coordinate a ride up to see the attack position, and also given the fact that the enemy threat in that area was pretty high. I tried for a couple days to coordinate an event with staff sections of RCT-7 and just couldn't make it happen. So, on the 2d of November at the evening battle update brief, I briefed that as 2-2's outstanding issue and said I really had to get up there to see the attack position. A couple hours later, Colonel Tucker stopped me and said, "Look, the personal security detachment and I are going on a battlefield circulation patrol tomorrow. We're going up that way so I want you to come with us and I'll get you in to see the attack position." So the next morning, Captain Beauchamp and I joined Colonel Tucker's battlefield circulation patrol and went on a combat patrol with them to the attack position. We started off at Camp Fallujah and went north along the military bypass and went to the attack position. It was exactly what we needed for a battalion mechanized task force: huge two to three square kilometers of open desert covered by a large earthen berm. Vulnerable to indirect fire, as it was only about 500 meters from the eastern edge of Fallujah, but it was the best location we could have. There were two Marine battalions in RCT-7 that had their attack positions farther to the north of Fallujah, but that made sense because their sectors were further west, so we were okay to go east more than north and establish our attack position there. I rode in Colonel Tucker's command light armored vehicle (LAV), which allowed me to stand up in the back and see everything while we were driving down the road. Going on this recon proved helpful later in the operation.

MM: When Lieutenant Colonel Newell and Major Reynolds arrived, did they issue an operations order?

JJ: Let me back up real quick. After we identified the attack position, Colonel Tucker decided he wanted to show me Fallujah, so we headed south over Route Mobile past Fallujah. By doing that, I was able to identify our sector completely. I was able to decide, just by visible inspection, that the railroad track north of Fallujah, which we had thought was going to be a pretty major obstacle, wasn't going to cause that much challenge for us. The railroad track was on a berm maybe three to four feet high, and a tank or Bradley could easily drive over it without any breaching at all.

MM: Let me get this straight. There was a railroad track on a berm, not a separate railroad track and a berm?

JJ: From my visual inspection there wasn't. I'll never forget it because, right after this, it was the first firefight I'd ever been in. We had been operating under the assumption that the eastern part of Fallujah was a shantytown. The overhead imagery sort of indicated that the buildings were more sparsely laid out and there didn't seem to be that much intel on sightings of enemy or reports of enemy in that area. But as soon as we passed the railroad track, we started taking fire – rocket propelled grenades (RPGs), machine gun and small arms fire. In the after-action report (AAR), the chief warrant officer in charge of the colonel's patrol estimated that between a section and a platoon of insurgents had ambushed us there. There were some unity-of-command issues because Colonel Tucker knew it wasn't his sector at that time. It belonged to somebody else, they hadn't cut it to RCT-7, and the warrant officer wanted to stay and destroy the enemy by calling in CAS and indirect fires. So we stayed on Route Mobile and got shot at for about two minutes while the two of them worked it out, and then they lost commo with the lead vehicle. As soon as everybody got their ducks in a row, we started heading out. That event said to me that the eastern portion of Fallujah wasn't exactly a shantytown. The buildings were of the same construction as the interior box, which are more heavily populated with buildings, but here they were just more sparsely laid out. There was definitely enemy presence there. They put a pretty good ambush on us.

MM: Did you have a hand in the final operations order that was published?

JJ: It's my personal belief that we never published a final operations order. We had an extensive rehearsal – a two-and-a-half to three-hour rehearsal – where everybody knew what they were doing. We also had a pretty extensive back brief after the rehearsal where the company commanders, in detail, back briefed their plan to the battalion commander. I think the back brief morphed into an op order. It was a very good back brief, but I don't believe there was a final op order or a final warning order that was published to the company commanders. The back brief and rehearsals were good techniques to make sure everybody knew what they were doing; but as far as an operations order published based on the colonel's directed course of action, I don't remember that happening.

MM: Can you tell me about what happened when Task Force 2-2 realized that the Marines were using this SIPRNET chat that went out even to their forward locations?

JJ: Yes, I would definitely like to talk about that. Part of my tasking from Major Reynolds was to find out how RCT-7 talked and conducted command and control. I was able to figure out that they used chat to communicate from battalion to RCT. I don't know what they used for battalion command and control, but their primary means of communication at the RCT level was SIPR chat. I understood that in the TOC by way of interaction with their watch officers and their battle staff. That's how they conducted operations. I didn't understand that they had the ability to position that asset forward in a tactical command post (TAC) or a forward command and control element, but that's what they had. I'm not sure what system it was or how they did it, but the RCT-7 FM command net was a pretty quiet net. We were pretty much the only people that talked on it, because the RCT conducted command and control over chat. It was very effective and we eventually had the ability to do that in our TOC at Camp Fallujah, where the battle captain and Major Erik Krivda were able to maintain situational awareness of what was going on across the RCT. But we didn't have that ability forward with us. I think that's one of the things that, had I recognized that fact earlier, it would have paid huge dividends for us in the fight. I wasn't aware of this, but I read in your interviews with Lieutenant Colonel Newell and Major Reynolds that they said a lot of their situational awareness came from the direct downlink that their media had, from the television stations covering the event. That just indicates to me that we didn't have very good situational awareness at the RCT level. We couldn't monitor what the other battalions were telling the RCT because they didn't call them on the FM net; they told them on SIPR chat. We had the ability to monitor that SIPR chat back at our TOC in Fallujah, but the only effective system we had to transmit messages from the TOC at Camp Fallujah to the TAC – which is where the colonel and the S3 were forward – was the Blue Force Tracker. This is a good system but slow. It's not an interactive chat program where I type something, somebody acknowledges and then asks for further details like a conversation. It's chat versus email, so it's slower. Even though our TOC and TAC were only separated by less than 10 kilometers, we had almost no FM communication between them. There was something that caused the radios not to work very well. The TOC had situational awareness at the RCT level but I would say the TAC didn't have it as good as it should have, had I figured out that we needed that SIPR chat system forward.

MM: Could the folks in the TAC actually pick up the FM radio and get RCT-7 on the phone?

JJ: Yes. When we wanted to talk to RCT-7, they answered.

MM: So there was somebody there monitoring the FM radio?

JJ: Right. They had an FM radio, and that's how Colonel Tucker figured out where Lieutenant Colonel Newell was during the fight and was able to come and see us every day during the fight. It was a quiet net and we only reported the significant events we had. I think the way we reported to the RCT over FM, they had a good understanding of what we were doing, but we didn't have a good grasp on what they were doing. Tom Mitchell and I switched out every few days. I did the first 72 hours and Tom did the next 48 and we switched back and forth about every two days after that. As the glorified radio/telephone operator (RTO) in the back of the S3's Humvee, I didn't know what was going on with the Marine battalion adjacent to us as well as we should have. The guys in the TOC did, because they were on SIPR chat and knew what was happening.

MM: Were you guys aware of the problems with the breach that 3d Battalion, 1st Marine Regiment (3/1) had getting into the city?

JJ: The events after we crossed the line of departure (LD) are very confusing to me. Once the battalion arrived and I ceased being an LNO and started being a battle captain, I became more of a glorified RTO. We had Blue Force Tracker, two FM radios, the high frequency (HF) radio. We had the driver, the S3, me, a gunner and an interpreter. There was no RTO there, so I became the RTO. I have all my original notes of what happened from the second we LD'd until I left 72 hours later. We could recreate these notes and look at them and be able to see what I wrote down when I was on the radio, but the exact sequence of events from LD until mission complete have morphed a little bit in my mind, based on different people's perceptions of events after the fact. After we got back from Fallujah, I became the operational writer for what happened in Fallujah. I took my notes, which covered the first 72 hours and then every other 48 hours after that. I took Tom Mitchell's notes, which did the same thing when he was the TAC OIC. I took the DA Form 1594 from the TOC – where the RTO and the battle NCO, under the supervision of Tom and myself, under Captain Krivda – I took those three documents, typed them up and made a minute-by-minute and sometimes a second-by-second log of what happened sequentially based on our notes. That became about a 35 to 40 page document that walks from LD to the end of the operation based on the notes taken at the time. Initially, I think that was a pretty solid document but I haven't seen it in two years and I don't know what happened to it.

MM: I actually have a copy of that here.

JJ: When it was initially produced, it was a very accurate minute-by-minute compilation, a digital copy of the handwritten notes we took. I have the notes right in front of me here. I'm not sure, though, that that document is as accurate as it once was, based on different people's perceptions of what may or may not have happened. But to answer your breach question, the Marines to our west were having trouble breaching. They did use our breach for their tank platoon and their medical evacuation (MEDEVAC) vehicles. We knew they were having problems breaching, but it didn't become evident to us until they called and asked us if they could use our breach, which they did and continued to do, which was fine. There was no real fatal funnel there at the breach because of that. It was just a simple event as they bypassed us and went about their business.

MM: Can you give me your opinion and your overall assessment of Task Force 2-2 in this operation?

JJ: I'd actually like to address some other things, if you don't mind.

MM: Sure.

JJ: From some of these other interviews I've read – and I've got them all sitting right here in front of me – I just want to go through and address some of these things from my perspective. In the end, you're going to write an article and you're going to have to pick which side of the story you choose to believe. Let's start with Major, now Lieutenant Colonel, Reynolds' interview. He talks about an Air Force-published grid box system for the Fallujah area of operations (AO), which existed. However, he states that we initially developed that and then the Air Force took it and produced it. I think it already existed prior to us building ours. When we got to Fallujah, we realized they had a better system than we did so we went with theirs. That document was great. It was overhead imagery with a grid box system for the entire city of Fallujah and it's what we used for command and control and reporting purposes. Major Reynolds seems to think that it started with us and then transformed into an Air Force product, but I'm pretty sure it started with the Air Force and ours just wasn't as good as theirs. Major Reynolds makes a statement on page eight of his interview that says, "Unfortunately, Jeff didn't get to see much, due to his position inside the LAV." He's talking about Colonel Tucker and me when we went to recon the attack position assembly area. I know we've already discussed this, but that's simply a factual untruth and I wanted to point that out. Major Reynolds and Lieutenant Colonel Newell both talk about the fact that we were enemy-oriented in Fallujah, where we wanted to destroy organized resistance instead of getting to a certain point on the map. But both of them also say that we wanted to get to Fran, which is Highway 10 running east/west across the middle of Fallujah, as fast as possible. It has always been my opinion that we were terrain-oriented instead of enemy-oriented, that our march objective was Phase Line Fran, not the destroying of organized resistance in our sector. This was evident by the fact that Marines backfilled us and, then, even our own tank company had to go back and destroy organized resistance in the sector we had fought through on the first day. We did get to Fran and that was important to open up that line of communications between Camp Fallujah and the city of Fallujah for resupply and MEDEVAC; but it does neglect the fact that we left organized resistance behind us – resistance that we had to go mop up later. Major Reynolds talks about how when Lieutenant Colonel Newell returned from block leave, we changed the course of action slightly. Actually, the course of action changed pretty much completely, going from two points of breach to one. Instead of having two companies conduct their own breach, having a battalion conduct a breach. That's a pretty significant change for a company commander, 72 hours prior to execution, to be told, "You're a support by fire," versus, "You're now a breach element." That was what Lieutenant Colonel Newell described to them when he briefed them after the division rehearsal. There are a few points in here where it talks about the loss of Ravens – our company-level unmanned aerial vehicle (UAV) – because somebody was on the frequency that we thought we were on. It's my understanding that the Air Force, Marine Corps and the Navy had Prowlers in the air that scramble frequencies. Has anybody else mentioned that to you?

MM: No, they have not.

JJ: That was my understanding of why every time we went to launch a Raven it fell out of the sky, which makes sense. If you can't talk to it over a radio, you're not going to be able to control it. Major John Petkosek, who became the battalion XO, came down to Fallujah for about three or four days at the end of the fight. He was brought in to improve the maintenance and logistical capability of the battalion, according to Major Reynolds. I think he neglects to mention the fact that Captain Jamie Friel and Captain Fred Dente, along with Eric Krivda, had been executing logistical operations that more than capably supported the battalion through the fight and continued to do so once Major Petkosek arrived. Those guys deserve a lot of credit for keeping companies in the fight. If something was broke, Friel and Dente got it fixed. If we needed supplies, Krivda was on the phone and they came in. From reading the interviews, it comes out like we needed help in getting our stuff fixed and getting the logistics squared away, but I don't really think Major Petkosek did a heck of a lot to change any of that. He spent the first three days in Fallujah at the TAC completely separated from any logistical element while Friel and Dente continued to fight the fight. I wanted to address that, because he doesn't give any credit to Friel, Dente and Krivda for making the logistics happen

– and that's who did it. Lieutenant Colonel Newell talks about when Captain Doug Walter came down to take command of Alpha Company, that he was definitely the right guy for the job, being a prior company commander before Captain Sean Sims took over. He really was the only one that could have stepped in and had any sort of legitimacy with the men at that point. Just reading the few interviews I've read, I would say Krivda's is probably the most accurate and most beneficial. He was in the TOC the entire time unless he was running special missions forward to bring people or emergency supplies forward, which he did quite often. But he was back at the TOC so he had some separation from the events to really understand what was going on. He talks about the fact that a Knight Ridder photographer photographed Sean Sims' body and got it out in the press. That was a point of frustration for all of us: the access the press had to what we were doing and the limited amount of supervision they had. Within hours of Sean being dead, his photo was on the Internet. Knight Ridder is the largest newspaper conglomerate in the Unites States, so it was pretty powerful to have their photographer sending things like that out. That was just indicative of our relationship with the reporters and media personnel. Major Krivda talks a lot about how we had so many of them, and I think that really played a role as far as getting our story out. Having CNN and Fox News embedded with us – and Scott Rutter went live as we crossed the LD and told the whole country what was going on. That really got the story out, but there's a fine line between when media access becomes too much versus too little. I think this incident with the photographer is indicative of the fact that they probably had too much.

MM: Did you get a chance to read the Jane Arraf interview?

JJ: No. I don't have a good opinion of CNN, so I'm not real interested in what she has to say. If it's worth reading then I might check it out. Something else Major Krivda talks about is the staff and, in Major Reynolds' interview, he talks about how 2-2 had deployed to Najaf in April, we had all done this kind of thing before, it was just another out-of-sector mission. 2-2 did do quite a few out-of-sector missions. There was Najaf, Fallujah, Charlie Company went to Mosul for the elections. But there's a significant difference between saying 2-2 did it and saying the staff did it. Just so somebody says it, the fact is that the staff changed pretty considerably in the month or so after we got back from Najaf, so I'm just going to walk you down the task organization of the 2-2 staff. When we deployed to Iraq, here's what the staff looked like. The battalion commander was Lieutenant Colonel Newell and that stayed the same throughout. The personnel officer (S1) was Captain Brian Ducote; he'd been in 2-2 for several years and had been the S1 for a while. The intelligence officer (S2) was Captain Rich MacDonald; he'd been with 2-2 for about two years at that point. The S3 was Major Jeff LaFace; he'd been in position since just after Kosovo, so he'd been around for about a year. Captain Adam Reese and Tom Mitchell were the two battle captains in the S3 shop. I joined the S3 shop kind of late in the ball game, right when I got to Iraq. The logistics officer (S4) was Jaime Friel and, like Ducote, he had been around for a while and had done a bunch of jobs. He took the S4 job in Kosovo, so he'd been in position for well over a year at this point. The S5/FSO was Tom Cobb, and he stayed in position throughout our tour in Iraq. He was actually the S5 all the way back through Kosovo so he'd been a member of the staff for a long time; and he was actually probably the senior member of the staff as far as time on staff goes. Major Adgie was the battalion XO at that point. It was a pretty seasoned staff when we went into Najaf, so people had been in position for a long time; they knew the systems, they knew how things worked, and they knew how to do their staff work. Captain Krivda talks about it in his interview, how 2-2 didn't have a staff standard operating procedure (SOP) or a planning SOP, or even a tactical SOP for that matter. But the staff had been in position for well over a year. They worked well together, they knew what they were doing and, led by Major Adgie as the XO, they were able to make things happen and get things done and plan and execute missions. But take a look six months later when we went to Fallujah: the only people that were the same were me, Mitchell and Tom Cobb. The entire staff had changed. The S1 was Captain Kamil Stalzkoper, who was a company XO and then took over as S1 after Najaf. The S2 was a guy named Captain Pemberton; he was brand new to the unit. And then Captain Natalie Friel joined us at this point as well. She pretty much served as the S2, even though she was junior to Pemberton, just because she had some continuity with the unit and knew what was going on. She became the S2. The S3, Major Reynolds, came to the battalion in July or August, so he had only been around about a month when we started planning for Fallujah. Captain Mitchell and I were still in the S3 shop, but Adam Reese had taken command of Charlie Company, so the senior battle captain was now Mitchell and that made a difference. The S4 was Captain Johnny Fortenberry, who had been previously the support platoon leader; and both Johnny and Kamil were both still first lieutenants at this point. Tom Cobb, again, was the S5/FSO and the XO was Major Petkosek. You can see the difference in the experience level of the staff when we went to Fallujah and how long the staff had worked together as a unit. Pretty much, Fallujah was the first event that the staff had done together, and I think that showed in the MDMP we conducted for Fallujah and the MDMPs we conducted during Fallujah. Lieutenant Colonel Reynolds talks about it in his interview where, at the end of each day of fighting, we would pull the staff together and come up with a plan for the next day. That happened, but it was more just telling people where to go and what to do. It wasn't actually an MDMP. It was a modified MDMP; it wasn't a real MDMP. Just from being a battle captain and a TAC OIC, there were several times when I thought we'd be briefing an op order and, as it turned out, we just kind of briefed, "Hey, this is what we're doing tomorrow," and not a very detailed plan several times. Did you talk to any of the company commanders, Kirk Mayfield, Paul Fowler –?

MM: They're on my list. They sent me a fairly detailed history, but I do want to interview them at some point.

JJ: I don't know if they'll mention it or not, but I know of one incident later in the operation when we were doing a detailed clearing of the southern section of our sector. After an op order, Doug and Kirk on the ground were like, "Hey, what are we doing here? All right, you go this way, I'll go this way." I think the staff's inexperience really put the onus on the company commanders to execute the commander's intent versus understand what the plan really was. They knew what needed to happen, but without their leadership and abilities things would have been a lot different. I think, for the most part, the company commanders probably would have been just as well off without a battalion headquarters.

MM: Yes, I believe Major (Dr.) Lisa DeWitt made a statement in her interview about how the battle was won by the company commanders.

JJ: As it should be. The company commanders, the platoon leaders and the squad leaders are who are fighting the fight. If you want to get a good insight on how the battle actually went, you should talk to a guy like Staff Sergeant David Bellevia – who's now out of the Army and who was one of the squad leaders in Alpha Company – or some of the platoon leaders.

MM: Isn't he up for a Medal of Honor?

JJ: I know he did some very amazing things that he deserves to be recognized for, but I don't know what the final result of that will be. He basically saved his platoon, cleared a house by himself, and killed a bunch of bad guys in between. If you ever go beyond your focus on the joint aspect, guys like him are the guys you should talk to. I have a different perspective than Lieutenant Colonel Reynolds and Lieutenant Colonel Newell have. Those squad leaders probably have the perspective of what really happened on the ground, them and the platoon leaders. Guys like First Lieutenant Jeff Emery and First Lieutenant Juan Meno from Alpha Company and the engineer platoon leader, Second Lieutenant (now First Lieutenant) Shawn Gniazdowski. He was attached to us the whole time in Iraq; he was a platoon in Alpha Company. He was the breach man. Just for a different perspective of what happened. The company commanders definitely fought the fight and controlled the fight. I felt, as a battle captain in the TAC, that I was just kind of taking notes and the company commanders were executing their missions as given the way they saw fit. Maybe that's how it's supposed to work, but I didn't think the command and control of the battalion was really that effective.

MM: Do you have any information about when Captain Mayfield's company actually took charge for a while and did the battle handoff with Alpha Company?

JJ: No. I wasn't present at that time. I do know it happened and it was a pretty awesome thing for him to do, but I wasn't there and I don't know exactly what was said. What I've read in your interviews, that's how I understood the situation as well.

MM: Is there anything else you want to tell me about the operation?

JJ: No, but if you have further questions, feel free to send me a note.

MM: Well, thank you so much for your time.

Captain Christopher Lacour
15 May 2006

MM: My name is Matt Matthews (MM) and I work for the Combat Studies Institute at Fort Leavenworth, Kansas. Today is 15 May 2006 and I'm interviewing Captain Christopher Lacour (CL) who was the assistant fire support officer (FSO) for 2d Battalion, 2d Infantry Regiment, or Task Force 2-2, during Operation Phantom Fury. If you could, please give me some background on where you were born, how you got commissioned, assignments that you had prior to going to Iraq.

CL: I was born in Raceland, Louisiana. I went to school at the University of Alabama and was an ROTC commissionee. I graduated in 2002 and went over to Oklahoma for a while and then, after completing the Officer Basic Course (OBC), I shipped out to Germany. I was a fire direction officer for the 1st Battalion, 6th Field Artillery (FA) Regiment, Charlie Battery, for about 15 months. I was a platoon leader for 1-6 FA, 2d Platoon, Charlie Battery, for about 18 months and then I shifted over to 2-2 Infantry.

MM: Could you talk me through how you ended up at 2-2 Infantry and what you were doing prior to Operation Phantom Fury?

CL: I was actually a recent addition to 2-2 right before the operation. I was a platoon leader in Ba'qubah for eight months when we were doing combat operations there. 1-6 FA rotates its lieutenants through different positions and usually we're attached to infantry. Ordinarily, your first assignment is as the FSO and then you go to the one unit. Lance McGill and I were on the reverse schedule of that so I would go be a fire direction officer first and then an FSO, so it was just my time to rotate out. I had been a platoon leader for almost 15 months and they wanted to rotate everybody through. The burnout rate was pretty high and they wanted to get a lot of guys combat experience.

MM: You were in 3d Brigade Combat Team (BCT), 1st Infantry Division (ID) under Colonel Dana Pittard and, of course, Lieutenant Colonel Pete Newell commanded 2-2. How was it working with those two individuals?

CL: I didn't meet Lieutenant Colonel Newel until I'd been in Fallujah for two weeks, and he said about three words to me. He asked me where I got my cup of coffee and that I needed to rustle him up a cup. For the most part, that was all the interaction I had with the man aside from assigning targets. I worked primarily with Captain Erik Krivda in the rear, Captain James Cobb and whatever Marine element we needed to work with to get the job done.

MM: When did you first find out that 2-2 might be assigned to this operation and how did the planning aspect of this go?

CL: I originally found out when walking back after playing football, when I was still a platoon leader, and I joked to one of my operations officers and asked him if he had any information about fire support stuff because I was really unfamiliar with it. I did it at OBC but I hadn't really practiced it, and he said I might really want to get good at it. I kind of made a Fallujah joke and he didn't laugh; he just looked at me really seriously so I said, "Oh, okay." Basically, Captain Cobb was doing the initial planning and the reason I was selected was because he needed a senior FSO on the ground there. I hadn't really integrated into any job in 2-2 yet. I was very new. Everybody else continued with the same schedule they were doing and they would be hurting for information operations (IO) a little bit. I could easily be put in that position. The reason Lance McGill wasn't chosen was because he was doing a bunch of financial work for them. So they just picked me; actually, I sort of volunteered. Anyway, I sat in on all the planning meetings. Captain Cobb was all excited and they all had this initial planning for Fallujah. Lieutenant Colonel Newell was still on R&R so Major John Reynolds drafted the initial plan, which was consequently completely scrapped – but the basic concept didn't change. We attacked from the north, we pushed through to Phase Line Fran, and then we make it up as we go after that – that was apparently the order of the day. Obviously, that had to happen because we had no idea what the Marines needed or what was going on on the ground. So during the initial planning stages, I remember sitting around with the sergeant major who was killed in action and the ops sergeant major who became the sergeant major for 2-2 – both really amazing guys. I can remember sitting around with Major Reynolds, Dr. Lisa DeWitt, Captain Jeff Jager, Krivda – basically the staff for 2-2. Major Reynolds was running the show as the S3 while Lieutenant Colonel Newell was away. So anyway, they put us all on a helicopter – Jeff Jager, Major Ken Adgie, who was the brigade S3, myself and I think one or two other people. They flew us into Fallujah, we got picked up, met the Marine commander and talked about the initial vague plans. We said we would refine it whenever Lieutenant Colonel Newell came back. They left Jeff and me there, we started integrating with the Marines, and everybody else went home.

MM: How long were you guys there doing the planning?

CL: About two weeks.

MM: Could you talk me through what happened there and what was your opinion of working with the Marines during this timeframe?

CL: They were really great to work with and it was great to experience that. We met the Regimental Combat Team 7 (RCT-7) commander, Colonel Craig Tucker, and he was absolutely fantastic as far as planning and tactical competence and running meetings. Jeff and I would try to coordinate with 2-2. We did have some Internet problems because the Marines and the Army use a different secure internet protocol router network (SIPRNET) and, let's face it, we just weren't the priority for the Marine Division (MARDIV). We worked it as best we could and the intelligence (S2) shop was really willing to integrate with us. Integrating with the fire support assets was pretty easy because the joint training the Marines and the Army go through makes it a lot easier because we all speak the same language, at least as far as cannon artillery goes. As far as air assets, they integrated me as best they could, but the Marines use pilots as their air liaison officers (ALOs) and the Army is just not built for that. We don't have that capability. So I learned the air support plan but there was nobody from the Air Force who could actually integrate with us and, honestly, the Air Force doesn't really know how to integrate. The senior enlisted guys that call for fire with the airplanes are not really that effective because they aren't planning on a battalion and brigade level. If they were there with me, I imagine they could. It's probably not that big of a switch for those guys, but I don't think the brigade had that ability. Well, we never really used air. I think we used it twice – shot off a Predator or a Shadow. It would have been nice to have an ALO there to work through how to integrate with Marine air and the Air Force. Jeff and I sat in on the planning meetings every night. We went to about 30 different briefings and Jeff would try to get an updated plan for what they wanted. Major Reynolds was trying, but when Lieutenant Colonel Newell came back he changed the entire plan. Jeff Jager actually knows more about what units were coming from brigade. The only interaction I had with Colonel Pittard – except for my time as a platoon leader, which was interesting – was asking for two howitzers. I asked Major Reynolds for that and I don't remember him pushing for it, but that's not his job technically; it was more mine. I pushed for it, the colonel said he was going to send down two howitzers, and that was the best thing he could have done.

MM: These two that you're talking about, are these the two Paladins that were actually used for the operation?

CL: Yes.

MM: So you were the one who first mentioned that they would be a good thing to have?

CL: Yes. I don't want to take credit for something that I didn't do, but I'm pretty sure I asked for indirect fire support assets.

MM: Right, because you knew that you guys were going to be the supporting effort and would probably need some of your own artillery because the Marines wouldn't have those assets.

CL: We were actually the last priority. I think it was the Black Jack Brigade that was doing the cordon, and actually I think they had a higher priority than us. We were the lowest of the low and I knew it was going to take over 35 minutes to get any sort of indirect fire support asset. The Marines don't have organic 120s, so the resupply of the 120 would have to come from 3d Brigade and that's tough to do, but they did a great job and pushed out a lot of ammunition for us.

MM: When you and Captain Jager were planning over this two week period, were you in contact every day with the Major Reynolds?

CL: He never talked to me. He just let us do our thing. He's not an artillery expert and, frankly, I don't think the way the infantry trains, say, at the National Training Center (NTC) ever prepares them for how effective artillery really is, so they don't really think in terms of cannon shells. They think in terms of stabbing and shooting and blowing things up with direct fire. They employ mortars but they didn't really understand it at the battalion or brigade level. And I was making it up as I was going along because it was a very unique situation and we were just adapting.

MM: Could you talk me through what happened once the operation is getting ready to begin, right before the breach and you guys are set up in your tactical operations center (TOC)? Can you tell me how the TOC was set up and if there were any communications problems in talking to 2-2 or to the Marines?

CL: I think Captain Krivda set up the TOC and it was amazingly effective, not to mention that 1st ID had amazing communications equipment. We had Predator feed access, which is usually a brigade or division level asset, pushed down to us at the battalion level. We had SIPR and NIPR. At Camp Fallujah, they expanded out so we were literally sleeping and working in a bombed-out old barracks building that hadn't been destroyed like the ammunition bunkers next to it. There was shrapnel and half exploded illumination rounds all over the place. We used this building, set up generators, our TOCs and our '577s, and we worked in a big horseshoe. So, if the closed part of the horseshoe is on the right hand side and the open part is on the left, on the bottom part of the horseshoe was where FA was. I had two computers, two radios and a printer; and then to my right the S3 station had a radio operator, a battle captain and then across from me was the S2 section. The room adjacent was where the personnel (S1) and logistics (S4) sections were working; and that actually worked out very well because they were working casualty evacuation and things like that. That kept our focus on the battle and not on who was getting wounded. We just slept on cots. The nice thing was that the Marines and I integrated our systems together, so we had what we called "combat chat," which was basically Microsoft Chat. I know Captain Krivda was reporting up to RCT-7 and, if he needed, to MARDIV on Microsoft Chat. Captain Natalie Friel at the time was monitoring from brigade to MARDIV intelligence channels and I was monitoring MARDIV fire support nets. So I had the Internet, I had the RCT-7 net, the MARDIV net, and I think there were a couple more. You could pull down from a thousand different channels; it was incredibly effective. I was the only person really talking because Captain Cobb really only had communications with us. He did not have communications with RCT-7 and his Humvee just wasn't equipped for it. There was no way they could talk to him. So that made it really effective although it was really difficult, too, because I didn't have a lot of manpower. It was me and a really great specialist who happened to get hurt on the convoy ride up there. He put his weapon out the window and somebody passed and it hit him in the arm. We had communications with RCT-7 for some air requests, but I was working through the fires net. For counterfire, it was me or my specialist clearing the area where they wanted the counterfire. We had to do ammunition requests initially through them, but then that started going through the S4. The only communications problem we had was only really when we were setting it up. It took about two days and that's just because the systems are a little bit different. The Marines provided us with some commo guys; they came in and fixed everything and it worked really well. We did have some generator issues, which in Iraq are nothing new, but they were pretty critical. From day one to day four, they were fine; and then by day five, they started going out. When they would go down, we could be out of the fight for like six hours.

MM: Because of generator problems?

CL: Yes, because there just was no power. It was a slow time, though. Had it been during the breach, it would have been just brutal. The nice thing about what we were doing was that we were almost organized as a howitzer battery as far as task organization goes. It's something the Army, I think, should do. Having two Paladins attached to a battalion – you don't get mass, but nobody really uses that anymore unless you're fighting the Soviets. Even in a high-intensity conflict, you could still mass if the battalion needed to because the battalion is still tapped into the Advanced Field Artillery Tactical Data Systems (AFATDS). But being direct support from battalion straight to the guns – I don't know if any major or lieutenant colonel FSO is going to be very keen on it because they're out of the battle. But as far as being good for soldiers, it's fantastic as long as the FSOs have planned in advance what the criteria are going to be and how to measure the forward line of troops (FLOT). The nice thing about Fallujah was that it was stationary, completely locked down, and we had a very good idea of where troops were. The Marines were able to communicate no-fire areas to us via the Microsoft Chat. They had places throughout the city, certain areas they didn't want bombed, and they could either ship it to our AFATDS or they could just send it to me and I'd built it in on FalconView. Not only did I have access to the no-fire areas for planning purposes, the guns had it as well, so it was an amazing system. It was probably the only effective thing that AFATDS did over there.

MM: Going back to the planning, do you recall anything the Marines put out about rules of engagement (ROE)?

CL: Yes. When I was working with RCT, this judge advocate general (JAG) there was in communications with MARDIV and I'm assuming the MARDIV guy was in communications with Central Command (CENTCOM). They were able to modify the ROE. I remember him saying that every vehicle that was moving was considered a car bomb. But as far as artillery level planning and air strikes, there were a couple buildings over there that were "protected"; but quite frankly, if we were getting shot at from a mosque or a minaret, it was an enemy structure at that point. It's against the Geneva Conventions to use protected sites for attacks. If you are, it's no longer protected and it was well known that that was occurring down there. People were shooting out of minarets and out of schools, they were holding families hostage. The ROE was very loose.

MM: Who came up with the "shake and bake" mission? Was that something new or something the Marines had done before?

CL: The "shake and bake" has been around since white phosphorous was invented. On a doctrinal level, to destroy a fuel depot you send in 155 VT, which means a high-explosive, variable-time fuse – so it explodes, punctures the fuel containers, and then you send in white phosphorous to destroy it. The initial "shake and bake" that I think the generals had their hands on wasn't a "shake and bake" at all; it was a screening mission for the initial breach. We were shooting low and most people don't screen over cities, but that area needed to be screened legitimately and needed to be screened with heat as well. [inaudible] had thermal but they had night vision, and I remember talking to a Navy SEAL or a Marine recon guy who said they snuck up to clear the berm on the northern part of the city. In pushing forward, they didn't have NVGs and they didn't have black chem lights; and so just as an experiment, they would break an infrared chem light and they started taking direct fire from the rooftops. It was pretty well known that at least some of the insurgents had Russian-made night vision, so the screening was necessary. I also remember that after we got hit at the second ambush area – and I can tell you what it looked like on maps and satellite imagery but I can't tell you what it looked like on the ground. Anyway, [inaudible] wanted to obscure the area because they were taking a tremendous amount of fire. We didn't have any felt-wedge white phosphorous left. The difference is, felt-wedge white phosphorous is airburst and it comes down like party streamers. The only other white phosphorous we had left was ground burst and that explodes like a regular high explosive on the ground. Then it kicks up a bunch of phosphorous to obscure and also sets things on fire so it adds a smoke screen effect. We realized we had a large bunker complex, so initially we were firing – and what I heard on the radio transmission and what they told me was that we were obscuring the second crossing of the linear danger area. Full tactics, [inaudible] in a danger area and conduct a breach, suppress and secure. So we were obscuring it and there just happened to be people in spider holes because the entire city was a gigantic, preplanned, waiting-for-the-invasion maze. And so whenever we pushed through, we simply shot white phosphorous as an obscurant; and then we decided to follow that up with VT in case anybody was firing at us from spider holes. We only fired two white phosphorous missions.

MM: I guess the whole white phosphorous thing becomes a big deal later on and so everybody always asks about it in the 2-2 sector.

CL: What supposedly happened was the Italian media came out with a pre-pared propaganda video, and I watched it when the State Department did an in-quiry. The real problem occurred when the State Department first said that we don't use white phosphorous in battle – but of course we do. So nobody in the State Department had any clue and they didn't ask anybody in the Army who had any clue, so they issued a statement and then people are starting to wonder. It was really, once again, the State Department doing an "awesome" job of running the military show. They just didn't understand. On top of that, I don't know what ex-pert these guys interviewed, but he called it "Whiskey Pete" and nobody calls it that. It's "Willy Pete." I don't know who this guy was, saying we killed civilians. There were no civilians there.

MM: Can you talk me through the good, the bad and the ugly of working with the Marines in your opinion?

CL: Sure. The biggest downside I saw was the availability of Marine air for 2-2 Infantry and for any Army unit, and it's not because the Marines are trying to snuff us out. One of the things I requested, which I don't think the RCT could have supported it – but had we had a Marine ALO attached to our TOC, we could have gotten air in a much faster manner. We had maybe five air missions, with the exception of the two gunships that were floating around at night who our Air Force guys could actually communicate with if we had priority. Not having somebody who was actually tapped into the system, who knows people in the system and how it functions, that made air not an option for us unless it was something big. It was never responsive. It took us a minimum of 30 to 40 minutes to get air as-sets, and we had to come into the system through the fringes. I would request air through fires who turned over their shoulder and talked to the ALO, but he never really talked to me – and I'm low priority and I don't really understand the terms he's using. The Air Force guy on the ground isn't at all tapped into the system; he may have met with the ALO once or twice. It's one thing to actually talk to Marine air; it's another thing to get cleared to request that the air come in. That was my biggest concern. If they really want to increase the availability of air and really make it more combined arms, they're really going to have to push an ALO to bat-talion level, just like they do to all the other battalions. If we didn't have those two howitzers there, we would have never had any indirect fire support except for 120 mortars – which may have to happen, but I don't see why. There's no reason to hold back assets if you have them.

MM: If you would have needed it, could the Marines have fired their towed 155s for you guys?

CL: They did once. They did a sweep in the zone in the southern part of the city after we discovered a large bunker complex, which was like 128 shells over a 500 by 500 meter area, and it worked out okay but I never saw the effects. Captain Cobb said it did. It wasn't exactly the most effective, but it did definitely suppress it. We had a very large varied bunker complex, but the problem is that a 155 penetrates about six to 10 inches in the ground so we would need something heavier. For the most part, Marine artillery is okay and they do a great job for the Marines, but the towed 155 is not as responsive, slower, and not as accurate as a Paladin. It can't be. A Paladin is a self-correcting weapons system, it gauges its muzzle velocity, it knows exactly where it's located. A towed 155 doesn't have the same capabilities and a Paladin clearly is responsive. They're air mobile. As far as the mechanized site, they're not exactly the highest speed. We could request missions for them; the problem was getting clearance of fires. With two attached cannons, our sensor-to-shooter time was maybe 30 seconds. To clear a Marine mission, it would have to go first to me, then to the Marines, the fire support cell for brigade and then, if that got approved – there was actually not a whole lot of organization in the artillery world. Usually you have centralized command and control and here we didn't, because counterfire was run by the Black Jack Brigade. So there were six Paladins next to our two Paladins and we never talked. I don't know who they were. I met them once, asked if we could set up in their area and they let us, but we didn't share ammunition or mission. They did strict counterfire and we did stuff attached to our assets. That was my question: If we have multiple counterfire missions, who gets priority of fire? Who gets priority of counterfire? A lot of the answers I got were, "We don't know." There were a lot of maneuver assets but there was no centralized artillery asset, which worked out well for us. But as far as the Marine artillery organization went, you could tell it was really ancillary; it really wasn't their primary focus.

MM: Is there anything else you feel is very important to get out there to young officers in the FA community in relation to this fight?

CL: The battery computer system (BCS) was a fantastic piece of equipment. Learn how to work your AFATDS. It works well at battalion and higher level, and maybe even at platoon level. All this nice digital fire support equipment they gave us – we didn't have to use any of it. We used nothing but voice. By the time you plug in an electronic mission, you could have already done two. In addition to that, between Microsoft Chat and FalconView, that's all you need to run a battle now.

FalconView is the best tool and I think young lieutenants need to figure out how to use it really effectively – how to set up an area they consider no-fire. That's about it.

MM: Well, that's super and I want to thank you for doing this interview.

Captain Gregory McCrum
28 July 2006

JM: My name is John McCool (JM) and I'm with the Operational Leadership Experiences Project at the Combat Studies Institute, Fort Leavenworth, Kansas. I'm interviewing Captain Gregory McCrum (GM) on his experiences in Operation Iraqi Freedom (OIF) and specifically Operation Phantom Fury in Fallujah, November 2004. Today's date is 28 July 2006 and this is an unclassified interview. Before we begin, Greg, if you feel at any time we're entering classified territory, please couch your response in terms that avoid revealing any classified information. And if classification requirements prevent you from responding, simply say you're not able to answer. For the record, Captain McCrum is currently stationed in the Philippines and we're doing a telephone interview. Could you please start by giving me some background on yourself: where you were born, where you grew up, how you got commissioned, things like that?

GM: I was born in Weymouth, Massachusetts, on 5 February 1971. My father was a Department of Defense contractor so we moved a lot during my formative years growing up in Pennsylvania, Ohio and ultimately ending up in Aiken, South Carolina. I came in the military in January 1990 as a medic with the South Carolina National Guard. I transitioned to be an infantryman and in January 1992 enlisted in the regular Army as a medic with the 82d Airborne Division, serving with Headquarters and Headquarters Company (HHC), 1st Battalion, 504th Parachute Infantry Regiment. I spent four years with the 82d, went through the Special Forces (SF) Qualification Course in 1994 and became a qualified SF medical sergeant in February 1996. I served with Alpha Company, 3d Battalion, 7th Special Forces Group (SFG) until April 2000 when I attended the Inter-service Physician Assistant (PA) Program at Fort Sam Houston, Texas, and was commissioned through Officer Candidate School (OCS) in May 2002. I went to the Medical Officer Basic Course at Fort Sam Houston in July of the same year and reported to HHC, 2d Battalion, 2d Infantry Regiment in Vilseck, Germany, in October 2002 until I left that assignment in August 2005. I'm currently serving as the Group PA for 1st SFG, Fort Lewis, Washington, with my current assignment being deployed overseas as the Joint Special Operations Task Force-Philippines (JSOTF-P) surgeon.

JM: Could you walk me through how you and 2-2 Infantry found your way to Iraq and how you first got alerted to the fact that there might be a joint operation launched in Fallujah?

GM: We received our deployment order for Iraq the day we redeployed from Kosovo, so it was about 24 July 2003 after a nine-month deployment to Kosovo. We had gotten in the night before and I opened up the Stars and Stripes the next day and got the deployment order for going to Iraq about six months later. We deployed to Kuwait on 13 February 2004 and stayed in Kuwait until 6 March 2004 when we did the road march from Camp New York, Kuwait, north through Baghdad and ultimately going to Forward Operating Base (FOB) Normandy outside of Muqdadiyah, Iraq. We arrived there on 7 March and got initial indications for operations in Fallujah around early October 2004. We got the warning order from division that said to plan for contingency operations and being sliced off to the 1st Marine Division (MARDIV) in Fallujah. It had yet to be determined what time we were going to be deploying but we started making preparatory movements towards splitting our operations or moving our operations completely over to Fallujah.

JM: What was your specific duty position at this time?

GM: I was the battalion PA for 2d Battalion, 2d Infantry. That was my assignment and that's where I had stayed for most of my career at that point as a commissioned officer, so I was the battalion medical officer for all intents and purposes. During that planning phase, Lieutenant Christopher Carlson, my Medical Service Corps (MSC) officer, who basically co-headed with me in 2-2 Infantry, did some of the initial planning in anticipation for the operation. We didn't anticipate the operation going off until after Ramadan 2004 so Chris took his mid-tour leave and that's actually when they decided to ramp up operations and send us to Fallujah. I guess at that point I was doing both medical platoon leader and battalion PA duties.

JM: Can you talk about who made up and how large the 2-2 medical team was?

GM: When we actually deployed to Kuwait we had 39 medics, MSC officer, myself and a Professional Officer Filler Information System (PROFIS) doctor from Bamberg, Germany, at the time. We had a grand total of 42 individuals.

JM: Major (Dr.) Lisa DeWitt was not the original 2-2 surgeon, is that correct?

GM: That is correct. Captain Alan Fields was our original PROFIS provider who was sent to us while we were in Germany. He did the initial train up at the Combat Maneuver Training Center (CMTC) in Hohenfels, Germany, and deployed with us to Kuwait. Unfortunately, he had circumstances regarding his medical credentialing that precluded him from having a continued service with 2-2 Infantry.

JM: When did Dr. DeWitt eventually join 2-2?

GM: She joined us on 2 April 2004.

JM: Can you tell me a little bit about her?

GM: How much time do we have? Lisa was an absolutely phenomenal asset to us in 2-2 Infantry. Unfortunately, the previous PROFIS provider had just had four years of medical school, one year of an internship and really had been thrown into a situation that he wasn't adequately prepared for. Really just getting into the world of trauma and not really being experienced with those types of injuries, he wasn't in the best place in terms of his medical career. Bringing Lisa onto our team and into 2-2 was actually a huge value-added benefit for us considering the 14 years of emergency medicine experience she had – and fortunately our personalities complemented each other well. We could work together well and could seemingly read each other's minds when we were running trauma cases. We could be on the same sheet of music and, without really asking for something, could have all the tools and the knowledge base we needed to save as many lives as possible.

JM: You mentioned that you initially thought the operation was going to kick off after Ramadan but obviously that didn't in fact end up happening. How did that impact your planning? Did that have any positive or negative effects on it?

GM: Right. I didn't really take the Ramadan holiday or festivities into account for any phase of our operation or our operational planning.

JM: Could you talk me through the planning phase itself? Did you feel you had adequate supplies and resources?

GM: Fortunately I had an absolutely phenomenal medical platoon to augment what we were doing. FOB Normandy was really in an austere location compared to some of the other locations. We were roughly an hour by ground – 20 or 25 minutes by air evacuation – from any other higher medical assets and our logistics lines were relatively long comparatively around Iraq. Knowing that, we kept a large amount of Class VIII medical stockage right there on hand at FOB Normandy so if we had logistics problems getting things out of Qatar or Balad, we could be self-sustaining for an extended period of time. When we saw the operation upcoming, we knew we had enough stockage up there to run split medical operations: operations forward in Fallujah as well as sustain operations on FOB Normandy with minimal impact as far as Class VIII medical supplies go.

JM: Were there any special preparations you had to go through in getting ready for Operation Phantom Fury?

GM: Not so much as far as training. We did do an initial evaluation and site recon with the US Marine Corps when our advanced party left out of FOB Normandy in October and drove to Camp Fallujah to interface with our Marine counterparts, seeing what assets we could actually draw from on Camp Fallujah. It was during that initial site survey when I finally got to see Camp Fallujah, link up with the Bravo Surgical hospital that was co-located there and see, logistically, how they would best be able to facilitate our resupply or getting us additional supplies or anything we may need. As it turned out, they weren't truly set up to really logistically support anybody but themselves. The Class VIII supply warehouse was located in Camp Taqaddum, which was 30 minutes west of Camp Fallujah. There really weren't any Class VIII warehouses or stockages on Camp Fallujah that were going to be able to sustain our operation that we could draw from. So in the initial planning phase of the operation, we said we would take with us two weeks' worth of supplies in our organic medical equipment sets, or MES chests, as well as an additional five-ton vehicle with approximately two more weeks of supplies enabling us to self-sustaining for a period of about one month. That was probably one of the key things that drove our planning there, so we could be a little bit more self-sustaining during the operation and wouldn't have to rely on long logistical lines from Balad Airfield out to Camp Fallujah. That was about an hour and a half to two hours flight time, and drive time was probably closer to eight or 12 hours, so that was probably one of the key things that went into a lot of our planning: ensuring we had the proper equipment in sufficient quantities for the upcoming operation in Fallujah.

JM: Could you talk generally about your integration with the Marine unit there? Were there any interoperability issues? Did they treat you okay?

GM: Fortunately we all had the one-team, one-fight concept and we got along well with our Marine counterparts. I actually felt bad for a lot of the Marines because they had to procure a lot of their own equipment. They aren't given the same equipment that the Army is. We got along fine, albeit they didn't have a lot of logistical support they could offer us as far as the medical side of the house. I did talk with the 7th Regimental Combat Team (RCT-7) surgeon who was on FOB Baharia and tried to get read in on the overall operational plan for what the Marine contingency was between 1st MARDIV, 7th RCT and 5th RCT. I was told the general concept of medical support was that they were co-locating 7th and 5th RCTs' aid stations north of Fallujah about five or six kilometers up on Main Supply Route Mobile (MSR) that was going to the north. They did not have the formal plan for execution on how they were going to advance the medical support closer into the city as the fight progressed farther into the city, so from their established aid stations, they weren't moving forward and progressing at the speed of the battle. Therefore, their logistical and medical evacuation lines were actually extending as the battle progressed, versus tightening up and getting shorter.

JM: Was there any talk about you treating Marines or were you just going to be treating soldiers from 2-2?

GM: I was prepared to treat any and all forces, both US and coalition alike, that were organic to our task force – in addition to should any other units bring casualties to our aid station. I was fully prepared to go ahead and execute that particular mission, but at no point did that become necessary. At one point we did have some Marine casualties who were in our task force as well as some airmen who had been wounded during the battle, but they were organic to us and we actually didn't take care of casualties from outside our task force. We weren't called on during the mission to execute that.

JM: Could you describe for me the setup and layout of your aid station? Also, what were your capabilities?

GM: We went in quite heavy as far as the medical complement goes for this operation. We had all the supporting companies: Alpha Company, 2-2 Infantry; Alpha Company, 1-63 Armor; the Brigade Reconnaissance Troop (BRT); as well as a large complement of HHC, 2-2 Infantry as a large component of the ground force for that assault. We took our M577 as our main treatment track which would have a complement of nine trauma chests, three sick call chests and two additional surgery sets that would be part of that vehicle, as well as litter stands, litters and all the command and control (C2). We had a redundancy of C2. We put two C2 radios in that track as well as two C2 radios in the M998 C2 vehicle. We took two M113 tracked ambulances, two M997 ambulances that had been up-armored, as well as the M923 five-ton as being part of the overall complement of the aid station. Each company that deployed within the battlespace of the city had an M113 tracked ambulance with it. Therefore, we had an armored vehicle that was forward for evacuation of casualties and we elected to use the tracked ambulances just due to their high maneuverability over rubble as well as their armored capabilities. Once we employed the aid station, we would position the tracked vehicle in line with the C2 vehicle that would be next to that on the right side and the five-ton would be on the other side of the treatment track. As we lowered the ramp, we had a standard operating procedure (SOP) that the chests were numbered, they would come out in a particular order and be set up in a particular order. Everybody knew what equipment was in what chest and it went progressively down the line. The airway chests would be first, followed by circulation and IVs and then surgical supplies and whatnot. The back of the track would be opened up and then there would be two litters on each side of the MES chests that were opened up behind the track. The tracked and wheeled ambulances would be on one side of the MES chest and that was basically the evacuation line. The other side of the chest would be a set of orange cones that would have our immediate, delayed and minimal casualties, and the expectant cone would be moved off a distance out of sight and ear shot away from the aid station. On the evacuation line, there were also urgent priority and routine cones to categorize patients prior to loading into the ambulances as we would progress them back to Bravo Surgical on Camp Fallujah. At night, we would mark the aid station with chem lights on top of one of our antenna masts. We did have a tactical operations center (TOC) extension, which was rolled up on the back of the track for use that enabled us to use white lights for patient care and give us a semi-controlled environment protecting us from dust and wind. We could be out of the elements and use a little bit more white light without feeling we were compromising the mission. Our medical capabilities largely focused on trauma resuscitation and advanced trauma management. We had the ability to perform limited invasive procedures to stabilize patients, including endo-tracheal intubation, surgical airways and chest tubes. A lot of what we do medically in forward aid stations is the initial evaluation and stabilization of casualties so that the patients are able to survive the transport to a higher level of medical care where assets exist to provide surgical intervention and patient hold capabilities.

JM: Was there anything that was particularly unique about your preparations or setup for this mission, something you did but wouldn't normally do?

GM: We broke with traditional doctrine in that we took both providers from the overall task force to Fallujah. That's why we fight better than our enemies: we don't adhere to our own doctrine. Traditionally, as per doctrine, you would have a main aid station established at a particular location and then you would facilitate sending out a forward aid station. We did this numerous times during our year in Iraq, where Lisa DeWitt would be manning the main aid station and I would man the forward aid station for a battalion or company-sized operation. Due to the intensity and the size of this operation, we actually requested a backfill provider from our forward support battalion to come up and provide that support at FOB Normandy. We took both providers with us into the city and that also allowed us, if necessary, to put a provider in the city to be with a particular element. We had that option, albeit we did not employ it during the operation. Another unique point about this operation was that as a heavy mechanized infantry battalion we had a total complement of six M113s within the city. Additionally we also had two wheeled ambulances and they were not a normal addition to the modified table of organization and equipment (MTOE). We actually acquired three of these vehicles while we were in Kuwait and Iraq. It offered us a huge benefit as far as speed of evacuation and movement of assets around the battlefield that we wouldn't traditionally have had.

JM: Can you pick up the story with what happens as the units blow the breach, cross the berm and combat commences? Where are you at this time and what are you seeing?

GM: There were three phases of the operation. We had the previous night – 6 November – where we proceeded to go north out of Camp Fallujah on what was a feint operation to get an overall feeling of what the enemy reaction might be to moving a large force and positioning north and northeast of the city, so we moved out with about 50 percent of what would be our normal execution strength for this operation. I took all my key leaders and Lisa as well. We departed the camp and took the exact same route we ended up executing the mission on. Therefore, drivers and some of the key leaders had an idea of the route they were going to be taking and some of the terrain they would be seeing once they were operational on the ground. During the feint operation, we established the aid station on the possibility we'd have casualties. We were not in the exact position we occupied on D-Day but we did see some of the overall lay of the land. We brought those key leaders back, did the final mission briefs, pre-combat checks (PCCs) and pre-combat inspections (PCIs) for all men and equipment – weapons – let everybody else get some sleep that night and then the next day we went and executed. We took the same route and moved north. It was a little bit more unique in that we ended up doing more of a daylight move in that particular portion of the mission. We ended up occupying our first logistics resupply point (LRP), which was LRP 1. We occupied that battlespace by force and were roughly 1,200 meters away from what was going to be the breach for 2-2 Infantry. We established the aid station, set up the MES chests and monitored radio traffic; and unfortunately we had to move that operation within an hour or an hour and a half of being established due to incoming mortar fire on LRP 1. During that movement north along the MSR, it appeared that the enemy identified our overall position, had some observation on our location, called in 82 millimeter mortars in relative close proximity to us and we incurred one minor casualty. The company commander was Captain Fred Dente, and he and I decided to move the forward logistical element and the aid station to a different location. We jumped about 750 meters away from the initial LRP and reestablished the aid station there where we remained most of the day until about 1930 – right about the time of dusk – after which we jumped back to a location in the vicinity to where we had established for LRP 1, about 1,000 meters away from the breach point. Closer into the elevated berm that was offered by the MSR Mobile to provide us with a little more cover from direct fire as well as direct observation from the enemy. This was LRP 3. I believe it was around 2100 to 2200 when the Army and Marine elements started using 155 millimeter artillery and our own 120 millimeter mortar platoon started engaging targets in the city to soften up the initial breach point on the northern side of the city. Bradleys and M1s that were with us on the eastern side of the berm started moving into their battle positions just north of the berm. The D9 armored bulldozers took mine clearing line charges (MCLCs) – which were the anti-mine devices with C4 attached to rockets – got those into position and then they started about a two-and-a-half to three-hour artillery barrage and smoke screen. That was a significant life-changing event you could say. The sheer power and intensity that goes into that type of conflict is something truly to be awed. I don't think you can go through something like that and really think of the 4th of July the same way again. It just pales in comparison.

JM: I think it was Jane Arraf who was saying she thought the world was coming to an end when all that kicked off.

GM: I would definitely say that it was hell's fury being unleashed. I don't think I would go to the point of saying it was the end of the world, but we were definitely putting some scunion down on the enemy at that particular point. About 2330 or so, they got the order to bring the MCLCs up and put those into position. We had been observing the artillery and preparatory fires from our vehicles, which certainly put a lot of reverberation into your chest. We were pretty close and you could definitely feel a lot of the shockwaves all the way back to where our vehicles were. The order came to button up because they were going to fire the MCLC into the city to open up that breach point, everybody did, and it was a very, very large explosion. I wouldn't call it the equivalent to the mother of all bombs, but it was definitely a significant blast they used in that breach. Once the MCLC went off, elements of 2-2 started to move through the northern breach into the city.

JM: You mentioned you were coming under some indirect fire. What kind of security did you have at the aid station?

GM: At all our LRPs, the medics' duties were to man radios and make sure they were ready for casualties. We gained all our organic security from the logistics support element that was with us, which came from our support platoon as well as our maintenance platoon, so they had the M88s – the tank recovery vehicles – .50 cal machine guns, anti-tank rockets. Everybody had their individual weapons, the support platoon had their crew-served and their squad automatic weapons (SAWs) mounted on their heavy expanded mobility tactical trucks (HEMTTs), and the HHC company commander had his command vehicle with a .50 cal mounted on it.

JM: It's my understanding that the first casualty you guys had was an Iraqi soldier who shot himself in the foot.

GM: Actually he was the second casualty. The first casualty was the gunner for the HHC commander's vehicle. The vehicle took a mortar round about two or three meters in front of the vehicle and he took some shrapnel in his fingers, so we stitched him up at LRP 1 prior to jumping to LRP 2. Once we were at LRP 2, the Iraqis brought over an Iraqi officer – I think a lieutenant – who had a self-inflicted gunshot wound to the foot. We did his initial treatment and the Iraqi Intervention Force (IIF) that was with us as part of the task force had a doctor, an ambulance and a couple medics. They ended up taking that soldier to the hospital.

JM: What was your assessment of the Iraqi soldiers? What kind of interaction did you have with them?

GM: We didn't have a lot initially. Their key leaders were briefed on the con-cept of the operation during the battalion's rock drill and I don't remember seeing them again until we were outside of the city. When we were at LRP 1 they did some initial staging next to us. I think everybody has that sense of nervous feeling or pre-mission jitters, but they seemed motivated and were organized. We actually didn't have a lot of interaction with them at the time.

JM: Was the first major casualty you received Command Sergeant Major Steven Faulkenburg?

GM: Yes.

JM: Could you talk me through what happened when they brought him in?

GM: I believe it was about a few minutes after midnight, I was up on the radio monitoring the command net and the initial call for a casualty came up on the radio. They said they'd received a casualty somewhere in the northern portion of the city just west of the breach and that they'd evacuated him into the medic track and were progressing him back to the aid station. About a minute or two after that, they said he was not conscious. They did give his call sign of being Ramrod 7 – which was Steven's call sign at the time – and about two or three minutes after that they informed us they were performing CPR en route. They arrived at the aid station about seven or eight minutes after we received that initial call saying he was being evacuated out of the city.

JM: Was there anything you guys could do for him?

GM: The track pulled up to the aid station, I jumped into the back of the track and Steven was on a litter on the floor with an ashen appearance. We quickly removed him from the track, brought him into the aid station and up onto the litter stands. The medics started to go to work and do what they were trained to do: taking the clothes off, getting ready to start IVs and getting ready to do endo-tracheal intubation. Lisa was there ready for that, to receive the casualty. When we took his helmet off, we saw he had sustained a gunshot wound above his left eye with exposed brain matter and tissue and there was no respiratory effort. We hooked him up to the EKG and he didn't have any cardiac activity or signs of life. Unfortunately, he wasn't a patient we could save.

JM: Was that a pretty standard SOP? You would meet the casualties initially and then take them back to Lisa?

GM: Right. We had established that I was doing most of the C2 as well as the provider portion of this mission, and I would receive the radio call and find out when and how many casualties were coming. I'd meet the vehicle with the casualties in it and do the initial triage there at the triage area; and depending on how many casualties, I would either come over with the casualty or continue to triage. If we had multiple casualties then Lisa would be working one and I'd be working the other. If we had one casualty then we'd both be working that particular individual jointly.

JM: Are you guys in full body armor at this time?

GM: This particular portion we were. They had just blown the breach and we were in the full kit.

JM: Can you tell me a little bit about the 17 or so IIF soldiers that were wounded?

GM: This was the next morning about 0700 – and this is a guesstimate because I can't tell you how much sleep I did get. I can, however, tell you how much I didn't get. Anyway, it was about 0700 and I was still up on the radio. I got the initial call that one of the individuals from Alpha Company had taken some shrapnel to the groin and was on his way back into the aid station. We received him at the aid station and he had some shrapnel wounds to the genitalia and the upper thighs. We were in the process of treating him when the IIF drove up with this large truck with an open back and proceeded to drop off at least 14 casualties on our doorstep without any advance notice. We dove into that, but we didn't have that many medics with us at the time. We had four medics who came with the aid station and then each ambulance had a driver and a medic with it, so we had about 14 of us at the time to treat these casualties. I was doing the initial triage and assessment. The medics were on the radio, doing treatment and trying to get an overall grasp of the situation. That was a lot of patients to drop on our doorstep at any one given time, but it went extremely well. There were no Iraqi casualties that were in a great chance of dying; these were individuals who would have survived regardless of our care. The emotionally significant incident, however, in the process of treating all these individuals and getting them categorized so we can evacuate them out occurred about 30 minutes into the treatment: that's when we started taking mortar and rocket fire into our location. We identified that it was coming from the east of our location, from these granaries that were about 25 to 30 kilometers away. We were taking large 107 and 122 rockets and mortar fire, which tends to be an emotionally significant event.

JM: You had to shield the patients yourselves, right, because obviously you had to take their armor off?

GM: Right. I think at a certain point we might have had our Kevlar and body armor off. We were close to the end of treating all these patients, categorizing them and figuring out how we were going to evacuate them and what their ultimate disposition was. Not one of the brightest moves I've ever made in my day, but I was standing on the ramp of the treatment track on the radio, with the battalion net in one ear and Bravo Surgical in the other ear. I'm informing Bravo Surgical what I have coming when I started to hear the first rocket come in. It just sounds like a freight train and the louder it gets the closer it is, so it was really a disconcerting thought. The medics started to get that uneasy feeling and were ready to start taking cover. I was standing on the back of the track, I take the hand mike out of my mouth for a second and yell for them to cover their patients, and it was one of those really cool things to see. All that training that was ingrained in them over the years they were doing medicine, they immediately stopped whatever they were doing and dove on all their patients to keep them from being further injured, which I thought was huge and I couldn't help but smile. In retrospect, as I'm standing on the back of the track yelling instructions in the middle of mortar and rocket fire, it probably wasn't the brightest move in the world. I guess hindsight is 20/20.

JM: Another US casualty you guys had was Staff Sergeant Todd Cornell, is that correct?

GM: While we were receiving mortar and rocket fire another vehicle drove up; and during a brief lull of getting rocketed and mortared, we were trying to package and load these patients up as fast as possible to get them into all the am-bulances and evacuated back to Camp Fallujah. We ended up receiving four more IIF patients there at our location as well as three KIAs that had occurred in the city, two of which were Iraqis and one was Staff Sergeant Cornell. We received those patients the exact same time we were packaging up the other patients, so we put those additional casualties into the two ambulances and took them back to Camp Fallujah. We were prepping the aid station to be jumped because we wanted to get out of our location because, obviously, it had been fixed by mortar and rocket fire. We took the two Iraqi angels we had and Staff Sergeant Cornell down with us to the next LRP and ended up jumping the aid station. In fact, I think that was the fastest we'd ever broken it down and gotten rolling: it took us about four or five minutes. We took the KIAs with us to what would become known as LRP 4, which was located at the cloverleaf.

JM: I wanted to ask you a couple things about Alpha Company. They obvious-ly lost their executive officer (XO), Lieutenant Ed Iwan, and then their company commander, Captain Sean Sims, shortly thereafter. Can you tell me a little about that and whether you had any visibility over Alpha Company in general after they suffered these tremendous losses?

GM: I'll tell you, that was a bad day. That was probably one of the truly bad days that really breaks your heart. It started out early in the morning as a relatively clear day and I think right about 0700 it was like somebody hit an alarm switch and all hell broke loose. It seemed like every weapon that could be fired in the city was being fired, which is when Ed got hit. The initial call that came back said he had been hit and they were driving him back to the aid station. Staff Sergeant Albert Harris was my senior medic for Alpha Company for that particular phase of the operation and he was bringing him back. He said Ed was in pretty bad shape. We received him into the aid station, did his initial triage and put him on the litter stand to do the resuscitation. We took off his body armor and his clothes and tried to get the initial IVs and everything on board. Lisa was doing the airway and I was doing the chest and abdomen and some of the other injuries he had incurred. Unfortunately when we took his body armor and his desert camouflage uniform (DCU) top off, he had large gaping pelvis and inter-abdominal injuries that we were trying to address. It was almost a complete transection of the thorax. During the initial phase of treating him, we found a rocket-propelled grenade (RPG) tail-fin that was still lodged within Ed. We called explosive ordnance disposal (EOD) over, which was located close to our position, just to determine whether or not the munition was still live. We were a little bit concerned because the insurgents don't always pull all the pins or truly prepare munitions for detonation, so therefore it might still be a live munition and might put our aid station and crews at increased risk. Fortunately, EOD was able to determine it was just the residual tailfin and we were able to evacuate him with it still in place. It was not causing any further abdominal injury. Lisa went back to Camp Fallujah during that particular evacuation leaving me in the city and she came back about an hour and a half or so later. I would definitely say his death hurt morale. Ed and I had been lieutenants together and I remember the day Ed got to the battalion when we were in Kosovo. Ed had had almost as many years in service as I did – being prior service – and seeing this really hurts morale a bit. The same thing when Sean was hit the next day. What do you say when you know somebody's wife and kids? It takes an emotional toll, and you don't get to process that information while you're in a battlespace. You just have to lock it away, throw it somewhere else and think about it later when you get back out. At the same time Ed was hit and we were evacuating him back, Sergeant James Matteson was killed. Sergeant First Class Daniel Bumbaugh was hit, Specialist Byung Yang who was one of our medics was hit, as well as one other individual from the scout platoon. The same RPG that killed Sergeant Matteson wounded all the other individuals who were in that vehicle. The next thing I know, we ended up getting all the soldiers from that vehicle at my position while Lisa was back at Camp Fallujah. I looked right, looked left, asked where Specialist Yang was and they all said he was still in the city and that he was injured. I was like, "Well, why is he still in the city?" He wasn't willing to leave his platoon without a medic for any phase of the operation even though he had been wounded in the hand. He treated these individuals, evacuated them to me and he wasn't leaving the city until he had a medic to replace him. So I looked to one of my medics, Specialist Moore, and told him to get on the next vehicle going into the city, replace him and get him back out – and that's exactly what he did. We ended up incurring numerous casualties that particular morning. You just don't have time to process the injuries and the deaths and those types of things. You have to just say "Okay, roger" and move on. Certainly the loss of friends and key leaders had an emotional impact on both Alpha Company and across the battalion. Everybody deals with these losses in their own unique way and uses different coping mechanisms in dealing with grief.

JM: You said Lisa went back to Camp Fallujah. This was when she accompanied Lieutenant Iwan's body?

GM: Well, don't confuse this. This wasn't Ed's body; this was Ed. He was still alive. We stabilized him to the best of our ability at the aid station. He had been intubated, we put the paralytics on board and he was still alive. He had IVs on board and we were trying to bring his blood pressure up. We had treated all his abdominal wounds and stopped all his major bleeding. The pieces of Ed might not have all been there but, in my mind, he was still alive when we got him to Camp Fallujah. He did make it to the operating room but unfortunately didn't survive surgery on the table. But up to that point he was still alive.

JM: This whole issue of civilians in the city – did you guys ever see any of those or other non-combatants?

GM: I actually didn't see any of what I would consider non-combatants in the city. I didn't see any or hear of any. There was a particular phase of the operation – I think it was the first night we moved into LRP 4 where the task force had collected up about 20 or 22 individuals within the city. These were all military-age males who had been found who didn't have weapons with them at the time and they came back and were being interviewed by the interrogators and intelligence people to find out what their overall role was. I did the initial medical evaluation because they all had bizarre injuries which weren't normally incurred in combat: more like from being locked up in a room or being beaten with sticks and wires and other forms of abuse. I didn't find out what their overall disposition was. I was more inclined to think they were probably individuals who, at one point or another, had taken up arms with the insurgency and after getting hit with artillery barrages or coming up against our assault into the city, they decided it wasn't something they wanted to be doing and left. We did have those individuals and they were treated well within their rights as individuals, but I didn't see any women or children. We did have six insurgents come through the aid station for care of different gunshot and shrapnel wounds. We did have contingency plans for the treatment and evacuation of civilians off the battlefield. We planned on utilizing the Jordanian hospital located approximately four kilometers east of Fallujah to receive patients; however we didn't have any civilians in our sector.

JM: From your perspective as the PA, can you give an overall assessment of the medical support provided and the operation in general?

GM: As far as medical support from 1st MARDIV, I didn't receive much. The level of support I received was from Bravo Surgical who received all our combat casualties and they were treated well. There could have been better patient follow-up or care there, but I understand they were a busy unit trying to return as many soldiers and Marines to the fight as possible. They were a great value-added benefit to the treatment of our casualties and I'm truly grateful for that. As far as what, if any, medical or logistical support I got from 1st MARDIV – we were really on our own. We weren't really brought into the overall plan or offered any medical evacuation (MEDEVAC) assets. They didn't bring any air assets devoted solely to MEDEVAC and our location and proximity to the city really precluded them from being willing to give us any type of air evac. When we were set up at LRP 4, we were 400 meters away from the city and they weren't willing to commit any aircraft for MEDEVAC. Fortunately, though, our evacuation lines were relatively short, averaging probably 15 minutes per run. What medical support I had I brought with me, with the exception of Bravo Surgical.

JM: When you say 15 minutes, you're talking by ground?

GM: That's correct.

JM: You did not have any air evac capabilities at all?

GM: That's true. I wasn't authorized the use of air.

JM: Were there any major lessons learned you have from this operation that you think you'll carry forward with you in your military career?

GM: I think I use them every day. I think there were quite a few. Logistically how I plan for particular operations – especially the more sustained combat operations and how I posture myself logistically probably have a lot to do with it, being a little bit more self-sustainable. I have nothing but high praise for the medics and individuals I had in the task force for being as highly trained as they were. I'm a little bit biased because I did all their training, but I had nine months in Kosovo working seven days a week during that deployment where you could see the smoke on the horizon and hear the war drums beating, so I had a captive training audience for nine months and medical training is not usually an important thing in the infantry world. But because I had this captive audience for nine months, we utilized that time to train medics for war. We trained mass casualty situations, evacuation drills, litter carries, doing trauma patients, going through trauma drills – and that paid me back in spades 100 times over during my time in Iraq. When we redeployed from Kosovo and got to Germany, they told us we were going to Iraq in six months – and medical training takes an immediate back seat because gunnery and everything else becomes a big priority for the infantry. But my medics were already trained at that point. We went through a brief period where we did some crew drills and night driving. We set up and took down the aid station repeatedly, doing sequential jumps, but our medical training at that phase was complete; and by the time we did the CMTC rotation in Hohenfels, they were already running like a well-oiled machine that made our rotation there go very easily. Then that just perpetuated the

122

whole time we were in Iraq. They only got better with time as they got exposed to more combat injuries and trauma patients. They only got better and they truly did amazing things while they were in Iraq. I took a lot of med planning things with me. I'm not at liberty to discuss some of the operations we're doing here in the Philippines, but I use my logistical med planning on a daily basis and a lot of those tactics, techniques and procedures (TTPs) I use here have been refined. I think you have to learn from some of your mistakes, learn from some of your successes, take away what works and scrap what doesn't and move on. I learned quite a bit there and I think a lot of my medics did as well.

JM: What were some of the challenges unique to this being an urban operation?

GM: There are probably a hundred different things. With urban combat, you're looking 360 degrees the whole time, and not just on ground level but also up in the structures above you. It's a three-dimensional fight that continually moves. It's a very dynamic and fluid environment. There were so many different components to that particular battle – between indirect and direct fire – that I almost don't know where to begin to answer that question. The logistical portion was certainly difficult. We were thinking about committing an armored asset into the city, not wanting to commit a wheeled ambulance into the city just due to the amount of shrapnel and rubble in the streets, not being able to get out through certain evac routes because we couldn't negotiate the rubble or tires being an issue – being flattened by pieces of shrapnel or something else. We just took a lot of things into consideration for that operation, came up with a plan and, fortunately, I think it was well executed. We didn't lose any medics or medical vehicles within that operation and we did everything within our power to treat every one of those individuals that we had there in Fallujah. The overall success of the patients we ended up treating: we unfortunately incurred the five casualties with Staff Sergeant Cornell who were KIA and then 74 other individuals above that who had been wounded but made it back. Yet while our overall casualty numbers comparatively were low, you still hate to lose good friends in combat.

JM: We've mentioned a number of individuals but are there any others we haven't mentioned that you think deserve special recognition for their service in this operation?

GM: I think every medic within Task Force 2-2 Infantry. I will always and forever tout the individuals I took with me to Fallujah, but I'm equally grateful to those I did not take with me who ended up staying back on FOB Normandy and ended up taking the fight to the enemy back in Muqdadiyah. It was the exact same job doing the exact same mission just in a different location, and that job was every bit as important for the rest of the task force that didn't deploy and still continued operations back in our own sector. I can't speak highly enough of all the individuals I had in that task force. I had some of the finest Americans I've ever known as far as the medics who were with me. I will truly forever be grateful to my driver and medic, Specialist Luke Millikin, for keeping me alive more than once. Specialist Byung Yang, Lisa DeWitt – and she didn't have to do that. I almost felt like I had to cajole her and every 90 days or so I would say, "You want to stay longer, right?" I think she was just playing me along because she had planned on staying all along; she would just make me beg every so often.

JM: Once she got her motorcycle her mind was made up, right?

GM: That was a pretty happy day. When she got her motorcycle, she committed. She was there for the long haul. Other individuals who were there: Lieutenant Chris Carlson, Staff Sergeant Esteban Alvarado, Staff Sergeant Albert Harris, Sergeant Wes Smith – I could list every single individual I had in that task force who were just outstanding people in every sense of the word. They did absolutely amazing things.

JM: Are there any other issues we didn't bring up about this particular operation that you'd like to talk about or other points you'd like to make?

GM: None I can think of off the top of my head. You have a copy of the paper I wrote after the operation, correct?

JM: Yes, I do.

GM: I think individuals could probably draw a lot of information from that paper as well. I can't think of anything I could add to this interview.

JM: Are there any assessments you might have of the battalion staff – Lieutenant Colonel Pete Newell or any of his guys up there?

GM: Honestly I think the battalion staff was certainly influenced by Lieutenant Colonel Newell and they were very competent and led us to a successful operation. I think I will actually give credit as well to Lieutenant Colonel Ken Adgie who was the battalion operations officer (S3) for an extended period of time – 2002 through 2003 – and who also served as the battalion XO. He had a bigger influence in forming the battalion staff and his influence had a big impact on this task force being as successful as it was. Not to take anything away from Lieutenant Colonel Newell or Major John Reynolds, but I think Ken Adgie had a significant impact in the overall mentoring of the 2-2 staff officers that stayed with the task force and in the actual methodical process of how they thought and successfully executed combat operations.

JM: Okay, thank you very much for your time today and for your service as well. It's greatly appreciated.

Captain Edward Twaddell III
28 February 2006

MM: My name is Matt Mathews (MM) and I'm an historian with the Combat Studies Institute, Fort Leavenworth, Kansas. I'm telephonically interviewing Captain Edward Twaddell III (ET). Today's date is 28 February 2006. This is an unclassified interview. Before we begin, I'd like to say if you feel, at any time, we are entering classified territory, please couch your response in terms that avoid revealing any classified information or simply say you're not able to answer. I'd like to start out with what your background militarily is and something about where you went to school, how you were commissioned, that sort of thing.

ET: I was commissioned out of the United States Military Academy, Class of '97, in May of '97. My first assignment was the 1st Battalion, 502d Infantry Regiment at Fort Campbell, with the 101st Airborne Division. I deployed with them to the Multi-National Force and Observers mission in the Sinai Peninsula in Egypt for six months. I went to the Captains Career Course. I went on to Fort Hood where I served in the brigade operations (S3) shop, 3d Brigade, 1st Cavalry Division, then moved down to the S3 shop in 2d Battalion, 7th Cavalry Regiment (2-7 CAV), where I served as the assistant S3 until I took over command of Alpha Company, 2-7 CAV, on the 6th of November of 2003.

MM: For the record, could you give me your full name?

ET: Edward Samuel Twaddell III.

MM: Okay, excellent. Now could you briefly describe how Alpha Company 2-7, and Task Force 2-7 in general, were committed to Fallujah – when you first found out about the mission, what you did to prepare for it?

ET: Throughout our tour in Iraq, 2-7 was cross-attached to the 39th Enhanced Separate Brigade (ESB), Arkansas National Guard. We were posted at Taji, approximately 25 miles north of Baghdad. In August of '04, I guess we were filling a rotation as the theater response force or the theater quick reaction force (QRF), or something to that effect. The whole issue with Moqtada al-Sadr began to develop and 2-7 was cross-attached then, I think, to the 11th Marine Expeditionary Unit (MEU), who had a responsibility for An Najaf. So we loaded all of our vehicles on heavy equipment transporters (HETs) and convoyed to An Najaf, not far from the 11th MEU. We gained a good reputation there with the Marines and – as I've been told, although I don't know for sure – when it looked like Operation Phantom Fury was going to kick off into a much more a direct conflict, as opposed to the low-level type of fighting that had been going on, the Marines asked for 2-7 by name. So I think there was some bit of reputation that went on with that. Taji and the area surrounding Taji was an economy of force mission for the 1st Cavalry Division.

Therefore, when the theater commander called for movement of a battalion, it was easier to pull 2-7 out of that area rather than, say, a committed battalion in central Baghdad and move them across the theater to whatever contingency operation had arisen. Is that what you're looking for?

MM: Yes, that's perfect. When you announced this to your men, how did they respond? Were they pretty enthusiastic about this mission?

ET: Yeah, they were. We were very proud that we had done as well as we had in Najaf in August. Alpha Company specifically had had two new lieutenants come into the company, joining us literally as we pulled out of Najaf, and they met us at the forward operating base (FOB) where we were hanging our hat until we re-deployed to Taji. So, they were kind of new guys in the mix and wanted to prove themselves.

MM: Were these the 1st and 2d Platoon leaders? And if you recall their names, could state those for me please?

ET: It was 1st and 2d Platoon. 1st Platoon was led by First Lieutenant, now First Lieutenant (promotable), Daniel Kilgore, and 2d platoon was led by now First Lieutenant (promotable) Michael Duran.

MM: And do you recall the name of the platoon leader for 3d Platoon, Charlie 3-8?

ET: First Lieutenant Matt Wojcik.

MM: Okay, great. Could you just talk me through, from day one, the entire scope of the operation for Phantom Fury, from when you guys did the breach until you withdrew from Fallujah?

ET: Are you talking from notification of mission –?

MM: Yeah, why don't we start there and just take it right up to November 8th. Just talk me through the whole mission and what you recall, what went right, what went wrong. I'm also trying to specifically come up with some ideas on your joint operations, on what you thought went well with the Marines, what you thought didn't go well. A lot of people I've been interviewing seem to be shocked that the Marines didn't have hardly any equipment, I guess is how most of them put it. So I was just interested in your observations on that, too.

ET: I've got a journal that I kept here, so I'm kind of flipping through trying to refresh my memory. Okay, we arrived at Camp Fallujah on the 3d of November. We left Taji at about 0430 on the 3d of November and then we drove. We didn't HET our vehicles to Fallujah; we just drove the tracks all the way there.

MM: So you took the Bradleys all the way there. How many kilometers was that?

ET: I don't recall off the top of my head.

MM: Do you have an approximate figure?

ET: I know we drove south from Taji along the main supply route (MSR) into Baghdad and then moved west into Al Anbar Province along Route Huskies.

MM: Did you experience any improvised explosive devices (IEDs) along the way?

ET: We did have an IED detonate behind us, between my serial and the last serial, but other than that we didn't have any issues.

MM: Now speaking of the serial, you had your company. Was Charlie Company 2-7 with you?

ET: Captain Pete Glass had serial one; he was the Charlie Company commander with 3d Battalion, 8th Cavalry Regiment (3-8). Serial two was Captain Jake Brown, Bravo Company, 215th Forward Support Battalion. I had serial three. I guess that leaves Captain Chris Brooke with Charlie 2-7 in serial four, but I might be mistaken on the order of march.

MM: Can you briefly take me through your arrival at what I guess Marines were calling Camp Fallujah, and how you linked in with the Marines and the prior planning for the operation?

ET: One of the lessons that came out of Najaf was the requirement for good tie-in once the warning orders had been given at that battalion, brigade, regimental level. Our reception to Camp Fallujah and our tie-in with the Marines seemed to go a lot smoother than it had in Najaf. So my assumption is that folks took the lessons learned from Najaf and applied them and did a lot of good cross-talk before we even left Taji to link in with the Marines. We had the quartering party already at Camp Fallujah that had established motor pool and established where our billets were going to be. When we arrived, it seemed to be pretty quick. We pulled right in, dropped the ramps, and said, "Okay, Alpha Company, here's your portion of the motor pool; do your maintenance and get the men settled in."

MM: Did you guys do any chalk walks or any planning with the Marines?

ET: Not at my level. I'm sure Major Tim Karcher, who was the battalion S3, Lieutenant Colonel Jim Rainey, and probably the battalion executive officer (XO), Major Scott Jackson, did.

MM: I'm going to be interviewing Major Karcher tomorrow, so that'll be super. Okay, can you talk me through, then, the plan? Let's say November 8th, you guys do the breach, and just take it from there.

ET: We actually got all lined up on the 7th. We left our assembly area and moved into the task force support area (TFSA) which served as our assault position, on the 7th. That was on the north side of the city. The time for crossing the line of departure (LD) was set for 0300 on the 8th.

MM: Was Task Force 2-7 the first to breach or was it simultaneous with the Marines?

ET: The Marines actually set the breach and were supposed open a lane, and then 2-7 was supposed to be the initial battalion through the breach and into the city.

MM: Did the Marines use the mine clearing line charge (MCLC) for this breach?

ET: We were pretty close and, as you're well aware, MCLCs will make a big boom. I don't recall hearing it detonate. I'm not saying they didn't use it. I did not hear a MCLC go off, but then again, maybe it went off and I wasn't paying attention or maybe I confused it with an aircraft strike or something like that.

MM: Was it 3d Battalion, 1st Marine Regiment (3-1) that did the breach that your company went through?

ET: Let me see here –

MM: I can find that out from Karcher. But after they blow the breach, it was Charlie 3-8 and then Alpha 2-7 and Charlie 2-7. Is that –?

ET: Yes. We moved south through the breach to a road that ran east-west along the north side of the city. Charlie 3-8 was first in the order of movement; they had the easternmost position. Our final assault position on that road from east to west was going to look like Charlie 3-8, Alpha 2-7 and then Charlie 2-7.

MM: In the initial phase of this operation, were you basically driving for Phase Line Fran, which would be Highway 10? Or just talk me through what you thought the scheme of maneuver was.

ET: I want to say it was Phase Line Fran, but we had to give up all our graphics when we came back, so –

MM: And that's what I'm dealing with right now. I really don't have solid graphics on 2-7. I'm hoping to get those. Now I do have solid overlays with phase lines from 2d Battalion, 2d Infantry Regiment (2-2), and I'm just assuming that they just extend west. I'm assuming everybody pretty much was on same sheet of music here.

ET: Yeah, 2-2 was immediately to our east; we were to their west. I believe you're right. I think we had either 3-1 or 1-3 Marines. I remember the regimental designation as being 3d Marine Regiment, 5th Regimental Combat Team (RCT), and I want to say 7th RCT was in there somewhere, but I'm not sure where precisely they were.

128

MM: Why don't you just talk me through what you remember of the fight once you got into the city, what went right and what went wrong.

ET: Once we came through the breach and got lined up on that east-west running road on the north side of the city, Alpha Company had the mission of being the point of the wedge, so to speak, as the task force pushed south. Once we seized our initial objective, which was the Jolan Park, or Objective Pennsylvania, we were to pretty much serve as an anchor and allow Charlie 3-8 (to our east) to march further south, begin to pivot to the east, and then end up directly south of us. So, we were to serve as a pivot point; and once Alpha 2-7 and Charlie 3-8 were set, 3-1 Marines was supposed to follow us through the breach. We were supposed to clear from north to south. Because the Marines weren't a mechanized force, our purpose was to allow them to move unhindered down south and then pass them forward through our lines to continue to press the enemy to the east. So, to recap, we were to seize Objective Pennsylvania. Once we had Objective Pennsylvania, we were to pass 3-1 Marines through us and allow them to continue south of us and then they were going to move off. Similar to Charlie 3-8, they were to swing to the east and continue a detailed clearance of their objective.

MM: So, did the Marines stay right on your tail for most of this operation? Or, because they had to clear all the buildings, were they kind of lagging behind?

ET: They were definitely lagging behind. Because they were a light force, I do not think that their planners understood how quickly 2-7 CAV was able to move as a mechanized force. A mechanized force has the ability to clear, but not in the detail that a dismounted light force does. So, when we pushed through the breach, I got the impression that the Marines expected we would be fighting for a good three or four hours. We encountered very light resistance throughout the night. Just a couple folks would come out and try to fire off a rocket-propelled grenade (RPG) or an AK-47 or something like that.

MM: Did your company take any casualties that first night?

ET: That first night, no. As light started to come up on the morning of the 8th, we started taking a lot of mortar rounds. I don't know whether to say the enemy was not willing to fight at night, through lack of discipline, or they realized that we had technology that they couldn't beat, in the form of our night vision and thermal capabilities. Maybe their thought was: "Well, let's wait. Let's take that advantage away from the Americans and fight during the day when we're on slightly better footing."

MM: Was the mortar fire you were receiving accurate at all?

ET: There was a big water tower on Objective Pennsylvania that the enemy was able to use as a reference point off of which they could adjust fire, and I'm sure they had observers that were able to walk rounds in once we were on the objective.

MM: In the northern part of the city there, were you given any sort of decent intelligence on who you might expect to find? Were these former Fallujah Brigade members or insurgents or foreign fighters? What did you think you were going to encounter?

ET: The intelligence we received suggested that the majority of fighters in Fallujah were former military, although there was an element of foreign fighters there. But there seemed to be a split between the foreign fighters and the locals, so to speak, of the Fallujah area. There was a question, and I don't think it was ever answered, as to the motivation of the enemy. The locals from the city, according to one theory, were just like, "Look, just get out of our city and go home, go away," whereas the foreign fighters were much more into killing Americans, the jihad, that kind of thing. Whether that was ever confirmed, I don't know. That was something that was floated out there as a theory, but again, as a company commander, I wasn't really concerned as to why they were shooting at my guys. My concern was: seize my objective, kill the enemy and get where I need to go.

MM: Did the intel help at all? 2-2 sent me a couple slides where they thought people were at, but someone told me that that basically went out the window as soon as they came in the city. Intel wasn't really able to place these guys for certain anywhere, was it?

ET: We templated a very dispersed threat rather than concentrations. We assumed that the enemy would rely heavily on snipers, forward observers, rocket attacks and direct fire attacks, and would not try to go toe-to-toe with us. Instead, they'd allow us to pass, fire us up from behind with RPGs and anti-tank weapons, use IEDs, vehicle-borne improvised explosive devices (VBIEDs) – things he had that could counter the protection that our armor provided us. That being said, there were several folks that tried to go stand out in the middle of the street with an AK-47 and face down a Bradley. It ended badly for them.

MM: Now I've got here that Alpha 2-7, you reached Objective Pennsylvania. Alpha 2-7 passes 3-1 Marines. On the 9th at 1800 hours we've got shaping operations. We've got Charlie 3-8 arrives on Objective Virginia. Anything you can recall up until that point?

ET: We had very light contact throughout the night, until such time as the light started coming up. As we cleared through and secured Objective Pennsylvania, we found a large cache of some rockets, mortar shells, C-4, a large VBIED, which we consolidated. Eventually we were tasked to leave Pennsylvania and we blew all that when we left. But we had passed 3-1 Marines through us by the time that occurred.

130

MM: I have Alpha 2-7 arrives on Objective Kentucky, Ohio. Does that make any sense? And I've got the date on that as the 10th, 0900 hours.

ET: Yes. The night of the 9th, I received a fragmentary order (FRAGO) to move back to the task force support area on the morning of the 10th to receive another mission. So we pulled out on the 10th, received the mission, pulled off of Pennsylvania on the 10th and received orders to conduct reconnaissance of Objectives Kentucky and Ohio, which are the two bridges that cross the Euphrates River on the western side of the old city. We conducted recons of Kentucky in the south without incident; no demolitions that we could see. I learned later that, evidently, IEDs had been rigged by digging them into the asphalt and either melting tires or putting asphalt on top of them. So I had explicit instructions not to go onto the bridges but to conduct a visual reconnaissance of the bridges. When we conducted that, we didn't see anything. But again, without going up onto the bridges, we just didn't know. I learned later, when they opened those things up, that, yes, in fact, they did find several IEDs buried in the bridge itself.

MM: So you basically secured Objectives Kentucky and Ohio and then, at 2100 hours that night, according to my sheet, you get a change of mission. Is that the FRAGO that sent you further south into the city?

ET: Yeah, we reconned Kentucky and moved north along Route Kevin to Ohio and conducted reconnaissance there. We came nose-to-nose with a Marine company; they were fighting from east to west and we were coming right up into their area from the south. So we did our recon as quickly as we could and got out of their hair, and then we pulled back south to Kentucky and set up a perimeter that we held until morning. And the following morning, I guess that'd be the 11th, I got instructed to pull back again to the task force support area. We spent the day refitting in preparation for another mission, which would become the movement to contact that Charlie 3-8 led. That would be the night of the 11th.

MM: Okay. I have here on one of my notes that on the 12th at 0900 there was heavy contact, and that appears to be Charlie 2-7 and Alpha 2-7. Could you explain what happened then?

ET: Yeah, I'll just read it right out of my diary here: "After spending the day planning, we moved out with Cougar (i.e., Charlie 3-8) in front of us on the night of the 11th. The mission was to continue pressing the enemy south of Phase Line Jenna. Cougar was to work one phase line ahead of us. We were to secure Route Henry south so that they, Cougar, didn't get cut off. We moved through the night, bounding one phase line ahead at a time with minimal contact. We were all incredibly tired and staying alert was difficult. As dawn broke on the morning of the 12th, we, Alpha 2-7, found ourselves arrayed from Phase Line Donna to Phase Line Isabel with about a section of Bradleys or tanks on each major intersection. Again, as

131

the sun came up, the enemy came out to fight. We began taking intense mortar and RPG fire. I received orders from battalion to consolidate south of Phase Line Isabel in order to get out of the way of an air strike that was coming in. As our forces became more concentrated – Cougar was working down south, Phase Line Jenna – the mortar fire intensified. Ghost 5, Major Scott Jackson, instructed me to take charge of the Cougar element – Captain Glass was refueling/rearming with half of his force at the task force support area – until Cougar 6, Captain Glass, returned to the battlefield." So at that time I found myself in command of my company plus half of Charlie 3-8.

MM: Was Captain Glass wounded at that time?

ET: No.

MM: Now, can you just basically continue the story from there? I guess this was 0900 hours on the 12th.

ET: I made the decision right there to maneuver this company-plus on the enemy rather than sit there and take mortar fire. Move on the enemy while we were waiting on the air strike, rather than sit stationary and eat mortars for the next unknown period of time.

MM: Were the mortars causing any casualties at this time?

ET: No, they weren't, but it was a matter of time before we had a direct hit on a track. I figured it was just bad for morale to sit there buttoned up and waiting for a direct hit. So Ghost 5, Major Jackson, said, "Hey, you're the man. Go."

MM: Now, Major Jackson, what was his position at this time?

ET: He was the battalion XO. I believe he's the deputy brigade commander for 3d Brigade now.

MM: You have this heavy contact and you move forward. Does the air strike eventually come in?

ET: I believe it did. Let me find my place here: "I decided to extend along Phase Line Isabel to Route Isaac and attack south to Jenna." So I had everybody all curled up on Route Henry. Rather than sit there all bunched up like that, my intent was to extend to the west and attack south to Phase Line Jenna. I figured this would keep us moving, make it more difficult for the enemy to call mortars on us while, at the same time, putting pressure on the enemy, allowing us to kill him with direct fire. 2d Platoon was on the west, 3d Platoon, Charlie 3-8 was in the middle, 1st Platoon in the east. Between 1st Platoon and Route Henry, Lieutenant Mike Throckmorton, who was the XO for Charlie 3-8, which set up what was available from Charlie 3-8, do the same thing as Alpha 2-7. So, from west to east as we pushed out from Isabel to Isaac, you had the 2d Platoon, Alpha 2-7, 3d Platoon,

Charlie 3-8, 1st Platoon, Alpha 2-7, and then whatever elements of Charlie 3-8, between 1st Platoon, Alpha 2-7, and Route Henry.

MM: As you started moving out as you were taking mortar fire, did you start taking direct fire?

ET: Yes, we did, as we began moving in the position on Isabel. I had mistakenly called Route Isaac "Route Jacob" in my instructions to Lieutenant Michael Duran, 2d Platoon leader, and as a result he was moving too far. I changed my instructions to him, got him pulling back. It was at that point, as I was changing those instructions to him, that my track got hit from behind.

MM: Is this the incident where your interpreter was killed?

ET: Yes, although he wasn't my interpreter. I had a tactical PSYOP team (TPT) attached to me for the fight and the interpreter was attached to them. So I had him available to me but he wasn't my interpreter, if that makes any sense.

MM: Who was in your track when this occurred?

ET: Staff Sergeant Doug Queen was my gunner. Private First Class Richard Cohlmeyer was the driver. Sergeant Brian Newman was the TPT team leader. Specialist Rankin, Sergeant Delhotal, as well the linguist we all called Izzy.

MM: My understanding is that this RPG came through the back gate of the Bradley?

ET: Yeah, it punched through the ramp.

MM: It came right through the ramp. Who else was wounded? I know the interpreter was killed. Was there anybody inside wounded?

ET: Sergeant Newman lost his left arm, just below the shoulder. Rankin and Delhotel took some small shrapnel injuries and Izzy was killed outright.

MM: Did you just consider this to be somebody got a lucky shot off?

ET: No, as we talked about it, as I continued to look at the hole in the ramp, it wasn't an RPG-7. It had some kind of penetrator. I'm not as up to speed as I should be on the various models of RPGs, but as you look at the back of the Bradley from the outside, there are the two M-231 gun ports. The RPG penetrated below the right hand gun port, sheared off Sergeant Newman's arm, passed right through Izzy, passed underneath the screen for the Force XXI Battle Command, Brigade-and-Below (FBCB2) system, and penetrated the turret through the turret shield. We had the turret slewed, I want to say to the 2 o'clock or 3 o'clock position. The penetrator passed through the turret shield into the ammo ready box and detonated a couple of high explosive (HE) rounds. How Sergeant Queen and I didn't catch any shrapnel, I have no clue.

MM: That's an incredible story. So you're convinced that that was not an RPG-7. You think it was some other kind of RPG or some other kind of anti-tank weapon?

ET: We found an awful lot of boosters for RPGs, to give them more kick. We had the reactive armor on the Brads to counter the more modern RPGs out there, but the ramp doesn't have those reactive armor tiles on it. If you looked at the ramp, the hole was – you could maybe fit a finger and a half into the hole. There was not a scorch mark on it that would indicate an explosion outside, so my guess is that there was a booster that pushed the penetrator through the vehicle.

MM: This event actually takes place on the 13th, is that correct?

ET: No, on the 12th, as we're moving everybody along Isabel to Route Isaac.

MM: And this is around the 0900 timeframe?

ET: That sounds about right. I've lost track of time.

MM: Can you tell me what happened after this incident, just talk me through the rest of the fight?

ET: Let me back up a little: "We began moving into position on Isabel. I realized I had mistakenly referred to Route Isaac as Route Jacob and 2d Platoon was moving too far to the west. Sergeant Queen, my gunner, was directing PFC Cohlmeyer, my driver, into position behind 3d Platoon, Charlie 3-8. As I looked down at my map to get oriented so that I could get 2d Platoon pulled back to Isaac, I saw a flash between my knees, the turret was filled with smoke, and I realized we had been hit. As we lurched to a stop, Sergeant Queen asked me if I was good to go. I didn't feel any pain and answered, 'Yes.' He was out of the turret checking on Cohlmeyer.... I called up Captain Hank Wiley, who was my XO, and told him we were hit. I passed as much info as I had, which was that we had two urgent casualties, one routine and one killed in action (KIA). I crawled out of the turret and hit the ground. As I got on the ground, Sergeant Calvin Smalley pulled up behind me. Sergeant Smalley was the platoon sergeant for 1st Platoon and was directing the fires of dismounts in all directions. Scott 'Doc' Cogil was on the ground treating Sergeant Newman."

MM: Were you still taking pretty intense fire at this time?

ET: No. We were shooting every which way, but I don't remember hearing rounds around me. So I think they shot, realized they had a successful hit, and then moved out before we could bring direct fire onto their position.

MM: Okay, now can you talk me through all the way up to the 20th. From my notes here, you have some heavy contact at 0900 on the 13th.

ET: Let's see: "Under suppressive fire from the Brads and dismounts, we got Newman and Delhotel onto Alpha 1-1 and got them back to the aid station. Policed up our gear, got it back in the Brads. Sergeant Smalley's Bradley had been hit, too, and was leaking oil. They got everything moved and back to the TFSA. When we closed on the TFSA, everyone headed right for the rearming/refueling point. I stopped in the medic's tent, unloaded Izzy's body. We spent the next couple hours getting the Brads and tanks straight, more bullets and more gas, etc. Cleaning out my track. About 1600, I sent 2d Platoon back. I went with them in the XO's track. Stayed out on Route Henry until 0230. On the 13th, came back in, swapped out with 1st Platoon and the XO." So I came back, handed the XO's track back to him, and I crashed about 0430. I got up about 10:00 on the morning on the 13th, I think. I don't think your timeline is correct. About 11:30, that's what I have here. Again, I don't know precisely what the time was. "About 11:30, 1st Platoon is still out with the XO, came into contact. Staff Sergeant Santillana's squad had chased an insurgent that they had seen running across an alley into a building. They seized a foothold in the courtyard, prepped the entrance with a grenade, and kicked in the door. Reports were that between 10 and 20 insurgents were waiting for them. Sergeant Abdelwahab was on point. He was immediately hit in the right leg and left arm. Specialist Howard was the number-two man. He grabbed "Abe," dragged him back. Simultaneously, the squad started taking fire from a sniper positioned across the street. Specialist Jose Velez sprayed the window across the street with a squad automatic weapon (SAW), stopped in the open to reload and was shot just below the neck in the right shoulder. Grenades came out of the original target house and exploded, wounding Sergeant Bristol, Specialist Goodin and Specialist Benny Alicea. Somehow they got everyone back in the Brads and began casualty evacuation (CASEVAC) back to the TFSA. I met them at the aid station where Captain Kevin Burnham and the rest of the battalion medics were waiting. Captain Burnham was one of the physician's assistants (PAs). By the time I got in the tent, Abe and Howard were stabilized and Alicea, Bristol and Goodin were outside. Their wounds were relatively minor. Sergeant Bristol was the least hurt of the bunch. I walked around to the side of the tent and talked with Goodin for a bit. Saw some activity behind the tent; walked behind it to see what was happening. The medics were carrying a body bag. That's when I was informed that Specialist Velez had been killed. He was the SAW gunner." I just circulated between the remaining casualties. Sergeant Santillana, the squad leader, he was unwounded completely. I've never seen anybody feel as guilty, I think, about that. He loved his men, and I think he felt like he should be lying there in the medical tent with them.

MM: What happened after this? Were you forced to get right back into the fight?

ET: Yes, we did go back into the fight.

MM: I've got a big block on my notes here that says, basically, from 0700 on the 14th to 17 November, Charlie 3-8 attacks in support of 3-1 Marines, and I just have a complete blank on Alpha 2-7.

ET: We rolled back out, but we swapped. As I said, Charlie 3-8 had pivoted and come to the west and they were south of us. Up until that point, we were arrayed from south to north: Charlie 3-8, Alpha 2-7, Charlie 2-7. Once this happened, it took a lot of guys out of the fight. We flip-flopped and Alpha 2-7 pulled back and Charlie 2-7 pushed forward. Charlie 3-8 remained at the tip.

MM: As you're progressing south here, did you find that the resistance became greater from the enemy? The 2-2 folks were telling me that there were some foreign fighters in their area on the southeast.

ET: The initial take was you had the two elements: you had the foreign fighters and you had the former military folks in the city of Fallujah. There in the Martyrs District, that was the area where my Brad got hit and where Specialist Velez was killed I heard reports, not necessarily confirmed, of interpreters identifying enemy KIAs: "Hey, he's a Syrian, he's from Russia, he's Lebanese, he's Saudi." I would be lying if I said that I could tell everybody apart.

MM: In the last days of the mission, were you guys pretty much working in conjunction with the Marines in clearing out the last buildings?

ET: No, we were very frustrated. I was very frustrated. Morale was pretty low after Velez died and the other six troops were pretty seriously injured. It was two hard days there that we were down vehicles; we were down some good troops. Everybody did get back in the saddle and they did great and wonderful things. But, all of a sudden, we're pulled back. Very minimal contact after the 13th. It seemed that we were much more of a route security force while the Marines continued on with the fight.

MM: Did they pull 3-8 back? Were they in the same boat?

ET: It seemed that 3-8 was also being held back. Pete Glass, he was an amazing commander. He was all about taking the fight to the enemy and we were all frustrated. Again, I'm not privy to what was going on at the regimental level or above that, but we all felt: we've got a mechanized task force that is sitting still. Meanwhile, we're listening to radio reports and hearing about great Marines getting hurt, not through any fault of their own, but they didn't have the protection afforded by armored vehicles. They're a light force. So we were very frustrated. It appeared that the whole force was not using the assets available to accomplish the mission.

MM: It's my understanding that the Marines really only had about a platoon of their own tanks, I guess, in each battalion.

ET: I don't know enough about how they were organized.

MM: So, in general, what was your observation of working with the Marines during this time period? Good, bad, ugly?

ET: They're all great Americans. I was amazed by their tenacity and ferocity in the fight, and the abilities of their noncommissioned officers (NCOs) to get things done. Overall, though, including Najaf, I was not impressed with their planning processes. When we went to the regimental rock drill, it seemed that it turned into a wargame session rather than the rehearsal it was supposed to be. Again, I'm just a company commander, and there are a lot of guys out there with a lot more brainpower than I have. But that's what I got from that regimental rock drill. I did not feel that there was good adjacent-unit coordination or communication between the Marines and units that they were working around. There's more than one occasion I can think of where I got calls from my platoon leaders: "Hey, Apache 6, is there anyone around you?" or "Anyone supposed to be around us?" "No." "Because I've got guys with weapons walking in the open one block to my east." "Okay, well, keep an eye on them." "Oh, they must be Marines because I can make out their Kevlar (helmets) and they're with a tank." They were doing the WWII squad-walking-behind-a-tank kind of thing.

MM: With their telephone, I guess, on the back.

ET: I don't know how they were communicating to the crew. I can't say no one knew where those guys were, but they were moving through our area of operations and nobody bothered to tell me they were going to be there. I was very concerned about fratricide as a result of poor adjacent-unit coordination.

MM: Well, that's significant.

ET: They didn't bother to call up and say, "Hey, Apache, I got two tanks and two squads moving south along this route, going to pass through your area of operations (AO). But just for your information, that's where we're going to be. We should be there about 1830 and we should be gone by 1900." "Roger that, man, no worries. You have a mission you have to do; I've got to guard the road. I got it."

MM: When I talked to Major Karcher, he wanted to know if I'd read Bing West's No True Glory book. He said, "If you want to find out what really didn't happen, read that book." Have you read the book?

ET: I have not, sir, no.

MM: Okay, because the Army's hardly mentioned in it at all, so –

ET: Yes, sir. I might have to get it, but I got so pissed off reading a couple pages. I was like, "This is crap."

137

MM: There's one page in there that says the Marines specifically requested Task Force 2-7. But other than that, they're pretty much overlooked. One more quick question on logistics: Did the Marines provide you with ammo, fuel, that sort of thing, or did you pretty much have to get that yourself?

ET: We got all our stuff from Captain Brown and his forward support company.

MM: And you're not sure where he was drawing that from?

ET: Major Jackson, the XO, and Captain Brown would probably be the guys to talk to about that.

MM: Are you still in contact with your platoon leaders during this fight?

ET: I keep in contact with Lieutenant Kilgore. I send an email message to Lieutenant Duran every so often, but I don't hear back from him.

MM: Because if you are in contact with any of them and if they want to shoot their story my way, that'd be super. We're trying to get all the information we possibly can on this. Any NCOs, anybody.

ET: Well, it happens, believe or not, that you've got my old first sergeant and you've got my platoon sergeant right there in Leavenworth with you.

MM: You've got to be kidding me.

ET: I'm not bullshitting you, man.

MM: Okay, let me get these names.

ET: You have formerly First Sergeant, now Master Sergeant, Steven Vigil and, unless he's been promoted, Sergeant First Class John Urrutia.

MM: And they're permanently stationed here at Leavenworth?

ET: Yes, they're part of the Battle Command Training Program

MM: Oh, really? I worked over there for 16 years. I was with the World Class OPFOR over there. Well, look, this answers all the major questions I have, but I'm sure that I'm going to be picking your brain as I start writing this. I'll probably be emailing you quite a bit to see if this is right or if this makes sense.

ET: Yes, sir.

MM: Well, is there anything else that you want to leave me with?

ET: Lieutenant Kilgore and Lieutenant Duran are still in – well, 2-7 was re-flagged 1-12 about the time I was leaving, but they're still down there.

MM: Okay, I will make contact with them. Thank you very much.

Captain Coley D. Tyler
20 April 2006

MM: My name is Matt Matthews [MM] and I'm an historian with the Combat Studies Institute. Today is Thursday, April 20, 2006, and I'm interviewing Captain Coley D. Tyler [CT], who was the fire support officer, FSO, for 2-7 CAV [2d Battalion, 7th Cavalry Regiment] during Operation Phantom Fury. Could you just give me some background on where you were born, where you went to school, how you got your commission?

CT: Yes, sir. I was born in Macon, Georgia, on February 6, 1978. Shortly thereafter, my father and I moved to Franklin, North Carolina, which is in the western half, in the mountains. I grew up there and went to high school there at Franklin High School. I was an all-around athlete. I played soccer, I wrestled and ran track. After high school, I applied to West Point and was accepted. I then spent 1996 to 2000 at West Point and graduated in May, commissioned in field artillery. Shortly thereafter, I went to the Officer Basic course at Fort Sill, Oklahoma, followed that up with Ranger School, and then ended up at Fort Hood, Texas, with the 2d Battalion, 82d Field Artillery Regiment, 3d Brigade.

MM: Could you talk me through your arrival in Iraq and how you linked up with 2-7 CAV?

CT: Not a problem, sir. When we first deployed to Iraq, I was the battalion intelligence officer for 2-82. The FSO for 2-7 at the time, it was his time to come up for command. So in September of 2004, I moved up to Taji where 2-7 was stationed with the 39th ESB [Enhanced Separate Brigade]. I took over from him and he came back to 2-82 and took command of our headquarters battery. That's how I ended up in 2-7 in September of 2004.

MM: Do you recall when you first heard about the mission that might be coming up and when you first linked up with the Marines and started to coordinate, do some planning for this operation?

CT: I heard of 2-7 previously with their operations in Najaf, and I knew that was where I was headed. Just keeping up as the intelligence officer, I knew things in Fallujah were bad and there was talk of a possible military operation. When I got to 2-7, I actually heard the rumors that since we had worked with the Marines previously, we would be the ones called if there was an operation. But at the same time, there was the presidential election going on and nobody was really sure if that would have an impact: would we go prior to the election, would we go after the election, or would we even go at all? We didn't have direct liaison authorized with the Marines officially, but they would give us information just to help us get into the mindset if we were called to work with them. They were getting the same type of rumors on their end too, that if they did do this, we would be one of the Army battalions that would be attached to them. A lot of it was rumors until maybe a week before we really started conducting operations.

MM: What do you recall of meeting the Marines for the first time and starting to really get into the nitty-gritty of planning this thing?

CT: Honestly, before I actually worked with Marines, I think I probably had the regular, stereotypical idea of what Marines were: not necessarily the brightest, that the Army was always better and smarter. However, I found the Marines were extremely intelligent, have a lot of common sense, and I actually enjoyed the way they ran their operation, almost more so than the Army. It was very refreshing to work with somebody outside the Army, but still in the U.S. Armed Forces. I have a newfound respect for Marines, and I thought of myself as being sort of a Marine after that. They really brought us in and treated us like their own. I really enjoyed working with them. I found them to be very, very good soldiers.

MM: Excellent. Let's start maybe 8 November. The Marines have blown the breach on the western side of the train station. Just tell me what you did, what you remember, starting from there, and let's take it all the way down to when you guys capture the Jolan District.

CT: Okay. Actually, can I start with maybe a few days previous, because –

MM: Certainly, yes.

CT: We actually sent a recon by force. I can't remember the exact day, but several days prior to the same breach location just north of the train station. I was just trying to get an idea of how tough it was going to be to breach and get into the city. We went in with about a company size, with one of my fire support guys, the air liaison officer [ALO] and myself, and we basically got into a little bit of a skirmish there at the train station in part of the city where we were going to breach. I called a lot of indirect fire on what we thought were suspected minefields in front of where we wanted to breach. I was trying to get that destroyed with fire so the engineers wouldn't be forced to deal with that when they actually did the breach.

MM: Who fired that mission for you and what kinds of rounds were these?

CT: It was Mike Battery 414 and it was regular 155 millimeter high explosive rounds. That was the fire support part of that and, of course, the tanks and Bradleys got into a little bit of a skirmish with their weapons systems. Then they withdrew and it looked as good a place as any to breach. Right before the breach happened, all the pre-planned targets had been reconned with UAVs [Unmanned Aerial Vehicles], and that sort of intelligence gathering had been going on for months previous. Within our rules of engagement, we engaged as many targets as possible to soften up the front four roads so, once we did the breach and got into the first few blocks, it wouldn't be so hard to get into and actually get a foothold, and not have to be stuck outside the city. A lot of that was controlled at the RCT, or regimental combat team, level with the UAVs and the other Marine regiments, because they were prepped right outside the city and we were rolling through them, through the breach, into the city. They were controlling a lot of that, basically softening up the first few blocks.

MM: Were you using any of your 120 millimeter mortars at that time?

CT: We used our mortars and also the Marines used our mortars quite a bit. All the fires were talking on the same net: Marines and Army. Of course, the Marines only had 60 millimeter mortars and 81s. So anytime 2-7 wasn't using our 120s, we just passed them over to the Marines and let them shoot. We ended up, through the course of two weeks, firing almost 1,000 rounds.

MM: When the Marines wanted to use the 120s, was it a Marine FSO that was calling in those missions?

CT: Yes.

MM: So you just handed them over to –

CT: Just handed them over.

MM: That's super; that some joint-ness there.

CT: Yes, sir. And honestly, it was as simple as one of them coming up and asking, "Hey, can we use your 120s, we're kind of in a bind?" And we'd say, "Yeah sure, go ahead and take them." They had their freq', so they'd talk straight to the mortars. It worked out really, really well.

MM: Where was the 155 battery located that you were also using?

CT: They were at Camp Fallujah, probably about 20 kilometers away from where we were, I guess.

MM: Talk me up to when you guys fight to take the Jolan District.

CT: Of course, all the buildings were numbered. All the maps were the same so, if you're talking to pilots, talking to guys on the ground, everybody has the same graphics; everybody knows exactly what you're talking about. A lot of times that does not happen. Everybody was using the same phase lines, and since we were first in, we were able to control the coordinated fire line. We'd keep it two CFLs in front of us. As soon as they rolled in, I was using the UAVs, looking about two kilometers in front of them, looking for deep targets, using the 155s, air with the ALO, and engaging targets up there. Then because of the city, the company FSOs that were actually on the ground with the maneuver units, it was very hard for them to see anything much more than about 1,000 to 1,500 meters, if you were lucky. So a lot of times, they would first use the 155s if they could. If it was a little too close or they didn't feel quite comfortable using those at first, they'd go straight to the mortars, talk directly next to them – and we were walking mortar rounds in on armor troops probably within 70 meters.

MM: So you were doing some danger close –

CT: Definitely, especially with the 120s. Now the 155s, I think probably the closest we ever got was about 600 to 700 meters away. A lot of times, the company FSO would see something and it'd be a little too hard for 120s or he wanted to engage it first with 155s, so they would just back up a little bit. I'd take the UAV, if we had it, look at the target and engage it myself with the 155s, and then get the assessment from the company FSO. After the volley was over, we'd pull back up and see what the battle damage assessment was. If we needed to reengage it, pull back; and if it was good, they'd move forward. That's the way it worked, that kind of systematic moving forward and reengaging the deep targets and the close ones with a combination of mortars and 155s.

MM: Now, the UAV that you were using, was that your own Raven or was that a Marine UAV?

CT: It was a Marine UAV and I think the Army calls it a Shadow. It was an intermediate UAV; it wasn't the Predator that has the Hellfires on it and whatnot. The Marines gave us the equipment to have a feed into our assembly area, right north of the train station. We could actually sit there in the TOC [Tactical Operations Center] and watch.

MM: So the TOC was actually seeing this and relaying that to you? Could you actually –?

CT: I was actually looking at it on the screen.

MM: From the TOC location. You could see it from your track?

CT: Yes, sir. We were too far outside the city; we were north of the train station. But with the UAV feed, I could see everything. It turned out to be a very effective way of observing and calling for fires.

MM: Were you co-located with the TOC most of the time? Or did you, at some point, have to go into the city?

CT: I went into the city on one big occasion. After things had calmed down, we had pushed south of the major highway that goes through. I think we called it MSR [Main Supply Route] Mobile. It goes through and it's a four-lane highway. Once our guys had pushed past that, the ALO and I went into the northern part to assess what we'd been doing over the past several days up to a week. In the city during the fight was all my company FSOs. The main fire support element stayed right outside north of the train station, and a lot of that mainly for the fact that it was so hard to actually see in the city. We were doing and calling more missions from outside with the UAVs than would have ever been possible. The support we were able to give them was much better from right outside the city.

MM: The RCT commander, Colonel Michael Shupp, just raved about the 120s. He thought they were the greatest thing since sliced bread.

CT: I think they're amazing. They're extremely quick and you can walk them in very close. They're amazing weapons and they worked very well for us. I'm really glad we could help the Marines out and let them use them.

MM: Did the RCT put out any rules of engagement before the operations started where you can't use this, you can use that, that sort of thing?

CT: Yes, sir. The ROE is and always will be very restrictive, and that was exactly the case for this operation. It was a good thing to have, but it also tied our hands. Conventional warfare, a lot of times, you just think you can watch the target, you've got intelligence on it, so you can just fire. Well, we couldn't shoot anything without having notice of positive identification. That made a lot of our planned targets not really planned targets anymore.

MM: How did that work? If you identified something, did you have to go to the task force commander and then he'd have to go to somebody?

CT: My task force commander was in the city basically the whole time. I had a lawyer that was attached to our battalion and he stayed with me and the ALO during the whole operation. Anytime we had any doubts about it, the lawyer was right there to either confirm, "Yes, this falls within the ROE, you can do this," or, "You might want to wait, see how things unfold before you do it." So, we had the lawyer watching the same UAV feed, hearing the same radio traffic. And he actually was a prior field artillery officer.

MM: Oh, that's super.

CT: He knew exactly what was going on; he understood how things worked. He was a tremendous help for us because we never had any fears about whether we were doing something wrong.

MM: That seems completely different to what was going on over in the east side of the city where there was some controversy about the white phosphorus rounds that were used over there.

CT: Right.

MM: Did your chain of command tell you guys that you couldn't use those?

CT: It never was brought up. There was never an instance where I felt, or really anybody else felt, that we needed to use anything different. We never had any instances where we probably wanted to use something else, so we never had to deal with that. I'm fully confident that if that had been the case, it would have worked out just fine; it would have been employed properly.

MM: Is there anything that sticks out in your mind, any big lessons learned that you want the soldiers out there to know about? Anything in this operation that worked really well or didn't work well?

CT: I don't know about the Marines, but we're a digital Army although we really didn't use it. We still used voice. I don't know if that's because I'm personally more comfortable doing that. On my end, we used voice; my company FSOs used voice. I think a lot of it, being in that type of environment, they didn't have the time to send digital messages. They could carry on with what they were doing while talking into the microphone and get the information back to us. So we didn't use digital, and I don't know if that's a bad thing or a good thing.

MM: When you handed off the 120s occasionally to the Marines, were they talking to those folks at that time?

CT: Yes.

MM: Okay, so it wasn't a digital thing with the 120s?

CT: No, no, it was straight voice. We did voice for everything. Like I said, I don't know if that's a good thing or a bad thing, but that's the way we did it and it worked well. Even with a lot of different assets, it can work, but that's up to somebody else to decide if that was a good or bad thing. I guess one of the biggest lessons I learned from a field artillery, fire support standpoint was the use of UAVs. They make a huge difference. It's an aerial observer that can totally change the way the battlefield looks. At first, I was kind of leery of calling for fire that way because I'd never heard of that before. We had used UAVs to look around and then the guy on the ground calls it. I ended up calling more missions than I'd ever dreamed of. I figured myself to be the guy who cleared the fires in the traditional sense and monitored what my company FSOs were doing. I never really thought I would get that hands-on into a battle like that. But myself and my ALO called more missions, talked more pilots onto targets than I would have ever dreamed – and it was the technology we have that made that all possible. It really helped out the company FSOs, too, who were only able to concentrate and see a block or two in front of them. I think if we didn't have that type of thing, the assets we brought to the fight – field artillery, fire support and air – probably would have been much more limited.

MM: My understanding is that, at one point during the fight, you guys actually went black on 120 millimeter ammo. Was everybody surprised you had shot that much?

CT: Yes, extremely surprised. The platoon sergeant for the mortar platoon, after we were all done and they were counting up how many rounds, he said: "I've never shot this many rounds in my career." He'd shot more rounds in a week or two than he had ever shot previously. Close air support was easy to use, coming from an Army background. CAS is not integrated into fire support like it is in the Marines. But the way they have it set up, it was extremely easy.

MM: What about Army aviation assets, did you have to call for any of those?

CT: We did, but they were all integrated with the Marines' fixed-wings and the Cobras. The way they had it set up with the different stacks around the city, when you needed air, they would come out from one of the stacks and they pushed your freq' – and we did that all over chat. Chat the air guys at the RCT, I'd say, "Hey, guys, I need air." Then, before you know it, "Okay, you're getting some air pushed to you and this is what it is." Before you know it, they're up on your freq', coming from somewhere. You never had to wait for it because it was all stacked real nice, and then you just went through the process of talking them onto the target, doing reconnaissance, whatever you needed them to do. And a lot of times, you get a feed from what they're looking at as well.

MM: Is there anything else that stands out in particular from this operation? Was there anything you thought maybe didn't go as well? Were there any problems that need to be addressed in the near future?

CT: I think specifically, for this information, we had two calls-for-fire nets when we started out. One was for battalion FSOs to talk to the RCT and then there was another one for company FSOs to do their calls for fires. They were supposed to monitor their calls for fire and approve it on the other net to the RCT. What ended up happening was everybody was on the same net doing everything. Sometimes it got crowded; too many folks were trying to do different things at the same time. Sometimes you just had to decide that, "Okay, I'm just going to use my mortars for now, and then when I get a chance to get in there, I'll do my thing." Because of ROE, clearance of fire sometimes could take a really long time. That was because the ROE was so restrictive; that's just the way it is. A lot of times, you can use other means.

MM: Did you get any sort of indication, by the time the battle was over, of how many foreign fighters and insurgents you guys had actually killed?

CT: There were numbers thrown around, not specifically for fire support or direct fire. But I think by the time we were pulled out, there were maybe 1,500 total enemy casualties. Honestly, I don't think too many people were concentrating on a body count. If it was clear that the Marines were able to do what they needed to do because we did our jobs, that was good enough for us.

MM: Well, I appreciate all your help on this. Thank you very much.

Captain Neil Prakash

20 October 2006

JM: My name is John McCool (JM) and I'm with the Operational Leadership Experiences Project at the Combat Studies Institute, Fort Leavenworth, Kansas. I'm interviewing Captain Neil Prakash (NP) on his experiences in Operation Iraqi Freedom (OIF), specifically Operation Phantom Fury/Al-Fajr in November 2004. Today's date is 20 October 2006 and this is an unclassified interview. Before we begin, Neil, if you feel at any time we're entering classified territory, please couch your response in terms that avoid revealing any classified information; and if classification requirements prevent you from responding, simply say you're not able to answer. Can you give me a little background on yourself to start out with? How did you get commissioned, where did you grow up, what have your duty assignments been and where have you deployed in the past?

NP: Sure. My commissioning source was Johns Hopkins University ROTC. I'd done Boys State in high school so there was a piece of the military that appealed to me before I even got to college, so when I got there I decided to sign up for ROTC. My parents had mixed feelings about it because they thought I was going to college to be doctor, but I sold them on the idea that maybe I could be a doctor in the Army. By the end of my junior year, though, I'd seen my first tank and decided right then and there that I was going to be an armor officer. At that point, I was already contracted so there was no way I was getting out of that and there was nothing my parents could do. Once they saw what I was doing and how much I liked it, they were very supportive; and once they saw my Ranger graduation, which was the biggest military thing they'd ever seen, they were really hooked after that. After that, I went to Fort Knox in January '03 and then went to Ranger School in the summer of '03. My first assignment was Vilseck, Germany, with 3d Brigade, 1st Infantry Division, specifically 2-63 Armor. I arrived there on 3 October and took over 1st Platoon. As soon as I got there we were prepping for gunnery. We did a Hohenfels rotation – like a mission readiness exercise (MRX) for OIF – and then we deployed in February. When I got back from Iraq, my wife was at Fort Hood with 4th Infantry Division and getting ready to deploy. Since my unit in Germany was getting ready to deactivate, I was trying to get a job at 4th Infantry Division so I could redeploy with her. I managed to do that with the help of a lot of people. I secured a job with 2-8 Infantry. Incidentally, 2-8 is the very unit that 2-2 relieved back in Ba'qubah, so everything has come full circle.

JM: For the record, Captain Prakash is currently back in Iraq and I'm talking to him today from Forward Operating Base (FOB) Kalsu, is that correct?

NP: That's right. I'm with 2d Brigade, 4th Infantry, with 2-8 Infantry, which they're now calling a combined arms battalion. I'm serving with Alpha Company, which is a mech infantry company, and I'm currently the company executive officer (XO).

JM: Can you talk to me a little bit about what you were doing in Iraq prior to Phantom Fury kicking off?

NP: To be honest, I was on two weeks of R&R when the company actually left Ba'qubah to go to Fallujah. Prior to that, it was September and October and the next big thing on our plate was the elections in January. At the time, as a tank platoon leader, I spent about half of my time doing main supply route (MSR) patrols, route clearance, where we'd go out in two tank sections. We'd just patrol the MSRs looking for improvised explosive devices (IEDs) and we also served as the quick reaction force (QRF) outside of the wire. The one thing about OIF II was the shortage of troops. One of the best and worst things 2-63 and probably all the other units had to do was micromanage at a battalion level in order to maximize the economy of force out there. When you're dealing with two-thirds of the troops that were there in OIF I, it really doesn't pay to have two separate tank sections operating in two different areas doing route clearance. If you're a battalion operations officer (S3), you always make sure there is a tank section from any given company at any given time – yeah, we're going out the gate every three hours, but at least there are two tanks outside the wire every three hours in a 24-hour period. At the time there was a lot of that going on. About half of my time was spent on my tanks rolling out two or three times a day. The other half was spent on Humvees with my platoon and we were doing a lot of fixed site security at the Joint Communications Center (JCC) with the Iraqi Army. In OIF II, there was a major shortage on armor and troops, so one week we were on tanks and the next week we were on Humvees, and then we'd give up the Humvees and jump on M113s. Every week it was either tanks, Humvees or 113s because our tank company only had four trucks so there weren't enough to go around. We were doing a lot fixed site security and MSR security. Presence patrol is a taboo phrase, but there were a lot of what you'd call presence patrols going on. If you're not taking contact and you're not actively searching out targets in a raid, that's a presence patrol. At that time, September had just gone by and 2d Brigade had just made a big hit with the operation in Samarra, which was like the mini-Fallujah. Are you familiar with that?

JM: Are you talking about Operation Baton Rouge?

NP: Yes. It was really just all of us watching and hearing from our buddies in 2d Brigade and just licking our chops.

JM: When did you first get word that your platoon might be participating in what became Operation Phantom Fury?

NP: We got word in October. I remember because our sister tank company, Charlie, had gone to Najaf twice. They went in April and in June and we were pretty jealous. We kept asking, "Why aren't *we* going?" The bottom line was they sent the company that didn't have an area of operations (AO) in a major populous region. We had an AO in the city of Khalis and we had to hold that down. But of course we still thought that was crap and we wanted them to send us. In October, though, they told us that they were going to send a battalion task force to Fallujah. At the time, none of the platoon leaders or platoon sergeants had gone on leave and I was getting ready to go on R&R. My commander said that, if this happens, it will probably happen when I'm on R&R, so I was like, "Screw it. Screw R&R. Let's do this thing." We were pretty amped up about it. There were a lot of politics surrounding the events, though, because it was obviously an election year. You had the 2004 elections and you also had Ramadan in November. I ended up going on leave on 17 October. By this time, my commander had said for me to go ahead and go because he said I'd be back in time, since he was now thinking the Fallujah thing wouldn't kick off until after Ramadan. So I went home on leave for two weeks and every single day all they're talking about on the news is Fallujah. Twenty-four hours a day that's all I see on the news. Anyway, about two days before I was supposed to return, I get an email from Captain (then Lieutenant) Chris Boggiano, who was then in Iraq on FOB Warhorse. He said, "Neil, I hear we're getting a tank section from Alpha 2-63. I hope it's your section." Well, I went home saying I didn't want to watch the news or read emails from Iraq or anything. I just wanted to be on vacation. But I wrote back and asked him what the hell he was talking about. He said, "Dude, we're going to Fallujah in three days." I was like, "This is bullcrap! I'm still here at home. You can't leave without me." So I sent an email to my commander and said, "You're not leaving for Fallujah without me, are you?" and he said, "Not if you get your ass back here in time." What I didn't realize was that I could have just gone to the airport with an open-ended ticket, got on a plane and I could have made it on time. I didn't know I could do that, though, and my commander didn't say anything about it so I didn't leave until 2 November. That was Election Day and I left Syracuse at 0600. By the time I got back to Iraq it was 4 November and they said my unit had already left for Fallujah. I was told to get to FOB Scunion and they would take care of me, so I went over there and they told me I had three hours to pack my bags. My platoon sergeant had left me a map under my pillow and they had already packed some of my shit for me, so I grabbed it and the bird came and picked us up three hours later. It was me, a sergeant and a couple privates who all were returning from R&R.

JM: Tell me about the process of getting integrated with the Brigade Reconnaissance Troop (BRT).

NP: That's funny because I was actually worried about integrating in general. I got on the ground at Camp Fallujah and was dragging my duffle bag towards the living area when I saw some of my guys. I gave them a couple high fives and said it was good to see them. Everyone was racked out because, the night before, they

149

did a huge task force rehearsal. I, on the other hand, had been drinking beers and partying and staying out late for the last two weeks, and now I'm supposed to lead these guys. The Army is so decentralized now that a section leader or a platoon sergeant can lead a platoon or section into combat, so these guys were ready to go with or without me. But how do you step right in without skipping a beat? I went in and talked to my gunner first. I had to wake him up since he had been out until four in the morning. He told me how we were task organized. We had two tanks. They cut me and my wingman off from my platoon sergeant. They kept his section organic to our Alpha tank company and brought me and my wingman over to the BRT. They took a pure infantry platoon of four Bradleys from the BRT, cut them in half, and sent two Brads to join my tank platoon sergeant in Alpha Company – my company – so now I have an infantry platoon sergeant, two Brads, two tanks and two squads worth of infantry. That was my first time working with infantry and Brads in combat and it turned out to be the best combination ever. As a matter of fact, I'm using it right now with my infantry company. I have a tank platoon attached to us. I just split the tanks and infantry in half and mix them up. Integration was funny. The infantry guys were pretty cool. As far as the BRT itself, there was no issue of integrating. My best friend in the unit there was Chris Boggiano. He had been in my tank company with me, and when he left he went to the BRT so it was like seeing an old friend. I was able to mix right in there with those guys and there was no issue at all.

JM: How were you going to be employed? How did you fit into the task force plan once you got there and got read in?

NP: When I first got read in on the initial plan, the idea was that the BRT was to screen line and soften the targets right off the bat. That was the simple piece. The BRT could handle that without much maneuvering and without much brainpower.

JM: This was using the Long Range Advanced Scout Surveillance System (LRAS) and things like that?

NP: Yes, along with the standard calls for fire. Being with the 4th ID now, I've realized that there are a lot of fun toys these guys have that we didn't have in Germany, like these commander's integrated thermal viewers (CITVs) and the improved Bradley acquisition subsystem (IBAS) that gives you a range as well as a 10-digit grid. Out there it was just LRAS that would give you a 10-digit grid, or if you're on a tank it was just laze the target and add the meters to your grid. But that was it. Soften the targets, stay static, observe, keep a low profile and hit anything that's moving. That was the initial part. Just from the briefing, though, it appeared after day one that we were just going to wing it. The way they were going to use me in the BRT was as an armor platform, as the element that could reach out and touch somebody. Otherwise it was just Humvee platoons and slightly more armored Bradleys comprising the BRT. Boggiano made a lot of money using the

LRAS and we could back up what we saw with the tanks and the 25 millimeter. What I didn't expect were the Marines at MSR Mobile and that initial screen line. From 0800 to 1900 the Marines were in Humvees shooting at buildings with M16s and I was like, "What are you doing, guy?" They said they were receiving enemy small arms from these houses facing MSR Mobile. We wanted them to just sit back and plug their ears. We were hitting these buildings we were taking small arms fire from with our main guns. The initial plan for the first half of the city was, as the entire task force moved north to south, the BRT and my tanks would bound from the northern part of the city all the way along MSR Mobile until we got to Phase Line Fran. What we learned out there was that, when you look at imagery, it may look dense, but when you're on the ground there's not much to it. There is no bounding because an entire tank platoon can secure two to four clicks on a straight highway overlooking a city in the low ground. It's pretty ridiculous how much you can screen line. There was no bounding per se.

JM: Had you operated in urban areas before with tanks or was this the first time?

NP: This was great because I had been in the Battle of Ba'qubah on 24 June.

JM: This was the battle you received the Silver Star for?

NP: Yes, but that was a platoon thing. There was nothing I did that really warranted that. It was just being caught in the middle of a hell storm, shooting everything around you and your platoon was doing likewise. The thing about Ba'qubah was that it was fast and they hit you hard from the front, the back, the alleys, the windows and the rooftops with rocket-propelled grenades (RPGs). I saw some dedication in Fallujah where some guys had some balls, but I've never seen anything like Ba'qubah where guys were sprinting up to your tank trying to lob grenades into your hatches. There were guys 40 meters away who would run up to the tanks, square up their shoulders even with our tanks, put that RPG on their shoulder and try to fire it at you. I haven't seen anything like that since. In a tank, you really have tunnel vision if you're in the hatch. You really have to be out. Even though you get chastised for it, you have to be out because your gunner has tunnel vision. The other thing is that the enemy really takes advantage of your flanks when you're in the alleys, which is why the BRT was screen lining on MSR Mobile. We were anticipating it to be a turkey shoot if it was going to be anything like Ba'qubah. If we'd known then what we know now, we should have engaged targets from the flanks as my element made the main assault into Ba'qubah, then move that flank screening element southward parallel to our main assault movement. However, we had neither the time nor the forces to do that then. Ba'qubah caught us by surprise and it was really a movement-to-contact mission. The BRT was set up on MSR Mobile and we were able to hit targets as they moved from north to south retreating from the division's northern advance.

What I noticed was that there wasn't much enemy fighting and there wasn't much enemy movement or any type of exfil from north to south as the task force cleared. I know this because we sat there from 1900 on 8 November all the way to 0600 the next day. We sat on MSR Mobile looking for targets to hit and there really weren't any. I don't fully understand where they were or what was going on. I figured other units must have been in a total firefight but I didn't see any of the enemy targets. I've read Staff Sergeant David Bellavia's and other accounts so I know there was enemy out there, but they must have stood in place and died because they weren't egressing in any way that we could see on the ground.

JM: At what point did you move off this mission and go forward into the city?

NP: At around 0500 we were sitting on the intersection of Phase Lines Fran and Mobile, which is a cloverleaf. We were sitting there and what we discovered was that the Army moved a hell of a lot faster than the Marines, because we were armor and mech. They had to catch up. We had city blocks divided up into Army, Marine, Army, Marine from east to west. All the Army units had now reached the halfway point along Phase Line Fran, but the Marines were still back up there. The bad guys were going to go left or right where the Army had already passed them and gone south. Why stay in front and face the Marines when you can just scurry left or right since it was unoccupied? We were sitting there at the cloverleaf looking due west into the city. The plan originally was to get to Fran and open that up as the line of communication because we were going to want to push fuel, chow and all our combat service support assets through there. That went out the window real quick and we ended up doing the logistical resupply point (LRP) on the safe side of the cloverleaf. Are you familiar with where the LRP was?

JM: Yes, I am.

NP: It was good and I was glad it was like that. It would have been a bad idea to bring logistics in there. So anyway, we get down to the cloverleaf and got our first taste of going into the city. When you're going into an area you're unfamiliar with, you should always let the tanks go first, then the Brads and then the Humvees. In this case, though, the Humvees went first and they started getting shot up by sniper fire. There were a couple scattered buildings as well as these barriers. There was concertina wire, HESCOs, bunkers and all this stuff the Marines and the entire coalition had previously put in there for themselves and the Iraqi Army, yet the city had not been patrolled for six months. No one had been there since 9 April when the Marines got hit really hard trying that ground assault they did to go after the Blackwater guys who got killed. So from April until November, the intel we had said there was no patrolling going on in the city, no maintaining of a presence at all. All these bunkers were either ready to explode, they were full of IEDs and or they were enemy strongholds, so we were just lighting them all up with the main guns.

After that, though, as the dismounts were trying to go forward, the Humvees were getting shot at. Captain Kirk Mayfield, the BRT commander, seemed really pissed off because he was getting sniped. Captain Boggiano had told me previously that Captain Mayfield had spent 16 years in light infantry. He hadn't messed with tanks too much so I would probably get free reign. It's great when you're a tank attached to the light because they really want to use you, but often times they don't know how. However, when the bullets start flying, it's just no holds barred and the gloves come off and all that good stuff. So he starts getting sniped and I call him on the net as we're moving down towards Fran. He's telling me about taking sniper fire and he's just pointing at houses and saying, "Shoot that shit!" so we just unloaded main gun rounds on all these houses he thinks he's taking sniper fire from. This was day two, 9 November.

JM: So basically you're using the tank main gun as an anti-sniper weapon?

NP: We used it for everything. On 8 November at 0800 when the first mortar round landed, Captain Mayfield told me to get up there on the high ground, on the berm. Just between me and my wingman, we went through 45 rounds in the first hour in Fallujah. This is before the task force even staged, let alone crossed the line of departure (LD) at 1900. You sometimes wonder what the appropriate use of force is, but Fallujah was just a joke as far as the amount of force we could use. There seemed to be no limit on main gun or .50 cal, so we were hitting every house we were taking contact from with main gun rounds. Why show them mercy, you know what I mean?

JM: Sure. Did you have any visibility on Marine units that were operating in this area? I assume they were not firing too many main gun rounds into buildings. They were doing a lot of dismounted clearing, weren't they?

NP: Yes. They were mostly dismounted. In fact, very rarely did I see Marine tanks. I think I saw them twice during the whole operation. The Marines were either not caught up to us, or if they did they were so far out of our sector that anything we engaged with direct fire didn't affect them. The only time the Marines came into play was with that fire mission that I'm sure Captain Boggiano told you about. That was where we called for fire on that building next to the mosque and ended up killing like 70 guys. I think that was 9 November as well. The first day going into the city we were starting to probe these buildings and getting sniper fire from them. Honestly at this point, it was really platoons operating independently, sort of, but with the commander's guidance. After awhile, though, that disappeared and it was really just platoons working together and everything was a react to contact. We did some probing and with the tanks you feel pretty safe. You kind of have to stick your neck out there when you're in the tank. I don't know who Captain Mayfield was talking to as far as what guidance he was getting. All I know is that he had his issues to deal with right there in that AO and that's what we were dealing with.

JM: Aside from the snipers, what sorts of enemy contact were you seeing? What was the nature of the enemy and what was your assessment of his capabilities?

NP: At this point I was pretty disappointed at their lack of aggression. The snipers were good. We're all high up on the cloverleaf a good couple hundred meters away from the city, so you can't see them but you can hear the crack and that was the sound of the bullet round hitting your tank. You're looking around and you can see dust kick up around your turret. The periscopes on the hatches are shattering because they're getting shot at. You're looking around, hollering at the scouts and asking them what's going on and they had no idea. We really didn't see anybody. There was maybe one guy we did see. The scouts saw him first and they lit up the house with Mk-19. Then I got there and, just for good measure, we put a few main gun rounds into the house. Captain Boggiano wanted to fire my tank so I let him climb up there and put a main gun round on the house. For my part, I wanted to shoot an AT4 so I got off the tank and he gave me one of his AT4s to shoot at the house. The contact at this point on the morning of 9 November was very limited. It seemed that we really advanced faster than the enemy expected and they were falling back to regroup. They weren't ready yet to stand toe to toe. That's what it seemed like on our end. Days later, when we got south of Isabella or Jenna, that was when we actually had guys going toe to toe with us.

JM: Can you talk to me about any significant or memorable events that occurred throughout that period of time?

NP: Are you familiar with the fire mission and how ridiculous that was?

JM: Was that when the near-fratricide incident occurred?

NP: No, that was later on.

JM: Chris told me about that.

NP: That's a good one. That's actually one of my favorites because it was just hilarious. What I'm talking about now, though, was on 9 November. It was the morning of day two. We were in the city about two clicks in from the cloverleaf, west on Fran. My two tanks are sitting there and there are two Bradleys in front of me. I noticed the "Bada Bing" stripper girl logo on the side – you know, like the strip club from *The Sopranos* – and I recognized it as Captain (then Lieutenant) Jeff Emery's Bradley. I figured we'd move up and go talk to him, so we drove up another click into the city. We pull up and see a sergeant in the hatch and I ask where Lieutenant Emery is. He said he was on the ground with the squads running around doing his light infantry stuff, so I told my wingman to pull back with me because my buddy wasn't there. So we pulled back and, as we did, with the Bradleys still in front of us, my gunner sees three to five guys running south to north across Fran and go into a building about two and a half clicks away. They all had RPGs and AKs. I couldn't believe it so I bent down to look and, sure as shit, there were three to five more guys who did the same thing. So I raced back up to the Bradleys, told them about the guys and asked them why they didn't shoot them. They said they didn't see them. So we shot a few main gun rounds in that direction but the window we had to shoot them was short, although we knew where they were going. I told my gunner to keep observing, I called it up to the executive officer (XO), Phantom 5, he says, "Roger, got it," and sends it up to Phantom 6. He told us to continue to observe and report. Well, an *hour* goes by and I believe Captain Boggiano suggested, "Hey, see if you can call for fire on this," so I called it up and asked if we could get fire. They asked for the grid and I said it was near a mosque, to which they responded that it was going to require a lot of approval and that I had to be absolutely sure about the grid before they would fire. At that moment my gunner said, "You know, sir, I don't know if this is such a good idea. They're asking you for a 10-digit grid and there's a mosque there. I don't want to see you fry." What happened was, back in the Battle of Ba'qubah, one of the vehicles my platoon engaged ended up having a woman in it and the investigating officers tried to blame my platoon for killing a family of eight, even though the car only had two people up front and one or two people in the back. They tried to say it was a family of eight in this little four-door Kia. Nobody was found negligent or liable in any way, but my gunner was still concerned about 15-6 investigations. He said, "I don't think you should call this. What if you go down for this?" So I began thinking to myself: "We have this whole city cordoned. These guys have no place to go. They're just running into a building and we'll just get these guys eventually." But as soon as I started thinking this, Captain Boggiano gets on the net and says, "My LRAS is seeing the same thing as you." I said, "You know what? Screw it." He said, "I will vouch for anything you say you see down there, because I see it too." What we ended up doing then was lazing it and I got a range of 2,490 meters, which I added to my map where I was and got my own personal 10-digit grid off that. I send that up to Boggiano and told him there was a minaret with a blue cap – and there were like five to 10 mosques all along this road. So he lazed what he thought was it, but he was off. Then he lazed the next the one and that wasn't it either. His grid was different than mine. The last grid he told me was only 300 meters off and I thought, "Perfect." These bad guys were going into a building and that building was in front of a mosque, so I told my gunner to laze the minaret that Boggiano just lazed and, sure enough, it was 300 meters back behind the building I was looking at. Now I was sure we were both looking at the same thing and I have a 10-digit grid from him now that confirms it. At that moment, there were guys running out of this building and they were pouring diesel fuel into the streets and then lit it on fire. This sent giant flames into the sky in front of this mosque. Captain Boggiano called me and said, "I'll give you an eight-digit grid off the LRAS. The guys on the fires net, though, are going to ask you for a 10-digit grid, so just add zeroes as the fifth and tenth digits in your eight-digit number and

I'll back you up." I said, "I'm with you, because I know what I'm seeing." The fires guys asked me if I was absolutely sure about what I was seeing and I said, "Roger." Captain Boggiano, being the scout that he was, had called for fire a lot but this was my first time, so he kept talking me through what to do. I called the fire guy – I think it was Ramrod 18 – and told him what I saw. I gave him the distance, the grid and the direction and told him to fire just one round. I told him the degrees were 267 but he asked me to give it to him in mils. I was like, "Ah shit! I don't know what it is in mils." All I knew was that there are 6400 mils in a damn circle and 4800 is 270 degrees, so 4700 must be 267, just eyeballing it. He said, "Roger, one round. Observe effects." So one round comes in and there was this guy out pouring diesel on the flames – and that one round landed right on top of his head. I was screaming, "Holy shit, that was right on target! Fire for effect! Fire for effect!" He said, "Roger, 20 rounds. Observe effects." Everyone on our net was like, "Holy shit!" You know, we were supposed to have this big, huge, famous barrage that was going to be the breach into the city on the LD, but it was a joke. That was like 100 rounds spread out over three hours, something like one round every 30 seconds. We were thinking, "That's the gayest barrage ever." These 20 rounds, though, were amazing.

JM: These 20 rounds – they were from the Paladins?

NP: Yes. These were from the Paladins back at Camp Fallujah. I know we only brought two Paladins so I assume the Marines were helping us with this, but I don't know. All I know is that they fired 20 rounds and I watched them all hit. Some hit the building and some hit just south of it, but every explosion that went off, it was like a volcano: three to five guys shot up like they'd come out of a geyser – and they were perfectly still, not waving or fanning their arms or anything. They were already dead as they were going airborne and blossoming out. Actually, I think there were bodies associated with about five to 10 of the explosions, but right off the bat that was like 30 to 50 guys that we killed. I gave them the numbers and Ramrod 18 was fired up and said to call for a repeat mission if we needed it again. I was looking at this place and it was just smoldering. There are very few times that I've ever felt sorry for the enemy, but this time they just got slaughtered. I don't know why I said this, but I said, "Repeat, 10 rounds." Right before this, a guy came out of the building, out of the gray smoke, and he's holding his stomach, dragging his AK by the sling, and he's gagging and retching; and just then, these 10 more rounds land right on top of his head. It was the funniest thing I've ever seen and I couldn't believe it. By the way, there were rounds hitting this seven-story hotel off to the left and the London *Telegraph* was there right behind me taking great pictures, seeing my two tanks just hammering this building with main guns. When the artillery hits that, Boggiano said one of his LRAS guys watched an insurgent on the seventh story rooftop just get launched off the hotel. My gunner also sees a guy get blown off the seventh story, but this guy hit the ground so hard that he bounced up about two stories off the asphalt. It was the most insane, surreal thing I'd ever seen, just watching these bodies fly. They looked like dolls. So anyway, we get the word that we'd done a great job, the building was destroyed, and the battle damage assessment (BDA) was 30 to 50 guys. There was a Major Johnson there who was the public affairs officer. Apparently he was running around looking for me and I was wondering what was going on. So I finally find him and he asked if I minded if someone from the London *Telegraph* talked to me. I asked what the big deal was. He said, "Do you know what happened?" I said, "No." He said, "That fire mission you called took out Omar Hadid." I said, "Who the hell is he?" He said he was the second in command to Abu Musab al-Zarqawi and was left in charge when Zarqawi left. They said that it was a great success. He then said the intel guys did their BDA and thought possibly 72 guys were killed. The London *Telegraph* guy said, "You need to tell me what you saw." I'm very paranoid about speaking with the media and getting myself in trouble, plus I didn't want to look like a warmonger either. I didn't want to look like I was bragging or anything. I was trying to keep it sterile, so I turned to Major Johnson and asked, "Can I tell this guy about the crazy shit I saw?" He said, "Sure, tell him everything you saw. This was a huge success. Tell him about the bodies and everything you saw." I said, "All right." So I told him everything I just told you, that this was the craziest shit I had ever seen, that it was awesome and that it was a great success. So that was a good day. Did Captain Boggiano tell you about when he was caught in the firefight on 11 November, where he got pinned down and called for my tanks to fire?

JM: He did, but maybe you can tell me about it from your perspective.

NP: It's less cool, though, from my perspective because we were just lobbing rounds. There was the easternmost road that first goes diagonally and then hooks and goes straight due south once it reaches the halfway point of the city. We were south of Phase Line Fran by a few hundred meters. Captain Mayfield told Boggiano to go down south to the southern part of the city because we were probably going to hit it in the next few days. He wanted Boggiano to recon it and stay out there out in the sand about two clicks from the city, so he went out there. We were just hanging around bored. Everything was quiet. All of a sudden, though, we hear that Outlaw 1 is on the net, he's in contact. I told Sergeant Terry, "If we just punch through this factory wall in front of us, we could probably see due south." So we punch through and see the four gun trucks out there. There's dust and dirt kicking up everywhere and I'm trying to get a situation report. I can see where Boggiano is shooting into the houses, which were a couple hundred meters in front of him, and Terry and I just started lobbing HEAT rounds into one of the houses. So then we called and asked if that was the house he was taking contact from and he said, "Hell yeah! Can you do that to every house you see?" There were about four to six houses in this open desert area that he was actually going to use to screen the city and we just started lobbing HEAT rounds. Boggiano described it as these big, long laser beams coming down on these houses. HEAT rounds arc very high because they're so heavy and we're lobbing rounds about 1,300 meters into these houses and successfully just blowing them out. He's looking at the houses from east to west and he sees the rounds enter from north and they just blow everything out the backside of the houses. He was so excited. When you're a tanker, there's nothing better than just blowing shit away with direct fire and being able to relieve others from whatever hell they're going through. We just had a good time. We didn't know how bad it was until later on when he described all that to me.

JM: I understand at one point that your tank hit a mine.

NP: Yes, that was around 12 November. On 11 November was when Lieutenant Edward Iwan was killed and the 12th was when Captain Sean Sims was killed. Is that correct?

JM: Yes, that's right.

NP: On 12 November we started the mission around 0700. We were now in the last click or so of the city, just clearing out the dug-in guys. This was where it was going to get bad. The infantry was going house to house and street to street, and if you were looking at the southern part of the city, we were on the east side of the city out in the dirt and 2-2 Infantry was in front of us. We heard on the net about Terminator 6 and what was going on. We were kind of confused because we were just sitting there letting the infantry do their fight. It was our job as the BRT to stay on the outskirts and just screen. All of a sudden, we hear that Terminator 6 isn't on the net, nobody knows where he is, and that's when Lieutenant Colonel Peter Newell, the task force commander, made the decision to pull everyone back and have the BRT just wipe the last click of the city down with artillery. I was pumped because I was told I was going to be the one to get to do it, and that Lieutenant Colonel Newell wanted me to fire for effect, left 50, fire for effect, left 50, fire for effect, and basically do that until there were no more houses to blow up. That's like the coolest thing ever. I was a 24-year-old lieutenant and I got to level a city with artillery.

JM: Christmas and your birthday all in one.

NP: Yeah, it's better than all of those. So I backed up in the desert about 300 or 400 meters. What I didn't know was that my actual organic company commander, Captain Paul Fowler, was still in contact in the city, so I had to continue to wait for the green light to go. While we were waiting with my wingman next to me and the Bradleys pushing down to the south, all of a sudden some rounds land about 100 to 200 meters in front of me. Meanwhile, Captain Boggiano is behind me with his Humvees doing his screen lining. He was looking due west into the city with me to his front about 1,000 meters. Anyway, I called up and reported that two rounds just landed in front of me. He said, "Roger. Avenger 6 is still in contact. He's calling for fire." I said, "Got it." It was friendly. At that point, another two rounds come walking towards me, this time about 75 to 100 meters out. I called and said, "The rounds are actually coming closer." He said, "Roger, I'll call them up on their net. Meanwhile, you get the hell out of there." I said, "Got it." I told Mewborn to back it up and, just as I said that, a round exploded right in front of my tank. My loader and I were sitting up on the turret with our butts on the hatches and I'm looking backwards and start screaming, "Go back, go back!" He floors it and we go in reverse, and I'm just waiting for the next round to hit us. All of a sudden, the whole left side of the tank explodes, the tank goes up a little, and both my loader and I fall into the hatches. So I'm on the turret floor, my feet are on my gunner and I'm reaching for the hand mike to tell them I'm okay, which I was finally able to do. I was cussing up a storm thinking we'd just been hit by friendly artillery. I get on the ground and look in front of me and my tank isn't even facing west anymore; it's facing north. The whole left side of the track had been blown off. I walk around the track and call my wingman forward. He tied his ratchet strap from his gun tube to the track. He was tying to lift the track up to try and drag it back to the tank so we can line it back up and fix it. At this moment, the recovery has already started, an M88 is about to come out to my location and then my wingman calls me over and says, "Hey sir, what the hell is this?" I walked over to him and there was a giant, yellow-beige doggie dish-sized disk under the track and there were two more under the track that he hadn't even raised yet. I was like, "That's a f------ tank mine!" He kicks it, the top pops off and you can see the explosives underneath and the pressure plate. He was like, "Holy shit!" I said, "Man, that's a tank mine. I think we're in a minefield!" My wingman starts screaming for everyone to get on their tanks right now. All the soldiers jump on their tanks and he realizes he has to do a mine plow job, so he kicks his gunner and his loader off his tank. He said, "It's not a safe mission. I'll just do this with me and my driver." His loader and his gunner went to me and my whole four-man crew was standing on our tank on the turret. He drives off and I see the M88 coming towards us, so I sprint towards the 88 and tell them to stop because we're in a minefield. He asked what they were supposed to do. I told him the mine plow was coming and it was going to plow a lane to the 88 and then a lane from the 88 to me and we could tow this thing out of here. I run back to my tank and am now standing on top of the tank with my five other guys. All of sudden, a sniper starts shooting at us. We were like, "Oh shit!" So we all get down and run to the east side of the tank and we're all crouched down hiding from the sniper. Sergeant Terry is coming back at us now and he's plowing the lane with the 88 in tow behind him. I look at him and he's screaming at us but I can't hear him over the plow. His face was red, he had this cigarette in his hand and he was spitting from his mouth he was screaming so hard. He was just bright red screaming. Then, as he was almost right on top of us, he said, "Get the f--- away from the tank! You never stand in front of a tank when it's plowing a minefield!"

Sure enough, mines are coming up from the soil and luckily none of us got blown up. We run around to the west side of the tank and we're hiding there as Terry was coming up on the east side of the tank. We were standing there waiting for mines to explode on our right hand side, and all of a sudden bullets start cracking around the tank skirt all around us as we're crouched by the tank. We were like, "Oh crap. We forgot about the sniper." Now the six of us are all crammed into the turret of our tank, which holds three. We were sitting there and we were like, "This is f------ ridiculous. Only in Fallujah and only in Iraq would you be pinned down by a sniper in the middle of a minefield. When would you ever think that would happen to you?" It was just the funniest thing. I mean, throw me a bone here. That was pretty wild. I know Boggiano pretty much thought we had exploded and died.

JM: How would you overall assess the role your platoon played and maybe the BRT in general? Do you think you were employed the best way you could have been? Were there ways you think you could have been better used?

NP: No, I don't think so. The way Captain Mayfield used us was great. I can't imagine it being done any way else. There were two things that went on. First of all, he pretty much gave me free reign. I think that was more the nature of combat, though, than the choice he had. Second of all, ask anyone from 1st ID or any of the tankers from Fallujah: this shit is easy when your orders are to kill everything in front of you and when you're limitless on fuel and ammo. Food and sleep? Don't worry about it. That's what we live for. I had that liberty and, as a light infantry company commander, Captain Mayfield had two tanks at his disposal. That's huge. After 12 November, the BRT became the main effort for 2-2. The tanks always led, the Bradleys were behind us – and we used the Bradleys like taxis, which was awesome. They came in behind, dropped ramp, brought infantry and then went back. The other great thing about the tanks when you're moving is that the tanks are always where the front line troops are in the BRT. The scouts were clearing houses and we were never behind them. We were always equal with them or in front of them, so you always knew your front line trace. There was a lot of friendly fire going on, though. My infantry platoon sergeant actually was shot at by his own platoon leader with 25 millimeter. I don't know if you heard that story.

JM: No, I didn't.

NP: On 10 November, we were getting ready to do a big push into the southern part of the city. As we were holding and waiting for the green light to go, Alpha Company 2-63 – the armor company that I came from – came parading right through our lane in front of us because their lane had been choked off. They cut in front of us and pushed down and then went back to the west, now they were back in their lane. We figured they knew where we were, so we pushed forward to get even with them. As we do this, we see a giant rocket that looked like one of those boosters from the Space Shuttle and it was sitting on an eight-foot berm pointing due east and slightly up. It wasn't wired to anything; it just stood alone. We called up and asked Legion 7 if he could go around us, go in front of that thing, hook up behind it and just shoot it with the 25 millimeter. He does and he shoots the thing and we were hoping it would just explode. Instead, he sets off the primer and that thing just launches into the sky. It went off like a Space Shuttle rocket. It takes off with bright orange flames and I was like, "Oh my God. That thing just went due east and Boggiano is out there." I get on the radio and call him and ask if a rocket just impacted out there. He said he was good and I was like, "Thank God." All of a sudden, 25 millimeter rounds start blowing up against the back of my platoon sergeant's Bradley and it was coming from his west. We realized it was Alpha Company's Bradleys – the ones that came from the BRT - that were shooting at us. I tell my loader to switch to the Avenger net and I say, "Cease fire! Cease fire! You're shooting friendly troops." The platoon sergeant over there gets on the radio and says, "Negative. We're not shooting friendly troops." I was like, "Who was just shooting due east with 25 millimeter right now, because you just hit us." My first sergeant gets on the net and says, "We were engaging an RPG team that just launched an RPG." I said, "Negative, you were shooting us. We just set off a rocket." I said to my loader, "Get me off this f------ net." I was so pissed off. But you can't get angry. If you think an RPG just got launched to your right, your first instinct is to engage. They knew we were there yet they still engaged, but that's the fog of war that no amount of technology can ever eliminate. I don't care what the Pentagon says. That's just the nature of it and you just have to accept it. Thank God we were in armored vehicles.

JM: How do you think you were supported by the task force in terms of logistics?

NP: I just got back from Diwaniyah and the Army has a new policy where it's like "whack-a-mole." I'm sure you've heard the term; it's sort of trendy to use but it's serious. In southern Iraq right now, there are no coalition forces other than a few of the military training teams (MTTs). So they sent this battalion task force, my company included, to go whack down these uprisings. It's great, but when you hammer these guys they squirt to other cities. Diwaniyah was the "whack-a-mole" thing; we had no maps or anything. It was just rush your ass off to another city where insurgents are flaring up with no imagery, maps, or preparation. But in Fallujah, let me tell you, logistically it was great. The maps were great and I had all the fuel and ammo I needed. I heard the rumors that we went black on ammo but everybody in theater was rushing to bring us ammo. I needed an IGV cable and this infantry battalion maintenance officer, who doesn't even know what it is, writes it down and gets it to me within 18 hours. That's unheard of. Logistically, the support for the Battle for Fallujah was just awesome and that's how it's supposed to be. When the troops are there and are getting ready to do their mission, the maps should already be there and you should start prepositioning the ammo. I'll say one thing, though: nobody thought we'd go through that much ammo. I don't know why that is. I think it was because nothing like Fallujah had happened before. I wasn't with 3d ID in the beginning when they took Baghdad, but this was just a shoot fest. Logistically they did great. At no point was I conserving ammo and I think that's how you have to operate. The Army is supposed to be effective, not efficient. It's a war machine, not a business.

JM: During this operation, did you have any interaction with any of the Iraqi units that were taking part?

NP: I only had two experiences with the Iraqis and they were really funny. One was at the very beginning. It occurred on the evening of 7 November, I think, when we did the walk-through rehearsal with everyone. The Regimental Combat Team 7 (RCT-7) commander was there, Lieutenant Colonel Newell was there, as were all the company commanders and platoon leaders. First off, the Marine colonel gave a speech that was pretty cool. Then Lieutenant Colonel Newel gets up and gives a pump-up speech that was good too. He said things like, "This is the closest you'll ever come to a battle between good and evil." It really fired me up. Then, though, this Iraqi colonel from the Kurd battalion gets up there and he starts talking in Arabic. The interpreter is interpreting every couple of sentences for him, but he starts getting more and more emotional and starts talking faster and faster in Arabic. As he keeps talking faster, he's not giving the interpreter a break and he's just going on and on. At one point, the interpreter actually taps him on the shoulder to stop him but he just swats the interpreter's hand away. He's got his finger pointed in the air, he's screaming and yelling, and then he finishes and just storms off. We're all sitting there and the interpreter didn't know what to do. Captain Boggiano said, "You know, I don't know what that guy just said, but I'm fired up!" It was the funniest shit ever. This guy was really emotional about it. It was great seeing leaders show some passion so we were all fired up. The Iraqis were clearly some pretty intense dudes and I think they were pretty fearless. On 9 November I remember them rolling up behind me and they did that blooming onion thing where they shoot in every which direction. Thank God we were in our tanks because we took a little contact from the hospital and they just shot everything. They don't really duck and cover. I had very little contact with them, though. As the BRT, we didn't have counterparts or have to hold hands with any Iraqis. Our task was just to be the forward element and be the reserve when 2-2 and 2-63 got tired.

JM: You mentioned the Marines a couple times. Do you have any other thoughts about the whole joint aspect of this operation?

NP: When you talk about adjacent unit coordination, I had to physically drive my tank over, get on the ground, link up with this Marine major and tell him where I was and where he was on the map. I told him he needed to halt his move because we're going to move west. This was on 13 November and we were just sitting there lighting stuff up. This was when the BRT became the main effort for 2-2 Infantry, and 2-2 had been the main effort for the whole eastern side to include the Marines. This was several days into the battle and the Marines were taking just horrible casualties. They only had 7.62 and 5.56, those weird shoulder fired rockets and that was it. I don't ever remember hearing or seeing the main guns go off on their tanks. From what I understand, the Marines used their tanks like pillboxes where the tank is just this weapons platform that the infantry can maneuver around. We ended up taking a lot of their AO and it got to the point where Phantom 6 was telling me to go make linkup with the Marines, who ended up being about a click away. I had to go out and find this guy, and they used something called mIRC Chat. They gave us FM frequencies but they never monitored them. As far as coordination goes, it was difficult.

JM: Do you have any general lessons learned comments about the Battle of Fallujah and what it accomplished?

NP: Back at FOB Normandy, Lieutenant Colonel Newell got up there and said, "What we do here with the after-action review (AAR) is very important. We are rewriting the books at the schoolhouse for the urban fight with an armored force." I was like, "Hell yeah!" People were saying that the age of tanks was over. In 2001, I was told when I was a cadet not to branch armor because tanks were going the way of the dinosaurs. I was convinced after the Battle of Fallujah, though, that we had proven that tanks and Brads can go anywhere. There was a point when I was going straight into the city and ran into these residential houses where I couldn't turn left or right, and I see Lieutenant Emery in his Bradley in a courtyard – and the courtyard is just slightly bigger than his Bradley. He saw me, did a 270-degree turn and got out of my way. I couldn't back up and I couldn't turn because of where the enemy and friendly forces were, but he was able to get out of my way. There's nowhere a tank or a Bradley can't go. The great thing about the city is that there are no canals. Cities are built on the flat desert. The area I'm in now makes it hard for movement, but down in the city tanks and Bradleys can go anywhere. I don't care what anybody says. So if I would say anything, it would be to not reduce the footprint of armor in any fight. We already know that tanks do great in open terrain. That's a given. But you don't want to reduce your footprint in the cities by taking away the armor. The enemy is getting more sophisticated with the explosively formed penetrators (EFPs) and the RPG-29s, and you can't beat the tank for crew survivability. As far as coordination was concerned, I think the reason we had enemy to our rear at the beginning was that the Marines couldn't keep up. Clearly right off the bat you have to do a better job of maintaining your front line trace. We did it great at the organic Army level, but at the joint task force level with the Marines we did a bad job of that. There has to be a better way. The Marines don't have tanks like we do, so how do you keep up with tanks and Brads? I don't know what the answer is. Do you slow the tanks down? If you do, you will lose the momentum that the tanks and Bradleys bring to the table. Right off the bat the Army should have spearheaded that. Even though it was a Marine AO, the Army should have taken charge and the Marines could have held and secured it. That's what infantry does best. They hold.

JM: Another thing I meant to ask you was: what kind of visibility did you have over the initial breach itself?

NP: All I knew was that it was going to be dangerous as hell and I was expecting a lot of friendly casualties. All we were told was that it was heavily defended and we were going to get tanks stuck in the trash and the scrap metal. I just had a feeling that we were going to lose a lot of people and I thought the BRT was going to be killing a lot of squirters. The death of Sergeant Major Steve Faulkenburg was a shocker. I don't understand how that happened. When we heard about it, everybody was kind of confused. Other than that casualty, though, things were a lot less violent than we thought they were going to be. We spent 10 hours dropping artillery on that city. What we realized was that you can get very close to your own artillery and you can basically drop artillery on top of yourself and still live. That's what we learned from the screen line.

JM: Are there any other parting thoughts you have about this battle or anything you might pass on to someone who's going to be a tank platoon leader in an urban environment?

NP: I have to say that I fell into a lucky bunch. My peers were people like Captain Boggiano and I had the latitude from my commander. My platoon was great. You asked about being cross-attached. I brought that up to my battalion commander back in Ba'qubah. I told my colonel how great it was to be cross-attached and said we should do this more often. He said, "You don't need to do that. There's no need to stay permanently task organized. How quickly did I split you up and then send you to the infantry and how well did you do?" I said, "We did real well." He said, "Did you have any practice or any training?" I said, "No." That's the one lesson. It's all about fundamentals and it's all about building blocks. You need to stay pure, you need to train with tankers and you need to maintain those skills. There's no use spending my time learning everything the infantry is doing. I know they're pushing for that, saying everyone is an infantryman first; everyone's a rifleman first. Negative. They have military occupational specialties (MOSs) for that. You can either have me as a tanker, doing that as well as I do, or you can have me as a grunt. But if you have me doing both, I'm not going to do either one as well as I would if I was just dedicated to one. On the spot task organization is the way to go. It's your tank company and you live and die by your tanks. When you're doing gunnery, that's when you learn those basic skills, fundamentals and instincts and you reduce your reaction time. When you put a tank section with an infantry section, it just seems more fluid because infantry will do what they do best and armor brings its firepower and survivability to the table right off the bat. I will say, though, that there has to be an innate level of competence that's built in with that leadership, and having guys as competent as Captain Boggiano on my left flank is huge.

JM: Thank you so much for your time today, Neil. It's greatly appreciated.

Command Sergeant Major Darrin Bohn
20 July 2006

CI: My name is Dr. Christopher Ives (CI) with the Operational Leadership Experiences Project at the Combat Studies Institute, Fort Leavenworth, Kansas. Today's date is 20 July 2006 and I'm interviewing Command Sergeant Major Darrin Bohn (DB) at Fort Benning, Georgia, telephonically about his experiences in the Global War on Terrorism (GWOT) and specifically his experiences during Operation Phantom Fury. If at any time we start to move into an area that is classified or sensitive and you're uncomfortable with your ability to sanitize your answer, just let me know that's something we can't discuss. Sergeant Major, would you state your full name and your current duty position and post?

DB: My name is Command Sergeant Major Darrin J. Bohn and I'm currently the 11th Regiment sergeant major at Fort Benning, Georgia. My rank and duty position during Operation Phantom Fury was the operations sergeant major and, about 10 or 15 minutes into the fight when Command Sergeant Major Steve Faulkenburg was killed, I assumed duties as the command sergeant major.

CI: When the fight started and in preparation for the fight, you were the ops sergeant major for Task Force 2-2?

DB: Yes.

CI: How long had you been in that duty position?

DB: I arrived there in July 2002.

CI: So you deployed with the battalion?

DB: Yes, I did. We deployed to Kosovo for nine months, returned and did our train up for Iraq. I deployed to Iraq as the operations sergeant major and Faulkenburg was the command sergeant major.

CI: So you and he had served together for quite some time at that point?

DB: I'd say about a year and a half at that point.

CI: Who was the battalion operations officer (S3)?

DB: Our battalion S3 during Phantom Fury was Major John Reynolds.

CI: How was the battalion task force S3 shop organized for combat?

DB: We had a light tactical command post (TAC) and a heavy TAC. The light TAC consisted of four Humvees with the S3, a couple battle captains, the fire support element, a security element and an Air Force enlisted tactical air controller (ETAC). The heavy TAC was two Bradleys and it consisted of myself and Headquarters 33 with a lieutenant/battle captain and Lieutenant Colonel Pete Newell and his Bradley. Headquarters 66 was just himself, his gunner and his driver.

CI: Where was the ground liaison officer from the Air Force and where was the fire support coordinator?

DB: They were in the light TAC with the S3.

CI: Was there a tactical operations center (TOC) as well?

DB: The TOC was back at Camp Fallujah where we were with the Marines. It was about 20 miles outside of the city and that consisted of the intelligence officer (S2) rear, Captain Natalie Friel, some more fire support guys, and some of the battle staff back there who were tracking the larger battle, which included the logistics officer (S4).

CI: Was this normally how 2-2 configured for a fight or did you decide to structure the command post (CP) organization this way?

DB: We went on some of the local missions around the Diyala Province, mainly Muqdadiyah, where we were stationed at Forward Operating Base (FOB) Normandy and there would be a mixture sometimes of the light and heavy TAC. It just depended on the mood or the mission requirements for how we would configure and go out.

CI: Were you involved in the planning of the joint operation with the Marines?

DB: I wasn't really involved with that. It was mainly just our task force specific, what we were going to do and how we were going to conduct the mission. I was not involved in the big picture with the joint task force.

CI: When did you get the warning order (WARNO)?

DB: Those dates are kind of foggy after all this time. I want to say about 15 days before we were going to leave FOB Normandy to go to Fallujah.

CI: So as far as you were concerned, your battle started when you deployed from the FOB.

DB: We experienced quite a few contacts with our convoy on our way there to Camp Fallujah. We stayed there about three days to finalize the plan and do some rehearsals. We went on a feint the night before we went in.

CI: Let's talk about some of those troop leadership procedures (TLPs) and prep for battle activities at Camp Fallujah. You close on Camp Fallujah – you had to fight your way down there basically, redistribute ammo, and make sure everybody is fueled up and such. Did you issue a fragmentary order (FRAGO) at that time based on an update of the tactical situation?

168

DB: We did issue a FRAGO on what we were going to do in Fallujah. When we left FOB Normandy, we did an order to get to Fallujah safely and then finalized the plan when we got to Fallujah. We did a huge rock drill before the rehearsals and that paid big dividends for us.

CI: Was it pretty much an Army only rock drill with the company commanders?

Db: It was. It was company commanders and I want to say we went down to the platoon sergeant level. We also had the Iraqi Intervention Force (IIF) there with the Iraqi battalion commander and his company commanders, to include the major who was the liaison for that group.

CI: You didn't mention any Marines. Were they involved in this rock drill?

DB: We had an attachment that was more of a sensitive site exploitation (SSE), kind of a human intelligence (HUMINT) team that was with us. We had no real Marine fighting force.

CI: What about a liaison element for command and control and things of that nature?

DB: No.

CI: Going back to the Iraqis for a second, did you cross attach any liaison officers (LNOs) with the Iraqis?

DB: No. The major in charge of the IIF had a contingent of noncommissioned officers (NCOs) that assisted him and he was on our radio frequency so we talked to him quite a bit. They were actually part of the fight for us. The major commanded and controlled for us and relayed his orders to the IIF battalion commander, so he was like another maneuver element.

CI: His subordinates were embedded in the force structure of the Iraqi battalion to help facilitate that. What other attachments did 2-2 have from the brigade? Was there an engineer slice or things of that nature?

DB: We had already had an engineer platoon attached to us in Alpha Company's task organization so we had just brought them with us. We had those guys from the beginning so they were an integral part of Alpha Company.

CI: What sort of capability did they bring? Did they have bulldozers?

DB: We actually had a mine clearing line charge (MCLCs) and a couple recharges. The Marines did give us a bulldozer at the beginning to help with the breach and we had the Scan Eyes – the little computer with the drone that we flew around.

CI: The Ravens?

DB: We had a couple Ravens that were just part of our organic task force in the S2 shop. I don't recall anything else. We did have a 155 battery of Paladins that was just totally for us that our brigade attached to us for the fight.

CI: Going back to the prep for combat and the TLPs, did any issues arise during the couple days you were at Camp Fallujah before moving to your assembly areas (AAs) that needed to be addressed in terms of command and control?

DB: Brigade actually sent down an LNO that was inside the Marine place who did some overhead cover for us, but I don't recall any sort of command and control issues.

CI: Were there any communications or computer issues? Did you guys go ahead and wicker up the radio network structure for your FMs? Did the Marines have Blue Force Tracker?

DB: They did have Blue Force Tracker and I don't recall any communication issues at all. The TOC at Camp Fallujah had a pretty big radio and sometimes it was a little sketchy talking to those guys because it was 25 miles away; but we had direct contact and we were always monitoring Regimental Combat Team (RCT) 7's frequency and the battalion commander talked to him frequently about our progress.

CI: Do you recall any issues with the battalion task force keeping up with the companies?

DB: No, not at all. The light TAC tracked it pretty well and the colonel and I were with the maneuver element, so we pretty much had a good idea on where the companies were and our friendly forward positions. I thought the battle tracking was done very well.

CI: From the way you just described that, I think I have a better appreciation for the rationale for the light and heavy TAC now. With your track and the battalion commander's track, you can move to the sound of the guns, so to speak, because you're armored.

DB: There were a couple times that the colonel and I found ourselves in front of the company so we had to go back. We were being a little bit overzealous. As the ops sergeant major, it was kind of strange because with my background, now being in a Bradley, you don't see that very often.

CI: You guys are given the ability to go to where the battle is without worrying about the thin skins and you can put those guys somewhere else. Walk me through the movement up to the AAs and the breach.

DB: The night before, I called it a feint but we reconned the route, did the same route we were going to take during the fight when we did the breach, and literally went up and ID'd the breach.

CI: Did you do this with organic elements?

DB: Actually it was the whole battalion task force that moved up and identified their AAs and their assault positions. We actually even tweaked the 155s where they would fire the smoke and everything else so we actually fired artillery that night as well.

CI: To get registered as well as assist in the deception?

DB: Yeah. I think it was a pretty good deception.

CI: What happened after you crossed the line of departure (LD)?

DB: We crossed the LD and Team Tank, which was Alpha 1-63 or 2-63, went up with the Abrams – Faulkenburg in tow with Alpha Company. They fired the MCLC and established a foothold into the breach. We sent the company through with the tanks to secure the objective right inside the breach and then moved Alpha Company up and basically started the leapfrog. The other Marines got bogged down in their breach and some of their systems may have failed, but when it's all said and done I believe the majority of the Marines used our breach to gain a foothold into the city and move up to their sector.

CI: Did that bring about any command and control issues? This was during the hours of darkness, correct?

DB: Right, it was during the hours of darkness but it really didn't cause any problems. We moved a lot faster than those guys because we were all mechanized whereas they had some of their tracks, but they were mainly dismounted. We were already pretty much into the city – at least a kilometer or so – where they could go through and sneak around and get to where they needed to go.

CI: How are the mech companies using their tanks?

DB: They're basically just going down the street and clearing a path for Alpha Company to come in and follow on and have their dismounted infantry clear building to building.

CI: What sort of resistance are they meeting?

DB: When we first entered the city it was kind of a light resistance, and I want to say it was the remnants of the Fallujah Brigade because we really didn't get into a huge fight until we crossed Main Supply Route (MSR) Michigan a couple days later. That was the main MSR that ran through the city of Fallujah.

CI: By daylight of the first day, is the whole battalion task force through the breach and into the city?

DB: It is.

CI: Did you coil up at daylight or did you keep moving?

DB: We still went through and cleared. The majority of the fighting was really at dusk and right at dawn. They took to the cover and hid during the day and in the middle of the night because they didn't have any advantage. There was sporadic gunfire from the beginning until we left, but the bottom line was that the enemy didn't really focus themselves on us until the early morning. Right when it was transitioning between night observation devices (NODs) and light is really when a lot of our big fights and engagements took place, and then at night right after dark. They may have eaten, had a full belly and decided to kick it off. We used the day to refit, refuel and rearm and get a little rest.

CI: I've seen references to hot refueling and rearming. Did the battalion S4 push a logistics package (LOGPAC) forward?

DB: The battalion maintenance officer (BMO), Captain Jamey Friel, he and his motor pool guys along with Captain Johnny Fortenberry who was the S4 – they were both shit hot, both those young captains. The S4 was an armor guy, Friel was an infantry guy and both were junior captains who hadn't been to their captain's career course yet, just doing phenomenal work keeping everything refueled and rearmed. They would bring it forward and we would fall back, get refueled and rearmed, and go right back to the fight.

CI: I'm assuming with a mech task force like this that your support is all heavy expanded mobility tactical truck (HEMTT) uploaded?

DB: It was.

CI: So they could move in that sort of terrain once the task force has gone through.

DB: Yep, and then of course the motor pool guys have their '113s that would pull security for those guys.

CI: Did the task force keep the '88s – the recovery vehicles – forward?

DB: They did keep a couple forward and each company had one as well, so they would have their own company thing so they would move the '88 up to recover a vehicle if needed. But surprisingly enough, I think we only had to do one real deliberate recovery on a tank. The rest of the vehicles held up pretty well minus a couple strapping a tow bar on a Bradley and pulling them back a little bit. For the most part, the motor pool guys really kept our stuff up to snuff.

CI: Back to the enemy resistance. Did it seem like there were individual fighters coming at the task force? Were there squads, organized platoons?

DB: I think it was more groups, maybe squad-sized or three-man teams. I don't recall a large sized element until we crossed MSR Michigan into the industrial area where we lost Lieutenant Ed Iwan and Sergeant James Matteson. We got ambushed up there by the mosque where we found the building that had the big mural on the wall that connected Abu Musab al-Zarqawi and the rest of Al-Qaeda.

CI: What day was this?

DB: I think it was day three.

CI: Is this the same ambush where foreign fighters were popping up out of spider holes?

DB: You're absolutely right.

CI: This is principally rocket-propelled grenades (RPGs) to initiate?

DB: RPGs and small arms. When we got ambushed in that one spot – and we really got caught in a gaggle for some unknown reason. It was a perfect kill sack for the enemy and how we ended up in it was a fluke. There were a lot of folks in this area and there seemed to be RPGs coming from everywhere.

CI: Which element of the task force moved into this kill sack?

DB: It was actually Alpha Company to the right side and then the tanks were on the left; and somehow the colonel and I ended up in the middle of the two task forces and we were kind of coming up on the side. I can't remember the phase line names, but we were just clearing up through the city and we stopped in this area. It was an open area and, hindsight being 20/20, it looked like a pretty damn good area for the enemy to hit us and that's exactly what they did.

CI: The first couple days of the battle seem to be characterized as the task force having the initiative. At any time did the initiative cross over to the enemy?

DB: Even when we got ambushed that day, they may have gotten one on us but I don't think they ever gained the initiative and put us on the defensive. We did fall back and regroup, and there was artillery and we dropped a couple 500-pound bombs on that area before we went back in, but I don't think we ever lost the initiative or the advantage to the enemy.

CI: Did Alpha Company fall back or did the battalion fall back?

DB: It was the battalion that fell back to the previous phase line and we started calling in artillery – the 155s that did a phenomenal job for us, to include the fire support guys. They dropped a lot of 155 rounds and a couple 500-pound bombs on what we thought was the suspected enemy stronghold with the little trenches going underneath the walls.

CI: For your close air support (CAS), did you utilize the Marine Air Ground Task Force (MAGTAF) or was this Air Force support?

DB: This was Air Force guys calling it in. The funny thing was that we had one Air Force guy attached to us and we started using the Air Force a lot to drop bombs; and at the end of the fight, we had at least four to six Air Force guys with us hoping to be able to call the last mission because we seemed to be the only ones out there using them and dropping bombs on our objective area.

CI: Do you think there may have been two air tasking orders (ATOs) then, one for the MAGTAF based on their organic air support and then a separate one for the joint forces air component commander?

DB: I always thought there was just the Air Force one. I wasn't aware of any of the Marines flying. They did have the Cobras flying around, but they were up pretty high. I don't recall any Navy ETACs calling in any CAS. It was just the Air Force guys we worked with and we didn't filter into the Marine sector that much. The RCT-7 commander made it a point to come see us at least once a day to talk about our future ops and the big picture and what he wanted from us.

CI: Operationally, was there any integration with the Marines? You mentioned they were principally light. Did they draw on the resources of the mech companies to help cut, so to speak?

DB: I want to say that day three and so on we would send a platoon over there to help clear some of their objective areas, so we actually went there and assisted them a couple different times on some hot spots.

CI: Would you say that mission emerged as opposed to being part of the original plan?

DB: It emerged because of our speed and mobility. We were at least a day ahead of them when it came to those guys fighting from building to building. I don't really know how much resistance they had down there, but I know that fighting from street to street as a light guy is pretty time consuming and very tiresome.

CI: Did this open up any seams and create an opportunity for the enemy?

DB: It may have, but we had the IIF following behind us doing some SSE and securing some of the key terrain features around the mosque, some intersections and some key buildings, so I don't believe anything filtered in behind us, but we would go through the city and then pull back. We called them gun runs. We would run down the street and try to receive fire to eliminate the pockets of resistance and then fall back to our company CPs and our battalion CP. The Marines were

174

just a little behind us because they weren't as quick as us and they didn't have as much firepower, so I don't want to say we caused some problems. If anything, we drove the majority of the enemy to their side of the city because, with some of the intercepts we received, the enemy was saying they were just getting the shit beat of them on this side of the town. We'd hear them saying they hit a tank and then another would just appear. They said it was a no-win situation for them, so they were saying they should get out while they can. A lot of the fighters may have fled through the Marine sector out of the city up by the lake and got out.

CI: The pace of operations is very different between the Army sector and the Marine sector, it appears.

DB: Yes, but it was never any problem for us shooting on their side. We had some restricted fire lines that we didn't want to cross and we actually chased a few guys over into their sector. I recall a mission of our Long-Range Advanced Scout Surveillance System (LRAS) up on top of the railroad, seeing some insurgents moving into the mosque in the Marine sector. They actually went back and lazed the target for the bomb to hit that part of the area where we killed a bunch of insurgents that weren't in our sector, because we were just further ahead of the Marines. I don't want to say there was a problem. There was no fratricide I was aware of with the Marines, either them shooting up behind us or us shooting across into their sector.

CI: With an Army pure task force – or when 2-2 is operating as a subordinate element of the brigade combat team (BCT) and everybody has Blue Force Tracker, everybody's on the same radio nets, you've established your fire support coordination lines and whatnot – it's a little different with a joint or combined operation. Did any extraordinary or unusual control measures have to be put into place?

DB: No, I can't recall any at all. I can't speak for the Marines and what they were doing, but we knew where they were at and their forward momentum either from the light TAC or from the colonel and me monitoring the RCT frequency. I don't recall any issues whatsoever when it came to fire control measures.

CI: You mentioned that when the command sergeant major was killed, the battalion commander had you switch hats.

DB: He did, but I don't think my role changed at all. We were in the middle of the fight. Faulkenburg was kind of the liaison with the tank company and he was supposed to pass the IIF through the tank company to their objective. I was in the heavy TAC with the colonel and, although it happened right inside the breach – I want to say seven to 20 minutes into the battle – I don't think it really changed the way my role was throughout the fight. I would go visit and try to instill confidence in the guys whether I was a master sergeant or the command sergeant major. It didn't matter.

CI: Plus, you're another set of eyes for the colonel.

DB: Right. I could tell him how the men were doing. I was dual-hatted but I didn't think my role or anything else had to change during that fight at all.

CI: Tell me what happens after this.

DB: I know we fell back and pretty much bombed it for the day with artillery. We went back through that night and it was pretty much towards the end of the town through the industrial area. We had set up our battalion TAC back behind the two companies and, that night, we went back and forth through the city where we were ambushed looking for people to shoot at us, threw in some pot shots and ran through the city to make sure we had cleared everything. When we got shot at, we would shoot artillery if possible, shoot the big guns on the Bradleys, and then dismount the soldiers to go and clear and eliminate the resistance. We did that throughout the night and, the following day, we went through and did some assessing. We would drive up and secure a position and have the guys get out and do some clearing. The tank company had two tank platoons and a motorized platoon with the scouts that we had.

CI: Your organic battalion scouts. Were they under armor or were they in Humvees?

DB: They were in Humvees.

CI: How would you characterize the most effective enemy resistance? Was it precision shooting, RPGs?

DB: It was RPGs.

CI: Any evidence the enemy had trained with these?

DB: Even in Afghanistan I was surprised that a guy couldn't shoot a rifle but, at a full sprint, he can shoot an RPG and pretty much hit what he's aiming at. Maybe it's like how some Americans put footballs in babies' cribs – maybe they put RPGs in theirs. They were pretty good with those.

CI: What about improvised explosive devices (IEDs) and mines?

DB: There weren't that many of them. If you recall, the Marines did a feint awhile back on the east side of the city and had a lot of those 2.75 millimeter rockets all lined up and daisy-chained to fire from the city out to the main MSR. They had a pretty elaborate system in our sector of IEDs and rockets that were all command detonated and rigged to go off. They had a couple land mines set up at key parts of the roads but they were surface laid as a decoy or put under some trash, so there were land mines out there and some mortars. We found that they would throw a brick with a rope outside a building and that acted either as a rally point or a weapons cache. Every place that we'd see these bricks outside the wall we'd either find a small weapons cache or some enemy personnel.

CI: How much indirect fire was the enemy using?

DB: They had a few rockets during the initial phase where they somehow were seeing where we had the casualty collection point and our other assets, like where we had the 120 millimeter mortars set up and they received rockets sometimes – and mainly it was the 60 millimeter mortars. I remember getting mortared at MSR Michigan waiting to go across, just five or six rounds, and then it would stop and then it would pick back up. Mortars weren't that effective and I only recall mortars being shot two or three different times. Some of the other folks, like the combat service support assets we had, did get rocketed for the first three days. It wasn't very effective but you could certainly say they were coming in.

CI: Do you think something that might have facilitated them as a target was that they weren't moving as aggressively?

DB: They weren't moving at all. They were on the other side of the road and somehow the enemy could see where they were and they were just lobbing pot shots at them.

CI: How was morale down in the companies?

DB: Morale was great. I hate to use Sergeant Major Faulkenburg's death – up until then, people were getting shot at, don't get me wrong, but I think it really woke people up when he got killed because, hey, if the sergeant major can get killed, this is some serious shit and they realized they had to get focused. Not that the guys weren't focused before then, but it kind of put everybody into the mindset that there was no coming back from this. And of course Alpha Company lost their executive officer (XO), Ed Iwan, and their company commander, Captain Sean Sims – and with a great American, First Sergeant Peter Smith, taking charge of that company. I even had to move my assistant operations guy to be the Alpha Company XO for a day or two until we got it all figured out with Captain Doug Walter coming from FOB Warhorse to take over the company. The morale was always good with the guys. They were fighting hard and winning and there were a couple times when it probably sunk in when they were sitting around doing nothing. But they were pretty busy and I thought morale was high all the time.

CI: Were there any issues with casualty evacuation or getting logistics pushed up to the companies?

DB: No, absolutely not. For some reason all that stuff worked flawlessly.

CI: I'm assuming it went according to doctrine with the first sergeants pulling that stuff up.

DB: Yes, the first sergeants would pull it up, and sometimes the XO would go back and pull it up depending on the situation and where we were at in the battle. We worked a lot of that stuff before we went to Fallujah, because every time we'd do a company or a two-company raid or cordon and search, we'd always push the assets up forward. It wasn't a strange thing for the '88s to roll out the gate, set some stuff up – whether for the enemy prisoner of war (EPW) collection point or to supply water or fuel. It was never a strange thing or a huge muscle movement to get those guys up, because they were always in the fight from the beginning when we crossed the border into Iraq.

CI: Was it routine at the company level to send a platoon or a Bradley back to bring the LOGPAC up?

DB: The first sergeant would bring it up with his '88 and a couple '113s, but mainly we didn't bring those assets too far forward. Platoons would break contact at a time and go back to the somewhat safe area to refit and rearm; and what was good about Camp Fallujah being 20 miles away is that we were actually getting hot chow mermited to the back. So the men, for the most part, were eating an A ration for breakfast and at dinner so we had a pretty good mechanism going. I'm not sure what the Marines were eating, but I know our logisticians were taking pretty good care of us.

CI: Were there any Class V issues, any problems moving ammo?

DB: We had a few issues with the 155 rounds. The Marines helped us out a little bit when we were in a pinch and, of course, they pushed some up from FOB Warhorse that actually were sent because General David Petraeus said people needed to get their heads out of their asses and send these guys some 155 rounds. We were probably critically low but we really didn't know it, although it all seemed to work out in the end.

CI: Clearly somebody thought the battalion was going to need that artillery or they wouldn't have been part of the task force, but the rates of consumption were higher than expected?

DB: Our two guns fired over 1,000 rounds, whereas the Marines had a battalion and they didn't even come close to what we were shooting. I don't know why that was. Maybe because they were light and they were running around, and when you have a bunch of light guys running around it's kind of hard to keep your forward trace going. We really used artillery a lot and we also used our 120 millimeter mortars a lot as well.

CI: Let's go back to your organic mortars. Did the battalion commander keep pretty close control of those? How were the mortars used during the battle?

DB: The mortars were employed as a platoon and they basically put the stop-gap between the 155s and the 120s. I don't know if that artillery battery that came with us was the very best, but there never really was a lag time when it came to a call for fire mission. The mortars fired about 700 120 millimeter rounds and those guys were mainly sending them on top of the rooftops and in some of the courtyards, whereas we focused the 155s somewhat on the buildings.

CI: I assume with a Bradley-based task force and the accessibility of thermal imaging and everybody has their NODs that you probably didn't shoot a lot of illumination, is that correct?

DB: Right. We did shoot some deep into the city but the Marines were a big fan of the illumination. I do remember seeing a lot of it but not from us as much.

CI: How was the battalion intel section able to keep up with the fight or, more importantly, help the battalion command team and the companies anticipate challenges hours out?

DB: Our S2 in the light TAC with Major Reynolds would do a lot of battle tracking and try to find out what was going on, but I think the real work horse was Natalie Friel back at Camp Fallujah tapping into some of these national assets and pushing them forward to us. She had control of a Predator and actually fired a Hellfire missile from Camp Fallujah to where we were running through the objective area, where she had seen some folks running around. She was running back and forth to the Marine TOC, tapping into some of the national assets, feeding them to the S2 guy and to the battalion commander so we could have a better and bigger picture of what was going on around us – the movements, some of the voice intercepts and so on. Both those two worked very well together with Captain Friel. It was a husband and wife team, by the way. Captain Jamey Friel was our BMO and Captain Natalie Friel was in the infantry battalion with us as one of our intel officers, which was kind of strange having a female captain in an infantry battalion but it worked out very good.

CI: Is it commonplace now for women to be in infantry battalions?

DB: I don't think so. I've been in the Army for 23 years and that's the first time I've ever had a female attached to an infantry battalion. We've had a couple medics, but never a female who was in the infantry battalion and deeply integrated into the planning and execution process. I don't want to sound like a male chauvinist jackass, but she was that smart and was immediately respected by the other guys for her knowledge and her know-how. It really didn't seem to matter.

CI: Intel was not only able to follow the battle but able to help anticipate and participate in the battle. Were there any communications issues? It sounds like you had connectivity pretty well.

DB: We did, and we had that system called Scan Eyes or whatever it was that we received right before we left. I really wasn't familiar with it, it really didn't work all that well for us, and our radios were sometimes a little sketchy from the city of Fallujah to Camp Fallujah, but other than that we worked through it.

CI: Let's go back to the battle narrative. We are up to day five and the battalion is continuing to keep pressure on the insurgents adjacent to the Marine sector. How did the nature of the battle change after the battalion fought through Alpha Company's ambush?

DB: The last couple days after the ambush and after we had finished clearing our section of the city, we sent a platoon over to help the Marines out until they finished up, and mainly we just went into more detailed searches of the buildings. We went through and did some SSE on some of the hot spots where we got hit pretty hard to try and gather some intel. The IIF was helpful in doing a lot of SSE, picking up some of the dead bodies and consolidating those guys so folks could pick them up. They also found a lot of documents. I don't really know what they were but people kept saying they were important so we kept pushing them up. Some of the civilians started coming out – and where they were hiding I have no idea – but a lot of them had freshly shaved faces and said they were here just guarding their homes and such, so that was kind of suspect. We did a lot of mop-up operations. If the guy really didn't look like he was going on, we would let him go to the mosque where they were getting a lot the civilians together; but if he looked sketchy or looked like he had been in a fight or was freshly shaved, then we would call the IIF, control him, and then turn him over for interrogation. The last couple days of the op were mainly just a mop-up/SSE operation.

CI: Did Task Force 2-2 have anybody attached to them at that point to assist with exploitation or interrogation or things of that nature?

DB: That small Marine contingent we had with us – about four guys – they went around and did some tactical questioning of some guys, but there really wasn't a lot that came out of that to my knowledge. We found a classroom that had an easel and a bunch of chairs with information that taught them how to shoot down helicopters and stuff like that. We also found a vehicle-borne IED factory. It was full of explosives. They had a green Chevy Suburban van that traced its origins back to Texas, but it was in there and the seats were gutted out, but it kind of looked like a contract vehicle that some of the civilian contractors were riding around in. We pushed some pictures up and stuff but no one actually came down to look at it to see what we found. There was a vice up there with a barrel in it, so it was a place where they were clearly up to no good – and that was in the industrial sector.

CI: At what is now the tail end of the battle, did the Marines come and relieve you in place? How did the battle handover go?

DB: They just spread out throughout the city and strong-pointed it. Some other follow-on forces came in and picked up some traffic control points. I want to say that when the 82d Airborne Division had gone to Fallujah for the first time, they had set up right outside MSR Michigan right at the overpass where the railhead ran through, and basically they just called us up on the radio and told us they had control of our sector. I want to say that a couple company commanders linked up with each other and shared some thoughts, and then we broke contact, went back to Camp Fallujah, and the Marines took over the whole city.

CI: What happened after that?

DB: There were a couple days back at Camp Fallujah to get cleaned up and wait for the HEMTTs to pick us up and take us back to FOB Normandy.

CI: Was there an after-action review (AAR) conducted?

DB: We did do an AAR internally but there wasn't anything real huge with 7th Army Training Command (ATC) that we were attached to.

CI: How was the movement back to the FOB?

DB: It was pretty uneventful. A couple HEMTTs breaking down and stuff like that and a couple wrong turns – pretty much standard operating procedure (SOP) going back.

CI: What stands out in your mind as the most positive surprise you saw during the prep or the conduct of the battle?

DB: I don't think it was a surprise but the soldiers were just outstanding. When they were asked to do something, regardless of the plan, those damn kids would pick anything up and make it look like a genius put it together. Those guys were just awesome, from the platoon sergeants on down and with the company commanders and platoon leaders inspiring the men to do great and wonderful things. Those guys never gave up, always had a positive attitude and brought it to the enemy 24 hours a day for the first three days. They were just non stop – kicking ass and taking names. They never doubted it or questioned it, they just kept on going. There were a few guys who stand out in my mind and those guys just get you up in the morning and make you proud to be part of an organization. Some of those things will never be known by anybody but were just absolutely amazing.

CI: What percentage of your subordinate leaders were Ranger qualified?

DB: We actually didn't have very many Ranger qualified NCOs at all. When Faulkenburg and I first got there, there were only three of us in the whole battalion. We had set up a little program and sent a few guys, but I would say when it was all said and done – enlisted-wise – there were probably six of us. It was a mechanized outfit and I always had my reservations about going mechanized, but those guys just need good leadership. No one wants to go to work and be a dirtbag and fail at what they're doing – and with good leadership and guidance, those guys shined. Lieutenant Colonel Newell and I, and Sergeant Major Faulkenburg in the beginning, really put a good comprehensive plan together before we left for Iraq. We knew it was going to be a ground fight, we knew there was going to be a lot of room clearing, and we knew the man with the rifle was going to win the battle, so we did a lot of close quarters battle (CQB) and close quarters marksmanship (CQM). With my background, I even ran a leadership program through the soldiers in the brigade that came to Vilseck. We ran them through a quick two-day CQB and CQM to get the other two or three battalions up to snuff where we were at. I still have guys coming up to me and saying they thought it was horse shit that they had to go through the courses in Vilseck but, that said, they wanted me to know that it also saved their lives and other soldiers' lives as well.

CI: Did you have any trouble getting the assets to do that?

DB: We had absolutely zero problems getting assets. Some of the close quarter optics and some of the M45 machine gun optics we didn't get until we got to Kuwait, so a lot of the guys weren't very familiar with some of the guns we eventually got before we crossed the border. But they knew how to shoot, they knew how to do a magazine change and they knew how to enter and clear a room. The only thing I really had heartburn about was when we were in Kuwait and we went through the Military Professional Resources Inc. (MPRI) thing. They had a memorandum of instruction (MOI) they had to teach that everybody had to go through and check the block – call it cover your ass. I don't know what it really was, but they were very inflexible on teaching military operations on urban terrain (MOUT). For example, a lot of those guys are ex-special ops and they were teaching the four-man stack with the guy going into the room and being a flyer, whereas I knew that our technique, expertise and training didn't allow us to send a flyer. I taught the strong wall technique so the soldiers knew when they entered and cleared a room that everyone in front of them was enemy and we didn't have a flyer going up. They were insistent that they teach that and I just thought they should really fall under the battalion's plan and maybe reinforce what we were doing up until then. I was pretty pissed off about that whole thing.

CI: Was there any opportunity to provide feedback?

DB: No. They said they had an MOI they had to do and they appreciated what we were saying, but that was what they were being paid to do and they didn't care what we thought. This was what their MOI said they had to teach us before we crossed the border. I'm a soldier and I've been a leader for a while. I see that it's my responsibility to teach my men how to fight and win in combat and I didn't really want to rely on a bunch of retired civilians to strengthen what my guys and I already knew. I took a little offense to it.

182

CI: You mentioned the close combat optics. I'm assuming there were issues in getting the laser target designators and white lights –?

DB: No, we did a pretty good job buying some flashlights. We got a lot of PQ2s and the older PAC4s before we left Germany and then got another big stash as the rapid fielding initiative (RFI) issue before we crossed the border. We ran a small arms master gunner course before we left where we had some guys come over and teach us how to use these.

CI: Who was your target audience?

DB: Team leaders and above. We made a couple platoon master trainers and they were pretty proficient at that before we crossed the border.

CI: Did you have access to ranges and the time to do that in Kuwait?

DB: We did have some ranges in Kuwait, but where the guys really paid big dividends was just running off some engineer tape in the field and doing some dry fire techniques, some magazine changes, and just getting their squad and platoon SOPs down for entering and clearing a room. Udairi had a great match site out there with cameras and the guys ran that very professionally. They were there to assist us but only when asked would they provide it, which was kind of nice. We basically took the tank company we had attached us at the time, and I focused on them because they were weaker than Alpha and Charlie, which were pure infantry.

CI: Did you end up with a mix of the ACOGs and the Aimpoints?

DB: We did have a mix of the ACOGs and the M68s.

CI: Did that work out for you?

DB: It did. We had the weapons quality with the ACOG and maybe a couple other [inaudible], and some of the shots that were really long were with the ACOG. It was a pretty good mixture.

CI: What about on the crew-served weapons?

DB: We had PQ2s and the M145 machine gun optics. The only thing I would've liked to have changed was the quadrant sight for the Mk-19 and, of course, the PQ2 on the .50 cal was a little rough and broke a lot and didn't hold its zero. So I just fell back to my Ranger battalion days with the guns [inaudible] and stuff like that, the quadrant sight for the Mk-19 to get that first and second round hit in lieu of trying to walk it in. With the AIM1 with the quadrant sight at night and, of course, the AIM1 with the .50 cal is a lot better as well.

CI: Those are authorized items, right?

DB: In a mechanized table of organization and equipment (TOE), you'd be surprised what's authorized and what isn't. We're still drawing M16A4s, whereas clearly the M4 is the way to go.

CI: You do give up a distance capability but –

DB: Well, in a city fight, distance really isn't that big of a deal. The compactness of the M4 really comes into play; and then you have the coax and the 25 on the Bradleys for your distance shots, plus we had the 240s as well. So I think we had that covered.

CI: When you guys got back to the States, could you tell if the infantry was going to stay with the M16A4 or were they going to a mix with the carbines?

DB: I think the Army is going to go with the carbines, but I'm not really in that big picture. My personal belief is that the carbine is the way to go.

CI: What was the most negative surprise you had from the move down from the FOB to Camp Fallujah, into the city and back out?

DB: I don't want to call it negative but there's always confusion when you're dealing with those corps assets when it comes to getting the HEMTTs – when they're going to show up, how many are you going to have – and then the quality of people who are going to come. When you're sitting in the back of that Bradley, riding back, there's always a big what-if and concern of what was going to happen. It was mainly just the support and getting back and then, of course, the information getting to the soldier level of when we're leaving – but that's been a problem throughout the Army for 231 years. There were really no big surprises. Just the unknowing of when you're going to leave, when the assets are going to show up and what assets are you going to have. You have the plan and then, of course, it always turns into a FRAGO of who you have and where you're going.

CI: Is there anything else you can think of that you'd like to get on the record in regards to leadership or TLPs or about the nature of the fight?

DB: No, not really. Not ever being in a mechanized assignment and not knowing a lot about the Bradley, I learned to really love that machine, to include the tanks in an urban fight. I always thought that, as an Airborne Ranger, it was a bunch of guys running up and door kicking, but when you have that tank and Bradley in support, it gives you a sense of comfort knowing somebody is there watching your ass. That's a pretty big gun to reach out and put a hurting on somebody. I think it's a big morale boost for the guys who are on the ground and, if they get in trouble, knowing those big assets can get you in and out of that area when it turns ugly. They're just a phone call away and there's not a whole lot that's going to stop them from getting there to get you.

CI: Thank you for your time.

184

Command Sergeant Major Timothy L. Mace
19 April 2006

MM: Why don't you go ahead and give me some background on yourself, like where you were born, where you went to school, your Army career up until Operation Phantom Fury started. Any assignments you may have had.

TM: All right, sir. My name is Command Sergeant Major Timothy Lee Mace. I was born in 1960 in St. Louis, Missouri. I entered the Army in June 1978, right out of high school, basic training, infantry AIT [Advance Individual Training], then jump school. My first assignment was in Italy as a paratrooper, second assignment was Fort Campbell, Kentucky. I did some time in the infantry there, then air assault school instructor for about two years. I went to Fort Bragg, North Carolina, for a straight shot of six years at the 82d Airborne Division. I became a drill sergeant and basically varied assignments. Training base, went to Korea, back to the training base, Fort Leonard Wood, Missouri, basic training. I went to the Sergeants Major Academy, went back to Fort Bragg, North Carolina, back here to the basic training brigade. Then I got activated to go and take over 2-7 CAV [2d Battalion, 7th Cavalry Regiment] about halfway through their tour, so I arrived in country in late September 2004. About five weeks later, my battalion was involved in the battle of Fallujah.

MM: Why don't you talk me through when you first found out that the Marines were going to use you guys and go into Fallujah.

TM: Well, a little bit of background. The battalion had fought in An Najaf in August 2004, so they had worked with the Marines before on a joint operation. As a matter of fact, part of the reason why 2-7 got selected was how well they worked with the Marines. They complemented the Marines with the assets the cavalry had. About the second week I was there, in Taji, I started hearing rumblings about we were going to go back to Fallujah and we've been selected. We started laying the groundwork. I went there myself with the S3 [operations officer], Major Tim Karcher, and the advance party just started getting the lay of the land at Camp Fallujah. Up to that point, the battalion had no experience in Anbar Province to my knowledge. So we went there, met our counterparts with the Marines, came back and they started planning. It wasn't certain they were going to have an operation. They didn't know when, perhaps in the upcoming future, but be prepared. About the last week of October, we were there on another reconnaissance and it started looking more and more like it was going to happen. We actually went down there for a planning conference. The day we got back was the day the battalion was alerted to load out, go to Camp Fallujah and prepare for future operations. We had a full-time fight on our hands at Taji, so it was a busy time for all.

MM: What was your impression of the Marines when you showed up? Did they treat you okay?

TM: Excellent. The Marines were extremely professional and I was very impressed with the 1st Marine Regiment, 1st Marine Division. The regimental command sergeant major welcomed me right off the bat. "Whatever your soldiers need, Camp Fallujah is open to you. If you ain't got it, you let me know and you'll get it." The Marine officers and staff officers, from the commander on down, just excellent to work with. No difference between the Marines and the Army as far as having common purpose, common direction, know what we had to do.

MM: How'd you personally prepare your soldiers for this action? In my opinion, this is the fight of the war right here. Did you have to do anything special to prepare them for this?

TM: No, actually not at all. The soldiers were battle hardened by Najaf, and that had nothing to do with Tim Mace. That was Lieutenant Colonel Jim Rainey and his guys. We had a couple new commanders, a couple changes in command, but they were in the brigade, so they were familiar with the people and the fight and everything like that. We had only received maybe one or two groups of replacements by the time I had arrived there, so we're talking about less that a dozen new soldiers – and a couple of those were combat experienced at another time and place. The soldiers were prepared for the fight and Najaf made them that way. What they were doing in Fallujah was basically Najaf on a more vicious scale. The soldiers continued their mission in Taji, patrolling, up until the time they folded in, prepped their vehicles and we loaded out. There was no time for any train up, other than when we got to Fallujah and actually started getting the battle plan.

MM: And you actually drove your vehicles to Camp Fallujah, is that correct?

TM: Some we drove and we moved others by HETs [Heavy Equipment Transporters], as I recall.

MM: Could you basically just talk me through your part in the initial Marine planning for the operation and up until November 8th, when they blow the breach and you guys go through?

TM: Our primary battle staff was involved in every regimental meeting of the two Marine battalions, 3-1 and 3-5. We were just another maneuver battalion under the 1st Regiment's planning process. That was mainly the officer battle staff NCO; they were doing that stuff, getting the orders. I will tell you there were no three finer officers in the entire theater for this fight than Lieutenant Colonel Rainey, Major Scott Jackson and Major Tim Karcher. All these guys are Jedi Knights, meaning graduates of SAMS [School of Advanced Military Studies], and they were actually making sure that what people were doing was doctrinally correct and was

186

resourced accordingly. We were just impressed to hear these guys. A little terminology back and forth: the Marines want us to do this, but what we should be doing is, that sort of thing. Whenever our guys had input like that, it was well received. The Marines said, "This is what we want you to do. Army: execute." Our officers took over and had a plan that looked good to me.

MM: Okay, the Marines blow the breach on the west of the train station. Talk me through the first day or two of the fight there as you guys head toward the Jolan District.

TM: We hurt them as best we could, and it was a pretty grand scale operation. I'm normally a foot soldier, airborne infantry. It was my first time in a mechanized force, so it was awesome to see how big of a scale this thing was, and just how much room you suck up trying to maneuver cavalry units. We rehearsed it on a smaller scale so everybody could get an idea of who was where and what they were doing. The preparation for the battle, we had Air Force, Army artillery, Marine artillery, everybody else prepping the battlefield. We led with our armor and they were going to do the plows and proof the lane, stuff like that. Charlie Company, 3-8 CAV, led by Captain Peter Glass, they were actually going to be the first ones in, lead with the M1s and then the Bradleys behind. From that point, I was with my battalion commander in his command Bradley, a two-man team: the S3 in one and the colonel in the other one. We were just following the lead assault elements through. Of course, the time schedule didn't survive initial contact. We anticipated, I think, somewhere around 2100, but the Army did not cross into the city until after midnight, 0100, something like that.

MM: So that puts you into November 9th.

TM: The operation started on the 8th, but by the time we were physically engaged with the enemy in their backyard, it was early morning on the 9th.

MM: Did you guys take a lot of fire as you were going in there initially, driving toward the Jolan District?

TM: I was not really on the net in the back of the commander's Bradley. What was happening to the lead elements, the commander and his primary staff could probably tell you much better that I could. I don't remember a heck of a lot of resistance or hearing anything like that. I do know that the commander and Major Karcher knew there was enemy out there taking shots. Major Karcher's Bradley actually creamed the guy that was lining Lieutenant Colonel Rainey's Bradley, our Bradley, up for an RPG [Rocket-Propelled Grenade] shot. So there was resistance out there, but the intensity, I really can't speak to.

MM: Is there anything that stands out in your mind during that initial 48 hours period? Any stories you'd like to get out there to folks?

TM: I've been in the Army 26 years and you always hear how good the Army is at executing, but it was awesome to see how everything followed the plan that Lieutenant Colonel Rainey and the Marines had laid out. It was a professional operation. When you have professionals with good equipment and good support who work well together going against a bunch of raggedly little muj', you're going to win. Everybody knew they were going to fight, and I'm not disparaging the enemy. They're brave in their own right, but they were just amateurs fighting professionals – and the professionals had the better toys.

MM: Did you end up at the bridge at some point?

TM: The battalion did, I physically did not. We had one company, either Alpha or Charlie, I'm not sure. It had gone over to the east end and secured that. I physically did not get to the bridge myself.

MM: Does anything stand out in your mind from when you guys get down to Highway 10, Phase Line Fran, the main highway that runs through the center of town? From there, up until I think you guys leave around the 20th of November – anything stand out in your mind on the second phase of the operation?

TM: We knew we were going to get where we were going to go, the question was just how long was it going to take us and how bad were we going to be hurt. After that, it was, "Okay, hold what you got." Then the Marines said, "Okay, we got them." We anticipated we'd continue to push all the way through that part of the city, we just didn't know when that was going to happen. We got to our initial objectives rather rapidly, all things considered. Then it was sit, consolidate, hold what you got, let the Marines do their thing. It was never safe in Fallujah, but it was not as bad as we thought it was going to be. And as things keep piling on, it was just natural: you have them on the run so let's do some exploitation, let's continue on. At that point, there was whole lot of waiting for the other shoe to drop. The colonel and I were in the city every day with the soldiers.

MM: Did you have any problems with combat service support operations?

TM: No. First of all, the battalion planned where they located the task force support area. It was close enough to be responsive, but they only took contact a couple of times, direct contact. It was only four kilometers, I think, north of the train station. So it was ideally positioned: access to the highway, access to the city, but not close enough that the enemy could really hurt us. Now, the support elements: excellent, just excellent. The tanks and Bradleys would come in daily battle damaged, black on fuel, black on whatever else. Whatever they had to do, they got the vehicles back in the fight quickly. I don't recall any vehicle being deadlined back there for very long, so the support element was excellent.

MM: Did the Marines provide you guys with chow or did you handle that yourself?

TM: Camp Fallujah pushed out one hot meal a day on most days, our guys would. It was prepared by the civilians working for the Marines on Fallujah. KBR [Kellogg, Brown and Root]. Our guys were getting the chow, our support element, and they were pushing it up to us nightly for the most part. That would be at the task force support area. They would also push forward to the train station, link up with the line guys, and push their chow to them. It was as good as can be expected in a fierce battle.

MM: A lot of the Marines I've been interviewing are extremely impressed by the 120 millimeter mortar that the Army had. Did you get to see that in action?

TM: The mortar platoon actually doubled as the commander's personal security detachment. They were going with the commander at the same time they were manning the guns. They went through a massive, I want to say, 750 or 850 rounds. They had to call for emergency resupply from 1st CAV because they were using so much. Because of the stuff we had, the 120 millimeters on the Abrams and the Bradleys and stuff like that, our mortars actually fired more missions in direct support of the Marines than they did of us. It was very impressive and they were ready. When you're getting a little bit of sleep at three o'clock in the morning and the mortars are firing, that wakes you up. They were only maybe 100 meters away from where our TOC [Tactical Operations Center] was. So it seemed like those boys didn't get any sleep for three weeks. They were constantly firing.

MM: The Marines were really impressed with the 120, the ones I've interviewed so far. As the battalion sergeant major, how did you handle your KIAs? You had Sergeant Jonathan Shields that was killed and Specialist Jose Velez. How did you handle that?

TM: In the Gulf War, fortunately, as a platoon sergeant, I never had a KIA, never lost a kid. Jon Shields was the first one I ever lost. I think it was November 12th around 2300 hours, Friday night, we got the call from TOC. Myself and Major Karcher actually went forward. It was an initial report, we got a flipped over tank, possible casualty, whatever else. We got there, the tank was inverted down. It was laying upside down at the bottom of the ravine and the rear deck area was actually on fire. Our PA [Physician's Assistant] was there, myself and Major Karcher. Major Karcher had to crawl underneath the tank to see if anyone was under there. He couldn't tell anything, so we had to wait until the FSC [Forward Support Company] guys came and righted the tank. Once they did, Sergeant Shields was on the ground. Myself, Major Karcher and a couple of the guys carried him off. The PA pronounced him dead at that point. It's rough. I'm not callus, unemotional, but it's not a surprise either. This is war, kids get hurt. The next day was war because we heard the gunfight happening. Myself and the commander and everybody was back at the TOC when this thing broke out. Not too long later, evac came in and we had guys wounded. They took Velez back behind; he was dead too. At the time, though, maybe it's easier when you're in a pretty intense fight, because you really don't have time to dwell on it. Afterwards, though, those are rougher.

MM: Did you know Command Sergeant Major Steve Faulkenburg over in 2-2? They were fighting over in the east side of the city.

TM: I knew the name, and I think I went to the academy with him, if I'm not mistaken, but not a close friendship.

MM: Because he was killed the first night of the fight over in their sector. Is there anything else that you'd like young soldiers to know or young NCOs from your experience being in this fight?

TM: The rivalry crap between the Marines, the Air Force, Navy – that stuff doesn't survive the first bullet. Everybody we worked with – the SEALs, the Air Force, tac air guys, the Marines, my counterparts, sergeants major in the Marines – it was almost like an automatic friendship. Great admiration for all the services, and that's doctrine; that's how we fight. It's easy on a battlefield when everyone is working towards the same thing. The soldiers were very impressive and I think a lot of that had to do with An Najaf. You're probably going to survive, but it's luck of the draw, so you might as well just put it out of your mind because you don't know. I did see one kid, one of the new guys that came in. A few days into the fight, we were downtown at one of the mosques and the colonel and the PSD and I ran into a little bit of fire getting to the mosque. The Marines and our guys were out there. Well, I saw this kid barf; he was looking like, "Oh my God." But the PFCs, the specialists, the E-5s and the lieutenants, that's the strength of the Army. All of our training and just leading people right paid off in that battle. I have great admiration for the Marines. They took the brunt of casualties because they were dismounted and clearing the stuff. We were under armor, we blew through and overwhelmed the enemy, so we were more well protected. Those guys had the hard job of going door to door, floor to floor. When I was talking to one of my counterparts at the train station, their aid station took fire a few times. There were several times daily right there, getting pounded, but you know, Marines are Marines: they're going to do the damn job. Very impressive. So all in all, how we train, our good leaders, good soldiers, and a good mission we believe in – and that's the thing. Everybody knew these guys we're fighting are not good people. They're just bad people, and every time you pulled the trigger, the world got a little bit better.

MM: Did somebody forward you the interview I did with Colonel Michael Shupp, the commander of Regimental Combat Team 1?

TM: No, sir, I'd love to see it.

MM: Yeah, I will send that to you today, it's really good. He thinks 2-7 walks on water and I think you'll really like it. It's a great interview.

TM: Good commander. Right off the bat, he just told you, "We're going to win!" Whenever Lieutenant Colonel Rainey and his staff came up, we saw him in the town daily, along with General [Richard] Natonski. The big boys actually got their feet dirty; they weren't hanging back moving stuff on a board.

MM: That's what I hear a lot of. You have the division commander and the regimental combat team commander and they seem to be out there seeing what's actually going on.

TM: The 1st Marine Division sergeant major came to see us every day at our TOC; and when we weren't at the TOC and we were in town, then you'd see him in the town. All the leaders were getting dirty. The III Corps commander and the III Corps sergeant major, they came to see us the day before the battle kicked off. Everybody supported but nobody micromanaged. Nobody was trying to grab a hunk of the battle. Everybody deferred to the Marines. Our Army chain of command, the commanding general, came to see us, so did the division CSM and General [Peter] Chiarelli. "Whatever you guys need, don't worry about. If the Marines can't give it to you, we will." Great support.

MM: How did you guys work the press? Did you guys have a bunch of embedded reporters with you?

TM: We had three that accompanied us in. They weren't in the commander's Bradley; they were with the S3. One of the guys actually got hit with mortar fragments when we were downtown that first full day, on the 9th. Full access. We didn't have any problems with them. Velez's death hit them hard, because the day or two before they were with that squad. So, they knew Velez, they knew the squad leader, they knew the guys. And the next day or so, one's dead and the rest are wounded, so it hit them personally.

MM: Earlier this morning, I was reading through the Chicago Tribune and Matthew McAllester, one of the reporters, has a great quote from you saying, "I feel for anybody who bought real estate here the past year."

TM: [Laughter] Yeah, those poor guys. If you had a house in Fallujah, you think Saddam's gone, life's going to be good, and the next thing you know....

MM: So you had no real problems working with the press or anything?

TM: I never tried to be a spokesman for the Army. I answered the questions, but the officers and commanders are much more well versed. But these guys could see for themselves that there's no dog and pony show. We're in combat, this is what we do. I got an email from my wife: "You ought to see what they write about this Marine who killed this guy or whatever else." To my personal knowledge, nobody did anything wrong, not the Americans. None of my guys did, and Lieutenant Colonel Rainey would not have tolerated it. But none of us would; we're not barbarians. It was a hard fight, it really was, and there was no mercy. You fired on us, you were getting lambasted. But if they were out of the fight, then they were out of the fight.

MM: Did you see any civilians running around? My understanding is that the city was pretty well denuded of civilians. I talked to a couple people that said they saw some here and there, but basically that city was pretty empty of civilians.

TM: Well, going into it, we were told that the only people there, for the most part, were there because they wanted to fight. Of course, there are always exceptions. But they were looking forward to it. Well, good, we're going to bring it on. See if you can handle it. The third or fourth day, we were downtown. As a matter of fact, I believe the 1st Marine Division commanding general. We were at a mosque, a site we had cleared and secured – and actually the Iraqi Army was in that area at the same time. You have the Marine two-star, you have the regimental commander, you have my battalion commander, everyone has their CSMs there, and they were meeting in the courtyard of this mosque. Here comes the word that the Iraqi Army was actually escorting a whole bunch of civilians – about 30 or 40 old people, a couple of military age – they were escorting them out of the city from south to north. We immediately secured the area because nobody's stupid. If they find out that a Marine general and Army and Marine commanders were there, they would try to take them out. We were just, "You're not coming near our commanders." That is the only time I personally saw civilians who weren't fighting.

MM: The Iraqi Army troops were actually taking them out of the city. Did you form any kind of impression on how well the Iraqi troops did for you?

TM: The morning of the 9th, they were coming into the city from the train station. Now, the area they were coming into was already secured by the Marines; we'd already punched through. These clowns started firing and maneuvering to enter the city. Our interpreter, a Kurdish guy, is yelling at them. I didn't see any bad things about the Iraqis. I didn't witness them in combat so I can't speak on how effective they were. But from my experience, what I've been reading, that was the embryonic stage of the Iraqi Army getting involved. I heard nothing bad about the Iraqis as far as not doing their job. And they were given a pretty easy mission. I think somebody smarter than me said, "Okay, get them in there, put an Iraqi face on it, but don't let the battle hinge on them because things could go to pot in a heartbeat." Given the baby-step mission to secure what the Army and Marines had already taken, I think they did well.

MM: How did your first sergeants do in all the various companies you were controlling?

TM: The first sergeants were, generally speaking, excellent. Nobody hung out at the rear, and that's the expectation. A lot of first sergeants: "Well, I'll stay back here or I'll just go in the first day." Well, if the battalion commander and the CSM are going in, you're going in too. That's that. Across the board, I saw and heard of no hesitancy whatsoever on anybody's part. Nobody tried to stay in the rear, nobody tried to stay in the building. Everybody that was in the fight, they were in the fight.

MM: Do you recall right off the bat what your PA's name was or the task force surgeon?

TM: Gosh, no, I'm terrible with names. I can picture this guy and he would kill me if he ever found out that I forgot his name, but I do not remember. I'd have to look up a roster.

MM: I'm eventually going to track them down too. Obviously, they did a bang up job for you guys.

TM: They did. As a matter of fact, we pushed part of our aid station forward, co-located with the Marines. We sent our surgeon forward and whatever else. At the train station, the Marines set up their aid station. They were taking more casualties than we were. The commander wanted to make our guys more responsive and he said, "Okay, let's help out the Marines." So we pushed part of our medics forward. I don't even know if they treated any Army right there at that Marine aid station, but they treated a heck of a lot of Marines; so again, more interoperability. Marine casualties are Americans, so we pushed our guys forward. The surgeons did super; all the medics were super.

MM: Well, that's what the regimental commander was telling me on an interview. He said that your guys saved a lot of Marine lives by putting his wounded guys on your armored vehicles and getting them back to the aid station.

TM: I have no doubt that it happened, but I don't recall if, say, Charlie Company pulled five Marines out. If they did, that does not surprise me. I'm sure it happened, but I just don't recall it. I do know that once they got to the aid station, whoever was manning it, Army or Marines, the kid got treated.

MM: Is there anything else you'd like to get out there?

TM: Every so often I read Al Jazeera, and I remember reading some of these articles about how it was barbaric and we were killing every civilians in sight – and that was a damn lie. It never happened. Propaganda, yeah, I know how it works and everything else, but there are people that actually believe it. Okay, well, I was there. And I'm telling you that except for those unarmed combatants – and they were left alone, escorted out of the city, protected – anybody else in that doggone city that died, they needed to die. I read that there was a lot of unnecessary damage, but there were a lot of buildings that were untouched. As a matter of fact, a majority of the buildings were untouched, as I recall. Maybe a little bit of superfluous damage, a piece of shrapnel or whatever else. But widespread destruction? That did not happen. Now, having said that, if a building contained the enemy, it was lambasted; it was leveled. JDAMs, direct fire from the tanks, whatever – they brought the wrath of God onto it.

MM: One of your NCOs, Sergeant First Class John Urrutia, I interviewed him. He said that when they got down by the southern bridge down there, they even went into a house and grabbed a few Zs; but when they left, they made sure everything was put back right where it was.

TM: Yes, John's a good man. Our guys did that. They took over the houses because it was protection from fire, but they didn't break things. A lot of the houses were already torn up by the enemy. But as far as tearing stuff up, our guys were either raised better than that or led better than that, or it was a combination of both. NCOs don't allow that kind of stuff to happen and neither do the officers. They didn't break things. Lieutenant Colonel Rainey set the standard right off the bat. We're not here to sink to their level, we're better than that, and the guys generally behaved, accordingly. I was very impressed.

MM: I'm going to be interviewing Lieutenant Colonel Rainey at one o'clock. I will, for sure –

TM: If you would pass on that the sergeant major was so impressed with his doggone leadership, caring for soldiers. He was aggressive but not foolhardy or reckless. I wouldn't want to fight him. You can pass that on, kind of as a compliment. I don't want to look like a cheese dick or anything.

MM: [Laughter] I will let him know. Well, look, I will more than likely, at some point, be emailing you back with a few other questions as I start to write this thing.

TM: Can you tell me if I was a lot of help for what you're trying to do?

MM: You were a great help, this is fantastic, because I want to make sure we hear from everybody. I'm even going to interview your chaplain, Jonathan Fowler.

TM: Well, he's down at Fort Jackson right now, good man. He was always, "Can I go into the city for a couple of days?" "Chaplain, I know you want to, but right now, we've only got one chaplain. We need to take care of you." And then a couple days later when he went in, it was: "You stick with me; nothing's going to happen to you." He wanted to go in with the assault element; he wanted to be with the soldiers; he thought that was his job. And that was his job but, "Chaplain, come on now, easy tiger."

MM: Well, look, I greatly appreciate this. Thank you.

194

Sergeant Major Peter Smith
6 June 2006

MM: My name is Matt Matthews and I'm an historian with the Combat Studies Institute at Fort Leavenworth, Kansas. Today is 6 June 2006. I'm interviewing Sergeant Major Peter Smith (PS) who at the time of Operation Phantom Fury was the first sergeant for Alpha Company, 2-2 Infantry. Could you please state you full name, where you were born and the circumstances under which you joined the Army?

PS: My name is Peter Lee Smith, I was born in Nuremberg, Germany, and I'm originally from Germany. I joined the Army in Nuremberg. I'm an infantry soldier, I have 16 years of service right now and I'm holding the position of sergeant major.

MM: Can you talk me through your career path up until you became the first sergeant for Alpha Company?

PS: I joined the Army in September 1989. I completed basic training and advanced individual training (AIT) in Fort Benning, Georgia. I was reassigned to Germany upon completion of AIT and they sent me to Baumholder. I was there with the 4-12 Infantry. I was stationed there for three years and upon completion of that tour I got orders to go to Fort Benning, Georgia, and Kelly Hill – a rapid deployment unit. I stayed there for three years and volunteered for the drill sergeant assignment, moved from Kelly Hill to Sand Hill in Fort Benning. I was a drill sergeant for two years. Upon completion of that, I received orders bringing me to Vilseck, Germany, and I was stationed in 2-2 for seven years. I got there as a sergeant first class. I did the platoon sergeant thing for three years and was given the opportunity to be the ops sergeant major for the operations (S3) shop. I did that for one year. I got picked up as a master sergeant and took over Alpha Company 2-2.

MM: When you took over Alpha, were they still in Kosovo or were you guys back in Germany?

PS: We were in Germany getting ready to go to Kosovo for the second time. I went to Kosovo the first time for nine months as a platoon sergeant with Bravo Company 2-2, came out on the first sergeant list while I was working in the S3 shop, and took over first sergeant around June, just in time to go back to Kosovo for another eight-month deployment.

MM: Could you talk me through what happened when your unit arrived in Iraq, who the leaders were in the company, and maybe take me all the way to right before Operation Phantom Fury kicks off?

PS: The special thing about this is that we came back from Kosovo around July 26th and found out the very next day that we had to prepare to go to Iraq. So our 30 days leave got cut down to 14 days and extensive training took place; we trained for four to five months in preparation for that Iraq deployment. We went to Iraq in February. We stayed in Kuwait for about two and a half weeks waiting for our equipment and, as soon as it docked, we downloaded it and headed north to Iraq. The sector we occupied was the Diyala sector. The brigade was at Warhorse and Task Force 2-2 was at Camp Normandy. Once at Normandy we did combat patrols, route clearances, and we reacted to information we got from people that came up to the front gate or the contacts we made in sector. We deployed to An Najaf and stayed there for approximately 14 days and did some missions there, had a big firefight in Ba'qubah and smaller firefights around that area. Then in October we received orders to prepare to go to Fallujah with Task Force 2-2.

MM: Was Captain Sean Sims your company commander at this time?

PS: Yes. During the whole preparation to go to Iraq, the company commander was Captain Doug Walter and he took us through our whole gunnery and the Combat Maneuver Training Center (CMTC) rotation all the way up to the day we were going to deploy to Iraq. Due to a medical problem Captain Walter had at that time, he was unable to deploy with us. I think he found out like a day or two prior that the doctor would not let him deploy with us and explained the eating habits he had to do in order to get rid of the problem. So out the door we got the new company commander, Captain Sims. The day of our deployment they told us that Captain Sims was going to take us down there.

MM: Had Sims been in the battalion up until this point?

PS: Not in the battalion. Captain Sims was at brigade. He worked with Captain Walter up there and he and Captain Walter were like best friends. They worked in the S3 shop at brigade or something like that. They knew each other very well, but the company and I didn't know him very well prior to him coming to the company on the day of departure.

MM: What were your impressions of him when he showed up?

PS: At the very beginning there was no impression at all because of the timeline we were under. Everybody was packing up and we were sitting up in the gym getting ready to get on the buses going to Frankfurt so we could leave. It was a non-factor at that time and it didn't really kick in until we got to Kuwait and we started talking and went over things. At the very beginning, everybody had a mission they had to do and we were more focused on getting out of there than on the new company commander at that time.

MM: Was Lieutenant Edward Iwan the executive officer (XO) during this time as well?

PS: Yes. Lieutenant Iwan came at the very beginning of our deployment. There was another guy that had prepped us and ordered all the stuff prior to us going. He set us up for success and Lieutenant Iwan stepped in and became the new XO.

MM: Do you recall if Iwan was actually in the battalion or did he come from somewhere else?

PS: He was in the battalion and I know he was a platoon leader with Charlie Company at one point and then he went to battalion. I think he was a mortar platoon leader and then he came to assume the XO position.

MM: Could you talk me through the first time you heard rumors that the Marines were going to use you down in Fallujah and maybe what happened with those rumors and what you did to specifically prepare for this mission?

PS: Everything was rumor control at the beginning. They were saying – and we saw it on CNN and Fox News – that there were things going on in Fallujah. They were talking about an Army force going down there and then the rumors got confirmed that 2-2 was sending a task force to go down there. At that time we had two infantry companies in 2-2 – Alpha and Charlie Companies – and we did not know who was going. Both companies prepared for the mission, but it wasn't said what company was going to go. Once we found out it was Alpha Company, the preparation for Fallujah was actually not that extensive. We were prepping all the time. There was gunnery going on and small arms qualification going on on a daily basis on the forward operating base (FOB). The only thing that was maybe a little more extensive was maintenance on the vehicles and getting ready to do the road march down to Fallujah. In Alpha Company itself, I had two infantry platoons and an engineer platoon that were going with us. They brought a tank company in that was going with us, some headquarters elements – but Alpha Company was the main effort for the mission.

MM: What happened as you went up to your attack positions and on the night the breach went in, up until your company breaches to the northeast of Fallujah?

PS: We road marched down to Fallujah; our Bradleys were put on lowboys and driven down there. We went into Camp Fallujah. On the way down there we were hit by a couple improvised explosive devices (IEDs) but nothing spectacular, and we didn't have any casualties at that time. We occupied a tent city at Camp Fallujah and stayed there for about a week prepping the vehicles and conducting troop leading procedures (TLPs). The individual soldiers were getting ready while key leadership went on recons to the outskirts of Fallujah itself.

MM: Did you have any interaction with the Marines during this time and, if so, what were your observations?

PS: There was a Marine general in charge of the whole operation. The task force command post (CP) was not set up where the tent city was; it was actually about two miles away in some buildings that were shut down. The company-level interaction with the Marines was non-existent at this time; it was all task force and higher. We did a couple rehearsals and Marine soldiers and leadership were there giving us guidance on what the whole plan was, but interaction on the company level or lower with the Marines at this time didn't exist.

MM: Could you talk me through when you actually move out to your attack positions and what happened with the breach?

PS: After sitting there for a couple days, we got the word that we actually were going to do the mission, so we staged the vehicles. Also adjacent to Task Force 2-2 was an Iraqi National Guard (ING) unit, and they were lined up with us right there at the motor park. We got orders to move out. It was barley dark when we moved to the northeastern side of Fallujah. When you look at Fallujah there's a highway that goes around it and that highway actually sits up about 10 to 15 feet higher than the surrounding ground level. We were on the far side and we couldn't see into the city at this time. We set up our tactical assembly area there, walked up onto the highway and then you actually realized how huge Fallujah was. Until you saw it you couldn't realize what a large urban operation this would be. We identified where we were going to do the breach and there was also a railroad track that went around Fallujah. At that portion where we were at, there were roads going in but the leadership determined we weren't going to use those because it looked like they were heavily mined, so they picked a spot across the railroad tracks and we called in artillery fire prior to going down there. There were heavy artillery attacks going into place and we waited until it got dark; and between 2200 and 2300 the actual breach started. The breach was put in and the engineers went in and cut the railroad tracks. A couple IEDs went off in the vicinity of the breach, but there were no casualties. Once the breach was in, it was marked and we moved through the breach with the tanks and Bradleys. I was still on the far side of the breach with the maintenance and the medics.

MM: Can you explain to me what type of vehicle you were in and who was with you?

PS: At this point I was in a '113 and I had another '113 with me that had my mechanics. The additional '113 held my medics and I had an '88 with me for any kind of recovery mission that had to take place. The company pushes through and they set up near and far side security on the other side. The breach is going well and there was sporadic gunfire coming from the inside, but the enemy had no night sight capability and there were no aimed shots at this time. This was when we had our first casualty – Command Sergeant Major Steve Faulkenburg. His mission during this operation was to bring the ING through the breach, due to the fact that they weren't that familiar with our marking system. When it was clear on the other side, he went through with his Humvee and waited on the other side, and the movement was probably 150 to 200 meters from the breach site to where he was. He started leading them through and the ING were sitting on flatbed trucks that were two-wheel drive. There were about 20 to 30 guys on each one of these. They got stuck on this side of the breach because there was sand, so they couldn't go through the breach. Sergeant Major Faulkenburg wanted to come back through, probably to find out what was going on and what was keeping them from coming across the breach. He exited that vehicle and wanted to ground guide the vehicle to turn it around and, at that time, the driver and the gunner of that Humvee couldn't see him anymore. It was dark and then they identified his body close to the Humvee. We actually don't know where the bullet came from, but I doubt it was a well aimed shot due to the night sight capabilities and what was taking place. It was pitch dark at that time.

MM: What was the reaction in your company to the sergeant major's death?

PS: What happened was that it came across the net, but not across the command net or company net. There was a special net set aside for things like this, that just certain leadership monitors to call up casualty reports and things like that. At that time, instead of calling these casualties killed in action (KIA), the task force came up with the code word "angel." It came across the net that we had our first angel and it kind of struck me hard. It probably wouldn't have struck me that hard if we had just said KIA like we did during the entire train up. There were problems between the two elements that were talking and one of them kept saying, "Repeat all after," and so they said we had our first angel a couple times. The way we identified him was by the last four digits of his social security number and his initials. So they said his last four and the initials were Steve Faulkenburg's, so S. F., and then they said his rank. At that time, I knew who it was, it struck me hard and I went in to go help evacuate him. He was already on the vehicle and then we took him through the breach and brought him on the other side where the forward aid station was located. At that time, it sunk in that this was for real. If hadn't sunk in yet, it definitely did after that radio conversation.

MM: Could you talk me through what happens after you get through the breach and with the fighting all the way down to Phase Line Fran?

PS: There were key positions they wanted us to hold so the units all pushed forward with our elements. The fighting wasn't too heavy at that time and a lot of this was because of the non-existent enemy night sight capability. But we still called in artillery and there was sporadic gunfire shooting at us so we returned with small arms, 25 millimeter and 120 rounds out of the tank. The positions that the battalion commander wanted us to occupy were actually seized pretty quickly, and the real fighting didn't start until it started getting light. What I liked about working with the Marines was how simple the plan was. The entire city of Fallujah was set up like a chessboard. There were different blocks and each block was numbered. So we knew where our left and right limits were and what the blocks were that they wanted us to start clearing. We were clearing from north to south and all the orders we received were very specific as far as where they wanted us to go. The order would say, "We want you to clear block 23 and 24." That was about all the guidance we got at the time and, to tell you the truth, we didn't need any more than that because the soldiers knew what they were doing and so did the leadership. So we just cleared those blocks, took out any enemy that was there, destroyed them, and just called up and reported when we were done.

MM: How were your soldiers performing as you got heavier into the battle?

PS: It was outstanding. It was very impressive to see the soldiers in action. The first three or four days there was hardly any sleeping. Everybody had rings around their eyes and nobody got a break until about day three or four. If you look at Fallujah, you can jump from one building to the next. They're all two to three story buildings and they have these big walls that go around the buildings so you can't look into any of the yards from the outside. There was fighting from street to street and house to house and clearing from room to room. Everything went well. The plan before we put any dismounts on the ground or in the buildings was to use our 120s on the Abrams or our 25 millimeters on the Bradleys. If we got shot at from a certain building, we'd bring the Bradleys up there and engage the buildings with them. At the very end, that's when we'd drop the dismounts and they'd move into the buildings. This was the way we trained. Looking at the size of the streets and the housing areas we had to clear, nothing prior to us going to Iraq could have prepared us for that. Every military operations on urban terrain (MOUT) site I trained on – if we were lucky, we had 15 or 20 houses and we had the whole company to clear those, or maybe even the task force to clear a built up area like that. In Iraq, we were clearing 80 to 100 houses a day with a platoon or a company-sized element. The tactics the field manuals (FMs) preach is for us to go into a two or three story house with a company, and that just doesn't happen because you have eight people and that's your mission. You can't leave a soldier in every room. If anything, we would leave a soldier at the main entrance while the rest of the guys cleared the remaining building. What actually made it dangerous was once you cleared that building, how do you secure it so you don't have enemy forces coming in the back and reoccupying them? Did that happen? I would assume it did, but once the building was cleared we'd bring the Bradleys on line and go to the next building. We took the risk of leaving those buildings abandoned at that time.

MM: It's my understanding that the morning after the breach, Task Force 2-2 is down on Phase Line Fran and the Marines are still at their line of departure (LD) – the Marines on your flank. Do you recall that being any kind of problem for your company?

PS: What I got out of the radio conversations was that the Marines had a hard time getting into the city and it was kind of easy for us due to the equipment we had. I was told that some of the Marine forces used our breach to get into their battle positions.

MM: That's a fact. They did. They had to take their MEDEVACs out and bring tanks in through the 2-2 breach.

PS: That's what I was told. We made pretty fast progress going up to Fran and, at that time, we came to a tactical halt. We had to go back and re-clear buildings we already had and sectors we already had. They did not tell us why we were doing it. Some of the leadership knew the mech units were going too fast for the dismounted elements – i.e. the Marines – but it's not that we were any better; it was just the equipment we brought to the fight compared to the Marines. They had wheels and they had the light armored vehicles (LAVs), but I don't think they had as much firepower as we did. The area we were fighting in was full of houses and then we hit the industrial area. I don't know what the area looked like that they were fighting in at this time.

MM: Do you recall having any problems with communications security (COMSEC), as far as getting new fills and load sets for your radios?

PS: The fills for us in Task Force 2-2 were not bad. I had commo with everybody at every time. We had a good commo platform set up and I could talk to everybody. The communications problems we had throughout the entire 12 months revolved around the fact that, as a normal infantry platoon, the modified table of organization and equipment (MTOE) tells you that you have nine single-channel ground to air radio systems (SINCGARS). What happens there is that you have two per lead vehicle. The lieutenant has two and the platoon sergeant has two, the two wingmen each have one, and that leaves three radios for the dismounts. And that's if none of the radios are down – and nobody guarantees that either. On the other side, you also get eight additional Humvees to that platoon with no radios and no comms. Now you have to determine what kind of operation this was going to be. Was it going to be Bradley or was it going to be Humvee? So you have to take everything out of the Bradleys and put it in the Humvees or vice versa. Once again, you should have two for your command vehicles, and now you don't have enough radios to go around in those Humvees – and we haven't even talked about dismounts at this point. Those are the commo problems we had. If we didn't have amplifiers to go into those Humvees, you weren't going to talk to anybody once you got out the front gate. You could talk from one Humvee to the next, but you can't talk to the rear. Those problems existed the whole 12 months we were there. I'm assuming it's been resolved by now. On top of this, you also need two radios to run your tactical operations center (TOC). We got some radios from battalion, but definitely not enough. Once we were down there, the communications inside the task force were pretty good. Talking to the Marines to our right flank was difficult or non-existent.

MM: Why do you think that was?

PS: On the company level, I knew there were Marines on my righthand flank and I could see some of them, but I didn't know what unit they were or what their call sign was. I didn't even know if our radios were able to talk to their radios. I think we had different equipment. Let's put it this way – during the whole entire fight down there, I was not able to talk to units outside of Task Force 2-2 except for somebody that worked for us. I was able to talk to the Air Force at one time when I put in a call for close air support (CAS). The roads went from north to south and east to west and we owned one road and he owned another. You just got on the ground and talked to the ground commander that was to your right flank and told them what was going on and what you were doing, asked them what they were doing. That was the way we communicated with them.

MM: Were you in the vicinity on the morning of 12 November when the complex ambush took place that killed Lieutenant Iwan?

PS: Yes.

MM: Could you talk to me about that?

PS: We were attacking from north to south and were in a more open area where we stopped at. We moved forward and came to a tactical halt, and the battalion commander came in with his wingman and there were news reporters there as well. We found spider holes there and the media was checking out the situation. I was parked back to the rear with the medics and my maintenance guys and people were on the ground talking. Lieutenant Iwan was up in the Bradley standing in the turret and was about to move his Bradley out of the way. To his north, one of the insurgents came up with a rocket-propelled grenade (RPG) and shot at the Bradley from about 80 meters away. The RPG didn't hit the Bradley; it hit Lieutenant Iwan in the midsection and didn't explode. Lieutenant Iwan fell back into the turret and then all hell broke loose. We then engaged 360 degrees. Small arms fire was coming and RPGs were fired at us and we started engaging back. The medic moved forward and I parked my '113 in the line of sight between where the RPG was fired and Lieutenant Iwan's Bradley. I got out of the '113 and went into the Bradley and pulled Lieutenant Iwan back. He was still alive at this time and you could see the fins of the RPG still in his stomach. What went on around me, I really don't know. I just know there were rounds impacting and a tank was burning somewhere. We did first aid and got him as quickly as possible into my medic '113. We closed hatch and drove out the same way we came in. On the way out, an RPG hit my .50 cal and knocked it off. I could barely hang onto it.

MM: Were you up in the turret of the '113 when that happened?

PS: Yes. I was behind the .50 cal firing our way out. I was leading the medic back out to the forward aid station and there was quite a bit of a drive back out. We were engaged the entire time with small arms and RPGs.

MM: You're in your '113 and your medic track is following behind you?

PS: Yes. Our troop hatch was open on the '113 so it was all open behind me. A piece of the RPG ricocheted off the .50 cal, went into the troop compartment and ricocheted back there. Luckily it didn't hit anybody. It was maybe 10 to 15 inches long and a two and a half inch around piece of metal that was just glowing hot. In the back, I had Sergeant Dove, an interpreter, and my driver up front. Luckily nobody got hit – I don't know how. Some of our equipment got burned. I don't know how many people were standing out there shooting. We just floored it and made it out of there as quickly as possible. We made it out to the aid station, downloaded Lieutenant Iwan at this time. The medics took care of him and we went back to the fight to see if there were any other casualties.

MM: Did the RPG that hit your .50 pretty much just take it out?

PS: I had to get my .50 cal replaced and it was taken out, but I didn't get that until after the operation was over. Luckily it didn't hit anybody in the back. I don't know how it didn't hit anybody, but it just didn't.

MM: When you drove back to the complex ambush site, what was going on when you got back?

PS: The firefight was almost over. People were pulling out and dispersing at this time. I think they recovered the tank that was burning and there was mass confusion going on. We were occupying defensive positions at that time.

MM: It's my understanding at that time that Lieutenant Colonel Peter Newell actually pulled everybody back about a phase line or two to get everybody reorganized.

PS: The reporters got pulled back to make sure they were safe. What orders Lieutenant Colonel Newell actually gave, I don't know. We set up defensive positions just a little to the rear, but not too far.

MM: The next morning rolls around after this complex ambush and Sean Sims is killed. Were you there when that occurred?

PS: At night, the way we operated was that we stopped at a certain area and occupied a stronghold – and that doesn't mean that the sun goes down and we all go admin. We accomplished the mission that was given and we go to a certain sector that we clear. We put our security out, operations are still going on until we accomplish the end state, and then we take over these safe houses. We pick houses that have good features – maybe three or four stories. We set the Bradleys on the outside and we occupy that house. The tops of these houses are flat and they have walls around them that are chest level high; it's like a fort. So we put people on top and we get our guards out and the Bradleys are positioned. Every platoon takes one of those houses and then we talk about what's going to happen the next morning. So when the next morning rolls around, we get refitted and we get fuel and ammo and come back. That's a 30 to 40 minute max turnaround. Then we get the order for us to start to attack and clear south again. Captain Sims and his security force – Specialist Seaford, Corporal Beretto (ph), an Air Force observer and a sniper team as well – they move a little bit further and ask the platoon he was with whether the house he sees in front of him was occupied last night. They say it was occupied by the Brigade Reconnaissance Team (BRT) or something like that, so he sets the sniper in position and Corporal Beretto (ph) is up there with the sniper team at this time. Captain Sims takes his security team and goes into this building. They do the four-man stack and walk in just to doublecheck that it was not occupied.

MM: So they were just going to check it again? They weren't going to go up to the roof or anything?

PS: I think they wanted to go up. I wasn't there at that time. I was a little bit behind them, but what I'm assuming is that they wanted to occupy that house because it was another house that was picked by a platoon to occupy. I guess he wanted to observe and see what was further down south. They went into the house the way we were trained and, at some point, they were engaged in that house. Captain Sims was killed, Specialist Seaford was shot and the Air Force non-commissioned officer (NCO) was shot as well. They were screaming and yelling. Corporal Beretto (ph) from the house next door came down and went into the house himself and pulled Specialist Seaford out, pulled the Air Force guy out and identified that Captain Sims was shot. The nearby platoon came over and helped clear that house. I don't know if they killed the insurgents in there or not. I don't know if there were any bodies found in there or not.

MM: Do you even know how many insurgents were in there?

PS: No. There was more than one in there, but there was a lot of confusion and a lot of screaming so I don't think a positive number of enemy forces could be identified in the house.

MM: Were the two that were wounded with him wounded seriously or could they return to duty?

PS: They were not life threatening. Both of them were still conscious and both of them were able to talk, but I think Specialist Seaford got his second Purple Heart at that time. After the Air Force guy was evacuated, I never saw him again.

MM: Talk me through what happened next. Your XO is killed and, less than 24 hours later, you lose the company commander. What happens at this point?

PS: At this point, we were still on our recon missions so the platoons had not yet left the positions that they occupied. Our new XO was Lieutenant Jeff Emery who was the 1st Platoon leader 24 hours earlier. He and I link up and go to the outskirts of town – where the tactical command post (TAC) was set up – to link up with Lieutenant Colonel Newell and get further guidance. When we get there, they already knew what happened from listening on the radio. We were given the mission to continue on with the attack and report Readiness Condition 1 (REDCON-1) as soon as possible. The attack took place around 1200 so that gave us about 45 minutes to get ready after the evacuation took place. We got those missions and there was no operations order because the city was like a chessboard; we were just given numbers for what we needed to be clearing. We went back to the safe house where the headquarters section was in and I went on top of the roof. I called in some fire missions to prep the objective. Before I left battalion, I talked to Captain James Cobb who was with the colonel and made coordination with him about what I wanted to do, where I wanted to go and where I wanted to call artillery.

MM: When you went up there to report to Lieutenant Colonel Newell at this time, it's my understanding that he actually made you the company commander. Is that correct?

PS: Yes, sort of. I was doing most of the talking and the lieutenant was there – and technically he outranked me. But he has like two years in the service while I'm the most experienced guy on the ground.

MM: So it was kind of an unspoken thing. Everybody knows that you're really the company commander now?

PS: Yes – definitely at battalion I think that was the impression. When we came back to the company, I went on top of the roof and called in fire missions to prep the objective. I finished that and went downstairs. Inside the compound of the building we were in, I had the four lieutenants there and they were all around a map discussing what actions to take next. The platoon sergeants were there and some squad leaders, section leaders and even maybe some team leaders as well. It was pretty crowded and they weren't arguing about what we were going to do next, but they weren't exactly all on the same sheet of music when I came downstairs. So I walked over to them, told them that the good idea bus stops here and told them what we were going to do. It was more important to me to show the junior leaders that we knew what we were doing and that everybody had confidence, so I basically took over, told everybody to shut up and gave them the plan. I told Lieutenant Emery – since he was the XO – to stay on company and platoon frequency and for him to go with his platoon. I was on company and battalion, so he would report to me, I would report to higher and I'll call in any kind of fire missions we need. We occupied two roads. We had two platoons on each and we said we would dismount when necessary to clear buildings and for everyone to give me REDCON-1 when they're ready. We did that and I called in to Captain Cobb and told him we needed a fire mission at this specific grid. To shoot an azimuth on the Bradley takes less than a second to get a 10 digit grid and I adjusted fire off that. The plan was for the left section to move out 100 meters and then come to a stop, then the right section moves out 100 meters and stops. They report to me and I call in an artillery barrage to our front. Once the artillery is over, I give a cease fire and we just leapfrog back and forth. The dismounts are in between the Bradleys and clearing the buildings when we go down there.

MM: So, you're basically commanding this company. Talk me through what happens up until when you guys finally leave Fallujah.

PS: During this attack, I was informed by squad leaders on the ground like Sergeant Joseph Bellavia that they identified 10 insurgents going into this big warehouse building, so we came to a stop and got a grid for this building. I called back to battalion and told them we needed fire support for this building and he said they would send us CAS and that that unit will drop down to my freq and talk to me. I was thinking to myself that if this actually works it will be awesome. To all astonishment, I actually talked to someone in an airplane above. When you do the train up, you're simulating that you're talking to somebody but there's really nobody answering you. This guy actually dropped down to my freq and talked to me and I was like, "Holy crap! What's going on here? This stuff really works." That was probably the most impressive thing that happened during this operation. I talk to this guy and I tell him what we saw. We gave him a grid but he can't really see it, so we have these command pointer things and we lase the target for him. He sees it and the next thing we know, there's a big explosion and the building is just rubble. We moved forward and put dismounts on the ground that were able to identify 50 to 60 corpses in there. It was very successful. All our other engagements during this were small arms, anywhere from three feet to 75 meters max. I don't think anybody engaged anyone with small arms over 300 meters. All the fire missions you called in were all danger close. So everything was danger close – and what made it difficult was that we had units to our left and right flank, especially to our right, that we weren't in communication with. So the fire we called in had to be very precise.

MM: Would you fire those danger close missions only when you were in your vehicle, or would you sometimes have to do that when you had dismounted guys?

PS: It was both. It depended on where you were. Usually the Bradleys were forward of the dismounts, and the dismounts had the Bradleys in eyesight when I called these fire missions in. They knew they were coming because there was a lot of talk, but of course there was a risk every time we called a fire mission, so it was very important that we knew where to call it in. Captain Cobb was phenomenal with it. Once the first fire mission came in, I adjusted off that; and everybody was still in the vehicles at this time so we just added 100 meters to each shot and kept doing fire for effect. It was executed like it was straight of the book. It was like rolling thunder coming in. It was phenomenal.

MM: Were you actually using a Long Range Advanced Scout Surveillance System (LRAS) to get your 10 digit grids?

PS: In the Bradley we have a precision lightweight GPS receiver (PLGR) and a laser range fire. The only thing you do is put the crosshairs of the Bradley onto the building, you hit the button and it tells you what the 10 digit grid is. To tell you the truth, the forward observer (FO) up there was a non-factor. We didn't need him. Before the Bradley, we'd dismount and send the FO on top of a roof with a security force. This takes time and the targets of opportunity go away, so it was way quicker to shoot an azimuth with the Bradleys and call it in.

MM: As this fight goes on, tell me how you handled MEDEVAC for your Alpha Company guys. Did you have to do that or did your medic track take care of most of those folks?

PS: The medic track didn't go anywhere without me, and it wasn't that they weren't capable of doing it. It was a security issue. He doesn't have any firepower and I have the .50 cal up front and there is an ADA with a .50 cal. I'm doing most of the land navigation on this and battle tracking, going where everybody is.

MM: How many wounded did you have in Alpha Company that you had to evacuate back to your field hospital?

PS: I think we had about three or four. Of course we had the two with Captain Sims, but that was only one evac mission. It wasn't that many. We had people with smaller wounds that didn't get evacuated. They went to the safe house, realized they were bleeding and the doc was able to patch them up right there. We had enemy prisoners of war (EPWs) that we evacuated and a couple enemy casualties – nobody that was killed – but some wounded guys, I brought them back as well. That night after Captain Sims died – the morning and the afternoon fight continued and we went to a certain phase line and we had another mission that night. For that mission, they actually moved us further to our right flank over to where the Marines were and we were supposed to clear some stuff over there. There was a little confusion there in that we had some head shed guys come out – not from Task Force 2-2, but somewhere else. We had to alter our movement plan to get around these elements.

MM: This was the actual attack where you guys did a passage of lines through 1-8 Marines and took over their sector?

PS: Yes. It wasn't out of our sector. We shifted further to the west and I wasn't told why we were moving over there. They just told us to go clear the sectors, so we picked the route. The only reason I knew it was because we came up to the headquarters section and I was trying to signal them to tell them I needed to get through with my Bradleys. They said nobody was coming through because somebody wanted to observe something, so we had to find an alternate route around them to get into position. That caused a little bit of a problem because I actually had to go off the road and in between buildings. I wasn't too happy about it, but we made it happen.

MM: You were still technically commanding the company at this time, correct?

PS: Yes.

MM: That must have been a very complicated maneuver.

PS: Yes. What was good too is that we didn't use maps; we used pictures from above so we were working off the actual picture that was taken of the area a couple days prior. It was pretty accurate. So we maneuvered around these guys in the dark and we got into position and started attacking south again. At this time, enemy fire hit us and one of our tanks kind of rolled off the road and broke a track. I went and found out where he was; and once the enemy saw we were having difficulties, we started getting shot at from every side with RPGs and small arms. We decided we weren't going to leave the tank there so we started the recovery mission.

MM: Did you bring the M88 down to get the tank?

PS: I didn't have an '88 with us, but Lieutenant Emery was talking to higher headquarters to get an '88, and then the confusion was how were we going to get that '88 over to where we were. They said they could find it, but we sat there waiting until Lieutenant Colonel Newell got involved. He was a bit upset about it, so I got on the radio and asked for a grid where the '88 was and said I would go pick him up. I got the grid and went back and maneuvered the '113 to link up with this '88 that was a couple clicks away. We linked up, came back and were able to do the recovery mission. We had people on the ground and everybody was getting shot at. This whole recovery took about six or seven hours.

MM: Was the tank pretty heavily damaged by the RPGs?

PS: No. Unless they have those armor-piercing RPGs, they just bounce off the tanks.

MM: So you just knocked a road wheel off or something?

PS: Yes. It didn't happen from the RPGs; it happened from going off into the ditch. The scary thing was that during all this we were getting engaged and, like I said, it took about six or seven hours but we did it and moved forward. There were some roadblocks in the way and then we occupied our phase lines.

MM: Is there anything else you can remember about this operation that you'd like brand new first sergeants to know? Any lessons learned?

PS: Not just with this operation, but everybody should have it in their mind frame that lots of stuff happens and you could be put into situations where you're in charge. Even if you're not all the way up front, you have to be battle tracking and you have to be ready to take over. The most important thing is to know where you are, being able to maneuver on foot and in the vehicle, call for fire missions and make sure they are precise and that you use the correct terminology, be able to spit out some mortars. Did I know if everything I was doing was correct? No, but I looked at the situation and came up with the best course of action I could; we went with it and luckily it turned out to be right. The stuff that was important in garrison was not so important while we were down there, while other stuff you kind of overlook while in garrison became very important down there. The tolerance level for me in some areas became zero when I came back. A good one was physical fitness. That was key. We aren't talking two minutes of sit ups and two minutes of push ups and a two-mile run. You're leaping from roof to roof, trying to get into buildings – so saying someone is an outstanding soldier but he just has a shortfall when it comes to physical fitness is unacceptable. If somebody can't hang physically then he endangers the rest of the squad or unit. We shouldn't be overlooking these things. Sometimes you have to cut people from the team to make the team stronger; at least then you have quality people who can get the mission done. You take calculated risks, you do what is right and you execute the way you plan. When you're training, a lot of leaders focus on the big missions – CMTC, NTC and stuff like that. You never see one of those getting canceled. But we go back to the expert infantryman badge (EIB) where we learn basic soldiering. It's easier to take that off your calendar than one of those other big events, and why is that? Because a lot of peoples' evaluations are depending on those big events, while the smaller stuff gets overlooked. In Iraq, everything depends on how your soldiers execute the mission. You can have the best plan, the best resources, the best of everything, but if your soldiers don't know their individual tasks, you aren't going to be successful. They're the ones going into the room, clearing the room, and they're the ones ultimately killing the enemy – not your plan. I think that's what we need to get back to and it seems like we are getting away from that nowadays. It seems like these big CMTC and NTC rotations are getting more attention. You go and do these big qualification exercises and what do you see while you're there? You see hatches up and the tank commander (TC) standing up so he can get a good view. Well, you aren't going to be doing that in Iraq. The hatches are clam-shelled and you can only see so much, but we don't train that way. Down there shouldn't be the time to figure out that your view is very limited compared to what you see at home – and we took casualties down there during the year for these exact things: people standing up and observing. Of course when you have any enemy whose main firepower is small arms, what's he going to do? He's going to shoot at that guy who's standing up in the turret. He can't destroy the Bradley, but he can get that guy. I don't want to say that was the thing with Lieutenant Iwan, because they shot an RPG at him and what's the possibility of an RPG hitting an individual soldier? We don't train that way and those are the learning points I bring back. When we train or when we shoot a gunnery or do a Table 12 or a dismount, you need to do it exactly the way you're told. Not what's convenient for you so you get the perfect score and all that. I'd rather have somebody go down a Table 12 and only meet the standard but do everything the way you would fight in reality, instead of exceeding the standard but using techniques you would never use in combat when somebody's firing at you.

MM: Thank you so much for your time.

Sergeant First Class John Urrutia
14 March 2006

MM: Why don't you go ahead and give us your full name and some background information on yourself. Then we'll focus on what you did up to operations in Fallujah in November '04 and what your position was during the fight in Alpha Company, 2-7 CAV [2d Battalion, 7th Cavalry Regiment].

JU: I'm Sergeant First Class John Domingo Urrutia. Currently I work at BCTP [Battle Command Training Program], but prior to that and prior to Iraq, basically I have a background in light infantry. I'd never been mechanized before I got to Fort Hood. I just came off of drill sergeant status and PCS'd [Permanent Change of Station] to Fort Hood. Prior to going to Fort Hood, I went through three months of Bradley training – since I'd never been mechanized before. Prior to going to Iraq, we obviously were into another transition to the M2A3 Bradley and also we went through our first JRTC [Joint Readiness Training Center] rotation with the Iraq insurgent background. I was a platoon sergeant at the time while we were in Fallujah for 2d Platoon, Alpha, 2-7, which was with Operation Phantom Fury.

MM: Where were you born and where did you grow up?

JU: I was born in Dodge City, Kansas. I was raised in Garden City, Kansas, up through high school, and I went to college at Northeastern Oklahoma, in Miami, Oklahoma. Joined the military in 1990. I went to basic training at Fort Benning and spent a year in the 2d Ranger Battalion. Other than that, I was at Fort Carson. I was in Hawaii. I was at Fort Campbell, in Korea, at Fort Benning and Fort Hood, and now here at Fort Leavenworth.

MM: I've talked to Captain [Edward] Twaddell and, as a matter of fact, he's the one that recommended I give you a call because we're trying to get everyone identified that was in this fight with 2-7 and 2-2 over on the other side. Could you just talk me through what you remember of getting the initial orders to go into Fallujah, how that worked and how you guys prepared for the initial assault – which I believe was on the night of 8 November?

JU: Right. Let's start from when we were still at Camp Taji. A lot of people were under the impression that we had a couple days to prepare to move out. You're talking about a whole battalion-minus moving from Camp Taji all the way to Camp Fallujah forward. We still conducted patrols up until 2200 the night before we moved, which would have been the 4th of November. I had a Bradley that had flipped over on that last patrol, so we had to go recover it, bring it back up, fix what was wrong with it and then sometime that morning we moved out. It was pretty amazing that we had less than 48 hours to pack all of our stuff, get ready to go, load up all our vehicles, load up ammo – the ammo that we thought we weren't going to be able to get – load up and then move out. For the convoy to Fallujah, we sent our vehicles on lowboys. We sent our crews – basically three men per vehicle – on the vehicle itself while they were riding on the lowboys, in case they made contact and so forth. Moving into Iraq from Kuwait, we didn't send anybody, so then we ended up waiting three months for our vehicles because the convoy had gotten hit. This time, though, we had put some bodies on there. Our dismount squad leaders and the rest of the platoon, we ended air assaulting into Camp Fallujah. Getting on some birds and going down to the airfield. Myself and my squad leaders and platoon leader – he rode with the vehicle.

MM: What was the platoon leader's name?

JU: First Lieutenant Michael Duran. He's currently the brigade specialty platoon leader. Once we got to Camp Fallujah, where we were based out of, we got the order. I don't know if you knew that we were also in Operation Pacific Thrust, which was Najaf. What made it easier for us were the maps that we received, down to the detail. Are you familiar with FBCB2 [Force XXI Battle Command, Brigade-and-Below]?

MM: Yes.

JU: We had those on our FBCB2 where we numbered and alphabetized the streets, basically. Once we received the orders, it was pretty clear that the tanks – which was Charlie, 3-8 – were going to go ahead and do the initial breach of the train station, across the railroad tracks. Obviously, we were going from north to south when we went in. My platoon was attached to Charlie, 3-8, so we were the first Bradley platoon in after the tanks had cleared.

MM: So they sent the first two tank platoons through and then you followed?

JU: Roger. That's the train station – so basically here's where 3-8 breached the train station and then tanks continued to move along the far left, which would have been the far east of the sector, with our platoon being the point for the Bradleys. I had another platoon from Charlie, 2-7 that was attached to us also. That was Lieutenant Palanco.

MM: How did it go that first night? Did you guys take a lot of enemy fire?

JU: Initially, when we were briefed about this, the insurgents had plenty of time to build up. We were running into a lot of IEDs [Improvised Explosive Devices] or a lot of obstacles along the roads, but when we crossed that railroad track and got on this main avenue, it was fine. We saw some movement over to our east, but we didn't take any fire. We didn't engage anything as we initially came paralleling the road.

MM: So once you did that and started south, how long before you had enemy contact?

212

JU: We must have only traveled a couple blocks when we started to see it. Now, our ROE [Rules of Engagement] was pretty simple. What we see is what we shoot. It was that basic. We didn't really encounter any IEDs. When we went in there, our SOP [Standard Operating Procedure] was that if we saw a vehicle in the road or blocking the road, we're supposed to shoot it with our 25s. We did, however, see a lot of two- to three-man RPG [Rocket-Propelled Grenade] teams roaming around.

JB: I guess non-combatants were not a factor, correct?

JU: No. It was dark when we went in.

MM: And they had pretty much evacuated the city by then.

JU: Yes. We were briefed that the ROE was: anything that moves, anything we see is fair game.

MM: Were your Bradleys and the tanks in this company taking some RPG hits?

JU: No, on the initial assault we weren't. We just encountered RPG teams. One thing we did encounter that we weren't used to was that we could see them moving and trying to flank us. Our plan of attack was to stay on the vehicles and to clear as far south as we could while mounted – without dismounting at all.

JB: Did you say that, initially, when you crossed the railroad tracks that there was a turn left?

JU: Yes, we crossed over here.

JB: And the tanks were in front of you?

JU: The tanks crossed, and once they crossed, they sent one platoon of tanks all the way to the far – that was somewhere right in here. So we could get lined up.

JB: Then everybody turned.

JU: Right, everybody turned and we cleared it. I know the rest of Alpha Company was in their sector when we crossed over.

JB: How was your field of vision in there?

JU: Field of vision was great with the thermals, obviously, and we could see quite a ways. Something we weren't used to was that there were a lot of buildings and this was an advantage to them. We could only see down this road, but it curved left and right or if there was a building there, we couldn't see any further. But like I said, we were spread out enough that we could see the other Bradleys to our left and to our right.

MM: Were you able to communicate fairly well – at least on your vehicle's radios – with everybody else?

JU: Yeah. We had no communications problems. As a matter of fact, the brand new platoon from Charlie Company, 2-7, they ran into an obstacle and they had to push it over into our lane, which was fine because the whole task force ended up having to push to the west a little bit.

MM: Could talk us through as the first night progresses and becomes November 9th? My understanding is that Highway 10 is actually Phase Line Fran –

JU: Yes.

MM: That was really one of your first objectives, correct?

JU: Roger. There was a park [Jolan Park] and that was our platoon's main objective: to clear that park. We had gathered intel that said that was where the insurgents would get together and have meetings or prayer or any big demonstration. It was a big open park and, on the maps we received of the park itself, we had a big market area. But as we moved that night into the morning, we encountered a little bit more. At one point, our rear track had a three-man RPG team literally within 10 feet of the vehicle. They were so close to him that he couldn't see them through his sights. When he moved his sight on them, all he could get was a blur. The platoon leader's vehicle, Lieutenant Duran's vehicle, actually shot the three-insurgent team. That's how close the RPG teams were getting to our vehicles.

JB: And everybody was still mounted at this time?

JU: Everybody was still mounted. We were basically in a holding area, letting everybody else catch up. We encountered about two or three of those teams that first night and into the morning.

MM: Were they able to get some RPG-7 shots off?

JU: No. They didn't even get any small arms fire off. Like I said, the plan was to stay mounted and clear as far as we could mounted, so we kept moving. We encountered very little resistance. Once we reached the park late in the morning, that was the first time we actually dismounted – and that was to clear that market area. Now, attached to our platoon were two Marine engineers, a lance corporal and a PFC.

MM: That's interesting.

JU: They had about 20 pounds of C4, which really came in handy as we got into the market. I can back up a little bit. Before we moved out, we had some combat cameramen and some regular news reporters. Our platoon didn't have any, but I know Alpha Company had a couple guys that were in there. We did have one photographer. He was an Air Force combat photographer.

MM: In your track?

JU: He was in the platoon leader's track. We did have some of those guys in there. Once we reached the market, we left our Bradleys. There was a little complex that overlooked into the park – the park that was the platoon's main objective. Once we dismounted and started to clear in the market, there were concrete walls that we didn't see on the pictures from FalconView – and that's where the engineers played a vital role. Obviously some of the buildings were a little taller and our key point was a big water tower near that three-story building. We could see the water tower, so that was our reference point. Once we got into this market, we started to blow holes through these concrete walls to work our way in there, and that's where our engineers played a vital role in helping us.

JB: So these walls were taller than a man's head?

JU: Oh yes. They were 10 to 15 feet tall.

MM: What did the Marines think about being thrown on a track with a bunch of Army guys?

JU: Actually it worked out pretty good. The lance corporal was like, "Hey, wherever you need me." When we did our PCCs and PCIs [Pre-Combat Checks and Pre-Combat Inspections], I checked that they already had 10 pounds ready to go, already wrapped the fuse and had timers on it, and all you had to do was pull them and go. We blew the first initial hole, and some of our soldiers had never been around explosives. And on the first hole, we used a little bit too much and we put a big enough hole so we could get through. If I remember correctly, we blew about three holes finally getting into the complex. A couple times, we had to blow the holes twice, because it left only a basketball-sized hole, so we needed some more C4. But they were enjoying it. They originally were from Camp Fallujah, the Marines who were attached to us..

JB: Was there any hostile stuff going on?

JU: Nothing yet on the ground. But we had our vehicles to the left of the park, up here on this main road here. I know the platoon leader's vehicle took an RPG hit, but they saw where it came from and shot into it.

MM: Did it penetrate his track?

JU: It hit the front of it. It didn't penetrate or anything else. We had to go a couple days later and change out the armor on it. Our Bradleys were equipped with armor.

MM: Right. The anti-armor.

JU: Right. The blocks were about 12 by 12 and it took out about four of them. Once we got into the complex was when we encountered our first insurgent. We entered the complex from the east. We saw the two-story building and there was a two-story building behind it. An open area probably about 75 meters by 100 meters. Like a big open complex. Lieutenant Duran took a squad-plus to the two-story building to overwatch. They hadn't entered the building; they were just overwatching the building while I went with the other squad to enter the rear two-story building. Once we got close to there, for some reason the speakers across the street from the park started blaring. Someone was talking. Didn't know what they were saying.

MM: Do you think this was something the insurgents had put up?

JU: I couldn't tell you that. We did have an interpreter with us who later told us they were just giving out warnings that the Americans were coming.

MM: So this was definitely a warning?

JU: Yeah. My lead squad with Staff Sergeant Nathan Scott went into the bottom floor of the two-story building. They didn't encounter any shots but the number one man, Corporal Willie Hudgens, went in to the left and trailing him was Specialist Lucas Bondo, who was our SAW [Squad Automatic Weapon] gunner. So basically our teams went in – two guys to the left, two guys to the right – and they didn't see the insurgent. He had hidden underneath a table and put like a door to hide – and when Specialist Bondo was standing there, he just happened to look and saw a body with a weapon, so he opened up on him with the SAW. He shot a couple of bursts into him. That's when I finally went in there and saw what was going on. We reported it and had one guy call it to the platoon leader. At that point, we started clearing and started finding more rounds, tubes. We cleared upstairs and there was nothing upstairs or the roof. But just in that little area there, we found over 500 mortar rounds and 30 or 40 155 and 130 [millimeter] artillery rounds.

JB: So one bad guy in a building with all kinds of ordnance lying around?

JU: Right. We found mortar tubes; we found surface-to-air missiles – like five of those. We found quite a bundle just in that area itself. Once we had cleared that building, Lieutenant Duran went ahead and moved the squad he was with and starting checking this garage to the left that had a fuel truck and two BMWs in it. They searched it, cleared it, continued to move and still didn't encounter anything. Went up to the building. Cleared the buildings. We found some grenades, some RPGs, some more mortar rounds and so forth and then –

MM: What did you guys do with this captured ordnance?

JU: We still hadn't done anything with it, we just knew it was there. At that point, I sent the squad I was with into a little shack and they found like 300 pounds of TNT or PE4 [conventional plastic explosive] – so we were finding all this stuff. Then we came back and started searching the vehicles. The fuel truck had three

155 rounds already rigged into the bottom. It had wire coming out that hadn't been connected or anything, but you could see the rounds inside there in the fuel tank. We found a black BMW and a blue one. The blue one was almost rigged up. Everything was set in there and had wires, but it wasn't connected to anything yet.

JB: These BMWs were POVs [Personally Owned Vehicles]?

JU: Yes, POVs. That was one of the things that was brought up: they thought there was a VB [Vehicle Borne] IED manufacturing plant.

MM: Right in that area?

JU: Right in that area. The black BMW was completely rigged up and ready to go. We found that the doors were also lined with C4. We found five 155 rounds underneath – where they had pulled the passenger's seat, it had a battery underneath it, and you could see wires running to it. It was in the completed stage.

MM: Did your guys just check that out or did you send the engineers in?

JU: We sent the Marine engineers around to say, "What can we move? What can we consolidate?" We didn't know we were going to be holed up in that area. The last thing we wanted was to be staying in an area that had all this stuff in it.

JB: So they acted like EOD [Explosive Ordnance Disposal] guys in a way?

JU: Yes. We were not EOD experts, but back in Taji we'd found so many IEDs that we kind of knew what to look for. But the ordnance we found in there, we only moved what the two Marines told us was okay. We started consolidating everything from the first building we went into and started consolidating everything in there. At that point, Captain Twaddell and the rest of the company were to our right – in another building over to us by the water tower. He was to our right and we were to the left. Captain Twaddell did call up some EOD personnel later on that afternoon and they came and checked out what we found. We found some more stuff and they said, "This can be moved. Don't touch this." We basically moved everything but about 10 to 15 mortar rounds that we couldn't move. We could move the C4. They disconnected some wires to the vehicles, so we could actually control that area. That was basically it. We did receive some mortar rounds where Captain Twaddell and them were sitting at. A rocket hit the building they were staying in, but it didn't explode. We didn't receive any fire or anything.

MM: At this point, then, you guys are pretty much in advance of all the Marine guys? They were kind of tagging along?

JU: Right. The initial plan was for us to get to the LOA [Limit of Advance] and then they could come in behind us and take over, but we still hadn't seen any Marines. It wouldn't be until the next day. We spent the night there. The next day was when we started to see the Marines pushup. My third squad leader, Staff Sergeant

Vernon Bigham, he took some fire, but it was friendly fire from a Marine. That was about it. We could hear their M1s moving forward of us.

JB: Were these Marines that were OPCON'd to [i.e., placed under the operational control of] you guys?

JU: No, these were the guys that were going to go ahead and leapfrog forward of us.

MM: Did they actually end up doing that?

JU: Yes, initially they did. So we checked out the park and there was nobody there. At the point when we went to this complex, we got attached back to Alpha Company. Now we get cross-attached back to Charlie, 3-8 to go ahead and move forward some more. Basically route reconnaissance, just patrol forward. That's when we started encountering a little bit more, the following evening, the 9th.

MM: Now, you initially went back to Alpha, 2-7 and then you were sent back to Charlie, 3-8. And at this point, you've been ordered to move down to Phase Line Fran?

JU: Past Fran. We were already past Fran.

MM: Please continue on with your story.

JU: We did the same thing. We got on line and we pushed forward. We were out there until the next morning. As we did this, we encountered some RPG teams, some fire, and basically whatever we saw we were taking it out.

MM: I think it was Captain Twaddell that told me – and maybe it was just his company that did this. Did you guys do any type of pull over to these bridges here?

JU: Yes. We get pulled back – there was a significant mosque, and we basically pushed to this mosque. I remember the mosque being right off the road. We cleared a route down to here. It was basically a run and gun. We run down this alley, down the streets, and shoot what we see, what we encounter. We pushed all the way forward again and then that morning, we got pushed back to Alpha Company again. Along here, we could see quite a ways. If notice on the map, it's pretty open and it was easy to detect personnel. Off this mosque, we could see a lot of bodies. People would be running in and out. I think it was Captain [Pete] Glass, the company commander for Charlie, 3-8. He ended up calling fire a couple times on this.

MM: You guys were being supported by a couple Army Paladins? Or were you getting indirect fire from the Marines?

JU: We're getting our indirect fire from our own mortar section.

MM: Oh, your own mortar section. That's what he calls for, okay.

JU: Myself and Lieutenant Duran, while we were sitting here, it was just becoming daybreak and we started receiving a lot of RPG fire from the buildings over here to our west. We ended up calling mortar fire and taking out a two-story building.

JB: I guess everybody had pretty much been up all night on the 8th?

JU: We had been up for about 48 hours.

JB: So then it gets to be the evening of the 9th –

JU: Right, and we're now going into the morning of the 10th.

JB: Everybody's still up.

JU: Well, we got one good night's rest back at the complex. But sometime that afternoon, we got pushed back to Alpha Company.

MM: Does that leave just two tank platoons?

JU: Yes. They also have the Bradley platoon with them, too. The big thing about being cross-attached to a tank company is they have to go back and refuel. We can stay two or three days without refueling, but they have to go back and refuel at least once or twice a day.

MM: Were they just shooting straight back north to do that?

JU: Yes, they were just falling back to this MSR [Main Supply Route].

MM: And they had set up a refueling point?

JU: Initially, our Alpha was about a kilometer north of the railroad station, and then once we did the breach and the Marines at this time were already in, they moved the fuel point back behind the railroad station.

JB: So I guess by the time you get two days into the battle, it's okay to move up to this MSR and you don't have to worry about –

JU: Yes. The Marines and the Iraqi forces were already securing that. Later on during the battle, MSR security ends up being our primary mission.

MM: Back to the fuel. Did you also set up your medical evac and all that? Was that there?

JU: The Marines had their medical evac down here. Our TOC [Tactical Operations Center] and all that was still back at the assembly area. They just moved forward a fueler and moved forward the FLAs [Front Line Ambulance].

MM: So your wounded would be evacuated by your '113s?

JU: Back to the railroad station, which would be transported back to the FLA, and then back to the assembly area. Part of the reason behind that is, from our assembly area to right here just to the north, there's a rock quarry or something.

There were a lot of deep holes, you have drop-offs, and it was real dangerous at night. Now, we still had to go all the way back to our assembly area to get water and chow.

MM: So you were supplying yourself. The Marines really weren't supplying anything?

JU: No. We were supplying ourselves. And like I said, we had about four days worth of water and four days worth of MREs [Meals Ready to Eat], so more than enough. Even though I was attached to Charlie, 3-8, I still would go to our first sergeant, not Charlie 3-8's first sergeant, and say, "Hey, I need water. I need chow."

MM: And that's First Sergeant Steven Vigil?

JU: Right.

MM: Yeah, he's with you here at Leavenworth. I was going to interview him, but he had to cancel today, but I'll get him over here at some point.

JU: So we get the call that we're going back to Alpha Company, 2-7. We link back up with Captain Twaddell and we're going to go check out these bridges that were supposedly rigged. When we got the word, we were told that there were some friendly forces on the west side of the bridges.

MM: Over in this hospital over here.

JU: Yes. So we knew there were friendlies there. We had an engineer – some guy to actually check out the bridges who was qualified. He wasn't with us. He might have been with Captain Twaddell or 1st Platoon. So we go down there and check out the bridges. We were given the order to stay and overwatch the bridges. At that point, we get attached two snipers, and I still have the Marines with me. We take up a house –

MM: Now, were these Marine snipers?

JU: No. These were our battalion snipers. These guys belong to 2-7. Basically they were already attached to Captain Twaddell, to the company, and they were riding with him and got crossed over to us. We took up a house near where we could see the bridge and we could basically see in all directions. Pretty nice house. You'd be surprised. We hung out there during the day. The normal SOP was to mark the top of our building with an IR strobe light and also a VS17 panel. We didn't encounter anything. That was another time we got to catch up on some sleep.

MM: When you were reattached to Alpha, 2-7 and started talking to the other men, had the rest of the company suffered any casualties along the way so far?

JU: No, not so far. At this point, from here is where we moved.

MM: I think I've got a map that shows the next move.

JU: Here's where we started to receive the beginning of our casualties. We start moving back. I stayed with Alpha Company. I might be getting my days confused. I don't know what Captain Twaddell told you.

MM: Yeah. He said everybody had a hard time remembering dates.

JU: It all blended in, and then for us it was extra hard because one minute I was with 3-8 and then the next minute I was back with 2-7. But on this initial push we did after we secured the bridges –

MM: So you came back down the road here?

JU: Roger. We linked up and pushed down. Myself and our platoon, 2d Platoon, was on the far west. Alpha Company had a tank platoon with them and they were going to be in the center.

MM: I'm assuming that tank platoon came from Charlie, 3-8 as well.

JU: It was Lieutenant Wochejck's platoon. Their 2d Platoon. We send a Bradley platoon to the armor and armor sends a platoon to the mech guys.

MM: Just a standard task organization.

JU: Right. A task organization, roger. We saw 1st Platoon, we saw the CO [Commanding Officer] and the XO [Executive Officer], but we never saw the tanks. We knew they were going to be in the middle but we never actually saw them. At this point, right before we started to move out, for some reason we started having problems with our FBCB2, so we had to revert back to our maps, which was no problem. We didn't physically make any contact with those vehicles, and with our FBCB2 you can tell where everybody is on the battlefield.

MM: It's your Blue Force Tracker.

JU: Right. I can tell where the next vehicle is, who is to my left and my right. When the platoon leader's or platoon sergeant's vehicle with FBCB2 goes down, that basically shuts down your wingman. That's going to play key here in a minute because we didn't see where the tanks were. At this point, the Marines are already up.

MM: They're side by side?

JU: They're right behind us. Some of them are a little bit forward of us and some of them are a little bit behind us. So we pushed forward and did receive some contact. The CO and 1st Platoon were already there and we were at the bridges. When we moved along across, we had to help a couple of the Marines out that were receiving RPG fire. They could pinpoint it but they didn't have the weapons capability to destroy it. So we stopped and did this about three times.

MM: Were the Marines kind of flagging you down?

JU: Yeah, flagging us down. When we finally get on the right sector, we start to move out.

MM: Everybody is on line.

JU: Everybody's on line. We start pushing forward and 1st Platoon started taking a lot of contact – that's where Captain Twaddell was.

MM: He was over here to the east and that's where his Bradley was hit?

JU: Roger. It's kind of simultaneous. His Bradley gets hit and we didn't know he had received any casualties because it was still running. Now, we're still pushing forward; nobody was telling us to stop.

MM: So the CO didn't call and say, "Hey, I've been hit"?

JU: He called and said he was hit, but we didn't know the damage. So 1st Platoon was still receiving contact, we're pushing forward, and that's when the XO, Captain Wiley, gets on the radio and says, "The commander's vehicle is down." He's now in charge. They had received some casualties in the commander's vehicle.

MM: It's my understanding, from talking with Captain Twaddell, that they're still not certain to this day what went through the back of his track. I don't think it was a 2-7 sergeant, but somebody in there lost his arm?

JU: One of the Air Force guys, right, and the KIA [Killed In Action] was one of his interpreters. At that point, 1st Platoon started to receive some casualties, we're receiving contact and we're getting pretty low on ammo.

MM: Were you just taking small arms fire?

JU: We were taking small arms fire and RPG teams. We still hadn't gotten an RPG shot at us. We're pushing and we see some Marines off to our left and to our right. That's when we get the call that we need to stop and hold our positions. I hear over the radio that they need to evac some personnel from the commander's vehicle. So we're going to regroup and pull back to this intersection up here. We're going to go back to the west – 3-8's over here now – we're going to come back to the west and regroup.

MM: But they're going to leave 3-8 down here?

JU: Roger.

MM: So what happens when the company gets up here?

JU: We see the tanks, blow by them and say, "Hey, did you get the word?" "Yeah, we got the word." Well, we blew by them and hung a hard left, continued to go, and then we get the call back, "Hey, we just passed the tanks and they're not moving. Do they know to come back?" He's like, "I don't know." "Okay, we'll go back and make sure. We'll police them up and head on back." Well, one of their vehicles was dead. They were going to have to tow it.

MM: A tank?

JU: A tank. One tank towing another tank.

MM: Had this tank been hit by anything?

JU: No, it just stopped. Not sure what happened. So when we turned around and came back, their tank crew is on the ground pulling security and you can see they're receiving small arms fire. So we pull up our Bradleys and start an overwatch. We basically do what we call a diamond. We go to all four corners and we watch while they hook up this tank.

MM: How many of the other tank crews had dismounted to go and hook the other tank up?

JU: All of the crews except for the driver.

MM: So they can't shoot; they can't do anything?

JU: Yeah. These tow bars for an M1 are massive, so they're trying to hook it up while pulling security. So we roll up and pull security for them. It's a little bit easier and they hook it up. We get the word that they're good to go – and we actually have communication with them now.

JB: So this is a tank platoon of five tanks?

JU: Four tanks.

JB: And one of them is down?

JU: One of them is down.

JB: So you've got all of the crews except the drivers – for all the tanks out there – trying to hook up the tow bar?

JU: Right. So we get the word to lead these guys out. At this time, I'm talking to the platoon leader of the tanks, Lieutenant Wochejck. Lieutenant Duran's radio went out and he had problems communicating so I'm now talking to the XO. I have communications with them on the platoon radio but not the company radio. I'm telling Lieutenant Duran what's going on and what we need to do. Well, they hooked it up, we started to roll and one of the pins broke or something, so we had to back up again. This time we have a little bit of mortar fire coming in. So we pushed the Bradleys out a little bit further and dismount some of our dismounts to help pull security a little bit closer, so they can just worry about hooking this tank up. So we get it hooked up and we start to move. At that time, we get the word that we need to cross-attach ourselves back to Charlie, 3-8, and I was like, "I can't do anything. We're low on ammo." We were black on ammo – we had none. So we go ahead and move back and we see 1st Platoon. They're near the MSR. We see them, we're escorting the tanks back, and we go back to the assembly area to get some more ammo.

MM: So you're going all the way back?

JU: Yeah, we're going all the way back to our assembly area. We get on the radio and we say, "I got the ammo. We're good to go; we're going back to Charlie 3-8." They're like, "No, you're staying. We're going to go back out as a company. So forget about going back to 3-8." At that point, the guys are relaxing. We're doing a little bit of maintenance and we get the word that 1st Platoon had taken a couple casualties and one KIA. We see 1st Platoon come by and you can see them unloading a couple of their casualties – and at this point, we don't know who the KIA is. Later on, the first sergeant shows back up and we get the word that we just took one KIA – Specialist Jose Valez. At this point, we still didn't know that the company commander was a casualty. We knew he was hit, had some casualties, but we didn't know KIAs or anything. So when the first sergeant linked up with the platoon sergeants, he let us know who was the KIA and the casualties and so forth. We're still holding there and we stay there overnight, and guys are taking the KIA pretty hard. Specialist Valez was our company armorer. One of my squad leaders had gone to basic training with him. This guy's been in this company for about five years, so the soldiers are taking it pretty hard, and basically you tell the soldiers that, "Hey, you can't let it get to you. You got to focus. We've got a job to do. You'll have time to say goodbye once we get out of here. First we need to get out of here safe." The next morning, we get the word that we are now going to take over Charlie 2-7's mission, which was securing the MSR.

MM: Is that what your company spends the time until the 20th doing?

JU: Yes.

MM: Is there anything that you could leave us with? Any particular stories that you could tell us? Any lessons learned? Anything at all that you want to tell us about this operation?

JU: You have to remember that that August before, we had already been in Najaf and had already been tested dismounted. We'd already been tested fighting in a city – and not only that, but also using our vehicles in a city and we'd proven that it can be done.

MM: And you had worked closely with the Marines on that particular operation?

JU: No, we were helping them out. They were on a different mission.

MM: So nothing at all like this?

JU: Nothing like this. Not saying it was easier – because none of this was easy – but we'd already been tested once. But the first sergeant was like, "Hey, you can't judge this like Najaf. Totally different." And that was one of the things that we kept reminding the soldiers: Najaf wasn't insurgents; it was religious fanatics. Fallujah was actually insurgents. It was difficult at times, and receiving that one casualty – it affected my soldiers more than I thought it was going to. We learned that also with the other KIA we had in our company: it didn't matter who it was; it affected everybody. Even if you knew him for two days or if you knew him for three years, it didn't matter.

MM: So you had that one KIA in the operation. Do you have any idea how many individuals were wounded? I know there might have been a few that were returned to duty.

JU: As far as the company, I know we had the one KIA – Specialist Valez. I know we had a sergeant that received a star for his actions in Iraq. He was wounded. Staff Sergeant Nicholson was also wounded. 1st Platoon had about five or six wounded. Specialist Watson was wounded. I can't remember any other names. But it was funny – after we got the change of mission and we secured the MSR, we'd rotate. 1st Platoon would go out 12 hours during the day and then we would go 12 hours at night – and we're just sitting in somebody's house that we took over. We'd resupply ourselves and talk about some of the stuff that had happened.

MM: So it must have been kind of a surreal situation.

JB: Are the occupants still there?

JU: No. The occupants were not there at all. But one of the things that was embedded into us – especially the area of Iraq where Taji was – we that these were people's houses. In fact, we moved to a different house. The house that we initially stayed in, we cleaned it up and put everything back just like we found it. A different house that we took over, we did the same thing, We might have used their sleeping mats if they had them in there, but when we were done, we would put them back, sweep, take all of our trash. That was one thing that was instilled into us – not just in our soldiers but to our higher-up senior NCOs: "We don't trash." People still have to come back and live here.

MM: Did you get the impression or did anybody tell you if you captured any of the enemy or anything? Were most of these people insurgents that you were up against or were there foreign fighters?

JU: We would often get a visit from the battalion commander, Lieutenant Colonel Jim Rainey, and some of the S3 [operations] and S2 [intelligence] guys would come and visit us. They would escort VIPs – maybe some Marine generals would come up. They would give us updates and say, "Hey, what you're doing is great." I know our S2 intercepted a radio message from them saying, "They're everywhere!" As a matter of fact, it was posted in one of the newspapers. "Fight for Allah. You've got to join together. If they see you out in the street, they're going to shoot you. If they see you in a house, they're going to shoot you. There's nowhere to hide." A strong message. I don't know if Captain Twaddell told you about it.

MM: Yes.

JU: This was the stuff that we're finding out. We've got these guys on the run.

MM: They were pretty stunned that you came in so quickly.

JU: Yes.

JB: So these are the bad guys saying that the Americans are everyplace?

JU: That we're everywhere and we're shifting –

JB: And that we'll kill them.

JU: "If they see you in a building, outside, wherever, you're going to get shot." And I know with 3-8, we had a couple people surrender and that was no big deal. We took control of them and pushed them back.

MM: Did you get the impression that most of these people were foreign fighters or insurgents?

JU: From what we heard from the lieutenant that worked in the S2, there were a lot of foreign fighters. And we encountered that also in Najaf, so it wasn't something new to us. As far as working with the Marines, they were great.

MM: So you had no problems?

JU: Nope. They took care of us pretty well, even when we were back at their camp. The two Marines I had were excellent guys. We'd mess with them; they'd mess with us. Basically just part of the platoon. As a matter of fact, I think they one-upped us because we had Wiley Xs and they were issued Oakleys for protection – goggles. I ended up trading my Wiley Xs with that lance corporal for a pair of Oakleys. We gave them some coins and so forth. They rode all the way back with us to camp and, before we left, they came and saw us. We even got two bottles of beer on the Marine Corps' birthday. That was back at Camp Fallujah.

MM: Do you have any further questions, Jim?

JB: I don't.

MM: I think that about wraps it up then. We appreciate it.

JU: Thank you.

JB: Thanks a lot.

Staff Sergeant Jimmy Amyett
31 July 2006

JM: My name is John McCool (JM) and I'm with the Operational Leadership Experiences Project at the Combat Studies Institute, Fort Leavenworth, Kansas. I'm interviewing Staff Sergeant Jimmy Amyett (JA) on his experiences in Operation Phantom Fury. Today's date is 31 July 2006 and this is an unclassified telephone interview. Before we begin, if you feel at any time we're entering classified territory, please couch your response in terms that avoid revealing any classified information. And if classification requirements prevent you from responding, simply say you're not able to answer. Could we start off with a little bit of background, where you grew up, when you came in the Army? Can you give me a thumbnail sketch of your military career up to the present?

JA: I joined the Army straight out of high school in Arkansas. I went to Fort Knox for Basic Training and then I was stationed in Schweinfurt, Germany, in 1-4 CAV for two years and deployed with them to Macedonia. Then I went to Fort Polk for a year to be with the 2d Armored Cavalry Regiment (ACR). I went back to Europe and did two years in Grafenwoehr where I worked at the Sabot Academy and the Close Combat Tactical Trainer (CCTT). When the war broke out, I volunteered to go back to the scout platoon, the Brigade Reconnaissance Troop (BRT) snatched me up and that's how I ended up back over there.

JM: What was the time period of your Operation Iraqi Freedom (OIF) deployment?

JA: I deployed early January with the advanced party and then we returned around the March timeframe. So from January '04 to about March '05.

JM: Where were you stationed and what were some of the major activities you guys were doing prior to Operation Phantom Fury?

JA: We were at Forward Operating Base (FOB) Warhorse in Ba'qubah and we did a lot of counter-mortar operations and a lot of raids – taking out suspected insurgents. A lot of sweeping operations and clearing out villages, looking for insurgents, palm-grove operations, counter-improvised explosive device (IED) operations, ambush and counter-ambush operations throughout the sector.

JM: When did you first get word that you might be participating in what became Phantom Fury?

JA: I had just gotten back from R&R and landed at Anaconda; and the minute I got off the plane the rumor mill had already started that we were going to Fallujah. At the time, my troop was in Salman Pak so I went straight there and they said we were going to Fallujah. We bounced around a lot in the BRT.

JM: Now, you all were a 3d Brigade asset, right?

JA: Yes, we were 3d Brigade Reconnaissance Troop.

JM: Once it was confirmed that you were going to Fallujah, what was the process for getting attached to Task Force 2-2 Infantry?

JA: For our little piece of the pie, it was more or less we got word we were going to Fallujah – and our platoon sergeant was on R&R at the time so our senior scout took over as platoon sergeant. It was just me and him getting the intel, getting the warning orders and getting the trucks ready. The troop commander did all the coordination with 2-2 and we were just prepping the platoon, getting them ready because a lot of them had left on R&R. We were at about 50 percent of our original strength.

JM: Was it just your platoon that was being attached to 2-2?

JA: No, our whole troop got attached.

JM: How large was your platoon and what kinds of vehicles did you have?

JA: Roughly we had around 20 people. It was a four-truck Humvee platoon and it was five people per truck. We ran into the issues of people going on R&R and emergency leave; and at the time, our platoon sergeant was gone and about five of our key figures, like gunners, were on R&R as well.

JM: The acting platoon sergeant, this was Staff Sergeant Nicholus Danielsen?

JA: Yes.

JM: So he was the platoon sergeant and you were the second-highest-ranking noncommissioned officer (NCO) for this platoon?

JA: Yes, I was.

JM: Who was your platoon leader?

JA: Lieutenant Chris Boggiano, who's now a captain.

JM: What were going to be some of your principal duties and how did you divide responsibilities with Staff Sergeant Danielsen?

JA: Even though he was the platoon sergeant, he was still the senior scout and he was a great guy who led from the front. He continued the duties of being up front and being the lead vehicle. I fell back to the rear in the very last vehicle where our platoon sergeant usually went and I just handled what the platoon sergeant usually did when we went out on patrols: checkpoints, monitoring the troop net, picking up anything the lieutenant missed. As far as the preparatory phase, we just worked hand in hand. He would go to the platoon sergeant meetings and other briefings and then he would come straight back to me. I would get the platoon hot on whatever came down – prepping, ammo, all that stuff – and we worked really

228

well together. It was a good platoon. I can't say we broke everything down as far as responsibilities were because we pretty much knew what we had to do and we covered each other really well, so we just shared everything. He was getting really swamped as the platoon sergeant so I just helped him out as much as I could.

JM: Were there any rehearsals or did you guys do rock drills once Lieutenant Boggiano got read in on the plan?

JA: We did rehearsals and rock drills until we were blue in the face and we really didn't get the gist of what the mission was going to be until we got down there. We got a warning order of what our role and responsibilities were going to be during the actual battle but it changed. Our mission actually changed the minute we got down there from what we were supposed to do originally.

JM: Can you outline for me what your original idea was of how you were going to be employed and then how that was changed once you guys got there?

JA: Our original plan of action was that, during the actual breach into the city, we were going to be escorting the bulldozers up to breach the HESCO barriers, providing security for them, and then we were actually going to move into the outskirts of the city and start clearing buildings. What happened was, we went on a leaders recon once we got down into Fallujah – and this was me, Staff Sergeant Danielsen, Lieutenant Boggiano and our executive officer (XO) all in one vehicle, along with a bunch of other vehicles. This was a 2-2 Task Force leaders recon and we took along our Long Range Advanced Scout Surveillance System (LRAS) truck. I was gunning and we had stopped just short of the cloverleaf because they had reported contact up there. So I began scanning and about four clicks into the city I identified two insurgents – one with a rocket-propelled grenade (RPG) and one with an AK-47. We reported it up to see if we could get an artillery strike in and, just from that one observation of enemy insurgents within the city, it really got the battalion commander and everybody else to see how valuable the LRAS was. So after that, our platoon mission got changed from escorting the bulldozers in to moving up onto the highway, observing the city, directing indirect fires and basically just catching insurgents hiding where they thought they were safe.

JM: For the record, can you tell me a little bit about the LRAS? What are its capabilities and why is it so unique?

JA: It's a thermal laser sight that you can see forever with. It's almost like a tank sight and when you scan with it, it can pick up hot spots. The insurgents would be like five clicks into the city, thinking they were safe, walking around on roofs, and you look through there and magnify in, hit the laser button and it'll give you a 10-digit grid and direction – basically everything you need for a perfect call for fire to take them out. And the whole time they have no idea you're watching them. It's mounted on top of the Humvee, looks like a big square box and it's probably the most valuable piece of equipment we had. We just decimated the insurgents with it the first day before the breach even started.

JM: What kind of weaponry did you have on the other Humvees?

JA: All the Humvees had dual weapon mounts. The lead truck had a Mk-19 and a 240B. The lieutenant's truck had a .50 cal and a 240B. My truck – the truck I usually rode on – had the LRAS and a .50 cal. The platoon sergeant's truck – the one I was riding on – had a Mk-19 and a 240B. We had a lot of firepower.

JM: Before we get into the operation itself, can you give me some of your impressions of Fallujah itself: the terrain and the overall operating environment?

JA: It was definitely different compared to what we were used to operating in. We had been operating in the palm groves back in Ba'qubah and, down there, it was wide open desert. There really wasn't any place to hide outside of the city. I just remember there was a four-lane highway running parallel to the city that we operated from and we just moved on top for the first couple days calling fire. The city itself was just like every other Iraqi city – buildings that were stuck together, narrow alleyways, and that was pretty much it. There was one main road that ran smack down the middle of it that connected to the cloverleaf and then you have the industrial center where you had more factory type buildings. The lack of civilians there was very eerie.

JM: I understand that it had basically been emptied of its civilian population by this point.

JA: Yes.

JM: That must have given you guys a lot of freedom. You didn't have to worry too much about hitting civilians.

JA: Yeah, that was really nice. We still worried about them, though. They said they were gone but you're never actually sure.

JM: This recon you went on where you basically demonstrated the LRAS – you said you identified a couple insurgents, but were you actually able to call in artillery on them?

JA: No, and I was really frustrated too because I wanted to get the first kill of the battle before it even started. Task Force 2-2 and the Marines were running off two different fills and the communications security (COMSEC) was different, so when they tried to call back up to get clearance of fire to call for artillery, they were getting nothing because Marine Corps command was actually running off a different fill. So those guys got to live another day.

JM: What was the nature of your interaction with the Marine Corps? Was this the first time you'd come into close contact with them?

JA: At this point, on a personal level I still hadn't interacted with the Marines at all other than just seeing them on the FOB. There was no operation with them up to this point.

JM: Can you talk me through the battle from your vantage point beginning with getting to the assembly area and prepping before the breach is blown?

JA: I remember we rolled out early that morning – can't remember which day specifically, only that I was tired. We got to the assembly area under cover of darkness and parked the vehicles. Off to the right was this giant slope and up on that slope was that highway I spoke of. We could hear sporadic small arms fire. This was early in the morning and the breach itself wasn't supposed to happen until that night. We were down there, the caffeine fix started kicking in and we were just chomping at the bit to get up there and start fighting. We kept looking over at Lieutenant Boggiano and asking him, "Can we go yet, can we got yet?" I was sitting there looking at the LRAS and, knowing what its capabilities were, was saying, "We just got to get up there." Finally we got the word to go. It was between 0700 and 0900 and it was so cool because the slope – it was about 20 meters up the slope we had to drive Humvees up, we're looking straight up at the sky and, all of a sudden, we crested the top and there was the city. We pulled my section up on the road and we just started fighting. The minute we pulled up on the road, we started receiving small arms fire. We got behind the LRAS, started identifying snipers and enemy insurgent positions, and then we just started raining down thunder on them using mortars and artillery.

JM: Would you be making the calls for indirect fire and for close air support (CAS)?

JA: We had a forward observer (FO) with us that, in my opinion, was worthless because we were already scouts. This was already our mission. So what we ended up doing –

JM: Was this an Army guy or Air Force?

JA: Army. The Air Force CAS guys were great.

JM: You had some joint tactical air controllers (JTACs) with you, right?

JA: Yeah, they were great – it was just the restrictions put on us as far as dropping bombs. We honestly didn't get to drop any bombs with our JTACs until a couple days later. We would find an enemy position or enemy sniper, lase it, get the grid and Lieutenant Boggiano would drop down to the fire net and call missions directly. Staff Sergeant Danielsen and I were doing command and control, positioning the trucks, returning small arms fire, trying not to get shot by the snipers who were just everywhere. They moved a Bradley up on the road, and when we saw that the indirect fires were taking too long, we'd run over to the Bradley and take the snipers out with direct fire.

JM: Were you calling indirect fire from the Paladins?

JA: Actually I'm not sure. I know we got a lot of mortars and, yeah, I know we did have some 155s coming in.

JM: Were these the 120 mortars?

JA: Yes.

JM: I've heard a lot of great things about the 120 mortars.

JA: Actually I liked shooting mortars better than artillery. When you call for artillery it takes about five or six minutes to get it in, but when you call for mortars you're talking two or three minutes tops, rounds in the air. The response time was just so much better. Artillery was good but it just took so long to get rounds in. It was really frustrating.

JM: Tell me a little more about this CAS issue. Were you requesting CAS strikes and they were just being denied?

JA: We didn't want to waste any CAS strikes so we were looking for really good targets. I'm guessing everybody was just so scared of fratricide that a lot of the CAS missions were getting nixed, or by the time they would approve a CAS mission the target was already gone. We actually didn't get to drop any bombs until later on in the battle when we were in the Queens District and were observing from there, where we were absolutely positive there were no American soldiers. We finally got the green light to drop a couple 500-pound bombs and leveled a couple buildings.

JM: Were these Air Force jets that were in a pattern that you guys were calling up to?

JA: From what the JTAC who was with us told me, he said they had them stacked above the city just waiting to drop. F-15s and F-16s.

JM: Was there any Marine air in the area?

JA: I really don't know. I didn't see any and I know we didn't get to utilize any if there was. I know what we eventually did use was Air Force.

JM: Did you guys actually witness the breach being blown?

JA: Yeah, we did.

JM: Can you tell me the good, the bad and the ugly about that?

JA: I remember they pulled us back a little bit from up on the interstate where we were observing the city and they fired the mine clearing line charges (MCLCs) off. It was this gigantic mushroom cloud and it was just thunder and fire. The Bradleys rolled through and we were looking through our night vision goggles (NVGs) watching; and the minute that first Bradley went through it was like the Fourth of July down there with small arms fire coming from every direction. At the time, I was really glad I was sitting up on top of that road and didn't have to drive through it with my Humvee.

JM: Were the Marines doing a separate breach at this time?

JA: Yeah. We had the far eastern corner of the city, the CAV had a breach going down through the middle and the Marines were on the far western side. All three elements breached at the same time, we watched those MCLCs go off, heard the vehicles going through and at the same time the whole edge of the city just started opening up with small arms fire.

JM: I understand the Marines had some trouble with their breach. Did you have any visibility on that?

JA: No, we didn't actually observe any of that. The Marines were so far out of our sector that we didn't see anything like that. I just know it was really frustrating waiting on them.

JM: So you're in an observation position. What was the next movement you made after this?

JA: I believe we were up there for two to three days and, as they were clearing through the city, we would push ahead of them up along that interstate overwatching. The next day that really sticks out in my mind was when they moved us down to the cloverleaf and we were observing the main road that split right down the middle of the city. From the push from the breach, they were just pushing all the insurgents south and they came out through the main road running through the city.

JM: Was that Phase Line Fran/Highway 10?

JA: Yes, I believe that was it. It turned into a turkey shoot. Tons and tons of insurgents were crossing the road and we just dropped artillery on them left and right. They would cross the road, get into a building thinking they were safe, we would observe them going in there and just started calling for fires on them. That went on for about two or three days. The first three days we were up observing the city and calling for fires on the insurgents, dealing with snipers, and taking out the mortar teams that were trying to hit the logistics resupply point (LRP) behind us.

JM: What rules of engagement (ROE) are you guys operating under at this time?

JA: Identify your targets, never shoot an unarmed civilian – we took the ROE that we had the whole time we were there.

JM: Do you think the ROE was just right, was it too restrictive or anything?

JA: I know on the Army side of the house our ROE was great. We could use every weapons system we had. The 25 millimeter, the tank main guns – if we needed it we got to shoot; we didn't have to call and request for missions. When we finally did interact with some Marines and talk with some of them on the ground, their armor units had a lot of restrictions. They had to call up and get clearance of fire to fire their 25 millimeters and their tank main gun rounds. I thought that was ridiculous.

JM: I assume they did too?

JA: Yeah, they were really frustrated about it. I was in awe because here we are fighting a major battle and these guys have to call up to shoot anything higher than a .50 cal.

JM: I understand the Marines were dismounted quite a lot more than you all were as well.

JA: That was my understanding too.

JM: They seem to have taken a lot more casualties because of it.

JA: I just remember having to wait on them a lot. When we finally entered the city and started dismounting through the industrial center, I remember we had to pull back a lot because the Marines were moving so slowly. The ones who were on the edge of my sector that I saw operating – when we moved into the city, we operated with dismounts and armor. When I took my section clearing, I had a tank with me. There were always Bradleys and tanks all along mixed in with us, so if we ran into a problem with a building, we didn't go running into the building; we ran up to the tank and had them take it out.

JM: Knock on the front door with a main gun round?

JA: Exactly. The way I understood it and when I saw them, the Marines were just operating strictly dismounted through the city and left their armor back in support, and when they ran into trouble they would have to call it up. It wasn't like us where we could just look to the left and ask the tanks to take a building out for us. So I know their movements slowed us down a lot.

JM: Did the nature of the enemy – his tactics or capabilities – represent any challenges to you in terms of calling indirect fires?

JA: At first not really, because they didn't realize the capability of the LRAS and they thought they were safe. There was one point, though, where we were calling in indirect fires that they started targeting the LRAS truck. I think they figured out what we were doing; and even the insurgents who were deep in the city started hiding a little better. I remember one incident where I was mad because it was my truck. I wasn't on it but one of my squad leaders was commanding it and the sniper shot out the headlight and kept shooting at my truck. I was getting mad having to watch my truck get shot at. We told him to back up in a defilade position and the sniper still kept shooting at him. We eventually ID'd the sniper and took him out, but it was obvious after two days that they knew what the LRAS truck was and they started adjusting their tactics to try and take out our observation.

JM: You mentioned taking your section and clearing – so you guys were actually employed as infantrymen, doing dismounted clearing and stuff?

JA: Oh yeah.

JM: Was that a definite change of mission or was that something you just fell into?

JA: We actually had prepped for that since the very beginning. We knew at some point that we were going to go into the city because they had given us the industrial area.

JM: The whole BRT had the industrial area?

JA: Correct. That was our sector and we knew that once we hit the cloverleaf we were eventually going to have to dismount. It wasn't anything we hadn't already prepped for. We'd been in Iraq since March, we were ready and the tactics hadn't changed.

JM: Can you tell me about any particularly memorable or significant incidents that happened when you guys were dismounted?

JA: One that does stick out in my mind and was an eye-opener for me was that everywhere we went we found an underground tunnel system that was used by the insurgents. We'd see all these tunnels we had to clear and I remember going down into these tunnels and they all had IED wires running from them. They had rigged buildings to blow and would hide in the tunnels and wait for us to pass, and then they'd blow up the buildings. I had my section all stacked on this door and was getting ready to kick it in when Staff Sergeant Danielsen called me on the radio right as I had my foot in the air. He said, "I found a building over here rigged to blow. Have you run into any of those?" So right then I stopped and checked the doorway, found this hole in the side and, sure enough, the door I was getting ready to kick was another building that was rigged to blow. That one stood out pretty good. I remember one of our soldiers – Specialist John White – the first day we dismounted he actually fragged an underground tunnel and, when the smoke cleared, I went down in there and he had actually fragged an insurgent who was down in there hiding. He was just down in there and we were right on top of him. I assume he was going to wait until we passed and then pop up behind us.

JM: Did you just drop grenades down these holes when you found them or did you ever get down into them?

JA: We'd frag it first before we entered and cleared it. I went down a lot of holes and they were all over the place.

JM: What kinds of caches were you coming across? Were they just in every building?

JA: Not in every building. I remember two large caches we found. One was mortar rounds and it looked like the guy was making an IED. It had an intercom system, a couple landmines, small arms rounds, a couple RPGs and a bunch of clocks that were taken apart with wires hanging out. It looked like he was rigging detonators for IEDs. We were clearing every building, every doorway and every house. It got so monotonous. There had been word of anti-aircraft guns in the area and, towards the end of the day, my section was stacked up on the last building. I kicked in the door and when I came through I had this anti-aircraft gun pointing right at me. At first I had the "Oh shit" feeling and then I was like, "I found the mother load!" And then I realized I still had to clear the building because it wasn't cleared. We found two antiaircraft guns, which I don't think could operate; they looked pretty old. But there were tons of 155 rounds, cases of ammo – it was a big cache. All through the town there were small caches, nothing big. A couple landmines here and there, a couple 155 shells. Those two caches are the ones that stand out in my mind.

JM: When you were clearing the buildings, did you ever have to shoot it out with anybody? Were these buildings abandoned?

JA: Most of them were abandoned. We really didn't run into too much resistance. Once we crossed Phase Line Fran, it was like random snipers here and there, but our main concern was buildings that were rigged to blow. That scared me more than anything. The 2-2 scout platoon had kicked in a door and a bunch of their guys had gotten shot up because there were insurgents in there with an RPK, so that weighed in the back of my mind a lot. You could frag buildings before you went in, but we learned a hard lesson that that was really stupid – because if you fragged a building before you went in, all it does is kick up dust so you need to wait five minutes for the dust to settle. What was a really valuable asset that I loved and was snatching them up every chance I got were flash bang grenades. Those are not something we normally got issued, but they were great because you threw it in there, it doesn't kick the dust up and gives you two or three extra seconds to get in the room.

JM: Where would you go to get these?

JA: When we came in to get more ammo. I told my driver to go get some more Mk-19 rounds and some frags and he came back with one case of frags and he also got some flash bangs. I told him, "Great. Go get more." Every chance we got we got more because they went like hotcakes. I thought they were a lot more valuable that a frag because a frag is only good if you know for sure that there's insurgents in the room.

JM: In terms of ammo or any other classes of supply, how do you feel 2-2 supported you?

JA: Our support was outstanding because I know we were burning through some ammo those first couple days. We never had a problem with getting rounds. 203 rounds started to dwindle down a little bit – and I don't know why – and hand grenades as well started to become in short supply as we moved into clearing the city. Other than that, there were plenty of small arms rounds, crew-served weapons and AT-4s. We could've used more flash bangs, but that was something we really weren't used to having. They were really great in that type of situation.

JM: You mentioned early on that there were some comms issues with the Marines. Did you continue to experience this and were there any comms issues with other Army units?

JA: That was solved a minute after the leaders recon. That was just something nobody really took into consideration. We honestly cut the recon short because of it.

JM: Did you have any interaction with the Iraqi units? I understand they were moving in behind you.

JA: Not really. I remember seeing them moving behind us and I was like, "Put them in front of us. Give me a little break." We really didn't interact with them at all. I guess they were just securing the rear flank.

JM: What about any fratricide or close calls you guys had? Were there any incidents?

JA: No.

JM: Are you able to get a sense of why, fortunately, there weren't any?

JA: They stressed fratricide so much and that was what you always thought about. When we were calling in artillery, we knew where all the friendly troops were and we already had restrictions set up of where we can't fire and what the sectors of fire were – and it was tough sometimes because you could see insurgents, see good targets, but couldn't engage them. We didn't worry about it too much. We just reported it and let the guys down there take them out.

JM: Your platoon had the LRAS. Did any other units have this system?

JA: For our troop, our platoon was the only one with the LRAS. The other platoon had their LRAS damaged by an IED attack a couple months earlier. We were pretty much the golden children with it for Task Force 2-2.

JM: None of the other companies even had one?

JA: No, not that I was aware of. From my understanding, we were the only ones with an LRAS in all of Task Force 2-2. But those things were awesome – especially for a scout. I do believe that was probably the most valuable piece of equipment we had next to the radio.

JM: You mentioned that some guys had busted into a building and taken fire from insurgents. Was this when Captain Sean Sims got killed?

JA: No, they weren't killed. They just received some rounds and were injured. It was Staff Sergeant Jason Laser and a couple guys behind him. They got hit in their plates so they were lucky – and it goes to show why we wear body armor. But that incident taught us that when we kick open a door, we needed to be mindful that there might be somebody behind it.

JM: Are you able to step back at this point and overall assess the role your platoon and maybe the BRT as a whole played in this operation, how you contributed to the 2-2 mission?

JA: The way I looked at it for Task Force 2-2: we orchestrated a raining-down death of artillery shells and mortars on the insurgents those first couple days. They thought they were going to be safe deeper within the city, but they couldn't hide from that LRAS. If they stuck their head up in a window or were on a rooftop, we saw them. Then, as the battle progressed on, we just cleared the industrial center.

JM: Were you the principal eye looking through the LRAS?

JA: When we first rolled up on top of the berm, I kicked the gunner off the LRAS because I wanted to play. I wanted the first artillery mission of the day. Staff Sergeant Danielsen and I just rotated out. I attribute this to our platoon sergeant, Sergeant First Class Jamie Loy, who wasn't with us – but Staff Sergeant Danielsen and I always led from the front. We wouldn't make the guys do anything we hadn't done or that we wouldn't do first. We stayed up behind the LRAS a long time the first couple days and we had all the other guys looking up at us like we were the big kids on the playground who took their toys away – so we finally let them get back on it. So besides me and Staff Sergeant Danielsen, the other guys who were trained on the LRAS were Specialist Brendan Sandmann who was on R&R leave. He came back in and got thrown into the battle about two days into it. We put him back on the LRAS because that was his truck, he was my gunner originally, and he was always behind the LRAS. Specialist James Taylor was also really proficient with the LRAS too. Between us four, we were usually on the LRAS.

238

JM: Is there any way you think you could have been better employed?

JA: Honestly, no. We're scouts and that's our job: to observe the battlefield, call indirect and send up spot reports. It was really the first time we actually got to do our job and have results as far as a scout's mission. In my eight years in the Army, that was probably the best mission I've ever had as far as doing a true scout's job – those first couple days when we were up there in that observation position.

JM: Were there any major lessons learned or takeaways you had from this operation that you'll carry forward with you in your career?

JA: I definitely have to say that close quarters combat (CQC) is such a major factor over there in the area we operated in and I've never let that drop. I'm an instructor now and I observe/control (OC) and train the National Guard and Reserves and get them ready to go over to Iraq. I harp on CQC because that's what you're fighting over there. The other thing we learned about were the flash bangs and I preach to these guys about them and tell them they have to get their hands on them if they can. I also tell them that the LRAS is one of the most valuable pieces of equipment and that they can do significant damage with it in the right hands. Cross training is important too as far as everybody needing to know how to do everybody else's job. Like I said, when the battle kicked off, the platoon sergeant was gone, the original LRAS gunner was gone and we had so many guys on leave; and then we just started rolling, accomplished the mission and didn't run into any problems because we always had done that. All the training and planning prior to that had paid off. Even though we never knew we would be going to fight in Fallujah, everybody always knew how to do everybody else's job and it made our platoon successful.

JM: Are there any other individuals you think deserve special attention for their actions in this operation?

JA: Staff Sergeant Danielsen obviously. He basically played two roles as the senior scout and the platoon sergeant. There's one more: my squad leader, Sergeant Mike Cowles. Since the platoon sergeant was on leave, Staff Sergeant Danielsen had his truck and the platoon leader had his truck. I took the platoon sergeant's truck, Sergeant Cowles took over as the commander of my LRAS truck and, between him and the lieutenant, they called in all the indirect fires – and he was just an E5. A PFC scout can call for fires but he really stepped up and shouldered his responsibility as a young E5. We just told him one morning that he was taking the LRAS truck and we were going to Fallujah, and he didn't have any qualms or questions or anything. He was really proficient and really professional. One thing he discovered about the artillery was that when we called for fire and then made our adjustments, they were seeming to be wrong. He figured out that the artillery itself back in the rear was doubling our corrections because they were afraid of fratricide. So we ended up having to counter that by – and I still don't understand that one at all. All it did was waste more time and more rounds, in my opinion, but he orchestrated that artillery really well.

JM: Did you have much interaction with Captain Kirk Mayfield?

JA: Oh yeah. Captain Mayfield was with us the first couple days. He was our troop commander so I saw him all the time. He was always right in the middle of things, always keeping us informed. But he was doing the troop commander thing and I was more worried about my platoon than about what he was doing.

JM: Do you have any comments about the whole joint-ness aspect? Any thoughts about how well the Army, Marine Corps and the Air Force worked together?

JA: I know the Army and the Air Force worked really well together. Those JTACs were great guys and they were awesome. They were right there, ready to support us in any way we needed and they had planes there ready to go. As far as the Marines went, it just seemed that every time I ran into them there were problems. They could definitely have used better equipment for one thing. It seemed like they always had more restrictions than we did and it almost seemed like they were more led by their officers than by their NCOs. In my platoon, you could take any one of my privates and he could lead a mission without any problem, but we saw some Marines up on the interstate that night and they couldn't really tell us what was going on with the city. We were receiving small arms fire and they were like, "Hold on, we have to go get the lieutenant, we have to get the lieutenant." Well, I didn't want to talk to their lieutenant; I wanted to talk to them. All in all, I'd definitely say that the Army and the Air Force worked really well together.

JM: You just wished you'd had permission to drop more bombs.

JA: Oh yeah, and I wish we'd had better targets for them too. That did seem to hinder us a lot. I remember when the battle first started we wanted to drop and we couldn't get clearance. That was frustrating.

JM: Are than any other aspects about this operation and your role in it that we didn't talk about that you'd like to mention?

JA: Not that I can think of. I think we pretty much covered it all.

JM: Well, thank you very much for your time today then. It was great talking to you and thank you for your service as well.

JA: No problem.

Staff Sergeant David Bellavia
27 July 2006

MM: My name is Matt Matthews (MM) and I'm an historian for the Combat Studies Institute at Fort Leavenworth, Kansas. Today is 27 July 2006 and I'm interviewing Staff Sergeant David Bellavia (DB) on his experiences in Operation Phantom Fury. This is an unclassified interview. If I start to get into anything that might be classified just say, "Hey, I can't answer that," and I'll understand what you're talking about. I want to start off with some background information on you – where were you born, where you grew up and went to school, the circumstances under which you decided to join the Army.

DB: I was born and raised in Buffalo, New York. I attended Franklin Pierce College in Rindge, New Hampshire, and the University of Buffalo. I joined the Army in the spring of 1999 and served in the infantry for six years, deploying to Iraq with the 1st Infantry Division's 3d Brigade stationed out of Vilseck, Germany.

MM: You had served, I believe, in Kosovo and in various other places before you ever got to Iraq in 2004, is that correct?

DB: That's right. Our unit in Kosovo was almost identical to what we brought to Iraq, with the exception that we deployed for KFOR 4B without our mechanized or armored assets. We did nine months instead of the six-month rotation. I have to tell you, with all sincerity, those were some of the most difficult and enduring days of my life. I could take two years in Iraq living out of a MRE bag over that. In Iraq we believed in our mission. We knew it was important and that we were needed to save lives. Human lives were in the balance in Iraq daily. In Kosovo, though, it was very difficult to maintain a presence in an area where absolutely nothing would ever happen. We were on patrols with soft cover hats and no vests, and you pretty much needed a written letter of consent to chamber a round. If it wasn't for the constant training it would have been very difficult to endure. The war was going on elsewhere and the talk around the campfire was that we were missing our fight. You can't be part of the Big Red One and not buy completely into the amazing history of this unit; but how could my generation face this great noble adventure if the Big Red One is guarding Mr. Mehmeti's chicken farm? It was criminal to miss the fight – and to be in Kosovo felt like a sham while other brave men and women were getting hurt. Morale was probably the lowest at that time, at least for me personally. Our leadership at our task force and company levels truly developed an ingenious plan. It would have been all too easy to lose focus on the next trip downrange, and we most certainly did not. Lieutenant Colonel Pete Newell, Captain Doug Walter, First Sergeant Peter Smith and Command Sergeant Majors Darrin Bohn and Steven Faulkenburg – these guys really made our nine months of pointless nothingness into a giant field problem with Iraq the dangling carrot to bait us. They would invent opportunities to air assault us into sectors, land navigate patrols, set up communications networks and drill casualty evacuations. The whole thing was training for the real world while in the "sort of but not really" world of Kosovo. The terrain got us in great shape and our enlisted men had mastered skill levels one and two by the end of the rotation. The leadership challenge for the small unit leaders had been met head on. Our success in Fallujah and during our whole year in Iraq was not bought and paid for by unit readiness training lanes in Germany or divine dumb luck. Rather, it was due to the nine months in Kosovo and the continued battalion-level focus when we came home. Our success was born from the fruits of outcome-based, goal-focused and purpose-driven leadership that started in Kosovo. This ethos, developed over time, emboldened the understanding that we are all accountable for each other coming home. That team building was essential to enduring the hardships of close quarters contact. Without that, we're just another unit in combat. I believe we shot more rounds than any other task force infantry battalion in the United States military, without a doubt. We stole ammunition. There'd be people who said, "Yeah, we don't want to go to the range today," so we just took it: 8,000 rounds here, 4,000 rounds there. And we literally would go on a 12-hour patrol and then we'd turn around and do bunker drills all night long.

MM: Can you talk me through when you first found out that you guys were going to have to go to Iraq in 2004? And also, who were some of the leaders in place at that time in 2-2 Infantry?

DB: Command was clearly picking up the training tempo and it was obvious that we were next to go when Kosovo ended. Family time was split between ranges and preparation. To be honest, I truly applaud our commanders and their ability to take the unpopular but professional approach towards family readiness groups (FRGs) and say basically, "If we don't train, we don't come home. Shut up and stop complaining. We'll be home when we're done." I don't believe that came out in actual memorandum form, but the point was clear. 2-2 didn't cut any corners before Iraq. We had a chip on our shoulder too. Everyone was talking about stabilization and sustainment operations. President Bush had landed on the carrier. No one even knew Abu Musab al-Zarqawi's name, let alone talked about it on Fox News. The UN headquarters was still up and running in Baghdad. The popular lay opinion was that we were going to open hospitals and clean water supplies. We wanted to be the Big Red One of our dad's war but we were widely considered a peacekeeping division. Then we started to read the names of the towns we were going to on the front pages of newspapers. When we started to hear on the news that the cities in our sector were getting hot, we got pumped up and the motivation while training matched the intensity of the training tempo and we knew we had something real special. War is horrific and ghastly. There are ghoulish images that we all endure and it's impossible to not be changed forever; but only in the midst of the worst mankind can produce can you truly see the beauty of human nature: self sacrifice, true honor, unprecedented loyalty – all the Army values displayed in person. When you have the chance to serve your nation with men and women you trust and love; when leaders two tax brackets above your pay grade carry rifles on the field next to you; and when you see your peers take bullets for you – that environment would motivate the most ardent anti-victory opponent of this conflict. We defended America and together put a lot of pure evil permanently out of business. This was truly the greatest experience in my life. I'm honored to have had the opportunity to fight this enemy during this noble time in my nation's history, but more importantly, to do it as a "Ramrod" in the Big Red One's 3d Brigade. I truly believed I was the most prudently lethal and professional soldier in the world when I wore that Red One patch on my arm, and my peers believed the same.

Lieutenant Colonel Newell was running the show at the task force level, and he was everything you could expect in a battalion commander. If you built a field grade officer in your garage out of parts, you would get Lieutenant Colonel Newell: square jaw, oozed confidence. If you beat him in the face with a shovel, his expression wouldn't change. Not a whole lot of laughing going on. No email exchanges after training. I spoke to the guy maybe six times in three years, and never small talk. He had expectations and we lived to exceed those. When he was happy, he went away. When he wasn't, he was in your living area telling your leadership about his displeasure. Command Sergeant Major Faulkenberg was always in our living area no matter what happened. You couldn't get rid of the guy even if you became a tanker. He was never happy, he always demanded things be better and was relentless about his own standards. He was the stereotypical Sam Elliott CSM Basil Plumley character in *We Were Soldiers*. A barbed wire personality, no nonsense. Had "been there" and "done that" on every continent in almost every unit. You never knew where you stood with him, though. In the field, his face was a red mask of veiny anger. You never questioned his loyalty or his passion for his soldiers, but I never knew if a slap on the back was going to be followed by a punch in the face. However, if strings of profanity followed by my last name is a mark of endearment, then I believe he loved me unconditionally. I would've gone through a wall for the man. They also brought in CSM Darrin Bohn who was a *huge* addition, because he came not only from Afghanistan but was the Alpha Company 1-75 Ranger Regiment first sergeant as well. His boys were the tip of the spear during Operation Anaconda and other epic battles of Afghanistan. He's a stud's stud. He really implemented a world-class close quarters marksmanship instruction course and I'm a walking, living, breathing reminder that it works. His training is the reason half my platoon is alive today. Unlike other units, CSM Bohn was teaching techniques ripped from real world firefights.

You get these Blackwater former SWAT morons who give vast dissertations from their urban room-clearing experiences on the Miami Dade Sheriff's Department. Give me a break. They seized little Elian Gonzalez out of a Miami condo and are now trying to reinvent the Army infantry wheel in Kuwait when you first get into country. When you hear about these other kids trying to go for head shots in close quarters, fly up walls like Delta Force, it's insanity. On the other hand, our guys under CSM Bohn were shooting center mass controlled pairs over and over again until the guy drops – and that saves lives. We strong-walled, put down controlled fire, overwhelmed, sustained, dominated, fixed and killed scores of insurgents in real world close quarters combat. No one jumped around with gravity boots down chimneys, so give the man the credit he deserves. CSM Bohn: what an amazing asset he was. There was also Major Ken Adgie who was the executive officer (XO) at the time. He gave outstanding after-actions reviews (AAR), had a wealth of infantry knowledge, and was another 2-2 field grade comedian. Ramrod NCOs and officers were full of scowls and vinegar before Iraq, but they were the best in the world at their jobs and they shaped a brilliant unit. You know, not a whole lot of chum-chum times at 2-2 back then. Major Adgie left and we got Major John Petkosek, and then we just started to gear up. What's great about Germany is that the faces never seem to go away. You have the Major Adgies here and then they end up showing up somewhere else in theater. In United States Army Europe (USAREUR), you never lose your guys. Once you have those relationships, you have them forever. We started to see guys trickle out and come back. We went with Captain Walter from February 2003 all the way to the day we left for Iraq.

MM: Could you talk me through what the company thought when you found out that Doug Walter wouldn't be able to go with you guys?

DM: I'm not a guy who gushes over officers in general. I don't believe that college makes you more adept at leading men in battle. You are not able to shoot more accurately because of a commission. That's lunacy. If we could get warrant officers to lead platoons in the infantry, I would sign up for 20 years tomorrow – but Secretary of the Army Francis Harvey doesn't take my calls. That said, Captain (now Major) Doug Walter is perhaps the most honorable man I have ever met in my life. I would put him in the inner circle. He is incapable of doing anything unethical and I really, truly admire him. I came to the unit under Captain Thomas Johnson who is a tenacious and in-your-face commander. Blunt and aggressive, he would lead the charge with a saber in his hand cursing the enemy until his last breath. Read Johnson's Silver Star citation for what he did during the battle for Ba'qubah in the summer of 2004 and tell me he shouldn't have a soccer field at Fort Benning. So having that predecessor, Captain Walter built on that aggression and instilled vast inner-company coordination and the organization of Bradley/dismounted infantry interaction that would be essential to fighting effectively in urban and rural Iraq. He would have four pages of notes on the way we reported things on the radio. He was meticulous in the training environment. Our platoons fought brilliantly with our mounted elements, and in urban contact that is what makes you devastating. Each and every leader you have, whether it's a senior NCO or a commissioned officer, you take something from them. In Alpha Company 2-2 we had very different personalities commanding us before combat tested us, and we were all better because of them. Captain Walter was the head coach when it all came together. He truly deserves the most credit and that's why I've always regarded him as the best. I really was looking forward to going to battle with Captain Walter in January 2004 but he got real sick with a severe stomach virus that comprised his immune system. We knew he was suffering and we saw his weight balloon. This is a guy who would punish us on six and seven mile runs. He was almost masochistic when he ran with us in company formations. To see him so sick, then, it was obvious to us all that something was seriously wrong. He went from being really heavy to frail because of the medication he was on. He was going through all these invasive medical procedures in Germany that were horrible. We all knew it, but he never complained. His wife is a nurse and her research is really the main reason he recovered. There was stress because of the fact that he never let on that his condition was life threatening, but we knew it could be potentially. We got our A bags, the wives are in the parking lot and he tells us he's not going with us the night we fly to Kuwait. It was really emotional. It was a tough one to take.

MM: At the last minute he's replaced by Captain Sean Sims. Could you tell me a little bit about that?

DB: Captain Sims had a stellar reputation. He worked at the operations (S3) shop with CSM Bohn for awhile and did a lot behind the scenes. I was impressed at his complete self confidence. He changed nothing from what Captain Walter had established. So many times a leader will burn the house down just to rebuild a different one from their predecessors, but he wasn't insecure at all. He had nothing to prove to us and he earned our respect under fire. He had a great personality, a magnetic personality: warm smile, funny guy. He would bust chops. He had a keen, razor sharp intellect and was articulate. Plus, he and Captain Walter had a deep personal relationship. Captain Sims observed/controlled a couple of our live fires so we knew he obviously was more than capable of doing whatever he needed to do as an infantry officer. He went to Texas A&M with Staff Sergeant Benjamin Richey from our 1st Platoon, Alpha Company. We figured it was going to be a pretty smooth transition. He showed up to Kuwait as our newly minted commander and had pink eye, which was then passed throughout the entire Alpha Company and subsequently the battalion. I remember much to the chagrin of our Special Forces physician assistant (PA), we started sharing all the extra eye ointment and pink eye infected half the brigade by the time we moved up north into Iraq. Captain Sims came up after having recovered from his initial bout and said to me, tongue in cheek, "Sergeant, you really need to be more careful about passing that stuff around." I accused him of leaving 2d Platoon alone, while he intentionally rubbed his eyes on my 3d Platoon and 1st Platoon's gear. I told him that in over a year with Captain Walter he never gave us pink eye and we all laughed. He said it would be noted on Captain Walter's officer evaluation report (OER). It was a near perfect transition.

MM: Let's now focus on your arrival into Iraq and anything that stands out in your mind that happened before you guys launched into Operation Phantom Fury.

DB: We took over Forward Operating Base (FOB) Normandy from Task Force 2-8 of the 4th Infantry Division. 2-8 Infantry named it Normandy because they were the first boots on the ground during D-Day; and like World War II, the division was going to be counted on to seal the deal. On our first mission as a platoon we took contact while still on our right-seat ride. This guy fired at us from a balcony not even 10 feet away, just missing Captain Sims and Staff Sergeant Colin Fitts. Captain Sims rolled with us that day and he decided to take us into the marketplace at night. The guy shooting at us gets off about four rounds before having a weapons malfunction. So he's correcting his malfunction, two of our guys fire back and we just sat there, eyes wide, "What's going on?" The 4th ID guys are saying, "This is a bad idea; let's get out of here." Captain Sims is on the ground and it seems like, "Holy cow! This is for real!" We all learned and grew together. Had that happened about three weeks later, we would've handled that area and the guy with the dirty rifle without pause. Captain Sims was extremely aggressive in the beginning of the year, and I absolutely loved that about him. Tenacious and cocky – it was really what we needed. Sims had a swagger that just let everyone around him know that things were going to be okay; and more importantly, he let his NCOs lead during fight. My platoon sergeant, Sergeant First Class James Cantrell, was the lead mounted Bradley element of most of the company and sometimes battalion set plays in contact. He never had issues with letting his NCOs do what they do best, and Sergeant First Class Cantrell was the best in the battalion. Cantrell would inevitably be making contact and reacting to contact on his own while Sims in the back would be issuing intent and direction to set up the next move in support. Sims was all about results and never about ego, and this worked flawlessly in our sector. Depending on who you talk to, our company killed well over a hundred insurgents over two days of fighting in April 2004. The mission was relentless and we were ready for it. We picked up after two days of fighting with attrition and moved into Najaf. We lost a great friend of ours, Staff Sergeant Victor Rosales, on the way to Najaf, which was horribly tragic. We loved that man. We all did.

MM: Was that an improvised explosive device (IED) incident?

DB: Yes, he was in the front cab of a heavy equipment transporter (HET). This guy was a Ranger, no-quit attitude and simply a wonderful man, a better father. His wife was also in our brigade. He had a little baby, was just a fantastic guy and a real asset. We lost him, and to lose him and not do anything there in Najaf really was devastating. I was very, very disappointed. Specialist Allen Vandayburg was killed in Buritz; he was from Charlie Company. Staff Sergeant Raymond Bittinger earned our division's first Silver Star that night and Specialist Nieves was killed a few days after that. We had been out in the desert 10 to 15 days doing nothing. But at the same time, we had cut our teeth on the intra-theater deployment. Again, a huge leadership challenge that 2-2 and 3d Brigade responded to. We were starting to lose guys; and with each loss we became more galvanized and tighter as a unit. We started to garner more and more swagger and that meant horrible things for the enemy back home. They would call us *"Wahed Mooshot"* (One Infantry) and it was nice to hear that spoken with the awe and reverence it deserved. Grandpa would have been proud to see us in the field wearing that Red One in battle. We were a sight to see.

MM: When you arrived in Iraq, was your platoon leader actually Lieutenant Joaquin Meno?

DB: No, we had Lieutenant Christopher Walls. He ended up being the mortar platoon leader in Fallujah.

MM: When did Lieutenant Meno come in? Was that a couple months prior to the Fallujah operation?

DB: That would be mid-to-late July 2004. Lieutenant Meno showed up and he was over at FOB Gabe with Charlie Company and Task Force 1-6 Field Artillery. He was actually with Charlie Company on the ground the night Specialist Vandayburg was killed in Burtiz. It was one of those situations where there were too many lieutenants for the leadership jobs. He came over and it was a perfect fit. Now, Walls was a West Point Ranger. The kid was like 6-foot-3 and 220 pounds of muscle. Everyone around the battalion would genuflect as he passed. He was a great platoon leader, but he looked the role and had the pedigree for greatness. Meno was a branch transfer; the kid was all heart and completely unafraid to express what was on his mind, which is sometimes not appreciated by all of command. But we thought he was great. He is Guamanian and very proud of who he is, where he comes from and will defend his point of view furiously. He also was a renegade in the sense that he really didn't care what feathers got ruffled in order to get the job done. I liked his us-versus-them approach. He valued his NCOs and, quite frankly, regardless of what his professional background was, Lieutenant Meno led us with uncommon valor. Every time we were hugging earth, getting pounded on from the enemy, he was feet away doing the same. What more do you want from a lieutenant?

MM: What branch did he transfer over from?

DB: I think finance. He kept it a secret until the end of the tour. It was the type of field where he didn't have any business being where he was but, I tell you what, you didn't notice it. He is going to be a great company commander, and that is an important role of the NCO: to help mold his young lieutenant to be an outstanding company commander. Meno is fearless and unrelenting. He won't back down from full bird or field grade. If they make all administration officers like Joaquin Meno, we need to start bringing them into the infantry. But they don't. So if by chance Francis Harvey is reading this, believe me, they don't.

MM: Talk me through what you and your men felt when you first started getting an inkling that you may have to go to Fallujah and help out the Marines.

DB: The first rumor was Sadr City in the summer of 2004. It was a rumor, but I really wanted that fight; I wanted something. The Najaf thing devastated me. Muqdadiyah was cleaning up and I really thought we could be used more and make a difference. I knew we could dent Anbar Province if allowed. It wasn't that we wanted attention; we just believed in the tenacity of the mechanized infantry company – and that is what Anbar needed. We had cut our teeth against the enemy. Muqdadiyah was like the "billion virgin giveaway" for the enemy. But more importantly, we wanted to fight and that's what we were there for. When we missed out on the Najaf fight and Najaf blew up again and then Samarra – 2d Brigade, 1st ID got Samarra, and then Sadr City went to 1st Cavalry Division. We heard it all: "Hey, you're going to Ramadi, you're going to Fallujah." When it actually happened, I was more than excited. I thought this was predestined, that this was what we were all born to do. I was extremely ready for this challenge. I thought our soldiers were going to be without peers and unflappable in the fight. As soon as the orders came down through to battalion, I started to see how gifted we were as a unit. We had guys who were thinking far outside the box. Captain Sims was lining up T-barriers and blowing them up with 120 millimeter gun tubes; CSM Faulkenburg was setting up Humvee doors and cracking them with rocket-propelled grenades (RPGs); CSM Bohn was getting back into a regimen of close quarters marksmanship. We started training more furiously, shooting more ammunition. It's ironic because you really can't be a subject matter expert on military operations in urban terrain (MOUT). No one knows what's going to happen inside a house fight. I studied SWAT doctrine from the Los Angeles and Chicago Police Departments and the early 1970s field manuals from the Army. It's funny because the early 70s MOUT was based on the lessons learned in World War II. There is always like a generation gap between when we start throwing things into our doctrine. They were teaching their boys in the late 60s and early 70s: "When in trouble, frag out and shoot like a madman." Today we are much more evolved, right? Yet when it hits the fan, we toss frags and shoot like madmen. High-intensity MOUT is without a script. You can't master golf and you can't master MOUT. You can, however, rehearse myriads of possibilities and hone basic fundamentals of close quarters marksmanship, and most importantly master the fundamentals of manipulation of your equipment. Magazine reloads, safety lever switching, etc. You set up circumstances to test your soldiers' ability to adapt to whatever situation, especially in casualty evacuations and buddy aid. But MOUT is very much a lesson in improvisation. Master the five-second firefight and leave the rest up to the enemy. When face to face, nothing can ever dominate the American infantrymen. Marine or soldier, Air Force or RTO; we're untouchable.

MM: So you guys arrive at the Marine camp in Camp Fallujah and the training then must really have intensified. Could you tell me about the rock drills and what sort of training you went through when you arrived?

DB: I'm going to be completely honest with you: I made sure my guys didn't do that. There was definitely training going on everywhere. You see these guys running around clearing houses, doing whatever. The thing about MOUT– and first of all, whether we were blessed or cursed, we had close quarters firefights in Muqdadiayh. We shot people in houses. My engineers were more combat tested than, quite frankly, the second platoon we dished out to the engineer battalion in exchange, just because of the way they were used and the sector they fought in. Our scouts were more bloodied than your average Army infantry unit. I'm not trying to sound like a braggart; I'm just saying that we had an area of operations (AO) that was extremely volatile and by handling that we developed tested techniques and tactics with regards to the urban fight. 2-7 will probably tell you the same thing. Then you've got your engineers, your field artillery boys and your tank crews – and 3d Brigade's in Ba'qubah and the Brigade Reconnaissance Troop (BRT) is slicing up their piece of the pie. We knew the plan when we left FOB Normandy. But extra training for Fallujah while at Camp Fallujah? When you boil it down, there are two ways you can go into a house: you have center-fed doors and corner-fed doors. The only thing you have to get into the head of Joe is that he has to acknowledge the fact that 90 percent of his fight against a maneuver-minded enemy is a psychological fight. They rely heavily on trying to intimidate you. As our populations continue to grow, urban areas will grow up and enemies of America will use these structures to try to neutralize our fighting methods. But they can't psych us out if our soldiers are ready for that type of battle. Once you determine that no matter what happens when that door opens you are equipped and trained to handle all of it, baring a Wes Craven film, you are golden. This enemy wants to engage you and run away, hoping you give chase. The enemy in an urban fight wants to lure you into making "inappropriate moves" and get you to chase him around the city, away from your mechanized support by fire base. A house fight really plays more into our favor than into the enemy's favor. By fighting us in the extreme close quarters, they're making the asymmetrical fight symmetrical. There, they're in a house – fixed – not running from phase line to phase line enveloping our positions. They jump into buildings and you have the choice. Do you have to clear it? Do you need to exercise precision or do you just want to lob some main tank rounds in there or some 25 millimeter high explosive (HE). This enemy thinks American warriors don't have the fortitude for the urban fight, and they are sadly mistaken. Our technological gap is neutralized to some extent, but what the enemy and some American politicians don't understand is that there's no such thing as a technological advantage in the urban fight. At some point, it comes down to your desire to destroy the threat that's in front of you. Everyone is at risk in the urban fight; nothing is bulletproof in the urban fight. It has never been world class technology that makes the American infantryman great; rather it's the American infantryman who makes the technology world class. We drilled into our kids' heads the fundamentals of CQB, but that doesn't mean you script how they enter and what they carry when they enter a building. Doctrine will tell you that you want your leadership and automatic riflemen towards the back of the stack; but if we didn't have squad automatic weapon (SAW) gunners in the front, we're losing at least four soldiers in Fallujah on day two. This is a five-second firefight. I would tell my guys, "We know what your index (trigger) finger can do, but what your thumb does is much more important (selector switch)." Muscle memory and manipulation of weapons, accuracy and fire superiority – that's what worked for us. "One man goes this way, two men go that way." I want shotguns and I want SAWs. I want AT4s and I want grenades. We must make sure our soldiers know how to read a room before they enter it. They must understand how to "cook off" grenades and how to toss them in concrete structures. We want our 240B machine gunners in the fight. We want our indirect assets of our 40 millimeter HE grenades. The fundamentals of room clearing are not things you can drill into soldiers' heads days before we go to battle. They are the things we learned in Kosovo and have taught for over two years. Like when your buddy gets hurt in a close quarters fight, you might not be able to give him aid. You've got to kill the source of that casualty. Get the bad guy or you are going to have more injured. You hear your buddy hurt and it sucks; but you eliminate the threat, secure and search the environment and then evacuate on command. It's all psychological – and once you empower subordinates to perform above their pay grade, they realize there's nothing they can't handle. Like professionals, they'll go out and execute. The enemy doesn't get it. We talk a lot about how this Islamist enemy has been fighting for generations and how new we are to this type of battle. In 2003, you may have had a point with that argument. In 2010 or 2012, though, I really would not want to fight an American infantryman in an urban situation. This generation today is unflappable in the worst situations imaginable. We never had the Grozny or the Berlin experiences to draw from as an Army. But now we have Fallujah, Ramadi, Tall Afar, Ba'qubah and Baghdad. I think we can stop telling Mogadishu stories about now. These privates will be far superior NCOs for that reason.

MM: So you and your squad are lined up, you've gone out of your attack positions and you're getting ready to blow the breach and go into Fallujah. Can you talk me through that first night?

DB: We got the go-ahead at 1500 that day that we were ready to roll. The Marines were asking if we were ready and we said we were. We're sleeping outside, gorging ourselves on MREs, drinking as much water as we could, getting some shut eye and not really knowing what a sustained urban fight was going to be like. No coming home for sleep and chow, 24/7 urban fighting, securing your six o'clock and focusing on your twelve and nine and three. It's challenging. My team leader, Sergeant Charles Knapp, and Lieutenant Meno ran off with the Headquarters and Headquarters Company (HHC) commander, Captain Fred Dente, and the chaplain, Captain Ric Brown, who was a super chaplain the entire rotation. The guy was praying with us and consoling us, literally on the battlefield and without a weapons system. He even got assaulted by ruffian Georgian Army soldiers at our Morale, Welfare and Recreation (MWR) at FOB Normandy. We really loved him. He's a great guy. Anyway, those guys do a quick Humvee reconnaissance on this berm. These mortar rounds just missed Captain Dente just a few feet away. We get a bunch of Paladins that crack over them and the guys told me they could see the binoculars twinkle in the distance and then that artillery round just puffed up pink. Our artillery, from the spotters to the shooters to the beautiful men who allowed the rounds to fly, they were crucial to keeping the enemy in one area to be flushed out. If we had to chase these insurgents from block to block, it would have been horrific. Their accuracy was spot on; and while they fired an absurd amount of artillery, it was still not enough for me on the ground. Our enemy might disagree, but he isn't available for comment at this time so they obviously did a great job. But the wait that afternoon for H-Hour was absolute agony. There are only so many Knute Rockne pep talks you can give when you're stacked eight to a man in a Bradley.

MM: So you're in the back of this Bradley and you're waiting for this breach to go. Were you able to see anything of the mine clearing line charge (MCLC) going off?

DB: We were checking it out before any of it happened. Our engineers were great the entire year because, first of all, they taught us how to blow our own stuff up. It was fantastic! We never needed explosive ordnance disposal (EOD) in our sector because the engineers were on patrol with us. They taught me, and at times perhaps they taught me too much. I loved the idea of coming up with different ways to get into houses and these guys were more than willing to help us out. So I checked out the MCLC, wanted to know how it was fired and what the rocket and the trailer looked like. When it was launched, you think, "Well, this isn't going to be anything." I've had a MCLC go off during training when I was outside and also when I was inside; and I have to say that inside is actually worse when you're so close to it. Staff Sergeant Bryan Lockwald was the engineer in charge of the MCLC. He told me he was more concerned about all the C4 he had in his M113 if they got hit to worry about the MCLC. He actually fired a second MCLC in the city. We had long talked about what would happen if you fired a MCLC down Main Street. The concussion would take out the first three stories on each side of the road. I thought it was awesome. The intense shockwave is actually that lethal, but to my knowledge that is the MCLC launched in an urban environment. The engineers from our Alpha Company did just that and God bless them for it. After that breeching MCLC went off, you probably had two minutes of nothingness and that's the last time I heard the still of the night in Fallujah until we left.

MM: So your platoon goes through the breach. At some point were you doing far or near side security?

DB: Staff Sergeant Biden Jim, a tanker with Bravo Company 1-63, was the lead vehicle in Fallujah on our side of the fight. His tank was A48 and he was in front of my Bradley. This guy was a Pacific Islander and really never got any credit for all that he did. Sergeant First Class Phelps, his platoon sergeant, did a whole bunch too, but tankers have the armor and no one wants to give them credit. If you see what happened to the Israeli Defense Forces armor in Lebanon, you realize that it's not just the tanks but the operators who are incredible. Staff Sergeant Jim was on point leading the way. We split our squads up by sections, Alpha and Bravo Sections. I was in Alpha Section and Fitts was with the Bravo Section, with 7 and 9. We just kept moving through and, I'll tell you what, it was really hard for the Bradley commanders to stay buttoned up like they were supposed to because we're trying to go with speed and you can just feel the Bradleys hitting soft sand and the resistance of them plowing the earth around and moving. You look out your periscope and you just see headlights with your infrared. Those Brads moved one inch off the chem-lit trail and, boom, there was some explosive, be it land mine or IED. It felt like the vehicles lifted off the ground. Sergeant First Class Cantrell's A37 had a small fire under its track leading up to the initial dismount.

MM: Did you have any difficulty with the railroad tracks that were blown up there?

DM: You felt everything you ran over. We got right up to the edge of the city, some idiot is bleeding over on our company net and it's a Marine. I hear Captain Sims lose his mind on the company net, and then I hear our whole platoon net lose its mind. We're on someone else's fire net. So the ramp drops, I send everyone out and we're maybe 80 meters from the city. My radio guy, Specialist John Ruiz, is ready to refill my radio and I said, "What the hell is going on?" They said the Marines had washed us out and they told us to get off the net. We actually had to do a communications security (COMSEC) changeover.

MM: You got to be kidding me!

DM: I swear, less than 100 meters from the city, right next to the breach. We were through and it was just a matter of organizing and getting everyone on line to grab our foothold. But we did a COMSEC changeover right there less than 100 meters from Fallujah.

MM: I've heard numerous examples of the Marine load fills not working and stuff like that.

DM: Right. Well, that's someone's purpose I'm sure. Whatever. Blaming who screwed up is pointless, but goofing on Marines is my favorite pastime. Seriously, everything was laid out well in advance at Camp Fallujah for all the detachments. We must have done six COMSEC changeovers before we left for the fight while at Camp Fallujah. I don't mean to bash the Marines and it might be our fault, but this was something that might have been handled a little smoother in retrospect. Whenever you work with another branch, there are always going to be issues no matter what you do. At this point, military historians will say that we're in the expeditionary era of warfighting. This is where we're all trying to be lighter, faster and more adaptable to the ever-changing environment of this global war. Now is probably the time where we should be performing more live fire, joint training missions with the Marine Corps and perhaps letting them get a hold of some quality equipment that would welcome them into the new millennium. It's shameful that they're so under-funded that they can't get basic issued gear. Seriously, we lifted night vision and Leopold scopes off the enemy in Fallujah. So it can be said, without hyperbole, that some of the insurgents had more modern equipment that our Marines did and there is no excuse for that. The days of amphibious assaults on a scale of what the Marines were designed to do are as long gone as phosphate sodas at the local drug store. Marines are being asked to do more and more offensive urban actions and need to be on a technological par with the rest of our world class military. Without that, you might as well leave them on the boats – and not the ones they "drove" into Fallujah, but the actual boat-boats.

MM: So you guys get through the breach and I think your first objective right there on the northeast side of the city is Objective Lion and you push down to Objective Panther that first night. Anything stand out in your mind from that first push? I guess you guys actually get through that breach a little after 1900. You're pushing and fighting all night to keep moving south, I would assume.

DM: First of all, it was an extremely dark night with very little natural illumination. The moon was nonexistent and, thank God, there was white phosphorous (WP) on the ground. We wouldn't have been able to see anything without that – secondary fires and other battlefield debris. My stomach's in a knot. I just want that first guy to start shooting so I can get it over with. I feel like my grandfather in World War II, that I'm literally living in an historical moment. We waited and waited and waited for the Iraqis to get their act together behind us. After about 45 minutes of standing there, it looked like the Marines were still all lined up and not moving. Someone just said, "Let's go! Take it down, first house, we're moving." Then a pretty good firefight broke out to our west, which I can only assume was the firefight that either preceded or was the actual the death of Sergeant Major Faulkenburg but it was definitely to our west. There was so much electrical wire from the bashed buildings. Captain James Cobb did an amazing job of prepping that area. A lot of kids still have fathers today because of his precision out there. During the day, you could see the way these insurgents were dug in; and without that relentless 155 millimeter barrage, we would've taken massive casualties. The front four buildings we were going into, which were completely pancaked – there were little spider trails and you could see fighting positions everywhere: dug in, overhead cover, even sumps on the bottom. Evidently FM 7-8 is available online. You could see where there was a garage, a car shop they would use, a little trench where you would change the oil – that was sandbagged with an RPK sitting up there. And this is the God's honest truth: I can't tell you how many bodies I saw in Fallujah, and every single one had a weapon in his hand and every one was either belt-fed PKCs or RPKs. There were very few rockets left around because they were more precious, obviously, than ball ammunition. A couple of my guys got caught in this electrical wire and for a brief moment there was some staccato fire from the distance. Staff Sergeant Fitts' squad had better position to identify the threat of the fire and he wasn't firing, so I trusted it was most likely stray rounds. But I was just having a heart attack thinking these soldiers were prone and in a huge danger area out in the open. I started to thrash a knife at the wire to free them only to be consumed in the tangle myself. We get into the first building, we get a foothold. I meet up with Fitts, Staff Sergeant Scott Lawson's there with his weapons squad, and Lieutenant Meno comes in. There are barrels of mo gas ready to blow, to isolate our thermals and night vision capability. There were newly-bricked walls behind doors and windows. Almost all the access that wasn't created by tanks and artillery was covered by the insurgents. They also made great strides to block our access to rooftops. Stairs would just stop and a seven-foot wall would block a door. I jumped into a window and found an oversized pineapple grenade on a door handle. Houses were empty, personal belongings packed in a hurry, stuff strewn across the floors. This one house had a serpentine-like maze of cinderblocks in the front yard with two sandbagged crew-served weapons overlooking from the roof. The only way out had a 130 millimeter round covered in flour. This took some planning. I was highly impressed and quite taken by the elaborateness of their defenses. Anyway, we get the call that Captain Sims was coming with his personal security detachment (PSD), we link up with him, 1st Platoon is still mounted up and we grab our first objective. No sooner than we do this, I see this dude with just soot all over his face. All I could see were his eyes, just two eyeballs walking. He's carrying a car battery like nothing's going on, his AK-47 smacking against his leg. I engaged him and Fitts – without a reticle aim by the way; he just had his night observation devices (NODs) on. But he shot three pump-action slugs that catastrophically ruined this guy's night. He was using my head as a tripod, unfortunately, but this was the first guy we hit. We move to the next building and I got a kid, Sergeant Knapp – the kid's an athlete. He can throw a grenade 40 meters on average and they almost air burst when he throws them. He's a great grenade thrower. He's a great baseball and football player. He tosses a grenade into this building across the street from where this guy was headed and, by the grace of God, our whole platoon piles in there and the whole thing was wired to blow. I've never seen that much C4 in my entire life. It looked like a log cabin, that's how many bricks were all taped together on the walls. It didn't take long. His grenade actually severed all the wires to the door. We came across our first building-contained improvised explosive device (BCIED) not even two buildings into the fight. It dawned on me that the guy we shot was heading towards the building. Knapp's grenade throw and Fitts' shotgun saved our platoon. With that much PE4 (Soviet C4), we would've been done.

MM: Can you talk me through your advance on down to your main objective at least initially, down to Phase Line Fran or Highway 10?

DB: The night went pretty slow and pretty much everything was tank or Bradley-killed. You would actually hear insurgents challenging Sergeant First Class Phelps' and Staff Sergeant Jim's tanks with AK47 fire and then, *Boom!* Silence. If it wasn't so serious it would've been funny. They were amazed at the enemy's brazen attempts to attack tanks. 1st Platoon threw a whole lot of fire in, but I have no idea how many they got. I know their Bradleys were racking them up and our tanks were doing the same. The AC-130 gunship and A-10s were active in the nights previous, as they were the first night, and we saw their harvest the next morning. I was most amazed by the audacity of the enemy. The editorializing by the tanks and Bradley crews after eliminating targets time and time again became the only way to keep focus. We get to the mosque and are going to bust in and let the Iraqi Intervention Force (IIF) search the inside as ordered. I shot an AT4, put up a Bangalore torpedo, put plain C4 on the hinges of this mosque's gate to breach into it and I couldn't even bust it. I was prepping a Javelin missile when Sergeant First Class Cantrell stopped the insanity and hit it with a Bradley. Nothing happened. Our orders were we couldn't enter and clear a mosque, but we could breach it so the Iraqis could come and clear it. So we were about 150 meters from Phase Line Fran at the Imam al-Shafi mosque at Objective Cougar. I shot everything we had at this door. Finally Staff Sergeant Jim just took his tank and peeled the wall back next to the gate. At any rate, the sun is coming up and my SAW gunner, Private First Class Alex Stuckert from California, yells for me, says he sees a guy. We're on a rooftop facing north, which is our six o'clock, because we're headed south and we've got limited security with the Bradleys facing south towards Phase Line Fran. We've got a pretty good foothold, BRT is somewhere to our east, and 1st Platoon is about 200 meters to our west. No contact, just a couple booms off to the distance. We started to see a hand move a curtain. There was a window in an adjoining building next to the building we're on the roof of. I asked Stuckert what he was talking about and said we can get at least an hour of sleep if he just chilled out. But then he sees it again and Lawson takes out his nine millimeter. Stuckert and Lawson put their nine millimeters in the window, engage it, and blood splatters the curtains. The wounded guy comes to the ground floor of the building adjacent to ours and, I'll tell you what, all hell broke loose. Things just erupted, he's screaming the entire time and there are echoes of return, either walkie-talkie foghorn/bullhorn or just people screaming. It was eerie to hear that as the sun was coming up, to realize how many people were behind us and how many people were moving towards us. I don't believe we missed them on the way through. I think in the vacuum with the Marines getting stymied, they just swung to the east and followed us up. Fitts took his squad and stayed on the bottom floor of a building next door. The bad guy building was in between Fitts' building and my building, and Fitts was to the west of me. I'll you what, he laid down a perfect linear ambush. He waited and waited, knowing we didn't have any idea of where he was – and I didn't want to fire not knowing where he was. He laid down an ambush and his SAW gunners cut down five or six individuals running right across the road. None of this was reported in the AAR. A Marine platoon was pinned down to the point where they had to put green smoke on the roof because they didn't know who was shooting at them. They were taking 360-degree fire. These guys were running across the T-barriers that were cutting off our advance to Phase Line Fran, so we shot TOW missiles at them – and nothing. Then we had people across the street from the mosque shooting at us from a distance of about 25 to 30 meters. The fire is coming quick and fast. Sergeant Warren Misa, Fitts' Alpha Team leader, gets hit in the face with a 7.62 tracer and I pulled it out with my Nomex glove. It was a piece of fragment but, my God, his face swelled up pretty good. Anyway, the moral of the story was we got a pretty good fight. That fight maintained its consistency until the BRT came up on the east flank, which would have been Captain Kirk Mayfield. Mayfield's Bradleys and tanks really just started taking over and you could just hear it. In that fight, somehow one of our gun tubes on a 4th Platoon tank got messed up; and to be honest with you, it was totally inoperable. The shield on his ammo carrier was broken as well. I'll tell you what, a Chinook came down less than five hours later and he got a brand new gun tube and fired without the shield protecting his ammo. So I couldn't say enough about the tankers. Anyway, I didn't really feel warm and cozy that we had that mosque locked down. One thing that was cool was I brought a 65-pound titanium breach ladder. It could be used as a ladder or a runway. They always thought I was retarded for bringing this thing. But we strapped it on the

Bradley. One of my corporals, my Bravo Team leader, Piotr Sucholas, actually got a Bronze Star with Valor (BSV) for retrieving that under rocket fire. But anyway, we put it across the other rooftop, the one where the bad guy was, and crossed maybe nine feet of alleyway with this thing. We opened up a completely different avenue of fire and Fitts used his advanced combat optical gunsight (ACOG), his marksmen just brilliantly. I mean, we were taking guys off left and right and it was really well done. He did an excellent job setting that up. I don't think we really won that fight but I think they stopped shooting at us. And until we get to Phase Line Fran, we're going to have to go backwards, flush this thing out and massage the battlefield a little better.

MM: When you guys did get down to Fran, the sun's up by this time –

DB: It was afternoon.

MM: You guys are taking some pretty heavy fire down there too, aren't you?

DB: We get to Fran and this guy comes running down the street from our west. 1st Platoon left the VS17 panel on one building and then went to another building, so they actually occupied two buildings. They had perfect fields of fire, whereas we were a little bit far to the east. So I could see their location but it was kind of forward of our location so we really didn't have the perfect area to defend ourselves or even put up any sort of a fight. But this guy running away from Headquarters Platoon and 1st Platoon ran right down the street into a building and detonated over 10 IEDs that were laced around telephone poles going up to Fran. A piece of shrapnel, a piece of the door lock, lodged into the genital region of Sergeant Lawson's team leader, Alan Pratt, and he was the first guy we medically evacuated (MEDEVAC'd). Debris was flying everywhere and there was nothing we could do. We knew he was in the building so we brought a Bradley up there to pound the windows and doors, which is what we learned in Muqdadiyah, but unfortunately the houses are like castles. We weren't really wanting to smash through walls at 40 miles an hour and deadline the Bradleys, so I took PFC Victor Santos, prepped a Javelin, and the battle damage assessment was that we engaged and destroyed one dude with a top attack. That was a great moment for the whole team.

MM: My understanding is that once you guys are at Fran, there's a little bit of a rearm/refuel and then you're ordered to go back and check out the area back to the line of departure (LD).

DB: 9 November was the morning of the mosque fight, so it was late at night. That day we lost Pratt to injury and then on the morning of 10 November – not everyone went back. First of all, everyone was loading up on ammo for the company. Certain people were grabbing things they needed that they were running low on. We got four crates of grenades because we were just throwing grenades everywhere. It was a grenade shower. I wanted to get the claymores in the fight. I just thought it would be the best static defense you could possibly have in a house. So we ordered a bunch of them but they just sat in the Bradley; we never used them. We got more AT4s, more 40 millimeter, Bradleys got fixed, the missile teams did a great job. Our logistics were perfect. On the morning of 10 November, we rolled back to the north and basically hit the areas that have now been cleared by, I assume, the BRT or the IIF. We were finding weapons caches in the middle of the street and I don't know if the IIF was grabbing them. We were finding bodies piled on top of each other and someone was going through and cleaning up the area. We were also finding different flags on different houses that mean different things. Bricks that are painted red have IVs, gauze and lidocaine and you name it inside. A few have rockets and land mines. It's like they're marking their egress routes. And there's so much to blow, you literally don't have the time. Our rules of engagement (ROE) are to destroy every vehicle because of the vehicle-borne IED (VBIED) threat. To make a long story short, it was just a tremendous amount of work and we get a call around 1700 that we need to be at Objective Wolf. That was the night of 10 November and that was 1st Platoon's call. They were supposed to show up but they got stymied with contact so they're handling their business. By the time 1st Platoon showed up at the scene, across the street there was a guy in the building heavily fortified. He shot Staff Sergeant Jason Laser and some other scouts. Laser got hit from behind. The round hit his M16 and his finger, a round went around his neck and one hit his Gerber tactical tool. It was ridiculous: these guys were so lucky not to have gotten killed. But again, there's nothing you can do when there are guys behind cover when you walk up the stairs.

MM: Had you been called over to Objective Wolf?

DB: There are two situations transpiring at the same time. The one that happened in the early afternoon, the scouts had made contact to the north. They cordoned the area and then Lieutenant Ed Iwan saw these guys run across the way into this block. He shot at these individuals, killed one, his 25 millimeter malfunctioned and, without even hesitating, he moved tanks and Bradleys to completely cordon this area. Now, simultaneously, we have probably a 350-meter lead on the Marine Corps at this time. They were to our west and probably a third of a kilometer north of our position as we are moving southerly. That's what it appeared because I'm going by the source of fire. Iwan gets out, he's sweating, we haven't had a whole lot of rest, we've hardly eaten, and this is the first day of the prickly heat: wet T-shirts, the ornery attitudes, the smells, the soldiering is really starting to hit hard, and our discipline is starting to be a challenge. It's a leadership challenge for the NCOs to keep these guys focused. Essentially our mission is to sweep this block of upscale houses, upper middle class homes. The Askari District is called the "Soldier's District" and all the Sunni officers lived in this area, so there's a whole lot of upper class homes. I remember Iwan said to Meno: "Hey, platoon leader, what you got? Give me a plan." And Meno said, "We're going to fire as many tank rounds as these guys have. We're going to 25 after that and we're going to shoot TOW missiles in at the base and pepper the outside of these buildings before we go in." High-explosive, anti-tank (HEAT) rounds are going through like three buildings of nothing but fire. We noticed in the mosque fight on 9 November that we were fighting guys who were wearing Kevlar and the same uniforms the IIF were wearing. We knew that; it wasn't a shock. The IIF have a red and a white piece of tape and they weren't anywhere near our front. So any guy in that uniform to our front was dead. But it did kind of freak us out. In the buildup training to Iraq, we're basically fighting our own defense. So now you have 19-year-old privates who are asking, "So, you're telling me if I shoot to the side of a guy with a small arms protective insert (SAPI) plate, that SAPI plate's integrity will be –" You know what I mean? We're essentially telling them how to destroy their only safeguard. So psychologically it's quite a challenge. So anyway, we go into these houses, we're about to get ready, and we're literally moving behind armor that's driving up this road. There's probably a 150-meter breach of nothing that's between a road, our side of the fight, Captain Sims and the scouts, and 1st Platoon's side of the fight. Meanwhile on the other side of the road, Sims has shot TOW missiles, 25 millimeter, tank rounds; he's hit it with artillery, AT4s, they're calling in an air strike as we move out and, literally, it's like the $6 Million Man. This guy is shouting in broken English, he's obnoxious, he's wounded three of our guys and we don't know how serious the wounds are. But it was pretty touch and go. We're on our side and we know we're fighting guys who are going to fight to the death. I'm expecting close air support (CAS) and artillery to come in at any moment. That was Sergeant Chad Ellis in the 6 track. He just got his 25 millimeter put back on, he shot a 25 and the wall collapsed after he shot a TOW. The 25 went through the wall, ricocheted to the west. The Marines unloaded in response on our positions, rounds impacting all around us. Meno is yelling on the radio, Cantrell is yelling back to him to check our fire. Chaos. The response of the fire was over two minutes. I have the DVD a reporter took of the exchange. Marine crew-served weapons fire chewed up real estate around us for a good chunk of time.

MM: These are all going against those particular houses that have been cordoned off that you guys thought these six or eight insurgents had run into?

DB: Negative. This was the fire that was coming from the Marine Corps.

MM: Oh okay.

DB: This is my argument: every five steps I took towards this structure, a parachute flare would go up. We would have complete isolation where the fires were inside homes and we still had enough cover where we weren't giving away our signatures at all. We're walking away from the hotspots of the town. There wasn't any electricity but there are still fires going on, so there are hotspots. We're doing our best to have our light discipline and these parachute flares are going off like every 10 minutes. What's going on? We're hearing on the radios that the Marines only have night vision for their squad leaders. Then Ellis' round goes off, and then from the origin of where the parachute flares came there was a tremendous amount of tracer fire. I'm putting it out there because it happened. The parachute flares continued and then some jackass in civil affairs (CA) pulls up a speaker system on a Humvee and starts blaring at max decibels the *Team America: World Police* movie theme song and the song by Dope called "Die, M-----f-----, Die." Now, this might be cool to some people, but when you're actually trying to focus men to go into each building and have the presence of mind to understand situational awareness, psychological operations (PSYOP) are really not needed.

MM: Who sent this guy down there?

DB: I have no idea. But he's playing the "America, F--- Yeah!" song, everyone's high-fiving on the other side of the street and I'm like, "What the f---, guy?" I was really adamant and I was really pissed off. Fitts was pissed, Lieutenant Meno was highly agitated and I was really trying to control myself. I had no idea what the hell was going on – Marines are shooting at us. We're finding American grenades, American Kevlar helmets, our old school Kevlar vests, American boots all over the place. At any minute we could have five wackos jumping out and blowing our heads off, and some asshole wants to play a soundtrack to this. You name it, this stuff was everywhere. I have no idea if I'm going to walk into a bunch of guys wearing an EOD suit with Browning automatics. I'm trying to focus these kids who are doing a really outstanding job of not losing their bearings. So finally we get to the side, we've been doing this and we've went through – Michael Ware from *Time* magazine says 10 houses as a nice round number, but we had done 75 percent of the homes and we're now booking towards the northern side of the complex. We're back to where the opening is where I can see the FOB, the commanding officer and everyone else and they're waiting on an air strike. A couple rounds are clicking off here and there but nothing big. So all these guys are waiting by their vehicles and we're watching them, they're watching us. As we move, I take point. Sergeant Knapp is my Alpha Team leader who sees a body. I see it simultaneously and we raise our weapons, snap off the rounds we need to snap off. It's a guy who recently lost his leg from one of the HEAT rounds and he's on the ground. The pucker factor's up now because we're in the bullseye zone and there are five houses left. So we did our enemy prisoner of war search on the guy. We're making sure he's dead, we search him. John Ruiz, my SAW gunner, turns his ankle on some bricks and goes down with a pretty bad ankle. I was kind of pissed off by the music so Fitts and I decide we're going to take a break for two hours. We're going to ice off Ruiz's leg and just tell these guys to chill out. Platoon sergeant is calling every five minutes, "Where are you at? What are you doing?" "We're at House 14, we're moving, leave us alone." Because we knew we were just smoked. We go into the next house and I find an RPG without any safety on it.

260

I'm pretty good with these things and I'm going to shoot this rocket down the street into one of these houses. They were like, "Dude, the Marines almost killed us all for a 25 millimeter. If they see an RPG, they'll kill us for sure." I argued that they don't have night vision so we have a chance. But I leave it on the road, put a chem light on it, and pull out the rocket and fuse so it's not armed. We literally go into the second gate and it's opened, which should have been a huge giveaway right there. Out of the 12 houses we went to, maybe four of the gates were open. We'd all seen signs of life there, but now we've been doing this about six hours and we think they're long gone. All I'm hearing is an AT4 being shot from a Bradley commander across the street. "What are we doing? It's pointless." So Fitts is kind of irritated with all our soldiers and he says, "I don't care what squad you're in, get in a file right now." He starts getting really pissed off and I start asserting myself to help him out. The guys walk in the building and open up the first door. Specialist Lance Ohle from Orlando, Florida, a SAW gunner, I don't have any idea how he manipulated – well, I do know because we drilled him to death on a SAW. This kid flicked that thing into fire, put a burst back, and Warren Misa pulled him out from the doorway and saved his life. Before I knew it, the weapons squad had pulled security on the outside of the house. I just saw fire coming everywhere. The wall that partitioned me from Fitts – the two doorways and behind this wall – it looked like if you took a campfire and threw a telephone pole on it, embers of tracer fire just going through everything and going everywhere, guys are screaming. And then I yell, "Cease fire!" because I figure it's Ohle and Misa shooting. Fitts says, "No, don't cease fire" and I'm like, "F------ cease f------ fire right now!" Fitts yells over to me, "How about you tell those f-----s on the other side of the wall to cease fire?" And I look above his head and start to hear a tremendous amount of machine gun fire coming from outside, and it's going through. Our cordon outside got hit from the kitchen – bottles and glass. One of our guys' whole face is swollen from glass and metal and he's screaming, "My eyes, my eyes!" Right then, I hear from the other side of the wall this f------ creepy insurgent son of a bitch mocking him and screaming, "My eyes, my eyes! Ah help me, my eyes," cackling all this shit. I tell you what, I was scared but I was absolutely f------ livid. I was just beyond livid. I called for a 240 and a SAW gunner to come in. Fitts and I would just come up with all these little TTPs. One that I had was I put a 240 gunner in the prone and a SAW gunner on one knee pulling rear security. I used the back of his heel to pie wedge that 240 on the asphalt. So I want to pie wedge the door with that 240B and, as soon as we do, PFC Jim Metcalf, SAW gunner, gets hit under the vest trying to move in. He falls down and I don't know his condition. Our radio guy outside, Rodriquez, who we kind of rented from HHC, says, "He's hit!" Then one after another. No one has any idea. Michael Ware is outside, I have Lieutenant Meno on my feet; he runs back and tries to get up. I see the guys through Fitts' room and the tracer rounds from the 240 are coming through the kitchen wall and going right over Fitts' head. So, someone's got to ceasefire so I tell the guy outside, "Just aim towards the base of the window, go long with the fire. Don't go high, go long." The next thing I know, I'm like, "Just give me the f------ SAW!" I threw my M4 across the floor, someone threw me a SAW, and Fitts said, "I need you." He was totally pinned down. This guy took three rounds and he's got three BSVs and a Purple Heart. Staff Sergeant Colin Fitts is an American hero; he's the bravest dude in the battalion by far. It's true; he's a stud. But there's nothing he can do, he's screwed. I'm there, I orient myself and just throw the bitch on fire and, I'll tell you what, it runs away on me. I'm just squeezing this thing down and people are just piling out, slipping on glass, falling. There are blood handprints, there's blood on the ground. I see Meno throw this Rodriguez kid in a toilet in the outhouse outside the gate. "Where's Rodriguez?" He goes back to the gate, picks him up and throws him in the road. We get back to the road and we're trying to find out where our guys are. As I'm in the house – and I'm the only one in there – I hear the confusion. I know what I have to do. I know no one else knows where I'm at and no one else can see what I can see. I know what it's going to take is for me to just completely f------ nut up. I just felt my heart beating a mile a minute. These guys are laughing at me. I can see their eyes and they're angry but they're smiling; they look completely evil. I can see their faces from the tracers. I'm getting low on ammo and I slow it down, my barrel is smoking, my flash suppressor is hot, so I ran out and threw down my SAW. I grab another SAW and blast from the front gate until that's out of ammo. I yell, "Give me an M16 with a 203." From the road, these dudes are shooting at us from the roof. Michael Ware says I got two guys on the first exchange. If I wounded one – he has better eyes than me. I don't see that happening. But anyway, I started prepping grenades and throwing them to Knapp. "Knapp, when you get it, you pull it, you throw it, no tape, no spoon. Pull the pin and throw it, pull the pin and throw it!" Finally I started pulling the pins for him, putting them in his hands and just said, "Throw as many grenades as you can!" and he threw maybe four or five grenades. I called for a Bradley, we started receiving more fires, Stuckert shoots his SAW, and people are now trying to get to a house across the way to get on line so we can at least fire suppressive from a roof. I come up with a plan, I bring seven up, and I'm just livid. I feel like a complete coward. Every five seconds I told these kids: "In an emergency we'll be unflappable. I will never not do what I ask you to do. I will not cower, I will not give in." I felt like an absolute liar and I was just fuming. I'm clenching my teeth, grinding them. Cantrell shoots his 25 millimeter and this shit wasn't going anywhere. He shot his coax. He's frustrated, I'm talking through a radio, I'm frustrated.

MM: The Bradley can't get a good shot because there's a wall there or something?

DB: It's not the wall – if the gate were a door to a room, it would be a corner-fed door. You have no space on the right side of this gate. Then there's an opening into a quarter-acre palm grove which is beautifully manicured: grass, it's got fruit trees, you name it. It has beautiful palms, well manicured. Everything is beautiful in the house, to be honest with you. I don't know how high the house is; it looks higher than the house next to it. I'm trying to get how many – did these guys run in from the kitchen; what are they doing? I yell for my team leader and look up and see Knapp telling the kids what to do. I'm really proud of my soldiers and my peers. I love these guys to death. I'll be honest with you, we're all replaceable. If you're going to look at a leader, the quality of a leader is that his kids are better than he is; and I'll tell you what: at that level, Knapp was better than I was. I felt he was completely competent to take over a squad and if anything happened, it happened. I yelled for two SAW gunners and Stuckert was right there but he had just shot around 200 rounds and I couldn't wait for him to reload. So Specialist Tristan Maxfield, great kid – who ended up almost losing a leg three days later – and Specialist Ohle, my two SAW gunners came out. Michael Ware is right behind me. He says I told him to get out, and I did. I wanted to scare him into getting out of there. The best motivation sometimes is false motivation, and I'm trying to convince myself and these kids that this is a great idea. Everyone's face is white. I hand a grenade to Maxfield and he almost misses the wall with it. It hits like twice on the top of the wall. I said, "Dude, if you can't throw a grenade, we're going to be in a world of hurt. You need to do it." So I start chewing his ass to let him know that I'm back, that I'm an asshole and I'm ready to roll, trying to get into character a little bit. And meanwhile I'm about shitting in my pants, I'm not going to hide it, but I'm putting up a great front. Lawson comes up to me and here's the quote the guy misconstrued. Lawson says to me, "I'm not going to let you go in there and die alone." That's what he said. My response to him was, "You're coming?"

MM: So Michael Ware had gotten that wrong in the *Time* magazine article then?

DB: Ware is extremely accurate, just his syntax was wrong. Lawson told me he wasn't going to let me go in there and die alone, and then he echoed it again that night after all this was over. He was like, "I couldn't let you go in there and die alone." We were both emotional. That to me was literally one of the most beautiful gestures I've ever heard. It also kind of pissed me off: "I'm not going to f------ die!" A kid on the road was screaming as we were taking fire from the roof: "We're all going to die! We can't just stand out here; we're all going to die!" I yelled back, "We're not going to f------ die!" That was said in the road. But Lawson said to me, "We're going in there and I'm not going to let you die alone." I said, "You're coming with me?" He said, "Absolutely, let's do this." He said, "All right." I used to tell my kids, "Charlie's Angels." Charlie's Angels was our little audible that when you walked into a building, it meant everyone's weapon was at the high ready, just like Charlie's Angels. It means your weapons are at the high ready and that's the only position you can have your weapon in a fight: at the high ready.

There's a two percent chance there's a manhole cover in there; but the chance of a guy getting a higher elevated shot off on you from a stairwell is a lot greater.

MM: So you agree that you told Ware to get the f--- out, that he's not –

DB: Yes, I did that in my most aggressive tone. I don't remember what was said. I do remember being kind of pushy with my barrel because I didn't want him to die and, to be honest with you, I had very little interaction with him up that point. I didn't know what his motives were.

MM: Did Ware say, "I'm coming with you" or something like that?

DB: He was bullshitting me. He would say he's coming and then say, "You know what? F--- this. You're absolutely right, this is stupid. I don't want to do this." Then I'd turn around and he'd be right behind me. I said, "Dude, what the hell? Get out of here." He said, "I will. You know what? Roger, you're right." Then I turn around again and he's right behind me! As we were in the house, he's right there: "I can't let you go. I have to see this. This is the most amazing thing I've ever seen." So I'm like, "F------ great," and I leave my two SAW gunners on the side of the house. My whole objective is to soften these insurgents up. They're going to run out of the house, I'm going to go in there like a banshee, I'm going to throw grenades, I'm going to make a loud noise, they're going to run out of the house and my guys are going to shoot them. I noticed at that point that Lawson's got a nine millimeter. "How many magazines do you have?" He said, "One." I said, "Dude, not cool." But whatever ended up happening, I turn the corner, I get low, these guys are whispering in Arabic and then they shoot a burst. I hear them talking to each other again and then the first thing I hear is the scream from upstairs. My heart absolutely stops right there. I'm sweating all over my leg. I'm like, "Oh my God, dude! I can do this, I can do this." I put my head down to peer the corner and this barrage of fire, accurate as all get out, takes a shot at the base of the wall. Bullet holes everywhere. I'm bleeding from my face, Lawson's bleeding from his face, my knuckles are red, I have my Nomex gloves on and I'm like, "Holy God, if I make another stupid mistake I'm done." It's one thing to die in the house but quite another to get shot in the carport. So, "Think, think, think." At this time, they'd started their "Allahu Akbar! Allahu Akbar!" and it was almost like a freakin' coward's chant. They said it over and over again and over each other like, "Row, row, row your boat." I looked over and he's twisting an RPG into a launcher. The only thing I could think of in my religion – and I'm a pretty religious guy – was under my breath from that stupid *Exorcist* movie. I'm repeating, "The power of Christ compels you!" I've become a shitty PG-13 movie. I start getting myself motivated and, for an instant, I think about that poor bastard who dies on his birthday. The family who walks through the graveyard and says, "Oh, that poor bastard." So I was like, "Okay man, f--- this! I'm going to do this, I'm not going to make it and I don't care!" In an instant I went from where my feet were 10,000 pounds to, "F--- it!" I was a coward in life and I'm going to die the way I should have lived – on my feet – and I don't care about anything. I got Lawson here, I got my boys outside, I love them, they'd do it for me and I'm going to do this now. I was completely fatalistic. I turned the corner and I'll tell you what, I couldn't feel a thing. I was squeezing my M16 and the RPG guy just dropped. They were firing RPKs, AK47s and whatnot. The guy who had two AK47s dropped one and went to an RPK, but his first burst was really left, long and high. I hit him. That's why I yelled, "Two f-----s down!" to tell Lawson, "Hey bro', we got it." I just got a foothold and that's all we needed. I hit this guy and Lawson comes over the corner of the door, shoots his nine millimeter into the kitchen, and it gets a retort of fire from the same guy I thought I had just killed who ran into the kitchen. The rounds are going through the room Lawson is in, and now he's out of ammunition.

MM: Was that kitchen door closed? It didn't go through the door; it went through the wall of the kitchen?

DB: It went through the inside of the room. He had one shoulder exposed. I was near the stairwell and my back was to a room I hadn't been in, so I'm using the stairs as cover from the kitchen. I've got a dead guy underneath me and I'm using that stairwell for cover. It looked like hot brass went into his interceptor body armor (IBA) and he starts beating on his leg and breathing hard. His whole face is sweaty. I look over him at Michael Ware and he's gone; he's completely gone. He's outside and I tell Lawson to go get Fitts, get me a shotgun and a f------ SAW and come back. He said, "Don't go anywhere!" I realize my back is turned and I can't have that so I drop my magazine and put another one in. At this time, Ware is outside yelling, "Sergeant Bellavia is dead!" They're hearing the guy in the kitchen groaning, Ohle's on that corner of the wall, Ohle thinks it's me, and so he's telling everyone, "Bellavia's hit, Bellavia's hit!" I get on the radio to Sergeant First Class Cantrell and he says, "Give me a situation report, goddamnit. What the f--- are you doing?" And I said, "Dude, I'm stressed the f--- out right now, I'm shitting my pants, and I'll give you a SITREP when the shit's over!" Enough is enough. He wants a SITREP and I'm in the f------ pillbox here.

MM: And at this time the platoon sergeant, the platoon leader, and Fitts and everybody, are they still in the building across the street? .

DB: I can still hear firing and they're trying to get into buildings by shooting locks and stuff. It took awhile to get into some of these houses. Most of these houses, in preparation for a northern invasion, they actually sealed all the doors and windows with locks and fixed grenades on door handles. It was an event to just get in one of these bitches. It really was; it took a lot of time. There was a closet to my left. My night vision is still on. The squad was to my left and I hear the flip-flops coming down the stairs.

MM: So you did have some sort of night vision capability at this time?

DB: At this point, I got my NODs working and everything's great. There's an elbow of a wall I backed into not knowing where it was, tripping over shit. But the dude comes into the room just using the wall close to the stairwell, blind firing his weapon, doing nothing but making echoes that were just piercing to my ears. It was just horrible. I'm scanning and I see tracer rounds going lengthwise in the room. I have no idea what's happening. I don't know what's happening because they're just shooting from left to right and I'm just shooting controlled pairs. I get to my third door when the injured guy from across the kitchen comes blasting into the room. He's shot and crawls back to the kitchen where we find him dead later on. I hear flip-flops coming down the stairs. The guy from the kitchen was noticeably bleeding and it's like dark brown from my PEQ2A. I'll tell you what, I don't know if he couldn't hold his weapon up or what the deal was, but it was quick. A guy from the stairs is making a sand paper noise with his sandals, he gives me a shoulder and I took the left part of his breast, just below it in the abdomen. He just crumpled and moaned. And then another AK47 came around the corner and I could hear him yelling like a female's scream. I don't really know what happened. That guy fell by the stairs. I could see him from the door for awhile. As the rounds were coming against the wall, the closet opens up and literally I don't see anything. As I move my head quickly, my NODs fall off my mount and are hanging by the tie down. The wardrobe doesn't land on the door. You know how a door is only supposed to open so wide? If you take two doors in the middle and "Y" them out, if you stepped out of the closet you could probably snap the doors out. The wardrobe fell on the inside doors and so it rested like a miniature TV. The dude was shooting through the closet and a little piece of wood went through my shirt and nicked me above the elbow. As I was wondering whether that was a bullet – what does it feel like? – and assessing myself, I rolled into the corner of the room on my kneepads and the rounds were just hitting the top and there were pieces of crap going everywhere. He runs across the bed and the only reason I saw this was because the wood was on fire, the clothing was on fire and the foam from the Iraqi mattress completely comes apart. He falls on his ass with his back facing the door of the room. As he was running, he had his AK47 under his armpit shooting backwards – completely inaccurate but creative nonetheless. I thought that was kind of freaky. But he's shooting backwards, he falls on his back into the door and I thought I hit him good. I hit him square and it was just the thunk of a fatal wound. He goes to his knees with his back on the thing, lifts his pelvis in the air and pulls himself to his knees, picks up and charges up the stairs. They're screaming in broken English and I'm screaming in Arabic. They scream back and I saw the look on his face as he left. I'm like, "I got this dude. I straight up have this guy, I know it." Then I ran up those stairs and I slipped a little bit. I don't know if it was water or the fact that my boot was dusty, but whatever the case may be, I slipped, a round went off. I met them on the landing, exchanged fire. The guy goes into a room. I was looking at him square in the eye and I can't see anything. The smell in the upstairs – it was cool and dusty like something was going on and it's giving off a burn. I'm completely panicked and I don't know what the hell is happening. I take my frag, pull the pin, and I throw the frag into his head. I hit him in the face with it. I then turn over and try to affix my NODs so I can actually see. I change another magazine, leaving it on the ground, and I hear a scream. I wait by the stairs, hear a door open and see, from just the illumination from the fires outside, a guy jumping up and down, screaming and firing his weapon until it's empty. He goes back into the little back room. Once I go back into that room, I can see from the fire from the foam mattress that I hit him in the head but the grenade traveled long, and the room is L-shaped. It rolled the other way and the grenade went off. I go in there and, to be honest with you, I'm smelling natural gas at that point. I'm swinging my rifle to whack him in the head. I make contact with him a couple times like Mark McGwire, baseball bat style. I hit him and he hit me with something metallic. I think it was part of a weapon. It completely cracked my tooth and, believe it or not, that pain caused my whole – when your NODs are on, and the new helmets especially are really light. When you put your NODs up or jolt your head, your whole helmet goes down over your eyes with those stupid new pads. So my NODs and my helmet were too heavy. I got hit on the side of the head, my NODs flew, my helmet was now in front of my face and I'm hitting him on top of his head with my barrel. I shot two rounds that went nowhere. I felt what was to my right, felt my arm hitting the dial of a propane tank, and I took my helmet and hit him on top of the head. He started screaming. When I hit him, he fell to the ground and I literally jumped on him to the point where I knew he was hurt when I put the left side of my body on his right arm. He completely quit. He didn't want to fight anymore. I was covering his mouth, telling him to shut up. His breath was horrible, just stale, nasty breath. The moral of the story is that the dude bites my left hand near the thumb knuckle through my glove. I open up my SAPI plate and hit him with the inside of my vest. He's screaming, there are people screaming downstairs and I have no composure at all. This is not a John Rambo moment. I'm really scared. I stand up and he digs into my leg with his fingers. I'm looking for my Rex Applegate Gerber knife: not a multi-tool, just a serious blade. I go to reach for it and he puts his teeth – I don't wear underwear and he bites me right in the genital region. I'm standing at this point almost straddling him, but it's dark and I have no idea where he is or where my position is. I try to dig into his eyeballs, and I don't know if it's sweat or blood but my gloves are not giving me any traction or feeling. I literally cuff him with my hands and I've got the thing on my belt. My IBA is now down to my arms and it's like I'm in a crucifix type of thing. My IBA is almost causing me to have little movement and panic. I stomp and kick at his left side and he quits. He gave up; he got limp; he fell back. He is screaming and in pain. I continued to choke and told him to, "*Es tes lem.*" I also told him in English, "I don't want to f------ kill you! Just shut your f------ mouth!" And he was crying when I put all my weight on his chest. I finally find his face and my groin is very sore when I laid on top of him to restrain him. He was in agony, his mouth was open and he was spitting. I covered his mouth with my hand and punched down on his clavicle trying to break his collar bone. He screams when I uncover his mouth. I let go a little bit, he started screaming again and I cover him back up. I don't know if he thought I was going to give him mercy, but in the struggle my Velcro knife case slid off my belt and was now on the ground next to his head. I hear someone yell down from above me in a panic. The man underneath me yells back. The more I put pressure on his left arm the more he goes limp. I flick my blade to the side and it snaps to the ready. I had never stabbed anyone before so I went down on him with a stabbing motion. I lost the grip on the knife and it went right across the base of my right pinkie finger. As soon as I let it go, a hot wave hit me and it smelled like rust. I put one hand on his mouth and other under his chin and just started to push like I was giving him CPR. The stream only got powerful when I pushed down and it opened up. I fell over and was completely exhausted. I didn't want to touch myself because I thought about AIDS or something. I was confused and scared to death. I didn't have time, or perhaps I was afraid to do a quick inventory of my parts. I couldn't see and I smelled natural gas. I walked outside, I'm screaming for Lawson and Fitts and I don't hear anything. They're yelling, "He's alive, he's alive!" downstairs. I can hear people from across the way getting excited. The next thing I know, this dude just lands. I don't have a weapon in my hands and the dude just falls from the third story balcony. He fell right in front of me. He fell on his knees, his AK47 magazines – the one that was taped upside down is empty – and we looked at each other for what felt like 10 minutes. His weapon is at least five feet away from him. I didn't know who was here for who. I was really just agitated at that point and I ran in the house. The whole room is full of smoke. I looked for the AK47 and I looked for the M16. I kick the M16 and I shoot him. He tries to run away instead of fight, so I shoot until I'm out of ammunition. He falls, the AK47 is nowhere near him and I figure he's dead or wounded and I put in my last magazine. As I do that, I look out and the dude has one leg over the water tank and one leg over the side of the roof. I got chunks of muscle ripped out of his quad. He looked like Johnny Taliban; he looked really sooty and hairy. But they're all Palestinian.

MM: Is that what they found out later? These guys were all Palestinians?

DB: They were flying Hezbollah flags, the green arm holding an AK47 under a yellow flag. Usually if you see that, you have to assume there's a lot of trouble. They bring their passport and their flag so there has to be some correlation. Anyway, he falls and just lands on a pretty big bush and does not move. I shoot a 203 round down that I didn't even realize I had and it blows up. I remember at that moment I also had guys who were downstairs on the corner. I never even thought about what I was shooting at. So I yelled, "Ohle!" and all of a sudden I hear shotgun rounds and Lawson comes flying up the stairs. He had an M4. All the guys I hit downstairs, Fitts shoots them again. Then he shot up the stairs and almost hits Lawson with buckshot. Lawson was flipping out. "Why are you shooting at me?" I was just smoking a cigarette in the corner of the room. I was completely out of my shit. One of the things I never really wanted to get into was: was he killed by what weapon or why didn't you just shoot him? But all in all, I shot and killed four individuals and one of them, I assume, was gravely wounded. But Fitts, Misa and Sergeant Hugh Hall went up to the next story and there was a metal door that was heavy and leaning up against a locked metal door. There were bricks that were removed. They all put their weapons systems inside the bricks and then just unloaded on them. There was a guttural moan and I assume that was a person. I assume from what they told me. I never saw it. I saw them shoot and I couldn't know if I was hearing that or another guy or what the case might be. To be honest, I was kind of off on my own. But I went downstairs and everyone's trickling in. I got on the horn: "They're all dead, they're all gone." We looked in the grove for guy number five and then all of a sudden I heard an F-16 do a ghost run. They yelled, "Dude, it's coming in, it's coming in! They're going hot, get out of here!" Everyone's pouring out of the house, we dug ourselves a little thing, and the bomb drops and nothing happens. We go back in the house and start spiking weapons and gathering bodies. As we're pulling the first two guys out, another F-16 comes in, you hear something drop but, again, you don't hear an explosion.

MM: Two duds?

DB: Two duds! Finally, we get all four bodies out. I was moving to find what's behind door number six and getting someone in the backyard. We lit up that entire palm grove, just all got on line and lit it up. So even if I didn't kill that guy, someone else did. They said, "Take a photo of it! No one's going to believe this shit. Take a photo of it!" So they took a photo of it. Then another F-16 came in and we all ran like bitches. All the Bradleys were now on line, we jumped in the Bradleys for cover and the shockwave just hit us. "Man, they're smoked!" "How many did you say were in there?" "Six" "Is there a possibility that there were eight? We'll check the last two houses." "We got six, dude. Is that good enough for you?" "That's plenty, good job." That was it. That's what I know. I really wasn't in an emotional state where I went through and checked pulses, and we don't confirm kills in the infantry. I know Hall doubletapped a guy in the kitchen. The guy was wrapped under a drape and Hall stepped on him. He shot him and then Lawson came in, "Is that guy moving?" But again, this was shit that we didn't really want Ware to see and we didn't want to talk about. Everyone ended up with BSVs.

MM: That's an amazing fight. I hope somebody gets off their ass and gets you the Medal of Honor. But we'll talk about that off line. Can you tell me about the following days when tragedy strikes the company – when the XO, Lieutenant

Iwan, is killed and then the death of Captain Sims?

DB: The only guy we lost in that was Sergeant James Matteson.

MM: And he was with the scout platoon, correct?

DB: Right. As a matter of fact, he did some really great stuff that day, 10 November. He killed an insurgent leaving a house his Mk-19. He's actually from West New York like I am. I met his father and got to share with him some stuff. Mr. Matteson is a great man who truly admired and loved his son, who was definitely a stalwart soldier. On 12 November we had a couple other objectives. We did some other stuff, we had some contact, took some enemy attrition and moved out to Phase Lines Jena and Ethan, I believe. Again, I'm in the back of the track and I don't have a radio at this point either. Somehow something gets fried and my radio doesn't work right. I can't hear anything unless I'm listening to my own radio and there aren't any charges out there. Fitts is on the mike for two hours, then I use mine for two and then he uses his for two because we didn't have a charger. We dismount under fire, I don't see anything as far as what happens, and Fitts tells me we're shooting our weapons systems. He asks me, "Did you hear about the XO?" I said, "No, what happened?" "He's dead." I didn't even know about the sergeant major at the time. This was the first news we heard. That night we heard about the sergeant major dying on the opening night and then we hear about Matteson dying. We got into a building that, from the bottom floor, looked like it could be a fortress. Unfortunately when we got to the second story, there weren't any northern or southern walls. It was completely without walls; it was in the middle of being constructed. But it was so high that we couldn't see that. Contact was coming from the west. Whether it came from Newell or Sims, we couldn't cross this road, this intersection, because it was Marine territory and we had to keep our fire control measures. And so we didn't cross the road, and these guys were literally in an alleyway on the other side of the road. Every time we attempted to cross the road, "You can't cross the road!" They're a kilometer behind us and there's no way I can shoot a recoilless rifle to my west and hit anything there. There's no one there. If the Marines were to our west, this wouldn't be happening. Do you know what I'm saying? We're south of Highway 10, south of Fran. We're in the industrial area, we're right at the end, and this shit is coming hot and heavy. We just got unloaded on. Swanson is to the east and, no shit, the enemy's got a Dragunov sniper rifle and it's very effective. It almost lifts his head. His 240B is up at a 45-degree angle as he's getting down for cover. That guy shot his upper assembly so he couldn't bring his bolt forward; it deadlined his weapon. So his 240 was gone. Then Knapp just started throwing a bunch of grenades; he was completely deaf. A rocket missed the side of the building and Knapp takes his helmet off, puts it on a spare barrel, and starts bringing it up and down to engage fire. They draw fire, they throw grenades, shoot a 203, then they get a Bradley in there and put rounds in the window and

270

the sniper stops. They actually went to a Warner Brothers method to get that guy. My kid, Maxfield, one of the bravest kids – he's in the prone with the SAW. There were just so many targets of opportunity. I got A39, Staff Sergeant McDaniel, who was bottlenecked behind Lieutenant Brian Hartman, who was the platoon leader for the 4th Platoon of tanks. For whatever reason, they couldn't maneuver around one of the tanks so they just stayed there. They had three Bradleys shooting, one tank shooting and one Bradley and one tank not shooting. The dismounts are just getting whacked. It was really frustrating. Fitts finally took the mike and went on all the frequencies. He really called that fight from the ground. Staff Sergeant Jim's tank crossed over and just started putting HEAT rounds. I really thought this guy was shooting a semi-automatic. His loader was just blasting and it looked like red paint hitting a wall 20 meters behind that building. It looked like shitty special effects. It was very effective but also gratuitous. I'll tell you what, though, the firing stopped. A rocket was launched, it hit the inside of a wall that we didn't have, so it hit a pillar and ricocheted backwards and hit Maxfield in his left ankle. It snapped his ankle and exposed the skin from the ankle to below the calf. He had hot, burning metal right on his quad. Ruiz jumped on top of Maxfield to shoot the SAW and our medic, Doc Lucas Abernathy, ran over and started treating him. No shit, Maxfield said something like, "Patch me up while I'm on my stomach!" And sure enough, he rolled on his stomach, Doc wrapped him, gauzed him and stabilized him while he was shooting his SAW. You really can't ask any more than that. He's a great kid. That was the one fight out of 12 that we didn't win on our own. Had it not been for artillery, which we had none of – and they wouldn't give us a CAS, which we definitely needed. If it wasn't for Staff Sergeant Biden Jim of Bravo Company 1-63 Armor, we're all dead in that fight.

MM: You were having a hard time getting CAS then?

DB: We had none whatsoever. I don't know if it was a matter of being too timid on the microphone, which is why Fitts grabbed it. He thought the people on the microphone, like Rodriguez, were being a little too timid. He grabbed the microphone and started screaming. They said, "Look, we don't have it, we're not getting it!" He said, "What about artillery, can we get that?" They said, "No." "Can we drive the tank a half block to the west?" I look over and I don't even see 1st Platoon dismounted. I'm looking and I see 1st Platoon's Bradleys but they're just moving their turrets. I asked, "Did 1st Platoon drop their kids off? Get them over here; get them in the company fight." "No, they're needed to block off this area." So on 12 November, the battalion got hit, they moved Alpha Company into position where they and the two tanks from 4th Platoon really took all of the brunt. The scouts were the ones who made contact and took a tragic fatality. Then Iwan was killed and then they pushed us forward. It would have been bad news had that tank not said, "I'm doing my own thing." An RPG got his shot right after Maxfield and it was a dud. It tic-tac-toed in the building and landed right next to Rodriguez's head. But Fitts really went above his pay grade on that one. Meno was brilliant in that fight. He was very calm, he gave the microphone to Fitts and was focusing on getting another 240 out of a Bradley to get in the fight. But I have to be honest with you: that was probably the worst small arms fight I've ever been in.

MM: After you get through this hellacious fight on 12 November, it rolls into the next day and my understanding is your company commander is killed, Captain Sims.

DB: Right. They say Captain Sims is going to show up and I say, "Great." I'm thinking he's going to tell us to shave. I really don't need to be told to shave because I've had a horrible f------ week. We're doing it pretty rough. He shows up and he's got a beard, a real Grizzly Adams beard. Far beyond needing a shave, he's got a *beard*. I looked at him and said, "I thought you were going to tell us to shave." He said, "I am," and we all had a good laugh. We were joking around and sharing some private humor involving some shit the Joes were doing and Captain Sims is there laughing. That was his personality. I asked him how he was doing with losing his XO. He said, "You know what, we'll just have to deal with that later," and it looked like his eyes were pretty red and bloodshot, so he was taking it hard. I showed him these two Campbell's soup can grenades I found and asked him if he wanted to see what it would be like if I threw them. And he said, "Hey, Sarge, do you think that thing has a fuse?" I answered: "You know what, I never thought about that." "Yeah, I think it's just a Campbell's soup can with a fuse in it." "Thanks, sir, I appreciate that." He probably just saved my arm. So we laughed about that. I was smoking a cigarette and he took me aside. An embedded reporter from the London *Telegraph* wrote two articles about our platoon, one of which was unfortunately about what happened right after. Captain Sims came up to me and said, "I heard what you did the other night. You have to be smart. You're not Audie Murphy, but I'm real proud of you." I was kind of touched by that. We went for a walk with him and Fitts' squad was on the left and mine was on the right. We showed him everything we found. That night after Iwan was killed, I found a tunnel and tried to crawl in it until I realized there wasn't any way to get out of it. We found a tunnel and we blew it with C4. We found a spider network. There was another building containing IEDs down the street and he said he wanted to go down. CNN was shooting some footage. They had these rockets that were SA14s that we found maybe four days prior. They're not 107s; they're shorter and about 35 to 40 pounds. They're all rammed into pipes and they were all pointed towards the east. He was really fascinated by this. The EOD and Air Force guys were with him. The Air Force guy said, "Yeah, those are SA14s." I said, "Yeah, cool, that's what I thought too." Anyway, he was looking at all this shit and then he walked past his Bradley. I was goofing on Specialist Joey Seyford because he had a piece of shrapnel in his face. Now, Seyford was shot in Kuwait in a training exercise. He got shot in the ass with a SAW, okay? Then he took a piece of shrapnel in his eye, right next to his tear duct. So he's got two injuries and one Purple Heart. He's walking to the bathroom before Najaf after being shot in the ass and he pushes the glass of the door through and cuts a tendon in his wrist. The guy's a walking time bomb, but he's a great, great kid. Essentially they walked down the street, my guys are upstairs on the roof and my brand new kid – brand new in sector – tells me he saw some people running from house to house. I called it up, it was relayed, then BRT got into a little bit of a skirmish and, from the first report, it looked like they were running that way. As soon as I went downstairs, Cantrell came downstairs. There was small arms fire real quick. About five minutes later, we're eating MREs, smoking and joking, and then Cantrell is screaming at the top of his lungs, "I need all squad leaders outside now!" I'm wondering, "What the hell is going on?" It was completely unnecessary to scream like that. Jesse Flannery, Fitts' SAW gunner, said, "I think he said the commander is dead." "What?" He said, "That's what I heard, Sarge." Then Cantrell left with the first sergeant and I don't have any confirmation at all. I was pissed off because Fitts had told him right before he left, "Hey, let *us* go." Sims basically told us, "Look, you guys have been through enough. You've had your fight, we can do our job." That really hurt. There's nothing those guys could have done. This bullshit about CNN's Jane Arraf pushing them into the line of fire is ridiculous. CNN had nothing to do with that. At that point, as a matter of fact, CNN was with the battalion commander. So that was absurd. The kids in the house didn't do anything wrong. Joey got shot in the leg and shoulder. Joey threw his M16A4 at the insurgent. He hit them with his rifle, he was so pissed off. Corporal Travis Barreto was an outstanding soldier. All these men would've died for each other. I hate people who try to overanalyze.

MM: So there was more than one in the room then?

DB: There were two guys under a blanket. He threw his rifle and then he got hit and fell back. The Air Force guy pulled him out of the door and got hit in the shoulder himself. I assume the exchange either hit the commander in the leg or the shoulder. But it hit him in the hip bone, and the way he rolled he was obscured and the line of sight was gone. So Corporal Barreto is on top of the building pulling security because our sniper broke his leg three days before that, or else he's the point man in that house. Barreto jumps down, over a fence, pulls Seyford and the Air Force guy over the fence, links up with a Bradley and, as he should, loads up his dudes, thinking Staff Sergeant O'Brien or Sami the interpreter is going to take care of Sims.

MM: Sami is Sims' interpreter I take it?

DB: Exactly. No one took Captain Sims' death worse than Sami. He was a former Republican Guard weapons sergeant and very handsome – looks like Andy Garcia. Very good looking kid, very loyal. I got to the point where I actually would hand Sami my weapon on patrol. This guy would tell us when people were lying, say this guy's a piece of shit, and if you open up that door they'll be bad guys there. But he was also an emotional guy. He wrote a message in the *US News and World Report* article about 2-2. He's the one who wrote the message on the wall saying, "I'm so sorry this had to happen to your town." But anyway, he ran across the street with O'Brien and actually came to the door shooting. He had chrome magazines that were as shiny as a '62 Corvette's wheels and they have given to Sami for his AK47. "Sami, you want these?" So he had a chrome magazine on his AK. He says – and I've never known him to lie – he told me he shot into the house and wounded a guy. There was a trickle of blood. He says there could have been three, but he's positive he saw two. They were both limping. There were little splatters of blood and he didn't know what the case was. He definitely saw that one of them had an M16 which he never even knew about. He said it was a Marine's weapon, and that made me believe he was telling the truth because we certainly weren't telling the world that we lost an M16. By the way, that was returned to us by serial number three months later. So when 1st Platoon shows up, they just don't know what the hell is going on amidst all the confusion. They don't know where Sami or O'Brien are at this time. It was just a horrible situation that transpired. That was tough to take.

MM: Talk me through the rest of the operation. Does anything stand out in your mind and particularly anything for young NCOs who are out there now? What do they need to know if they're going to go into this kind of situation?

DB: I just got back from Ramadi and the biggest problem there is: we don't know whether we want to level a house or risk hurting the innocent neighbor next door in order to kill a bad guy. We need to make a decision as a nation and as a military as to what we're doing in the urban fight. It is almost like we're a bipolar military now, so concerned as to how we will be perceived that we second guess ourselves before we fire a round. We can't conduct combat operations like that and expect to do anything but run in place. I mean, the Iraqi Army is leaps and bounds beyond what it was in 2004. The Iraqi police are making progress. I'm just really concerned at seeing so many people stateside who appear to be enjoying the prospects of America's defeat in Iraq. The General Anthony Zinnis and the Congressman John Murthas are quick to tell you, "I told you so," but not so quick to come up with real world solutions to what is plaguing our success in the region. Debating 2003 talking points and talking about torture is not going to solve how our nation deals with counterinsurgencies in the future.

MM: If there's anything else you'd like to tell me, feel free to do so or we can wrap it up now.

DB: As long as I'm free to do so, someone has got to state the obvious. I want to talk about micromanagement of leadership briefly. I would like to speak for just about 95 percent of my peers when I say that I'm personally and professionally ashamed by the vapid cries for attention – masqueraded by concern for troop welfare – of my former proud 1st ID commander, Major General John R.S. Batiste. In recent months, the man has been on more talk shows than the guy who claims he fathered Anna Nicole Smith's baby – and even that guy I find more convincing at times. Look, it was Batiste's very own brainchild, concoctions like the Victory Standard, that talk about personal responsibility in the absence of failed leadership. If you can't change the world as a division commander, then the best thing Batiste ever did for his country was to retire from its Army. Only losers make excuses. While Batiste wants to talk about how handcuffed he was as a division commander by his secretary of defense, I would like to mention the time he told me and my peers to shave our faces before we ate the first hot chow we would have in over 10 of the most agonizing days of urban fighting in modern American history in Fallujah. After we were properly shaved, only then we were ready to share a photo with Danger 6 and he could finally properly console us on the record regarding the sergeant major, the XO, the team leader and the beloved company commander we bagged earlier in the week. I think even Donald Rumsfeld would've let the scraggly kids eat first. Duty First!

MM: I greatly appreciate you taking the time to do this interview. I'm going to go ahead now and turn the tape off and we'll talk a little bit off line.

Staff Sergeant Matthew Horgan
25 July 2006

JM: My name is John McCool (JM) and today is 25 July 2006. I'm with the Operational Leadership Experiences Project at the Combat Studies Institute, Fort Leavenworth, Kansas, and I'm interviewing Staff Sergeant Matthew Horgan (MH), US Air Force, about his experiences in Operation Phantom Fury. This is an unclassified interview. Before we begin, if you feel at any time we are entering classified territory, please couch your response in terms that avoid revealing any classified information; and if classification requirements prevent you from responding, simply say you're not able to answer. Could you first tell me a little bit about your background, where you grew up, how you got in the Air Force, your military career up to the present?

MH: I grew up in the city of Pittsburgh, Pennsylvania. I played soccer since I was about five and was put on state teams that are called select teams. You go through a selection, you're picked up for soccer and you travel around, playing other select teams. It's a level above high school, skill wise. I did that for many years then went to high school. I didn't play high school sports; I stayed with the select soccer. I dropped out of high school in 10th grade, just wasn't interested in it. At 17, I entered college and played soccer there. I went to a Division III school called California State University of Pennsylvania for two years. I left there, went to a community college for a semester and then joined the military.

JM: Can you give me a brief sketch of the duty positions you've held, the units you've served with, any deployments?

MH: I originally came in the military to be a survival, evasion, escape and resistance (SEER) instructor but I didn't like the teaching aspect of that. After that, I tried out for tactical air control party (TAC-P), which is my current job, and went through that process and the 14-week school in Florida. It basically teaches you infantry skills and a little bit more. My main job is communications and calling in close air support (CAS). I deployed for Operation Iraqi Freedom (OIF) with the 173d Airborne Brigade to northern Iraq, came back for a couple months, and then went back with the 1st Infantry Division (ID) for our first rotation, which was four months. We ended up staying about five months, came back to Germany and then went back to Iraq three or four months later for a third rotation. That's when Operation Phantom Fury kicked off.

JM: What was the period of time of this third rotation?

MH: I got back to Iraq in October 2004. We went to Salman Pak for a little while and then got pulled back from there to go to Fallujah.

JM: What unit were you assigned to?

MH: We were assigned to the brigade, but most of our operations were with the Brigade Reconnaissance Troop (BRT).

JM: Captain Kirk Mayfield was your BRT commander?

MH: Yes.

JM: Were you assigned to a specific platoon?

MH: No. Whoever was going to be most forward or whoever they figured was going to get into trouble, that's who they put us with.

JM: I see. When did you first hear there might be an operation that eventually became Phantom Fury?

MH: When I got back for the third rotation, some of our joint tactical air controllers (JTACs) were coming out of Samarra and the guy I was replacing was the one who told me about it, that it was about to kick off.

JM: Can you talk me through the preparation and planning phase of this? What kind of visibility did you have and what was your role in planning?

MH: I was made the noncommissioned officer in charge (NCOIC) of the teams that were going in for the Air Force, and two of the guys were higher in rank than me. I knew the BRT and was with 2-2 Infantry for four years here in Germany, so I knew all the staff there. They let me take what I wanted and what teams I wanted to take with me. We ended up taking a team from Hawaii. We took a battalion air liaison officer (BALO), a tech sergeant, which is one rank higher than me. As the BALO, he came to Operation Phantom Fury a couple days late just for planning purposes. We didn't realize we would need a BALO; we thought we would fall under our typical chain of command. But when we got down there we realized everything was totally different. It was like a new type of CAS scenario going on.

JM: Were you part of a pair of JTACs who were assigned to the BRT?

MH: Yes. Typically whenever we go forward from the base, we go with one JTAC and one guy who's in upgrade training and he'll be a JTAC in the next couple years.

JM: Like an apprenticeship?

MH: Yes, we call them 1C4s. When you first come into our job, you start as the radio guy, the driver – they would basically protect us if we were calling in air support; they would be the shooter. We also had a Guard unit that was under us when we went down there. They were Staff Sergeant Greg Overbay and Senior Airman Michael Smyre; they both got injured in the beginning part of the battle.

JM: How did you feel you were integrated into the BRT and into Lieutenant, now Captain, Chris Boggiano's platoon?

MH: I knew all those guys real well just from being back there with them in Germany, from deploying and training, Combat Maneuver Training Center (CMTC) rotations and stuff. We all knew each other fairly well.

JM: Can you describe the pre-mission planning process and how you thought you were going to be employed?

MH: A lot of the information we got came from the same scenario: Samarra. How they would set up the roads as phase lines. We'd do our portion, which is making maps and overlays. We'd start handing out all our information to the Army guys and then they decided they wanted to put their own spin on the maps since it was their operation, so we helped them make all the maps for it. We were with the same unit in Salman Pak so we just stayed with them when we got back to Forward Operating Base (FOB) Warhorse. We stayed with the same unit we were with and then we went to Phantom Fury with the same guys.

JM: Where were you going to be located while the battle was taking place?

MH: We had to be somewhere in the vicinity of the ground commander – Captain Mayfield in this case – but Lieutenant Colonel Pete Newell was the ground commander and above him was a Marine general. We have to be somewhere where we can get an "okay" to drop a bomb. We just can't go out and blow stuff up; someone's got to approve it.

JM: Can you talk me through this approval process and how a typical call for CAS would go? How did you go about doing that and who would give you the approval?

MH: For myself, I would call in CAS anytime I thought we needed it. You could use different tactics; you don't just have to drop a bomb when you're doing CAS. You can have the airplanes come lower and scare the people, and a lot of times that works. We call it a "show of force." Other than that, a couple times the Army would ask us to get some airplanes, but most of the time we already had them coming.

JM: Were you also calling in strafing missions too?

MH: Yes, I called in a couple strafing missions.

JM: What kind of platforms are we talking about here?

MH: Any fighter aircraft that comes; we train with every one of them.

JM: What ones were used in this battle?

MH: F-18s, F-16s, F-15s, AC-130s at night, the Marine Super Cobras.

JM: What were the primary targets you guys were looking at during the planning phase? Were there particular areas you were going to be working in?

MH: Yes. We had the whole eastern side of the city. If you drew a line, we had the eastern side. The [inaudible] guys were more in the city and we were on eastern edge of it with the reconnaissance team. We were mostly south of the rest of the people.

JM: Who were the Guard guys attached to?

MH: They fell under me and we decided to put them with 2-2, since Senior Airman Sean Mitchell and I had been working with the BRT for the last couple weeks.

JM: Can you talk me through the battle once it commences from your vantage point? What was your role, how many air strikes did you call in and what were the effects of them?

MH: Probably eight hours before anyone else moved, we started; we breached up over the berm into the city. We had priority of fires so we could call in air support at any time we wanted. The targets at that time were just random one or two people, so we didn't drop any bombs or call in any air on that. At night the AC-130 would come in; and since no one was in the city except other people we didn't know about, they controlled the AC-130s – the special ops guys who were sneaking around. We stayed up there for a couple days and then started moving around the eastern side of the city. Our job was to keep anyone from coming out of the east and we were watching the east/west roads as the battle was moving north to south. So if anyone crossed the roads where we were at, we had a fire support guy with us and had the ability to call in artillery as well as CAS.

JM: Were you calling in 500-pound bombs?

MH: Yeah, all the bombs we dropped were 500 pounders and all the strafing was 20 millimeter.

JM: Were these from AC-130s mainly at night and there were other strafing missions called during the day?

MH: The only CAS I did was in the daytime. At night, we tasked the AC-130 up to the BALO, who was with Lieutenant Colonel Newell at the tactical command post (TAC). Sergeant Mikalodos (ph) would control the AC-130s at night because we were only getting about a half hour to 45 minutes of sleep in between watch and patrolling in the city.

JM: Were you in a vehicle at this time?

MH: Whenever we deploy we take our own Humvee. We have every satellite radio, HF radio to talk to the Navy. We talked to the airplanes and helicopters. We could call Florida if we really wanted to on our radio.

JM: Did you have any communications issues?

MH: The only comms issues we had were down in the city, and that was because the buildings were masking everything.

JM: Were you principally targeting buildings with these 500-pound bombs?

MH: Some of the information getting passed back to us – one of the missions we did we had to abort the airplanes because we were talking an airplane onto a target and were going to mark our own position with smoke. Somebody overheard us on the radio and decided that everyone should mark their position with smoke. The plane called back to me and asked, "What's the deal with all the smoke on the battlefield?" He just couldn't pick up the target anymore. There were probably 10 vehicles that had all popped smoke at the same time.

JM: What was your personal proximity to enemy forces? How close were you to the actual fighting?

MH: We definitely had one enemy sniper who probably was within 300 meters of us. We took, I think, 18 rounds to our vehicle and at least three of them hit our windshield. Whenever my driver, Senior Airman Mitchell, would pull up his binoculars to try to find him, he'd actually shoot the binoculars – but the windows stopped it of course.

JM: Do you guys have a .50 cal or anything in the back of your Humvee?

MH: We actually had the worst Army person in the world to be our gunner. He wouldn't fire back. I tried getting him fired twice – and our Air Force commander who sent us down there wouldn't let us get in the gun turret because we wouldn't have any CAS if one of us got shot. Before we left, he said absolutely under no circumstances were we to get in the turret, which didn't go over well with us. But now everything has changed for our job. We have to be trained for crew-served weapons so we'll be able to man our own guns, which is a good thing because our Army gunner actually played dead on us.

JM: Was this different than your deployment in OIF I or any other rotations?

MH: No. Earlier in the rotations, our Humvees didn't have a gun turret in them. It was just a turtle-back Humvee and the radios take up all the space for a turret.

JM: So during this operation, were you guys ever firing personal weapons, like M-4s?

MH: Yeah, we fired those. We were clearing buildings. When we were doing CAS we weren't actually firing our weapons, but the rest of the time we were.

JM: But you were not, at any time, allowed to man crew-served weapons?

MH: Our commander didn't want our role being the gunner. My driver's job was to drive, plus he had to man the four radios we have to be on at all times. We split the responsibility, so I would man two of them. I would talk to the airplanes and helicopters and he would talk to our request net where we got the airplanes from and to the Army net, which was three different channels at once. We had the Army commander's net and we had to be on the fire support net.

JM: Did you have any visibility on the death of Captain Sean Sims, the Alpha Company commander, and the wounding of Staff Sergeant Overbay?

MH: No. Earlier in the battle when 2-2 breached, Senior Airman Smyre was the driver for Staff Sergeant Overbay and he had a rocket-propelled grenade (RPG) go through his armored Humvee. Both of his legs got shrapnel in them so he was pulled out of the battle, and this was maybe that first night. Then a couple days later, Staff Sergeant Overbay was actually with Captain Sims when he got shot. Staff Sergeant Overbay got shot at the same time when they were breaching the house.

JM: Was it that they thought the building had already been cleared or something and went in? Obviously it hadn't been.

MH: I think it was a manning issue. Because of not knowing, training-wise, how to approach that big of a city, everyone split up and they just put smaller teams in the houses. I think that's what happened, but I'm not sure because I wasn't there.

JM: Would you consider most of these to be danger close missions?

MH: For artillery, we had a lot of danger close ones. I wasn't uncomfortable dropping the bombs. I dropped them closer earlier, but we were dropping more bombs so it was a different effect. At no time was I unsure that we were too close to the bombs. I thought we were pretty much out of the way.

JM: In talking to Captain Boggiano, he said something about wanting 500-pound bombs dropped but that that was being overruled by Captain Mayfield. Was this your understanding as well?

MH: Yeah. They turned off a lot of the bombs we wanted to drop. I think we only got off eight and we probably phoned in a request every two hours for 10 days.

JM: What was the reasoning behind that, as explained to you? Why were they called off?

MH: The way I understood is that they wanted to shoot artillery at it, which didn't make any sense to me because CAS was more accurate. Our main focus was trying to limit the collateral damage and artillery just throws that out the window in an urban environment.

JM: I'm just looking at an email here that Chris Boggiano sent us. He also said that since Captain Mayfield wouldn't allow that, "I got the Air Force guys to get someone else's permission to do it."

MH: We went through Lieutenant Colonel Newell for approval to drop it. My chain of command goes from me to Lieutenant Colonel Newell to our BALO, who was with Lieutenant Colonel Newell, so I just called my BALO and asked him to ask Lieutenant Colonel Newell if we could drop it. We needed ground commander's initials for that one particular bomb.

JM: What one was that?

MH: It was just danger close.

JM: Was Lieutenant Colonel Newell more responsive to your requests?

MH: Yeah. I worked with Lieutenant Colonel Newell a lot and I actually fell under him for about two years back in the rear. We did a lot of CMTC rotations together, plus anytime we left FOB Warhorse we would go up to his FOB and make sure they were all right and see if they needed us to do anything. We had a great working relationship with 2-2 and their staff.

JM: Can you share any overall assessments of Lieutenant Colonel Newell?

MH: He's an awesome person and leader. Every time we go out, we're by ourselves – two Air Force guys in a big sea of Army – and he's always the guy who would help us out, see if we needed anything, get us a place to sleep whenever we showed up at his base, and made sure we were fed. He was always looking out for our best interests and it just continued when we got down there. We were just happy we had him as our commander. There was also Captain James Cobb who was the fires commander for Lieutenant Colonel Newell, and I've known him for quite awhile. He and Sergeant Hayden (ph) are both the fire support guys at 2-2. Those were probably the two most important reasons we had such a good relationship with that battalion. We were always training together.

JM: Had you worked with either Captain Boggiano or Captain Mayfield before?

MH: Captain Mayfield was in the 3d Brigade tactical operation center (TOC) when I first met him. He wasn't in charge of the BRT when I was working with them earlier. I can't remember the commander's name but he got promoted to major so they moved him out. He was the first commander of the BRT in Iraq. I didn't know Captain Mayfield's role when he was in the TOC. I believe he was part of the S3 shop and then he got moved to the BRT right before Salman Pak, right before my third rotation started. I knew him from the TOC, but I didn't know him from being out in the field working with him.

JM: How would you overall assess the Air Force's role in Operation Phantom Fury? Do you have any general thoughts about how well you were employed or if you could have been better employed?

MH: At one point we wanted to separate ourselves from the fire support guy. In the beginning of the battle, it seemed to make sense to keep us together because we're on the outside of the city. A couple days into the battle, though, they wouldn't let us go into the city – which is where we needed to be to call in all the air support. They wanted us to stay on the outside of the city and that limited us in our abilities. The forward observer's role was similar to ours, but whenever you get into an urban area I don't think we mend as well as we should.

JM: What about the whole joint-ness aspect of this operation: how would you assess that?

MH: For us, every day, day in and day out, is joint work. Working with the Army on this particular mission was kind of weird because we had to work with the Marines also, and the Marines and the Army weren't talking. We actually went to a staff meeting between the Marines and ourselves just for CAS. At that time, it was probably less than 24 hours before the battle was to kick off and my younger airman pointed out that no one was on the same frequency together. The Army and the Marines couldn't talk together. So we let them know that they were on different times so they could talk together, or else they might not have talked through that whole battle. It was chaos. We pointed out, "Hey, you guys are on different times." So for us, it was pretty easy. When we got into the city, the Marines and the Army weren't sharing information. We went through a minefield that the Marines knew about – and they were on our flank. If they were talking, we would have never gone through the minefield.

JM: Could you get Marine air or was this just Air Force?

MH: In Samarra back around August, before our battle, they came out with a new concept called Keyhole CAS. I can't really get into that too much, but we adopted the same thing in Fallujah. It's where you're basically sharing assets. So I could call in any available aircraft.

JM: Was Marine air more or less responsive than the Air Force?

MH: The Marines operate a little differently where they're calling up each channel just to request the air. With the Air Force, though, I can just call directly to the air support operations center (ASOC) and request air. The Marines have to call it through everybody. I've had situations where, from the time I keyed the hand mike to the time I got off, it was 42 seconds and the airplanes were checking on – and the Marines are still talking to the company level if you're down at the platoon or squad. It's just a lot quicker for us, and we use satellite radios whereas they were using HF radios. It's like the Vietnam era. We have the same radio, we just don't use it; it's outdated.

JM: How was the battle different from your having been there in the role you played?

MH: We were able to take out a good amount of people at the end of the battle when they weren't so worried about us dropping bombs. I guess we had proved ourselves to them. But they started approving all our requests. I got credit for over 100 people, for calling in air strikes on them.

JM: So, 100 personnel were basically destroyed.

MH: Yes.

JM: Did you have a sense of enemy tactics, the level of their capabilities?

MH: They seemed pretty determined to win but towards the end I think they just gave up. There were a lot of people talking about how they would just keep running out after the same RPG and the Bradley would just keep hitting them, then another guy would come out to grab the same RPG and the Bradley would mow him down too. I don't think they clearly understood that they were getting annihilated. Then we got reports that they had intercepted a cell phone call, which said they were scared to come out of the buildings. If they stayed in the buildings we'd come in and get them, and if they ran out we'd drop a bomb on them.

JM: Had you operated in a major urban environment before?

MH: I have dropped bombs in an urban area but that was the first battle I've been in an urban area. It was still pretty new. Before it would just be targeting one building, but this was every building for every block as far as you could see, so it was like a rolling battle.

JM: Knowing this was how it was going to be, did you make any special preparations?

MH: For urban CAS, no; it's all pretty similar to us. For us, we don't want to drop bombs on ourselves, on any friendly troops, and make sure we hit the right building.

JM: Are there any major lessons learned you personally or the Air Force generally took after Phantom Fury?

MH: I sent up a huge after-action report (AAR) about what happened. I wrote it a couple days after we had been pulled out and I haven't any clue what happened to that AAR. I haven't heard a word about it. If we're going to get an Army driver for our vehicle or if we're going to get an Army gunner, make sure it's not the guy they just don't want with them, because that's what usually happens.

JM: And that's what you think happened?

MH: That's absolutely what happened. They even told us – not the commanders but the younger guys. It's just a guy they didn't want there.

JM: You said he played dead at one point?

MH: Yes. I think he got demoted twice. Over that whole timeframe he got promoted and demoted – and this was only about a month long. He's not a real squared-away guy.

JM: Are there any other individuals you think deserve special recognition for their actions?

MH: Oh definitely. My IC4, Senior Airman Mitchell, definitely didn't get enough recognition.

JM: What was the nature of his contributions?

MH: He was on point all the time. Anything I needed from him he was right there. He's actually here too if you wanted to talk to him as well.

JM: Sure, maybe we can schedule a time with him as well. That'd be great. How long after Phantom Fury did you stay with the unit?

MH: I'm actually still with the same Army unit. I'm actually on the same team with Senior Airman Mitchell right now. I left in December, right after we got back, and they brought in a guy to replace me. I wasn't supposed to go on that rotation, but my NCOIC asked me to go as a favor to him. I went down with him and they brought a newer, less experienced guy down to replace me and get him some experience.

JM: Are there any other aspects about this particular operation you want to draw attention to or that we haven't talked about?

MH: I just think the joint-ness, with everyone talking on the same sheet of music. There were too many little meetings going on without one big meeting – for whoever the ground commander was to say, "Hey this is what's going to happen." All the information was passed down to the lowest level and you kind of had to rebuild what was going on.

JM: Is this something you've noticed before or is this a unique problem for this particular battle?

MH: No, a lot of times it's like that. In our job, we need to know the whole picture. And if we get stuck in with a battalion, we don't get the whole big picture; we just get the battalion's picture. If we're going to drop a bomb that's going to affect the guys next to us, we need to at least have their frequencies so we can contact them. We had to run through the fields just to talk to the Marines next to us so we could get on the same frequency. The Army didn't even have that information. They were on totally different fills anyway, so they couldn't have talked regardless.

JM: Had you worked with Marines before?

MH: I've worked with Navy before. It was different this time because everyone was there: Navy, Marines, Air Force and Army. It's just shocking that they weren't talking, especially in that high profile of a battle.

JM: You said you wrote up this big AAR? Were there any other highlights you wanted to mention that you can talk about in an unclassified manner?

MH: I just brought up giving us a bad gunner and the communications glitch between the Army and the Marines. We had a lack of training, not as far as CAS goes – just with the Army and Marines standard operating procedures (SOPs), how they were going to enter a building and things of that nature. There wasn't anything really set up to explain how they were going to do something with a JTAC with them. I don't think they thought that deep into it. At brigade level, they have plans for where your ALO is going to be and where all those Air Force people are. But when you get down to the lower levels like company and battalion – and the troop we were with doesn't have a plan to have a JTAC with them. That's definitely stuff they have to think about.

JM: All right, if there aren't any other issues we'll conclude the interview here. Thanks very much for your time and for your service as well. It's greatly appreciated.

Sergeant Wes Smith
13 August 2006

JM: My name is John McCool (JM) and I'm with the Operational Leadership Experiences Project at the Combat Studies Institute, Fort Leavenworth, Kansas. I'm interviewing Sergeant Wes Smith (WS) on his experiences in Operation Phantom Fury. Today's date is 13 August 2006 and this is an unclassified telephone interview. Before we begin, Wes, if you feel at any time we're entering classified territory, please couch your response in terms that avoid revealing any classified information. And if classification requirements prevent you from responding, simply say you're not able to answer. Could you start off by giving me a little bit of background information on yourself – where you were born, where you grew up, where you went to school, how you entered the Army – things like that?

WS: Okay. I was born in 1974 in Birmingham, Alabama. When I was about six, my immediate family and I moved to Florida and I was raised there until I graduated high school in Plant City, Florida; and as soon as I graduated I left for the Army. I went to Basic Training at Fort Leonard Wood, Missouri, in August '93 and then in October '93 I went to Fort Sam Houston, Texas, for the medical specialist Advanced Individual Training (AIT). I was there until February '94. My first duty station was Fort Lewis, Washington, where I'm currently stationed, and I was in a ground ambulance unit in the 62d Medical Brigade from '94 until 2000. In 2000 was when I reenlisted, went to Germany and was in 2-2 Infantry from 2000 until we returned from Iraq. Now I'm back here at Fort Lewis with 1-38 Infantry, 4th Brigade, 2d Infantry Division, the Stryker Brigade Combat Team (SBCT).

JM: What was the time period of your deployment to Operation Iraqi Freedom (OIF)?

WS: We were there about a year. I remember we left on Valentine's Day and we returned maybe one or two days after Valentine's Day the following year.

JM: So this is February '04 through February '05?

WS: Yes, sir.

JM: What was your duty position during this time?

WS: When I was in Iraq, I was in the evacuation section of the medical platoon. There were quite a few of us actually and we had some attachments from the 201st Forward Support Battalion (FSB) that were added to our section. I was an M113 crewmember, evac noncommissioned officer (NCO), and my primary assigned company was Alpha Company, 2-2 Infantry.

JM: Before we get into Fallujah and Operation Phantom Fury, could you tell me a little about what you were doing and where you were located prior to?

WS: While we were first there during set up, we were pretty much assigned to the aid station. If there was a big company mission, then they would send an evacuation asset out there with them. Sometimes the forward aid station would go with Captain Gregory McCrum, the physician assistant (PA), and his treatment team and maybe one or two evacuation assets. A lot of the time in the evacuation section we would pull a 24-hour shift in the aid station on Forward Operating Base (FOB) Normandy in Muqdadiyah. We would monitor radios and if patients came in during any time throughout the night, we would notify Captain McCrum, Major (Dr.) Lisa DeWitt and the treatment teams. We would be involved in calling in air evacuation for any casualties we had in the aid station. Also, we were just helping out if the treatment teams needed it with treatment. My driver and I were attached to Charlie Company at the time. I believe it was in March into April, and Charlie Company was out in a town at their own little base that they had. It was called Camp Comanche. This was right before Najaf started and they sent the task force to Najaf. We had gotten hit at Camp Comanche pretty hard for about two or three days. I want to say it was around 7 to 9 April, and it seemed like they were trying to take over that little camp. Once that was over, Lieutenant Colonel Peter Newell pulled Charlie Company out of Camp Comanche and we pretty much left it, went back to FOB Normandy and the next day they were getting ready to go to Najaf. I did not go on that mission because I was still at Camp Comanche. I stayed back as sort of a rear detachment on FOB Normandy in Muqdadiyah while the rest of the task force went to Najaf and sat out there for a couple weeks. Also as part of the evacuation section, we'd go to the retrans site that was up in the mountains. We spent about a week there with our field artillery attachments. We had some communications stuff up there on a hill so we could send our signals out farther to retransmit if we had any patrols out. That was a real boring duty. After Najaf, we'd gone out on a couple small company missions, cordons and searches, but we never really saw anything. We had gone out with Major DeWitt a few times on civil affairs (CA) type missions to pass out stuffed animals, little types of medical supplies or any treatment we could give – and that's about all we did up until Fallujah when we got really busy.

JM: When did you first hear that 2-2 Infantry might be participating in this operation with the Marines?

WS: I first heard about it around October or November. There were some rumblings about it. We had been put on standby and were supposed to start getting our stuff together because we may be going somewhere. I didn't really know for sure until we got our op order and they said who was going and what tentatively we would be doing. When it gets trickled down to us, all we hear about is the kind of medical coverage that's needed, who we are going to support, what we're going to bring out and stuff like that.

JM: What was the degree of planning, rehearsals and training that went on once you found out you were actually going to be going to Fallujah and be involved in this major urban operation?

WS: We only had a little bit of prep time, but we were always prepared anyway. There was vehicle maintenance to be done. We had a couple of our 113s that were non-operational so we had to hurry and get those fixed to where they could move. We had to pack up the aid station, our trauma sets and sick call sets. We got a couple briefings from the chaplain. Captain McCrum gave us a lot of information on how the opposing force was operating, things we may see on our level in terms of trauma and injuries.

JM: What were some of the concerns you had, things that were weighing on your mind as you were preparing?

WS: My time at Comanche was pretty nerve wracking, but this one – considering the way it was getting put out to us – I thought it was going to be 10 times more intense than the couple days we spent getting shot at at Comanche. I was concerned about how I was going to be covered. As a medical evacuation asset, under the Geneva Conventions we're not allowed to have any crew-served weapons. I had an M16 and my driver had his so we had to figure out if we needed escorts, how deep were we going to be going into the city, what type of stuff do I need to look for there. I needed to keep my head on a swivel.

JM: Your responsibilities were going to be, as needed, to go into the city in your 113 and retrieve casualties?

WS: Yes, sir. I was to be in First Sergeant Peter Smith's back pocket at all times. He was the Alpha Company first sergeant, and wherever his vehicle went, I was right behind him.

JM: Can you talk me through what happens as the units blow the breach, cross the berm and combat commences? Where are you located, what do you see and basically what's going on?

WS: We sat out in an assembly area for what seemed like forever, waiting for it to get dark. My driver got some sleep. I tried but I was running around checking on the guys, keeping in contact with the first sergeant and the aid station. Once it got dark and we started rolling out, you could see the prep fires from our mortars and the artillery.

JM: I understand there was quite a fireworks show.

WS: Yes, it was. It was amazing. We sat behind the breach a couple hundred meters. We could see and hear once they breached into the city and started firing. We could see it, but I don't think any sort of return fire was coming our way. We would creep up a few feet and then would just sit and I'd listen to the radio, keep an eye out and it seemed like we did that for forever. I don't know how long that went until we finally pushed up through the breach. I think we were sitting right at the breach or just a little forward of it when they brought Sergeant Major Steve Faulkenburg back through after he got hit.

JM: Do you know how he was actually evacuated? Was it one of the other medic teams that brought him out?

WS: It was. He was in another medical 113 track and I believe that track was part of 1-63 Armor. When they came through and saw my track and First Sergeant Smith's track sitting there, they thought we were the aid station so they were yelling for help. There was so much going on and I was yelling back down, asking what's going on, telling them that we weren't the aid station. They're yelling for air evac and we didn't have any air support so I asked them what they needed me to do. First Sergeant Smith told me to stay put. I think he knew and he went down and found out what was going on. He escorted them back to the aid station and we just sat at the breach for awhile until First Sergeant Smith could get back and we could push forward.

JM: The whole task force didn't have any air, is that right?

WS: That's correct, sir.

JM: All the evacuations were going by ground?

WS: Yes, sir.

JM: Who are the first casualties you guys actually encounter and treat?

WS: The first that my crew encountered were our Air Force air controllers. Their Humvee got hit by a rocket-propelled grenade (RPG) and it went through the driver's door down by the floorboard, hit his foot and went through the engine panel. They pulled the Humvee up; it was barely running but they got it to us and transferred the driver to my 113 where I treated his foot. The RPG didn't explode and take his foot off but there was some damage to his foot. It was most likely broken so I wrapped it really good and we took him back. That was the very first I saw while we were there. I saw a couple Marines later on that night driving the big D9 bulldozers; they got hit with an RPG and had some minor shrapnel wounds that we treated and took back. For that first night, that's really all my crew saw as far as casualties.

JM: You mentioned the Marines. Had it been something that was talked about beforehand that you guys would possibly be evacuating Marines as well?

WS: Yes, sir. We knew they had their own sector but we didn't have any big engineer type vehicles with us so they attached two of those bulldozers to the whole task force. We were the closest to them when they got hit, so when they brought them in we weren't surprised that they were there.

JM: These were just Marines who were attached to 2-2, though, right? They wouldn't be Marines who were in the other battalions?

WS: No, sir. They were the ones attached to us.

JM: Did you ever treat or evacuate any Marines who were not attached to you?

WS: No, sir. Not personally.

JM: Could you explain what the standard operating procedure (SOP) was for being alerted that there was a potential casualty? Would this come down from First Sergeant Smith?

WS: Yes, sir. We stayed on the same radio frequency and they would call First Sergeant Smith, but I was listening in on the radio so I heard what was coming. There were a couple times that they would come back in a vehicle and we didn't know they were coming, so that kind of caught us off guard. Luckily it was minor stuff; it was nothing life threatening that we were unprepared for.

JM: Did you ever have any comms issues with the first sergeant's track?

WS: Not at all, thank goodness.

JM: What was the next major event after treating the Air Force guys?

WS: The next major event occurred early in the morning once we had gotten into the city and established a command center for Alpha Company in one of the buildings. Some engineers who were attached to one of the infantry platoons in a building adjacent to us had an incident that wasn't combat related. One of the guys was pulling guard up on the roof and fell through a hole from the second story. He was a 240 machine gunner and so he had that big gun and all his gear on, and that wound up being one of those surprise ones we didn't get commo on. Their platoon medic was on the scene and treated him and sent somebody to come look for us while we were trying to catch a couple Zs before our guard shift. They kind of surprised us and I was a little disoriented where I was at, wondering who was yelling at me, but we went to pick him up and transported him back to the aid station.

JM: How long of a trip is it back to the aid station?

WS: It took five to 10 minutes.

JM: I guess it varies by how deep in the city you were, but what was shortest to longest?

WS: Shortest was maybe about five minutes and the longest was probably about 10 to 20 minutes depending on the severity. If it wasn't life threatening, we didn't have it floored so we could maintain safety for ourselves and whoever may have been around. There were a lot of personnel on the ground a lot of the times.

JM: When you go into the city, how worried are you about general force protection issues, seeing as you didn't have any crew-served weapons with you? Did you come under fire at any time?

WS: Once or twice, but it was sporadic. We had First Sergeant Smith's track in front of us, a maintenance track behind us that also had a crew-served, and they kept pretty good cover on us for the most part. The most fire we had taken ourselves was the Lieutenant Ed Iwan incident when we were evacuating him.

JM: Can you tell me a little bit about what happened with Lieutenant Iwan, the Alpha Company executive officer (XO)?

WS: We had just finished pushing through a section of the city and were in a big square – there were buildings on all four sides. Lieutenant Colonel Newell's Bradley was there, Sergeant Major Darrin Bohn's Bradley was there and I believe we were in a holding pattern. It wasn't totally light outside but it was light enough to see around us and we were just sitting there listening to the radio. There was an M88 maintenance track behind us – the big ones that can tow Bradleys and Abrams – and they started shooting their .50 cal machine gun behind us. I turned to see what they were shooting at and they were messing with the machine gun and the ammo tray, and so I figured they were just doing a test fire. There wasn't really a lot of radio traffic so I figured everything was fine. Then a couple of M16s went off behind us. I had turned to cover our rear with my M16 and out of the corner of my eye, about 50 to 60 meters to my right, I saw a streak come flying down this alleyway and it seemed like it was head level to the ground. It looked like a laser beam that came flying through and I watched it and saw it hit Lieutenant Iwan's vehicle but it didn't explode. Because of the light conditions it was a little hazy, and I didn't know he was standing up in his turret when this happened. I didn't see an explosion so I thought maybe it hit the reactive armor that was on the turret and sort of fizzled out or bounced away, because there was no radio traffic. My driver asked me if I had seen that and I said yes, that it looked like it hit Lieutenant Iwan's Bradley. He was wondering if Lieutenant Iwan was okay and there was still nothing on the radio. Then the Alpha Company commander, Captain Sean Sims, came up on the radio and was calling for Lieutenant Iwan, and he called two or three times with no answer. I thought maybe he was down on the ground and didn't have his radio. The last time Captain Sims called he sounded angry, like he couldn't get in touch with Lieutenant Iwan – and that was when his gunner came up on the radio and all he said was that the XO was dead. I perked up and told my driver, "We need to get up there *now*!" So we pushed forward and pulled behind Lieutenant Iwan's Bradley. Lieutenant Colonel Newell's Bradley was parked behind it and we went in between them. Once we got up there, I had my ramp dropped and I was getting off the track with a litter. They were pulling Lieutenant Iwan's body out onto the ramp of the Bradley and I just went into tunnel vision. What shows up in my mind the most is that I could see through him and see the Bradley's ramp on the other side, and I just told myself that this wasn't good. I was told later by Sergeant Major Bohn and Lieutenant Colonel Newell's gunner that we were taking small arms fire as I was down there trying to get him on the litter. I had help from Staff Sergeant Albert Harris who was the Alpha Company senior medic at the time and was inside Lieutenant Iwan's Bradley when it happened. He had pulled him out of the turret and got him out onto the ramp for me. I helped Staff Sergeant Harris get a field dressing put on Lieutenant Iwan and that was the best we could do for him at the time. I got him onto my 113, got my helmet back on so I could try to contact First Sergeant Smith – and I had lost track of him because he had pulled up earlier before the incident happened, up towards the sergeant major's track where they were having a meeting or something. I just took off by myself to pull up there once we found out what happened. I had trouble contacting him, couldn't get him on the radio and I couldn't roll without him, not having a weapons system. So we were stuck there only a minute or two but it felt like 30 minutes because we needed to get Lieutenant Iwan out of there fast. So I'm yelling for First Sergeant Smith and Lieutenant Colonel Newell's gunner is yelling at me because we had parked right in front of his gun and he couldn't shoot down the alleyway where the RPG came from.

JM: Are you still taking small arms fire from that direction as well?

WS: Yes, sir. I don't know how close it was coming to me. Like I said, I had that tunnel vision, but they said it looked like a cowboy movie or something, that I had stuff kicking up all around me when I was trying to get him up. I didn't realize that until later and my knees went weak when I heard it. We took RPG fire and more small arms fire on the way out once we linked up with First Sergeant Smith, because our only direction of travel to get to the aid station was down the alleyway that the RPG came from. I was down inside the track with Lieutenant Iwan so I wasn't up outside and couldn't see where it was coming from, but my driver was talking to me. He had his seat down and was looking through the periscope as he was driving. He said an RPG blew up right in front of us and we rolled over it as it exploded. We didn't take any damage from that. First Sergeant Smith said that one hit his weapons system on top of the track. It missed his driver and hit the barrel of the weapons system and bounced off, and I believe the weapons system took some damage. For that whole trip I was down inside trying to work on Lieutenant Iwan with his dressings and just yelling at him. It was so noisy so I was screaming at him. I had my hand on his shoulder and I was telling him, "XO, you're going to be okay." I could tell he was barley breathing. He had a weak pulse that I could get in his neck. A 113 is bumpy and loud and stuff was falling everywhere inside so it was hard, but I could get a weak pulse. He wasn't conscious but I was hoping he could hear me so I was screaming at him the whole time, telling him we were getting him to the aid station, that he was going to be okay and that we were helping him. At the same time, I was trying to contact the aid station and it took a few tries because I was yelling and I was scared. I was crying a little bit and I'm frustrated because I couldn't get the aid station on the radio. Finally they came up and I didn't let them know who it was, just said we had a serious abdominal injury due to an RPG coming in – and it took maybe five to 10 minutes to get there but seemed like an eternity. I didn't know the RPG was still in his abdomen. We had gotten the dressing on and, due to the extent of his injuries, there wasn't a whole lot I could do on that trip because it was such a short time. I just made sure the dressing was on him and tried to catch any bleeding I could. That dressing was covering the RPG so I didn't know about it until we had him offloaded and I heard Captain McCrum call for explosive ordnance disposal (EOD). That's when someone let me know that it was still in there and I broke down after that. Because it was so bumpy and we were going so fast that, if we'd have hit something just right, it could have gone off in the patient compartment.

JM: What was the delay in getting a hold of First Sergeant Smith?

WS: He was on the ground at the time. I didn't listen but they told me he was actually at the XO's track and was helping to get him out. I think he opened my litter for me. I don't know, though, because I had that tunnel vision and was focusing only on Lieutenant Iwan. I guess I was ready to go before he could get back to his track and there were so many vehicles there and so much going on that I didn't see him, but finally he caught hold of me and was ahead of me, so we just caught up to him. The maintenance guys were behind us and we headed out.

JM: How soon after this are you back in the city?

WS: We stayed long enough for me to clean my track out. There was a lot of blood and I had to exchange litters and compose myself. That was my first real serious incident since being there, so it took a lot out of me. I know the first sergeant was a little troubled so he hung around there for a little bit to find out the status of Lieutenant Iwan before he was evacuated further back to Bravo Surgical on Camp Fallujah. We were there maybe 30 to 45 minutes before we headed right back out to the city.

JM: Is the next major incident when Captain Sims is killed?

WS: Yes, sir. There were a couple small things like an RPG hit a rock and kicked it up onto a guy's ankle and broke it – minimal stuff. It was always little stuff in the lulls between the big stuff.

JM: A quick question before we get to Captain Sims. Are you ever treating or evacuating any Iraqi soldiers that are attached to 2-2?

WS: Not personally. Of the Iraqi Intervention Force (IIF) guys, the only one I ever saw was the guy who shot himself in the foot before we even rolled out. I don't know if that was by accident or on purpose.

JM: I think it's just been described as a self-inflicted gunshot wound. What about any non-combatants? Did you even see any?

WS: I don't know if they were unlucky non-combatants or actual combatants, but just the guys left on the side of the road as we were pushing into the city. There was nothing we could do for those guys. After Captain Sims got killed, I helped with some combatants at the aid station because the company was back there; but as far as being out in the city dealing with combatants I, myself, didn't treat any combatants or non-combatants.

JM: So Alpha Company loses their XO and was it the next day that Captain Sims was killed?

WS: Yes, sir.

JM: What was your visibility on that?

WS: We were back at the aid station. We had taken one guy who had a twisted knee back there and it seemed like there was a lull in the fighting, so the first sergeant got down and was talking to Captain McCrum and Major DeWitt. I went and saw Sergeant Jennifer Amato who worked at the aid station. It was almost like a break when we got word that we had casualties coming in, so First Sergeant Smith climbed in his track, we jumped in ours and were headed straight out there. We actually caught them coming in a Bradley and it was Captain Sims' radio operator and our other Air Force guy, Staff Sergeant Overbay. They were in the Bradley.

JM: They were not evacuated by medics?

WS: No, sir. They call that casualty evacuation (CASEVAC) if it's a non-standard medical evacuation. We caught them halfway so we turned around and followed them to see what had happened. We were there for a little bit, briefly helped out with their treatment, and then First Sergeant Smith came and got me and told me we had to go back out there because there were more casualties. So we jumped in and as I'm putting my helmet on to hear the radio and get moving, I could hear the traffic that said, "Terminator 6 is down. Terminator 6 is down. We can't get to him." So my reaction was that we had to get there *now*. I told the first sergeant that we had to get moving, pick it up a little bit. We stopped just short of a phase line and I was wondering why we were stopped. Was this it? It wasn't clicking with my map of where we were supposed to be headed and we stopped at the heavy tactical command post (TAC) where Sergeant Major Bohn and Lieutenant Colonel Newell were set up. The first sergeant got down and was talking to the sergeant major and I ran up and said, "First Sergeant, we have to get there!" And he said it was too late. I walked back to my track, told my driver what was going on, and we sat there for awhile while the company was trying to reconsolidate. For that incident, I never saw Captain Sims' body. They already had him packaged and in someone's Bradley by the time we made it up to where the rest of the company was and they had sent a vehicle. Sergeant Amato, Sergeant Wolf and our medical platoon leader – Lieutenant Chris Carlson – were on that vehicle to come and retrieve Captain Sims' body and take it back to the aid station for processing. After that, we sat for awhile. They brought the company together and reconsolidated. At the time, First Sergeant Smith and Sergeant First Class Ryan – because we couldn't just stop; we had to keep going because we still had that section of the city that we needed to get cleared. We had that mission to complete so they took the reigns; and from what I could see, they did a pretty good job so we could finish that little part of the operation.

JM: This is First Sergeant Smith, and who was the other person you mentioned?

WS: Sergeant First Class Ryan. He was part of Alpha Company. He was a platoon sergeant for a while, but at the time he was moved to a staff section within the command group. I believe he was in the heavy TAC with Lieutenant Colonel Newell and Sergeant Major Bohn.

JM: I don't know what kind of visibility you had on this, but Lieutenant Jeff Emery was the senior platoon leader and normally the senior platoon leader would take over since Iwan, the XO, had been killed and now Sims, the company commander, as well. What was the command relationship between Emery and Smith? Was Smith the acting company commander?

WS: I'm not really sure what role he played. Lieutenant Emery was 1st Platoon's platoon leader and I think he was wearing two hats. I believe you're right. I'm not sure what position he took, but I think Sergeant First Class Ryan jumped in to give the first sergeant a hand. I just noticed because he used to be in the company when I was a platoon medic; he was my platoon sergeant for that platoon. I thought it was funny that he had come back over to the company because I knew he had gotten moved to a different section.

JM: So your understanding was that it wasn't a formal thing. No one said, "Hey, First Sergeant Smith is your new company commander"?

WS: Not that I could see down at my level. I was always in the first sergeant's back pocket and he had moved [*inaudible*] on one of the Bradleys. I don't remember if it was Lieutenant Iwan's or Captain Sims' vehicle. He left his track with his gunner – Sergeant Eric Dove – and since I always was in the first sergeant's back pocket, I was a little concerned about how I was going to operate with just them and not the first sergeant to follow. But it worked out in the end. We weren't out there that long before we got pulled back to where the aid station was and they had a company assembly area. That's when Captain Doug Walter came back and took over the company.

JM: Had you known Doug Walter when he was the previous Alpha Company commander?

WS: Yes, sir. I was his company senior medic when we were in Kosovo so I was pretty excited to see him come back. I know he had some medical problems and thought he wasn't deploying with us, so it was kind of a shock to me when he showed up out there and assumed command again of the company.

JM: Yeah, and other people we've talked to have said it was a very pleasant surprise to see him again.

WS: Yes, sir. He had come out, it was dark and I was trying to get some shuteye. The back of my track was open and I heard, "Hey, who is this?" and I was like, "It's Sergeant Smith; we're the medics." He asked to use my radio. I didn't know who it was, but I said sure; and once he came in I saw who it was. He called battalion, gave a report and I remember it sent a shiver up my spine. I'll always remember that. He finished his report, had his head in his hands and he was looking down at the floor. There was a pause, and after the pause he said, "This is Terminator 6, out." And that just sent a shiver up my spine because I remember him being Terminator 6 in Kosovo and here he comes and takes over again. I thought he was an excellent commander in Kosovo so I was glad to have him back, especially after all that had happened.

JM: How do you think Alpha Company as a whole dealt with these tremendous leadership losses?

WS: They took it hard on the level of the soldiers and the NCOs. I'm sure the officers did too, but because of their positions I don't think they could show it as much. As far as the soldiers and the NCOs, they took it hard. I took it hard myself. They had brought some combatants into the aid station and there were four to six of them and they were messed up pretty bad. They had been in hiding for a few days and had been caught coming out of wherever they were hiding. Their wounds were pretty bad off because they'd been sitting for a few days untreated, so they brought them to the aid station and I went over there to see if I could help out. I was angry, and I know a lot of other people were as well. Major DeWitt actually yelled at me. I had a field medical card and was documenting treatment and there was a Marine or some type of naval intelligence guy who was there interrogating as they were getting treated.

JM: These are insurgents you're talking about?

WS: Yes, sir. He was asking questions and I was mad because we had these guys coming in. I said, "Ask them if any of these guys were the ones who killed my commander and XO." Well, Major DeWitt was standing next to me and she yelled at me and said, "Sergeant Smith, you're better than that." As medics we have to treat injuries no matter whose side they're on. We have to give the same standard of care whether it's a US soldier or an insurgent. So she yelled at me and kind of hurt my feelings a little bit so I dropped what I was doing and walked back to my vehicle in the assembly area. That's when I saw that a lot of the guys were mad and they started crowding around the aid station, saying they wanted to go shoot the insurgents. I was like, "We can't do that. I'm pissed too. I just got yelled at, but we can't do that. You guys need to stay back." Some of them looked like they didn't care who was around. They looked like they were going to go up there and do something to those guys for what happened to Lieutenant Iwan and Captain Sims. After they had been treated and taken away, they calmed down a little bit. The chaplain came around and talked to them and I talked to some of the guys. They looked to the medics as not just plugging holes and giving band-aids; they seem to think of us as psychologists and counselors too, so a couple of them came over and expressed their feelings. It was hard for me to console them because I was feeling the same thing and we're not trained for that type of counseling when we're at Fort Sam Houston learning how to be a medic. I believe Major General John Batiste also came out that day and walked around, talked to some of the guys in Alpha Company while we were there. That was the most I had seen as far as casualties on our side for that operation. It was getting close to the end of our operation, we had cleared the rest of our section and it was just the same routine – follow the first sergeant and pull a little bit of guard at night. We found a big weapons cache either the day before or the day we were pulling back. They blew that and that was huge. They told me that Captain Walter was around there as it was going off, there was ammo blowing up and stuff, and they were like, "Oh, man. We're fixing to lose him too." After that, I remember going back to the camp, doing some debriefings and getting ready to pack up to leave.

JM: Do you have any idea how many times you went back and forth into and out of the city?

WS: Three or four times a day. Not all the time with patients, just knowing I had to follow the first sergeant around if he needed to come back for something.

JM: Did you ever keep track of how many guys you evacuated from the city?

WS: I believe it was nine or 10, maybe 11 total for the operation that I evacuated myself. There was more CASEVAC from non-standard vehicles and from 1-63 which was on one of our flanks. The IIF guys had their own evacuation assets and they came back a couple times.

JM: After the battle, did you guys do any sort of medical focused after-action review (AAR), evaluating how the operation went and the medical support that was given?

WS: I had a little input on that. Most of the hotwash was the infantry side of the operation. In the unit I'm in now, we stress that we really need a big input on some of this stuff because they seem to forget about us until they really need us – and that's usually when something has gone wrong. I had a little bit of input and told the first sergeant certain things that we needed to do. For example, if we could keep a certain same route or I would ask him to keep me informed so we could prepare for what we may see casualty wise or anything like that. I would sit in on the op orders before the mission. We have a little paragraph for medical support and that's usually the first sergeant's job on missions. He's ultimately in charge of the support side – ammo resupply, CASEVAC – so during his little brief of the op order he would let us know how we're evacuating, call signs, all that stuff.

JM: How do you think the medical support went as you look back? Did you have adequate supplies? Were there any inefficiencies that you noticed?

WS: I believe it went *very* well. It was a blessing that the aid station was set up so close because it cut down our evacuation time. From point of injury to a level of higher care – which would be the battalion aid station – that shorter amount of time from injury to next level of care can make all the difference in the world.

JM: Apparently the aid station came under some indirect fire and they had to jump a couple times. They were *really* close.

WS: Yes, sir. They were right over the berm a lot of times. There was a big highway that turned into the cloverleaf and there was this raised area the highway was on. They were behind that raised area and we were right on the opposite side of it operating in the city. Towards the end, once we had gotten towards the end of our sector of the city, I know they jumped and were set up at a gas station. That was a little bit farther of an evacuation time because we would take the hardball road and would have to go back through where we already cleared, jump on the hardball and follow the highway to it. There was a shorter route to it but it was through this dust bowl. We would have to stand up out of our vehicles and the vehicles in front of us would just kick up so much dust that it was impossible to see where we were going.

JM: Are there any other individuals you think deserve recognition for their contributions to this battle that we haven't mentioned?

WS: Anybody working in that aid station was exceptional. Our attachments – Sergeant Amato, Sergeant Roger Wolf, Sergeant Ellen Smith, Specialist Ivy Marks – they were all from our FSB and they worked great with our treatment teams. That's the medical side. As far as being out in the city, Staff Sergeant David Bellavia was an amazing guy.

JM: Actually, we just talked to him a couple days ago and, let me tell you, that was an incredible interview.

WS: I'll bet. I talked to him when I was at the NCO Academy at Fort Sam Houston back in February because he's preparing a book on the operation and had everybody's story but the medical side of it, so we kept up an email relationship for a bit. Any of the guys in Alpha Company – I'm fond of them because since I've been in 2-2 I've been involved with them in some way, being their senior medic during two Kosovo rotations and their evacuation NCO for Iraq. There are so many names.

JM: Are there any other issues about this operation, the medical piece or your role in it that maybe we didn't discuss that you'd like to focus on, or other points you'd like to make?

WS: It was a trying experience for me. A lot of my training paid off for that operation and I credit Captain McCrum for a lot of that. They only teach us so much at school after Basic Training, and a lot of our further training came from the PA and Major DeWitt. They tried to teach us everything they knew, almost working at their level because the platoon medics and us are the ones who are right there when the incidents happen. They taught us a lot. It taught me a lot about myself and I was pleased that my training paid off. I got a Bronze Star with a V device for the Lieutenant Iwan incident and I'm really pretty humbled by it because, from my perspective, I was just doing my job. That's what I was there to do. If we weren't out there, who knows what would have happened.

JM: Well, thank you so much for your time. It was great talking to you and I appreciate you sharing your experiences with us.

WS: Thank you for contacting me. It was a pleasure to give my little bit of it.

Jane Arraf
3 April 2006

MM: My name is Matt Matthews [MM] and I work for the Combat Studies Institute at Fort Leavenworth, Kansas. Today is 3 April 2006 and I'm interviewing Jane Arraf [JA], who's currently on leave from CNN as the Edward R. Murrow Press Fellow at the Council on Foreign Relations. I'd like to start by getting some background information on you. Where you were born, where you went to school, your assignments, that type of thing.

JA: Sure. I studied journalism at Carleton University in Ottawa and that's sort of like the Canadian equivalent of the Columbia School of Journalism. Then after I finished, I went to Reuters in Montreal, ran a one-person bureau there, and then moved to New York and worked for Reuters in New York, reporting in places like Haiti and Bosnia. I was then appointed bureau chief in Jordan just before Saddam Hussein invaded Kuwait; and when he actually invaded Kuwait, it turned into a much different job than the one I applied for. During the '91 Gulf War, I was in Jordan. The first winter after the war, I went to Iraq for the first time and thought it was the most fascinating, challenging place I'd ever reported from. I moved back to the States in late 1993 and worked for Reuters in New York and then Reuters Financial Television as a correspondent in D.C. In 1997, I joined CNN to open their first permanent Baghdad Bureau. I stayed there for kind of a difficult three years, in which I was the only Western correspondent based in Iraq, and then moved to Turkey to open a bureau in Istanbul for CNN. I was then asked to go back to Baghdad, which I did, and then I was expelled a few months before the war by the Iraqi government for a protest I'd covered that they'd warned everyone not to report. I went back to Turkey to cover the debate there over whether to allow U.S. troops in the country, traveled through Iran, and spent the war on the front lines in northern Iraq. After Baghdad fell, I made my way back to Baghdad as bureau chief. Then in 2004, I became senior Baghdad correspondent and essentially spent all of my time traveling throughout Iraq, mostly embedded.

MM: Did you cover the April 2004 Fallujah fight that the Marines were involved in?

JA: I did not. I watched that unfold from Baghdad. Actually, I didn't watch it unfold: I was in Najaf at the time embedded with Army forces fighting the Mahdi Militia.

MM: Could you talk me through how you became involved with going down to Fallujah and getting embedded with 2d Battalion, 2d Infantry Regiment, with Lieutenant Colonel Pete Newell and the S3 [operations officer], Major John Reynolds?

JA: Sure. We had covered Lieutenant Colonel Newell's unit extensively when they were in Muqdadiyah. We'd been embedded with the brigade in Ba'qubah under Colonel Dana Pittard who told us that we might want to see the progress they were making in training Iraqi forces in Ba'qubah. So we spent a couple of weeks in Muqdadiyah. I thought what 2-2 was doing there and the rapport that Lieutenant Colonel Newell and his team had developed with the Iraqi National Guard at the time was really quite impressive. When Fallujah came up, it was clear it was probably going to be more dangerous than anything any of us had covered before, so dangerous that the networks decided to pool their footage to minimize the risk. In fact, journalists were dropping out once they were told by the Marines what it was going to be like. I thought it really should be covered from the point of view of the Army, which was going in with the heavy armor, as well as the Marines, so I proposed a second team that I would have covering Fallujah with Lieutenant Colonel Newell – because we knew them, essentially trusted them, knew how they operated and they knew us. I thought, rather than be embedded with a random unit where we didn't know what access we'd have, it would be the best possible way to cover that battle. So that's what we did. I had quite a difficult time convincing CNN that we needed that coverage, because the main effort was supposed to be the Marines and this was seen as a bit of a luxury. But eventually they let me go and it ended up being extraordinary. I think the coverage would have been a lot poorer had we not been with Task Force 2-2. Had we not been with them transmitting those pictures, the world wouldn't have seen the initial assault into the city.

MM: That's remarkable that they thought the fight would be more with the Marines because, from my research so far with 2-2, it just seems like the most amazing fight of all the fights I've researched so far.

JA: That's interesting. I think you probably know that the media sees things pretty simplistically. This was going to be a Marine effort, basically, so all of the focus was on the Marines as opposed to 2-2. And even though we told them this was going to be the initial assault paving the way for the Marines, that doesn't really sink in until you're actually there and you can show them pictures of what's happening.

MM: I've interviewed a lot of people from 2-2 and from 2-7 CAV [2d Battalion, 7th Cavalry Regiment] that were over in the west, and I seem to get the impression from those interviews that the Marines didn't really want the press around. Did you get that impression as well?

JA: It varies immensely, because after 2-2 went back – and we went back with them for the memorials – we jumped over because I wanted to stay in Fallujah and see what happened after the major fighting was over. We went to a Marine unit. It really varies depending on the division you get, the regiment you get. The Marines as a whole are perhaps less welcoming than the Army as a whole, but within individual regiments, I had nothing but amazing embeds with RCT-7 [Regimental Combat Team 7], for instance. So during Fallujah, it really made a difference who you were embedded with. We had two of our people embedded with the Marines. One of them was dis-embedded because of three basic things they said he had done – and a couple of them might have been in dispute. One of them was that he ran a story that a senior Iraqi Army official had defected and gone back to Kurdistan, had given up, and basically said, "I'm not going to be a part of this," after seeing the plans for Fallujah. He believed that he ran it by a senior Marine official who said it was okay to report. Well, the Marines decided later that it wasn't okay to report – so whatever you want to make of that. The thing that was the final straw was that he reported which direction the Marines were moving and, at that point, the assault was well underway and it was quite obvious. I'm pretty sure I reported the same thing with the Army after clearing it with the Army, but the Army and the Marines have very different rules about what you can report. There were several instances in which we had cleared everything – and we didn't even have to clear things because we were right there with the command element. The proximity was so close. You basically knew what you could report and what you couldn't report, and unless there were really serious questions, you automatically knew it was okay. It was quite obvious which direction the troops were moving in, but someone with the Marines reporting the same thing was dis-embedded. They may have had their own considerations, but those considerations weren't apparent even to the Army we were embedded with. I faced that several times, where I'd been cleared to report information and use video which was perfectly fine with the Army. But when we got to the stage where it was to be transmitted – and that was under military censorship run by the Marines – the Marines had a problem with it, even though we made clear to them that it was fine with the unit we were embedded in. So that was a frequent problem. The reporter who went in with the Marines replacing our correspondent who had been dis-embedded stayed just a couple of days and then left - saying he never received the support he needed from them to cover an infantry unit.

MM: Did you get the impression that soldiers were more forthcoming or more honest when you interviewed them, or do you think they held back if they knew that the press was there?

JA: It really depends. As I said, I've really been embedded for most of two years so I've done hundreds and hundreds of interviews. What I tend to find is that you start off with a unit that may distrust you. I don't actively work to win their trust because, one, it's a full-time job; two, it's a bit manipulative; and three, I'm really busy doing my real job. But at the end of it, what they generally say is: "You know, we don't like the media, but you're okay." So something happens in that process where they see you're serious, they see you're sincere, they see you're trying to tell the truth, and they become somewhat less guarded generally. There are those who will never trust the media and there are those who will never trust specifically CNN – and those are people who probably won't be terribly forthcoming. But in terms of the battle going on around you, a lot of the coverage I did wasn't so much based on interviews. It was trying to capture those moments either in battle or when the battle paused, or those moments when soldiers were reflecting on what was going on. That's less of an interview and more of just being able to capture something that's naturally happening.

MM: What do you think is the connection between the news coming out of Iraq, current U.S. public opinion and the lagging support for the war?

JA: I see the administration and [Secretary of Defense] Donald Rumsfeld and others trying to blame the media for the negative perception of what's happening there. It has a link, certainly, when you see news that's not perceived as positive everyday. It does give you a certain impression of how that war is going, but the news you're seeing is true. It's impossible to put it all in complete context. In television, for instance, in a two- or three-minute piece, you very rarely are able to get across the fact that shops opened and people went to school and people went to work today, even though there was a suicide bomb, although I always try to weave that in. The argument we get over there from military commanders or soldiers is, "This is so different from what I'm seeing; the media must be lying." Yes, we could report a school or clinic being built, but the argument usually goes that that's the only thing we should report. If I were to report a clinic being built and ignore the fact – as we saw today, for instance – that there were 120 clinics that were supposed to be built that will not be built because the reconstruction money has run out, that would be entirely missing the picture. I think this has become so politicized that this is the most difficult story to cover that I could ever have imagined. Not just because of the dangers in Iraq, not just because of the complexity of the war and Iraqi society. It's the intense politicization here in the U.S. where everything you say is taken as a political statement.

MM: Let's go back to Fallujah for a minute. John Reynolds left me with a bunch of film footage and just a truckload of photographs, a lot of them of you, your producers and I assume your assistant. Was it always in the back of your mind that, at any moment, you could have been killed during this fight?

JA: Oh, sure. It was in the back of my mind, and I tried to instill that in my producer, Arwa Damon, because I wasn't sure that was in the back of her mind. I remember before the assault started, they did shaping operations and there were mortars and artillery all night long. It really felt like the end of the world. It sounded like the end of the world, and at that point we'd been through quite a lot. The

306

battle in Najaf where we were mortared every night, the battle for Samarra where we were under small arms fire for hours at a time, but this was nothing like that. We were sleeping in these cots - trying to sleep - and I woke Arwa and told her that I really needed her to know that we could very well be killed and that she didn't have to do this. She basically said, "What do you mean I don't have to do this?" I think she thought I was stating the obvious or that I was a bit nuts. I didn't get the impression that she had absorbed the fact that we could easily be killed or maimed. I think if you're going to do that, you have to know what the worst-case scenario is and accept it, as opposed to doing what a lot of people do, which is to say, "That could never happen to me." It was always in the back of my mind and I tried to remind her so she could make a choice. I'm not sure how well that lesson stuck but everyone deals with things differently. She was extraordinarily brave, as was our cameraman/editor Neil Hallsworth, and he realizes the danger and wants to go back. I'm going back, and Arwa will go back as well into situations like that. I think everyone deals with it in a different way, but there was so much death and destruction around us that it would be hard not to keep in mind that, yes, we could be killed at any time.

MM: It's my understanding that you and your crew were right in the middle of that complex ambush that killed Lieutenant [Edward] Iwan. Could you briefly describe that experience for me?

JA: It was an ambush and there was firing all around. Niel Hallsworth, our cameraman, and I would take turns popping up out of the hatch because there wasn't a lot of room. He had to take video. You know, when you're doing TV, there's no way you can just sit in a Bradley; you actually have to put yourself in harm's way to get the pictures. And I needed to know what was going on because I was doing live reports. So we were told to basically put our heads down, which we did, and then – did they tell you about the part when Michael Ware –?

MM: Right. He was on another vehicle, on a Bradley, and he was trying to get over to the vehicle you guys were in, or something to that effect.

JA: Yeah, and he believes that the lieutenant turned around to wave to him - I'm not sure if he did - and, shortly after that, the RPG [Rocket-Propelled Grenade] ripped through him. At that point, we were still in the hatch, Niel was shooting, and they said to me, "Don't look at this." And, of course, I had to look. So I saw him on the ground. We didn't use the footage where the RPG hit. There was no reason to. I don't think Neil filmed him on the ground - we wouldn't have used that part of it. The image, though, was so seared into my mind that I'd thought for the longest time that it was so vivid because I saw it on tape. I hadn't, though. When we went back to Muqdadiyah for the memorial, one of the guys said he used to grow flow- ers. I hadn't known that about him. There are so many things in that war, in any war, that are so unbearably sad that you can't begin to describe or explain them, but it's details like that that make people understand.

MM: Did you consider that to be the biggest scare of your career?

JA: Well, Neil, Arwa and I had been through a lot of these things. Nothing like the intensity of Fallujah, but in Najaf we were mortared every night and there were RPGs that would land so close to us that you would be showered with concrete chips. We've been in ambushes with small arms fire and RPGs where I really thought, "This is it. We're going to die." We were in the Palestine Hotel when a rocket was launched into the room across from mine. I could go on and on. Fallujah was absolutely horrific - terrifying at times - but the thing about reporting is that you really have to focus on what you're seeing and what you're telling people at the time. The same way Neil focuses on what he's seeing, because things sort of narrow and being afraid is a luxury you can't afford, so you just do whatever it is you're doing. I think it probably sinks in later. And it's not so much the danger and the fear; it's that horrible soul-destroying aspect of seeing so much destruction. That's the worst part. The first time I really had a sense of what war could do was when the U.S. launched cruise missiles against Baghdad under Saddam. I lived in the Rasheed Hotel and, when the missiles hit, all the air was sucked out of the room. All of a sudden, that view I looked at every day was gone: buildings that had taken months to construct gone in an instant. Watching the Marines fire TOW missiles a few weeks later into a row of houses in Fallujah, it was the same sort of feeling. You can't help but be in awe of that terrible destructive power, but it's always a defeat, always a failure, when you have to come to that.

MM: What did you think of the commander of 2-2, Pete Newell, and his S3, John Reynolds? Just your observations of being with them on this battlefield.

JA: They were amazing. I think Major Reynolds – now Lieutenant Colonel – and some of the others started out not terribly happy that we were going to be embedded with them. It's not like a traditional embed. We were actually in the same deserted house. Their TAC [Tactical Command Post] was basically all around us, so there was really not very much they could hide from us – although not being military people it's not as if we would have understood the significance of everything we were seeing anyway. But there got to be a real trust there, which was due to Lieutenant Colonel Newell, who is an extraordinary person. It's hard for me to talk about it with distance, I think, because we really got to know each other very well and there's a certain amount of affection combined with the immense respect I would have had even if I hadn't known them so well. I thought that they were both extraordinary, and it was an amazing look at just how adaptable you have to be as a commander and a leader. We were there when Sergeant Major [Steve] Faulkenberg was killed. That was one of the toughest things I'd ever seen: Colonel Newell having to go on and make decisions when the sergeant major had just been killed and not deal with that part of it. I have immense respect for Lieutenant Colonel Reynolds because he isn't someone who will try to give you easy answers or pat answers. Neither is Lieutenant Colonel Newell. They're both extremely intellectually honest, which is something I was really grateful for.

MM: Did you get the impression that Fallujah was pretty much denuded of civilians before the November attack? Everybody I talk to in the military is like, "Hey, the great thing is that we got all the civilians out."

JA: Well, they can't say they got all of the civilians out. We saw some civilians. I reported on a body, for instance – it was clear to me later, and I should have known it at the time, that it was a woman lying under there. I could only see her hand and I didn't know it at the time, so I said we couldn't tell, but I found out later it was a woman. However, there were very few civilians – and that was actually my biggest fear going into it, that this would be a battle where we would see civilians being killed and caught in the crossfire. But we hardly saw any in the initial assault. The only thing we really saw were insurgents, presumably, and dead insurgents and dogs roaming around. However, I believe other reporters embedded with the Marines ran across civilians. And when we stayed with RCT-7 in those waning days of the battle, there were quite a lot of civilians there, and that was one of the huge challenges for them. There were people who had stayed and put up these signs on their houses that said, "We are family" in the hope that soldiers or Marines wouldn't attack their houses. We were in the industrial section and, in the area we came in on, there were very few civilians. That doesn't mean that was the case for the whole town, but in general, compared to the first battle for Fallujah, there were very few. They either had been driven out by the insurgents or had left in preparation for the battle.

MM: Did you or CNN get involved with the issue of 2-2 firing white phosphorous rounds? Was anybody complaining about that? I guess some of the European press got a hold of it, and I talked to Captain [James] Cobb, the fire support officer, and he said he was being raked over the coals on the Internet over some article he wrote about the "shake and bake" missions.

JA: Well, the uproar came about because the military denied using white phosphorous on official levels. They said, "We never used white phosphorous." As you know, rule number one in dealing with the media or the public, as soon as you're found out to have lied – even if it's because you were misinformed – nobody ever trusts you again. The whole thing about white phosphorous came out because an Italian television station got a hold of photographs that seemed to show insurgents and/or civilians with white phosphorous burns. Then the military said, "No, we never used white phosphorous." But then they came back and said, "Well, yes, we did use white phosphorous, but only against insurgents." I felt really stupid because we were actually in fields where there was still white phosphorous burning and it wasn't clear to me at the time that these were fired by 2-2. I think it was probably clear to my cameraman, we just never discussed it at the time – nor was it an issue at the time because we didn't see any bodies where people had suffered the effects of it.

MM: You can actually see it going off in some of the night footage. As they blow through the breach on the first night, you can actually see it in an airburst.

JA: You know, you're absolutely right. I just didn't connect it with the later controversy with the white phosphorous.

MM: Did Pete Newell or John Reynolds say anything about it at the time?

JA: I'm sure they would have treated it very matter-of-factly. I know we did a story in a field with a warehouse where they were looking for insurgents. We were with them and there was white phosphorous still burning in that field. I think I might have referred to it in a stand-up because it was very dramatic, but I didn't connect it at the time with anything that would be controversial.

MM: So you weren't getting any pressure from your bosses back in the States to find out what was going on about it?

JA: No. That whole issue didn't come up until just a few months ago.

MM: That's why Captain Cobb was asking me who I was and why did I want to know this. Is there anything else you can tell me about your time in Fallujah and anything that struck you or impressed you or horrified you?

JA: Yes. Just in a big picture sense, it was an example of an embed working, and there were a lot of factors that had to come together for that. Part of it is, I think, the chemistry of somebody like Lieutenant Colonel Newell. I just have immense respect for him and Lieutenant Colonel Reynolds and the rest of them. I have immense respect for all of them, and even more respect after the battle: because they had the foresight and that certain amount of courage it takes to trust the media. Now, they knew us personally and trusted us, but it still takes a leap of faith to let people in that closely. Our reporting was pool footage, but it was our footage that was given to the pool. So without those pictures, without that reporting, people would have had a much different view of that initial assault in Fallujah. You would have had a lot of stories saying, "Yes, the American troops are killing civilians." I did not intend to be the person helping the military by saying there were no civilians that I could see, but that was part of the backdrop of it. What horrified me? As I said, the almost total destruction of the city. They flattened that city. The other thing that disturbed me greatly – although I kind of understand why this happens: there was an article that appeared in Rolling Stone magazine with Charlie Company.

MM: I have that here. By Janet Reitman?

JA: Yeah. The initial version of that went a lot further, because these guys all got together and decided that actually we were part of the reason their company commander died. They felt they had to babysit us; and had they not been babysitting us, they would have been able to protect him. It was a rather large group of journalists they were with, but they focused on me and Arwa. I contacted Lieutenant Colonel Newell, because as you can understand, this was incredibly upsetting. He said to me, and to Janet, that this wasn't the case at all. They were tasked with doing this, they were in a different sector, and it wouldn't have made a difference. But it's that perception, in some cases, where they don't really understand why they have to deal with us. Some of them do, but not all of them. Enlightened commanders understand that it's also an information battle; and not only that, but we're fighting for the same things. Things the Army and the Marines are fighting for, we as journalists believe we're fighting for a strong democracy in terms of transparency. We won't promise and we won't – if we have any credibility – be cheerleaders for the Army or the Marines, but we do promise to be accurate and faithful to what actually happens. We believe that's really important to the overall mission so that Americans know what war is and can make informed decisions about it. A lot of the guys on the ground don't feel that, and I can understand why they feel they needed somebody to blame.

MM: And that was Captain Sean Sims that was killed. It's my understanding that he went into a room they thought had been cleared and, as it turned out, an insurgent had crawled back in there. I don't see how they could have blamed that on you guys. Did you get a chance to meet Sean Sims?

JA: Yes, we did; he was a nice guy. The other thing that sort of disturbed me was they had a lingering impression that all we did was lecture them about not using the word hajji. It sounds like a really small thing, but it is not. It's an example to me of how the military is needlessly creating enemies and, three years later, is still not getting the cultural context right. And it's not political correctness; it's survival. You cannot use that term as an insult and not expect there to be consequences. Arwa and I are both ethnically Arab and we sort of feel this intrinsically, as well as know it intellectually. So it's really hard to stand by and watch these guys make enemies by doing that sort of stuff, so we tend to mention it to them in a friendly way. Out of all the things I've seen in Iraq, and I've seen a lot of horrible things – because basically I've spent the last three years going to the site of suicide bombs and car bombs and covering battles. You know, I'm not sure where I was going with that sentence. I think what I was starting to say is that Fallujah was like nothing any of us had ever seen. And in the middle of it - particularly towards the end - in between the moments of terror, there were long periods of intense tedium where you're standing around for what seems like forever waiting for the next moment of potential terror. You get into these conversations about things like how not to use the word hajji, and then the shooting starts again.

MM: They're just not paying you enough money for that.

JA: Well, it's not something I hope I ever have to do again, but I will. But I felt really lucky to be able to be there and see it as it was actually going on. To witness it.

MM: Did you get to spend any time at all with the Iraqi battalion that came in behind you guys? There was a Major Fred Miller that was the advisor for that unit.

JA: I'm trying to think which battalion that was. We spent a lot of time with the Iraqi battalion that Lieutenant Colonel Newell was working with.

MM: He said at one point there was a Spanish reporter who actually spoke Arabic and was able to interpret when he ran into some of these guys in a building. It was the 2d Iraqi Battalion and they're all coming in on little light trucks. I was wondering if you had any comments on their performance and if you got to talk to those guys at all.

JA: We tended to talk to them quite a lot. We did see that unit there and in some other places as well. I remember seeing them in their unarmored vehicles with the Iraqi flags and being incredibly moved and proud of them and saddened. Some of those guys we had actually seen during the battle of Samarra, so some of them we already knew. As you know, the Army thought it was a major accomplishment when they didn't actually run away – and some of them are very brave. Compared to U.S. soldiers though, they're not very well trained. I always thought that one of the most dangerous places to be in Iraq – given all the dangers that can surround you – is actually with Iraqi forces, because they really have very little muzzle discipline. I've seen cases where they've shot each other accidentally. As bad as things are now, I often think about what it was like in 2004 when there were simultaneous uprisings in the south by the Mahdi Army and Fallujah kicking up at the same time. That was when a lot of the Iraqi security forces collapsed. I'm not sure, given the pressures on Iraqis – the threat of being kidnapped, blown up or assassinated – that if we were in their shoes we'd keep showing up to be policemen or soldiers.

MM: In one of these interviews I have, you can hear the physician's assistant, First Lieutenant Greg McCrum, just as they blow that breach that first night, the first casualty – as he's whispering into the film there – is apparently one of the guys from the Iraqi battalion with a self-inflicted gunshot wound.

JA: They also were not terribly well equipped. It's not as if they had armored vehicles.

MM: Right, or night vision devices and that sort of thing. This has been fantastic. Our transcriptionist will type this up and we'll email you a copy.

JA: That's really kind.

MM: I think I've covered it all. I do have one other question that one of our interviewers wanted me to ask. While you were over there, did you make any attempts to report on the success stories of new schools and ribbon cuttings and positive reconstruction efforts?

JA: Every time someone says success stories or good news stories, it really drives journalists insane. We like to think of it as, "We report the news." I know a lot of you don't see it that way, but having said that, there wasn't a lot of that with Task Force 2-2. Is the interviewer asking whether I reported on success stories of ribbon cuttings and new schools during the battle for Fallujah? If so, I have to think that that's not a serious question. In fact, to be perfectly honest, people who ask questions that way generally have decided that the media is only covering "bad news." We make every attempt to report the news - good and bad. If you want someone to focus only on ribbon cuttings or schools, that's not really a journalist; that's someone else entirely. We stayed with 2-2 for the battle and went back with them for the memorials. Then we came back with RCT-7, and there wasn't a lot of that (new schools and ribbon cuttings) with RCT-7 either. They were still fighting insurgents even weeks after and were trying to pay compensation claims. We covered extensively the relief efforts to get food to the civilians in the city. I'm fascinated by Fallujah and it haunts me in a sense. I went back to see what had happened a couple months after and they were doing a lot of reconstruction. I did a lot of stories that didn't get a lot of air in the United States because Americans, that week, were more interested in the girl who was missing in Aruba. We actually went back to the house where we were with Lieutenant Colonel Newell, that they had actually occupied during the battle. The family had moved back in; it was fantastic. I think they thought I was a bit deranged. I was so happy to see them back I couldn't stop smiling at them.

MM: Did you get the impression at all that there was any sort of animosity between the Marines and the Army? From the people I've interviewed so far, this seems like a model of joint warfare where they all seemed to get along.

JA: There was a lot of that, but again, I think a lot of that is personality. Lieutenant Colonel Newell intersected with RCT-7's territory and Colonel [Craig] Tucker.

They're both incredibly smart so they got along and were all on the same page. I think there was a certain frustration on the part of the Army when they had to delay operations at a couple points, when the Marines were moving more slowly than they thought they'd be able to move. A few logistical quirks – at some point, there really wasn't enough hot food. I don't know enough about that to know whether that's a major thing or a minor thing. I know it's not ideal, but I don't know if it's inevitable.

MM: While you were out there on the battlefield, did you get a chance to meet the task force surgeon, Major Lisa DeWitt?

JA: I did a great story on her. I mean, the story was great because she's a great person. She is amazing.

MM: Everybody I've interviewed has said she's the greatest thing since sliced bread.

JA: It was a really poignant story, I thought.

MM: Did you do a special on CNN about her?

JA: Yeah. It was a very long piece, by CNN standards. I think it was about six or seven minutes long.

MM: I've got to dig this up.

JA: Yeah, let me know if you have trouble finding it. She's really fantastic. The thing about Lisa is that she desperately wanted to be there - to be where she would be the most useful. She made a point of going there and she made a point of staying. She was a civilian so it wasn't all that easy for her, but she was terrific. I'm not sure she realized what a difference she made there.

MM: I hope to interview her sometime this week. She's only available on weekends.

JA: The Marines gave the Army beer on the Marine Corps' birthday. There was this amazing sound when they popped open these beers in the field and they were the first beers they'd had for months and months. It was just really funny. And poignant – some of the guys drank to their buddies who'd been killed. I think it's hard for civilians to understand how soldiers and Marines both simultaneously honor their dead by keeping them always in their minds and, at the same time, accept casualties far more than civilians do. There is a huge cultural difference between the Marines and the Army, but I think what bridged it, in this instance, in Fallujah, was the skill of the commanders, because you could tell they were all on the same page. Colonel Tucker, who dealt a lot with Lieutenant Colonel Newell, I thought he was extraordinary as well, as far as the agility you have to have in the fight he was facing. He was doing a RIP [Relief in Place] with the guy who was replacing

314

him and he said something which I think is really key and characterizes the best commanders – and it's something Lieutenant Colonel Newell used to say as well. They would tell people coming in: "Don't assume every Iraqi is your enemy." And that is really typical of how Lieutenant Colonel Newell operated and part of the reason I think he made such a success of the cooperation with those Iraqi forces.

MM: That's excellent. Thank you very much for your time.

Glossary

AAR: After-Action Review
A&L: Administration and Logistics
AIF: Anti-Iraqi Forces
ALO: Air Liaison Officer
ANGLICO: Air and Naval Gunfire Liaison Company
AO: Area of Operations
AST: Advisor Support Team
ATC: Air Traffic Control

BCT: Brigade Combat Team
BDA: Battle Damage Assessment
BMO: Battalion Maintenance Officer
BRT: Brigade Reconnaissance Troop

C2: Command and Control
CAS: Close Air Support
CFL: Coordinated Fire line
CMTC: Combat Maneuver Training Center
CO: Commanding Officer
COMSEC: Communications Security
CP: Command Post
CSH: Combat Support Hospital

DISCOM: Division Support Command
DSN: Defense Switchboard Network

ECP: Entry Control Point
EOD: Explosive Ordnance Disposal
EPW: Enemy Prisoner of War

FLA: Front-Line Ambulance
FLE: Forward Logistics Element
FO: Forward Observer
FOB: Forward Operating Base
FRAGO: Fragmentary Order
FSB: Forward Support Base
FSC: Fire Support Center
FSCC: Fire Support Coordination Center
FSO: Fire Support Officer

GPS: Global Positioning System

HEAT: High-Explosive, Anti-Tank

HESCO: A company specializing in pre-fabricated protective structures
HHC: Headquarters and Headquarters Company
HUMINT: Human Intelligence

IBA: Interceptor Body Armor
IED: Improvised Explosive Device
IIF: Iraqi Intervention Forces
ING: Iraqi National Guard
IO: Information operations
IP: Initial Point
IPB: Intelligence Preparation of the Battlefield
IR: Infra-Red

JTAC: Joint Tactical Air Controller

LAV: Light Armored Vehicle
LD: Line of Departure
LNO: Liaison Officer
LOA: Limit of Advance
LOC: Line of Communication
LRAS: Long-Range Advanced Scout Surveillance System
LRP: Logistics Resupply Point
LZ: Landing Zone

MANPAD: Man-Portable Air Defense
MARDIV: Marine Division
MCLC: Mine Clearing Line Charge
MEDEVAC: Medical Evacuation
MEF: Marine Expeditionary Force
MNC-I: Multi-National Corps-Iraq
MNF-I: Multi-National Forces-Iraq
MOS: Military Occupational Specialty
MOUT: Military Operations on Urban Terrain
MPAD: Mobile Public Affairs Detachment
MSR: Main Supply Route

NCO: Non-Commissioned Officer
NIPRNET: Non-secure Internet Protocol Router Network
NOD: Night Observation Device
NVG: Night Vision Goggles

OPCON: Operational Control

PA: Physician Assistant
PSD: Personal Security Detachment

PSYOP: Psychological Operation

QRF: Quick Reaction Force

RCT: Regimental Combat Team
RIP: Relief in Place
ROE: Rules of Engagement
RPG: Rocket-Propelled Grenade

S1: Personnel
S2: Intelligence
S3: Operations and training
S4: Supply/Logistics
S5: Civil-Military Operations
S6: Communications/Electronics
SAW: Squad Automatic Weapon
SIGINT: Signals Intelligence
SINCGARS: Single Channel Ground to Air Radio System
SIPRNET: Secure Internet Protocol Router Network
SPO: Security and Plans Officer

TAC: Tactical Command Post
TACON: Tactical control
TAD: Temporary Assigned Duty
TCP: Traffic Control Point
TDY: Temporary Duty
TF: Task Force
TOC: Tactical Operations Center
TOW: Tube-launched Optically-tracked Wire-guided
TTP: Tactics, Techniques, Procedures

UAV: Unmanned Aerial Vehicle

VBIED: Vehicle-Borne Improvised Explosive Device

WP: White Phosphorous

XO: Executive Officer

About the Project Team

Mr. Kendall D. Gott retired from the US Army in 2000, having served as an armor/cavalry and military intelligence officer. His combat experience consists of the Persian Gulf War and two subsequent bombing campaigns against Iraq. Before returning to Kansas in 2002, he was an adjunct professor of history at Augusta State University and the Georgia Military College. In October 2002, he joined the Combat Studies Institute where he researches and prepares articles and studies on topics of military history. His book-length works include *In Glory's Shadow: The 2nd Armored Cavalry Regiment During the Persian Gulf War, 1990-1991*, *Where the South Lost the War: An Analysis of the Fort Henry-Fort Donelson Campaign, February 1862*, and *Breaking the Mold: Tanks in the Cities*. Mr. Gott is a frequent speaker at Civil War roundtables and appeared on a History Channel documentary on the Battle of Mine Creek, Kansas, and the documentary *Three Forts in Tennessee* by Aperture Films.

Mr. John McCool is the administrator, editor, and senior interviewer for the Operational Leadership Experiences Project which is an oral history enterprise based at Fort Leavenworth's Combat Studies Institute. The OLE Project team conducts, transcribes, and archives interviews with military personnel who executed key operations in the Global War on Terrorism. Mr. McCool possesses a Master of Arts Degree in History from the University of Kansas and has a demonstrated background in both public and oral history. He has participated in several collaborative projects to include Web-based development endeavors. Mr. McCool has focused his research and writing interests on a wide variety of modern American political, diplomatic and military history topics.

Mr. Matt Matthews joined the Combat Studies Institute in July 2005 after working for 16 years as a member of the World Class Opposing Force (OPFOR) for the Battle Command Training Program at Fort Leavenworth, Kansas. Mr. Matthews graduated from Kansas State University in 1986 with a BS in History. He served as an infantry enlisted man in the Regular Army from 1977 to 1981. He was a Cavalry officer in the US Army Reserve from 1983 to 1986; and an Armor officer in the Kansas Army National Guard from 1986 to 1991. Mr. Matthews has coauthored numerous scholarly articles on the Civil War in the Trans-Mississippi to include *Shot All To Pieces: The Battle of Lone Jack*, *To Play a Bold Game: The Battle of Honey Springs*, and *Better Off in Hell: The Evolution of the Kansas Red Legs*. He is the author of Global War on Terrorism Occasional Paper 14, *The Posse Comitatus Act and the United States Army: A Historical Perspective*. He is a frequent speaker at Civil War Roundtables and he recently appeared on the History Channel as a historian for the Bill Kurtis production entitled Investigating History. Mr. Matthews is also the former mayor of Ottawa, Kansas.

Dr. Christopher K. Ives serves as an interviewer for the Operational Leadership Experiences Project. He possesses a Ph.D. from Ohio State University. Dr. Ives works as a defense and business process consultant. His *Knowledge and Strategy: Operational Innovation, Institutional Failure, US Army Special Forces in Vietnam 1961-1963* will appear in April 2007 (Routledge/Taylor and Francis Group). He is a retired US Army Reserve officer with an extensive background in Special Forces as well as general purpose forces C4I. Dr. Ives' next project is a paper for the 2007 Society of Military History annual conference titled Continuities and Combatants: Counterinsurgency in Vietnam.

Ms. Colette Kiszka acts as the Project Technician and Transcriptionist for the Operational Leadership Experiences Project at the Combat Studies Institute. She uploads the completed oral interviews onto Fort Leavenworth's Combined Arms Research Library website. She has an extensive administrative background that has led her to work in and around the US Army for over 25 years. As a retired Army spouse, she feels most at home within the military environment and thoroughly enjoys working at Fort Leavenworth, Kansas.

Mrs. Jennifer Vedder is a Military Analyst currently charged with transcribing interviews for the Combat Studies Institute's Operational Leadership Experiences Project. Mrs. Vedder possesses a Masters of Science Degree in Health Care Administration and has previously served as an officer on Active Duty in the Medical Service Corps.

Ms. Jennifer Lindsey is an editor for the Research and Publications team at Ft. Leavenworth's Combat Studies Institute. She is a graduate of the University of Kansas with a BS in Journalism/Broadcast News. She spent many years as a television news producer for NBC, ABC, CBS and FOX in Kansas City and San Diego. She has also worked as a freelance writer in corporate communications and for numerous publications.